'In this work we are provided with a much-needed breadth of approach (and thus a breath of fresh air) to understanding the problem of mental illness. The use of the broad approach including the questions brought by the interest in <<urhomelessness>> all contribute to the considerations so needed in our field.'

John Strauss, MD, *Professor Emeritus of Psychiatry, Yale University*

'In this acute and moving analysis, the authors explore a crucial feature of many who suffer from what has traditionally been termed "schizophrenia": feelings of utter homelessness, of wandering lost and alone in an uncanny world that offers no sense of safety or emotional sustenance. This is a work of deep empathy and marked iconoclasm. It opens new avenues for research and reflection – also for more effective forms of treatment, both in therapy and on a societal level.'

Louis Sass, PhD, *Distinguished Professor, Department of Clinical Psychology; Graduate School of Applied and Professional Psychology (GSAPP) Rutgers University*

'Wide ranging and beautifully written, one of the standout achievements of this phenomenological work is its engagement with culture, both at a more macro level (informants in Israel, Palestine and the US), and in its attention to the nuanced ways in which cultural contexts infuse and shape the experience and existential import of psychosis. Both those who agree and disagree with Kamen's underlying thesis of urhomelessness will find a text rich with insights and provocations positioned to unsettle tired phenomenological tropes and break new ground at the intersections of subjective experience, culture and religion, and identity.'

Nev Jones, PhD, *Assistant Professor, School of Social Work, University of Pittsburgh*

RECONCEPTUALIZING SCHIZOPHRENIA

This volume presents a novel, international research study that reconceptualizes schizophrenia through an investigation of ways in which the first-hand experiences of those living with a diagnosis differ from conventional diagnostic definitions.

Offering insight into the history of psychiatric taxonomies in general and the invention of the schizophrenia diagnosis in particular, *Reconceptualizing Schizophrenia* maps the emergence of uncertainties about the empirical and conceptual status of contemporary diagnostic systems. Particular focus is given to the heterogeneity problem, or the problem of wide empirical variation within and between disorder categories. At the heart of this book are interviews with mental health service users with psychotic-disorder diagnoses in New York City and Jerusalem. Through a detailed portrait of their existential and socio-institutional worlds, the book unveils a way of being-in-the-world characterized by the experience of feeling profoundly vulnerable and unsafe in an inhospitable world as well as foreclosed from belonging to one or more human communities. As this psychological portrait of *urhomelessness* unfolds, the reader becomes slowly aware of the relationships between psychotic experiences – often thought to be bizarre or 'un-understandable' – and the timeless ways in which all humans seek to dwell in the world.

Making an important contribution to the phenomenological-existential literature on psychosis, and demonstrating interdisciplinary and transcultural approaches to understanding anomalous experiences, this volume will be of great interest to researchers and scholars of transcultural psychiatry, clinical psychology, and critical theory.

Sarah R. Kamens is a clinical psychologist and interdisciplinary researcher whose work focuses on the phenomenology of emotional distress, including the distress that results from structural disparities and psychosocial marginalization. Alongside her colleagues in the Society for Humanistic Society, Dr. Kamens explores possibilities for diagnostic alternatives in the mental health professions.

THE INTERNATIONAL SOCIETY FOR PSYCHOLOGICAL AND SOCIAL APPROACHES TO PSYCHOSIS BOOK SERIES

Series editor: Anna Lavis

The ISPS book series seeks to capture these developments in the field by providing a forum in which authors with a variety of lived and professional experiences can share the significant value of their work. Complemented by international and national conferences and publication of the journal *Psychosis*, this series is central to the activities of ISPS and their global reach. It comprises books with a variety of empirical focuses and with differing experiential and disciplinary perspectives. Although diverse, the range of books combines intellectual rigour with accessibility to readers across the ISPS community. We aim for the series to be a resource for mental health professionals, for those developing and implementing policy, for academics in the social and clinical sciences, and for people whose interest in psychosis stems from personal or family experience.

To support its aim of advancing scholarship in an inclusive and interdisciplinary way, the series benefits from the advice of an editorial board whose members are drawn from across the ISPS community:

For more information about ISPS, email isps@isps.org or visit our website, www.isps.org.
For more information about the journal *Psychosis* visit www.isps.org/index.php/publications/journal

Finding Hope in the Lived Experience of Psychosis
Reflections on Trauma, Use of Power and Re-visioning Psychiatry
Patte Randal and Josephine Stanton

For more information about this series, please visit: www.routledge.com/The-International-Society-for-Psychological-and-Social-Approaches-to-Psychosis/book-series/SE0734

RECONCEPTUALIZING SCHIZOPHRENIA

The Phenomenology of Urhomelessness

Edited by Sarah R. Kamens

Routledge
Taylor & Francis Group
LONDON AND NEW YORK

First published 2023
by Routledge
4 Park Square, Milton Park, Abingdon, Oxon OX14 4RN

and by Routledge
605 Third Avenue, New York, NY 10158

Routledge is an imprint of the Taylor & Francis Group, an informa business

British Library Cataloguing-in-Publication Data
A catalogue record for this book is available from the British Library

Library of Congress Cataloging-in-Publication Data
Names: Kamens, Sarah R., author.
Title: Reconceptualizing schizophrenia : the phenomenology of urhomelessness / edited by Sarah R Kamens.
Description: Abingdon, Oxon ; New York, NY : Routledge, 2023. | Series: ISPS (the International Society for Psychological and Social Approaches to Psychosis) | Includes bibliographical references and index.
Identifiers: LCCN 2022046513 (print) | LCCN 2022046514 (ebook) | ISBN 9780367151713 (hardback) | ISBN 9780429055454 (ebook)
Subjects: LCSH: Schizophrenia--Diagnosis. | Psychiatry--Methodology. | Phenomenological psychology. | Psychiatry, Transcultural.
Classification: LCC RC514 .R3823 2023 (print) | LCC RC514 (ebook) | DDC 616.89/8--dc23/eng/20230125
LC record available at https://lccn.loc.gov/2022046513
LC ebook record available at https://lccn.loc.gov/2022046514

ISBN: 978-0-367-15171-3 (hbk)
ISBN: 978-1-032-47366-6 (pbk)
ISBN: 978-0-429-05545-4 (ebk)

DOI: 10.4324/9780429055454

Typeset in Times New Roman
by MPS Limited, Dehradun

Dedicated to the participants

CONTENTS

ILLUSTRATIONS

Tables

Figure

CONTRIBUTORS

Sarah R. Kamens, PhD, January 2023, Private Practice, SUNY College at Old Westbury, Department of Psychology; Wesleyan University, Department of Psychology; Yale University School of Medicine, Department of Psychiatry; Fordham University, Department of Psychology.

Frederick J. Wertz, PhD, Private Practice, Fordham University, Department of Psychology & Fordham College at Lincoln Center.

Jessica Yisca Baris Ginat, MD, Herzog Hospital, Department of Psychiatry, The Jerusalem Mental Health Center, The Hebrew University of Jerusalem Medical School.

Ryan Scanlon, MBA, Fordham University, Department of Psychology.

Jillian Minahan Zucchetto, PhD, Fordham University, Department of Psychology.

Faith Forgione, MA, Fordham University, Department of Psychology.

Ileana Driggs, LMHC, The Gateway School; Fordham University, Department of Psychology.

Lia Kamar, MA, Ness Ziona Mental Health Center; Interdisciplinary Center Herzilya.

Katherine Sullivan, BA, Fordham University, Department of Psychology.

Caroline Silva, BS, University of Houston, Department of Psychological, Health, And Learning Sciences; Fordham University, Department of Psychology.

Oren Matar, MA, Anaplan; Tel Aviv University; Independent Researcher.

Mary Beth Quaranta Morrissey, PhD, MPH, JD, Yeshiva University; Fordham University Global Health Care Innovation Management Center; Fordham University Graduate School of Social Service; Finger Lakes Geriatric Education Center at University of Rochester Medical Center.

David Miller, PhD, Private Practice, Maimonides Medical Center, Wellness Recovery Program.

Lyra Ward, PhD, Maimonides Medical Center, Wellness Recovery Program.

Tal Shachar-Malach, MD, Sarah Herzog Hospital, Department of Psychiatry.

Jacob Kader, PsyD, Private Practice; Manhattan Psychiatric Center.

Pesach Lichtenberg, MD, Jersualem Mental Health Center; Soteria Israel, The Hebrew University of Jerusalem Faculty of Medicine, Department of Psychiatry; Herzog Hospital, Department of Psychiatry.

John Strauss, MD, Yale University, Department of Psychiatry.

FOREWORD

At what level of understanding can psychiatric disorder best be understood? Several efforts have been attempted: biological ("psychiatric illness is an illness like any other"), descriptive (the symptom diagnostic criteria of DSM-III), and intrapsychic (the psychosexual stages and deviations in Freudian and related theories). The elusiveness of the answer or answers has often led to accepting the belief determined according to the powers of the proponents rather than because of careful inquiry. This volume pursues a different approach to this problem that is both fascinating and potentially extremely important.

In the current effort the authors utilize what they call a "phenomenological-existential" approach to the understanding of psychiatric disorder. Although the attention to criteria is obviously important, it seems to me that what is even more crucial in any approach is the attempt to answer the question, "what is really going on here anyway." In this volume the level of answer comes to focus on an underlying psychosocial process, what the authors call urhomelessness. Whether or not their answer finally proves to be the optimal one, this search and research opens up the major question of what is the most crucial level of the problem, not assuming ahead of time that we know, an assumption that seems to me not just premature but misleading and mistaken. Thus, even in their inquiry, without knowing the results, the approach used by the authors is a breath of fresh air that promotes a diversity of approaches, observations, methods and hypotheses.

The special value of the broad approach taken by the authors becomes apparent already in the first chapter. Rather than the usual myopic effort often made at reviewing the history of psychiatry focusing only on a narrow range of official efforts that is taken by most texts, these authors take the broader approach looking at the wide range of attempts that have been made by a wide variety of investigators, clinicians and theoreticians. References to the works of Denys and Foucault for example are included with the more traditional authors and concerns for considering the role of symptoms, underlying processes, and concepts in understanding and classifying disorders. This provides a further refreshing opening up of inquiry, indeed brushing past the usual range of hidden assumptions towards a real attempt at understanding the diverse possible ways of viewing this field along with their conceptual underpinnings.

In the second chapter, specifically on schizophrenia, this breadth of consideration is again a beautiful feature. The consideration not only of various symptom criteria but also of heterogeneity, "comorbidity," biological and cultural features, even homelessness and the possible "normal" experiences of "voice hearers" reflects not just some overinclusiveness of detail but an essential base for considering that fundamental problem of "what is really going on here anyway." These broader considerations are so crucial that I believe any tendency to ignore them will just defeat any efforts to create a real science of the field.

Subsequent chapters about the concept of urhomelessness and its nomadic, settled, and destitute moments are important descriptions and elaborations of the basic condition. Chapter 10 extends this inquiry by placing the individual experiences in their cultural context, suggesting the range or factors, social as well as psychological that are important to understanding urhomelessness.

Further chapters deal with the relation of urhomelessness to diagnostic concepts, to various approaches to understanding mental illness and subjectivity, ideas of recovery, community-based treatment and other topics. But rather than consider each of these in turn, it is important to note the wonderful impact of this work on reconsidering the mental health field more generally. By disconnecting their conceptions and research from the usual narrow paths of inquiry, the authors free themselves and us to take more distance so that we can see our field from a broader point of view. From this perspective, it is possible to follow the authors as they refocus us, not starting with the usual emphasis on symptoms or preconceptions about the possible psychologic, biologic, or social aspects of disease, but rather starting from a different point, "urhomelessness" and to see what our field looks like from that perspective. It seems to me that such an effort of "decentering" may be just what is required to help us escape from our revolving attempts going from one traditional viewpoint to another, to another, and returning again to the first, in order to rethink what we are dealing with, really to reconsider "what is going on here anyway." The value of such a reflective approach and the cross-cultural interview data used to elaborate it is impressive indeed.

Strauss John

ACKNOWLEDGEMENTS

This book is the outcome of collaborations between multiple co-investigators in both the United States and Israel–Palestine. While the contributions of our research team members are reflected in the co-authorship of individual chapters, it is also important to acknowledge the invaluable insights, generosities, and contributions of those who humbly and kindly offered their expertise. Some are named here, and some, for reasons of privacy/confidentiality, are not. This project is the result of all of these contributions – named and unnamed, spoken and unspoken. For those unnamed, I hope that this book is a way for you to be heard.

The origins of this book can be found in a dissertation project that was defended on April 13, 2016, at Fordham University in New York City. Indeed, this book owes its existence to many wonderful researchers and scholars at Fordham University. It is a project that would not have been possible without the unparalleled methodological expertise and dedication of my graduate mentor, Frederick J. Wertz. Nor would it exist without the dedication of the following talented and outstanding research assistants and co-investigators: Rebecca Dienstag, Ileana Driggs, Faith Forgione, Lia Kamar, Oren Matar, Jillian Minahan Zucchetto, Mary Beth Morrissey, Ryan Scanlon, Caroline Silva, and Katherine Sullivan. I am also tremendously grateful for the insights, wisdom, and patience of my other dissertation committee members: Margaret Andover, Rachel Annunziato, Monica Rivera-Mindt, and Louis Sass. This book also benefited from the camaraderie of The Qualitative Milieu at Fordham: Miraj Desai, Bojun Hu, Emily Maynard, Batya Rotter, and Nicoletta Skoufalos. Early stages of this project were supported by the Fordham Graduate School of Arts and Sciences (GSAS) Research Fellowship in 2012–2013. I am very grateful for this invaluable support, which allowed me to concentrate on developing my research plan.

This project would also not exist without the generosity, faith, and willingness of our hospital co-investigators in New York: David Miller, Lyra Ward, and Jacob Kader, and in Jerusalem: Pesach Lichtenberg, Yisca Baris Ginat, and Tal Shachar-Malach. These investigators and clinicians kindly shared their time and their working environments in order to help this project come to fruition. I am also deeply grateful to Abu Sbeih Hisham and Tyseer Razem, who generously provided expert translation, consultation, and Jerusalem-based wisdom; our data analysis was tremendously enhanced by their truly invaluable talents, insights, and expertise.

I am also tremendously grateful for the support and encouragement received during my predoctoral internship year from supervisors and colleagues at the Yale School of Medicine, including Thomas Styron, Erika Carr, Rebecca Miller, Elizabeth Flanagan, Larry Davidson, Anthony Pavlo, Patricia Fountain, Lisa Cross, Annie Thomas, Ben Cooley Hall, and Michael Hoge. For encouraging me to disseminate this work, I am also indebted to another very special person from Yale, John Strauss.

Student research assistants at SUNY College at Old Westbury provided very helpful feedback on a draft of this book as it was nearing publication. Thanks to Jade Hang, Brianna Kelly, Denae Wheeler, and Olivia Ryan for this feedback.

Many others have supported this project along the way. Specifically, this book has benefited from the invaluable insights and wisdom of Laila Atshan, Despina Constandinides, Bitya Friedman, Kelly Gawel, Nev Jones, Angel Malone, Blair W. Morris, Haviva Pedaya, Elizabeth Pienkos, Ariana Reines, Johanna Schütt, and Slavoj Žižek.

Last but certainly not least, this book would not exist without the support, patience, and encouragement of my amazing family and friends. I am particularly indebted to Donald Kamens' invaluable wisdom and guidance, Jenny Wilner's unparalleled support and eagle eye, and Udi Aloni's incisive insights. Most of all, I am grateful to my little one who, although born after this book was completed, has since taught me about the timelessness of existential homes.

INTRODUCTION

Sarah R. Kamens

This book tells the story of a human experience that we have named *urhomelessness*. The term urhomelessness is new, but the experience is not. The place of urhomelessness along the timeline of human history was not our focus in the research project presented in the book, as our study was a psychological investigation and not an historical one. Nevertheless, from the perspective of those who experience it, urhomelessness often seems as old as time itself.

What is this subjectively timeless experience? Urhomelessness is a unique way of being-in-the-world characterised by the twofold experience of feeling (1) profoundly unsafe in an inhospitable world and (2) unacknowledged, such that the experience of basic belonging to one or more human communities is eclipsed or foreclosed. Urhomelessness, in other words, is an experience of tremendous vulnerability as well as inescapable alienation.

It is important to emphasise that the sense of safety and belonging that are lacking in urhomelessness are of a very basic, foundational nature. The person experiencing urhomelessness sees the world as fundamentally dangerous, yet also inescapable and often encroaching. There is a stark feeling of being unacknowledged by others as a person with basic rights to sustenance, shelter, safety, and love. *Urhomeness* is our term for what is lacking, namely, the experience of basic existential at-homeness in the world of others.

There are three interrelated facets or moments of urhomelessness that we named *nomadic*, *settled*, and *destitute*. The nomadic moment of urhomelessness is a fundamentally exilic and diasporic way of being in which the person wanders through the world-at-large. In the settled moment, the person stumbles upon an imaginal means of securing urhomeness. In the destitute moment, the person relinquishes the search for basic existential safety and minimal communal belonging. These three moments, which will be described at length in this book, are non-discrete, overlapping, and can occur successively or simultaneously. For some persons, only one moment occupies the foreground of experience; for others, the experience of urhomelessness is characterised by an oscillation between two or all three.

DOI: 10.4324/9780429055454-1

We came upon the experience of urhomelessness through a research project in the field of clinical psychology, and more specifically a study of the experiences of culturally diverse persons carrying a psychotic-disorder diagnosis. It is not incidental that the structure of urhomelessness was discovered in this way. For over 100 years, various behaviours and experiences that sometimes occur in urhomelessness—but not its core existential structure or essential features—have been viewed as features of a psychiatric disorder called 'schizophrenia.' As a result, the story of urhomelessness cannot be divorced from the story of the schizophrenia diagnosis. That is, therefore, where this book begins.

The schizophrenia diagnosis

Contemporary clinical discourse on the diagnostic concept of schizophrenia is troubled by the spectre of a large, proverbial elephant. Indeed, in a review of the conceptual literature on the 'schizophrenia'[1] diagnosis, psychiatrists Keshavan et al. (2011) compared extant interpretative models of the disorder to the Indian parable of six blind men who touch different parts of an elephant and disagree as to whether it is a fan, a rope, a tree trunk, a wall, a snake, or spears. In the authors' own words:

> [...] the concept of schizophrenia as a disease entity, which has survived for over a century, is still mired in controversy and remains unsatisfactory to researchers and clinicians. The central roadblock to progress in this field is the lack of a cohesive, integrated model that incorporates the known facts of the illness. (p. 3)

Similarly, in an overview of central empirical findings and theoretical models of schizophrenia, Kurtz (2015) wrote that:

> the field of academic research in schizophrenia has been riddled with what have been labeled 'elephant footprints in the sand,' high-profile findings pointing to the origin of the disorder and covered by major news outlets, only to be found spurious with additional studies. (pp. 3–4)

What is this enigmatic elephant that tramples through the field of schizophrenia research, unseen and misunderstood?

Schizophrenia is one among many diagnoses comprising the current diagnostic paradigm in clinical psychology and psychiatry. The paradigm is represented and expressed in the *Diagnostic and Statistical Manual of Mental Disorders* (DSM; APA, 2013). The oft-cited quote—an old one, from Plato—in discourse about the empirical status of this paradigm is that it does not 'cut nature at its joints.' From this perspective, schizophrenia is one example of a human experience that has been ‘carved out’ or defined in imperfect ways. Some, in fact, have proposed that it might not be a single ‘disorder’ at all. Schizophrenia might be multiple experiences, all lumped into one, or a set of biological vulnerabilities that arises only in specific environmental contexts. It might be a family of related outcomes that, in teleological reversal, have been mistaken for their own cause. It might be the product of social inequalities. Or it might be no disorder at all, a phantasm of our scientific and clinical imagination. Definitions are even more tenuous across cultures, where conceptualisations of thinking, the mind, and the self—concepts used to define schizophrenia—do not always carry the same epistemic meanings and sociocultural implications as they do in the Western world. Researchers are now grappling with heterogeneous theories, findings, and perspectives surrounding a disorder category that once—not too long ago, in fact—unified the psychiatric profession with beliefs in its singularity and pathognomonic biological indexicality across cultures and time. Over the years, the empirical elusiveness of that biological indexicality has become clearer.

That is not to say that most professionals have thrown up their hands. The typologies of psychological distress in the DSM and the International Classification of Diseases (ICD; World Health Organization, 2019) continue to be utilised as a guide by clinicians on an everyday basis. Controversies notwithstanding, they have offered clinical researchers a common ground from which to study potential biological aetiologies, social determinants, and epidemiology.

Some researchers continue to hunt for the biological indices of symptoms that, it is believed, will reconstruct the diagnostic architecture of psychiatry brick by brick, from the bottom up. Others have sought new approaches entirely. Yet in the fervent search for biomarkers, present-day psychiatric scientists continue to gloss over the one source of data that has been the basis of research since the birth of psychiatry and related mental health disciplines. This source of data is lived experience.

Clinical diagnosticians base the majority of their decisions about the presence or absence of mental health challenges in observing, communicating with, and understanding expressive behaviour—in particular the person’s verbal descriptions of his or her lived experience. The utility of any future biomarker will necessitate its meaningful correspondence to identifiable and coherent characteristics of psychological life. In order to examine the ways in which verbal reports might contribute to ‘cutting nature at its joints,’ it is necessary to employ rigorous qualitative procedures that allow for the examination of psychological experience within the very contexts that it is lived. Qualitative methods for psychological research have gained traction in recent years as psychologists have become familiar with their provision of tools for rigorous, data-driven description (Wertz, 2018; Wertz et al., 2011).

Phenomenology as a research method

The research project presented in this book began as an exploration of the differences between the ways in which schizophrenia has historically been defined and experiences of persons who carry the diagnosis. In order to conduct this exploration, we used the qualitative method of phenomenology. Phenomenology is a rigorous research method for the study of human experience and structures of consciousness. Originally developed by Austrian mathematician and philosopher Husserl (e.g., 1913/1962, 1939/1970, 1948/1973), phenomenology has been systematised for contemporary social-science research by Giorgi (1975, 2009), Wertz (1985, 2005, 2010, 2015), and Wertz et al. (2011), among others. The primary focus in phenomenology is on lived experiences and their meanings. It follows that at heart of this book are descriptions of lived experiences that were derived from interviews with culturally diverse persons who had been diagnosed with a psychotic disorder. We wanted to understand the heterogeneity of the schizophrenia concept from a psychological perspective, through the first-person accounts of lived experience. Employing the data-driven method of phenomenology—which does not start with a hypothesis or theory—when we began our investigations, we had no idea where we would end up.

Organisation of this book

The chapters of this book, which are co-authored by members of our research team, are organised as follows:

The first two chapters provide the historical, scientific, and scholarly background to our research project and the book as a whole. Chapter 1 establishes the historical background, starting with the birth of psychiatry as a discipline and then tracing the ebb and flow of ideas about mental illness from the late 18th to the early 21st century. The first chapter also details the development and eventual popularisation of psychiatric diagnosis as a cornerstone of the profession. Also in focus are contemporary uncertainties about the empirical and conceptual status of the conventional diagnostic system, with particular focus on the heterogeneity problem—the problem of empirical variability within and across symptom profiles—and recent calls for a 'paradigm shift' in psychiatric taxonomy.

In Chapter 2, we provide an overview of the literature on schizophrenia, the focal diagnostic category in this book. Debates surrounding the schizophrenia diagnosis, sometimes seen as the quintessential example of madness, have often distilled and epitomised debates surrounding the psychiatric diagnosis more broadly. Particular attention is given to findings from cross-cultural research suggesting that psychosis is not experienced in the same way across place and time. We also summarise the neuroscientific and genetic research on schizophrenia before describing newly proposed and alternative models for renaming, redefining, and/or retiring the schizophrenia diagnosis.

In Chapter 3, we summarise previous phenomenological research on schizophrenia, starting with the work of Karl Jaspers in the early 20th century and proceeding through the work of Wolfgang Blankenburg, R. D. Laing, Louis Sass, and others. Going beyond diagnostic descriptions and their labels, these researchers have sought to understand the lived, subjective experiences of persons carrying a schizophrenia diagnosis. Their descriptions often differ vastly from the ways in which signs and symptoms are defined in the DSM and ICD.

We introduce our international, qualitative-phenomenological research project in Chapter 4. We first describe the project's methods, including its participants, procedures, and approaches to data analysis. The findings of our project are then the focus of Chapters 5 through 10.

Chapter 5 provides an overview of the findings by describing the *general psychological structure*, which is a depiction of the essential experiential characteristics of urhomelessness (see Giorgi, 2009; Wertz, 2005). The experience of urhomelessness was shared by both inpatient and outpatient hospital participants with a psychotic-disorder diagnosis.

The three moments of urhomelessness—*nomadic*, *settled*, and *destitute*—are detailed in Chapters 6, 7, and 8 (respectively).

In Chapter 9, we describe urhomeness, or the experience of living in recovery, as an immanent possibility along the continuum of urhomeless experiences. We also describe the ways in which the general structure was partially or fleetingly lived through in the experiences of comparison participants who did not carry a psychotic-disorder diagnosis.

Chapter 10 describes the findings related to cultural experiences, including both cultural heterogeneity and similarities. Although qualitative trends emerged within specific demographic groups in our sample, future research is needed on these trends due to the limited size and diversity of our sample. There were also unique patterns of cultural experience that corresponded to each of the three moments of urhomelessness, as well as patterns of cultural experience that occurred across the sample. Altogether, our findings suggested that urhomelessness is a fundamental potential of human experience that is always present, despite the fact that it is not always actualised in the foreground of experience for a given person at a given time.

The final four chapters consider our research findings in the context of previous clinical, phenomenological, cultural, and socio-epidemiological research. Chapter 11 focuses on the implications of our findings for diagnostic systems and the empirical dilemmas that beset them, including the heterogeneity problem. The potential contributions of phenomenological research to resolving taxonomic dilemmas are considered, as is the relationship between the present findings and the extant research on a psychosis continuum.

Chapter 12 considers the ways in which our findings build on previous phenomenological studies of psychosis. Although recent phenomenological research has focused on 'self-disturbances' that are located within the individual, urhomelessness occurs at the experiential intersection between person and world.

Next, Chapter 13 addresses some limitations of our project and offers directions for future research, with particular focus on participatory and social justice research methods. Last but not least, Chapter 14 considers the broader implications of our project for enhancing interventions given our important finding of the potential for urhomeness in the experience of all persons, especially community-based and social-justice approaches focused on creating safe, habitable, and welcoming environments. This final chapter also considers the proverbial elephant in the room through a consideration of recent socio-epidemiological research.

Through the research study presented in this book, we discovered ways in which our contemporary definitions of schizophrenia have strayed from—and sometimes even exacerbated—the experiences of those they were intended to characterise. By juxtaposing conventional definitions of schizophrenia with phenomenological understanding and descriptions of first-person accounts, it might seem, at times, that this book is comparing apples with oranges.

That is because it is.

In fact, that is what this book is all about.

Note

1 Quotation marks around words such as 'schizophrenia,' 'mental illness,' and 'psychopathology' denote the scientific instability of these concepts; quotation marks are eliminated after their initial use for purposes of parsimony.

1

PSYCHIATRIC DIAGNOSIS IN HISTORY

Sarah R. Kamens and Frederick J. Wertz

It has been said that the history of schizophrenia is that of psychiatry as a whole (see Scull, 2015; Woods, 2011). The scene or background for our reconceptualisation of the schizophrenia diagnosis is thus the history of psychiatry as a discipline. In order to lay the groundwork for later chapters, this chapter presents a brief overview of the history of psychiatric ideas, starting with their ancient precursors.

The birth of psychiatry

The first written descriptions of what is now called 'psychopathology' date back to the ancient world. Early accounts include an Egyptian description of dementia in 3000 BCE, a classification of mental disorders in the Ayurveda from ancient India, and various references to mental distress in texts from ancient Greece (Keeley et al., 2014). The Greek physician Hippocrates (460–370 B.C.E.) and the Roman physician Galen (129–200 A.C.E.) believed that mental distress was caused by imbalances in bodily 'humors,' elemental fluids that were thought to be the basis of health and illness.

The early history of psychiatry can perhaps best be traced through the development of its institutions. Although European and American psychiatrists often date the founding of the first psychiatric hospital to the construction of Valencia's Hospital de los Inocentes in 1410 (e.g., López-Ibor, 2008), psychiatric hospitals began to appear in the Islamic world as early as 705 A.C.E. (Youssef & Youssef, 1996). The invention of psychotherapy in the West was predated by the Persian physician Al-Razi (841–926 A.C.E.), who is also credited with an early theory of mental distress as neuropsychiatric disease (see Muazzam & Muazzam, 1989); in contrast, during the Dark and Middle Ages in Europe, psychological suffering was largely viewed as a religious or supernatural phenomenon. Later, in Europe's early modern period, philosophical accounts of the mind (e.g., Descartes, 1647/2008;

DOI: 10.4324/9780429055454-2

Kant, 1781/1999) and medico-scientific views of psychological suffering and unusual behaviour began to reemerge (e.g., Burton, 1621/2001).

According to most accounts, the birth of psychiatry in the Western world did not take place until the late-18th century, when physicians began to assume custodial roles in European 'lunatic' asylums (see Foucault, 1965/1988; Kurtz, 2015; Shorter, 1997). For approximately 100 years (1770–1870), during what is sometimes termed 'the great nineteenth-century lockup' (see, e.g., Shorter, 1997, p. 48), the asylum industry boomed in Europe and the United States. The new doctors of the mind, then known as 'alienists,' increasingly described mental distress and unusual behaviours in medical terms. The result was the birth of the medical model of mental distress, a system for describing and treating psychological distress as pathophysiology, i.e., as disease.

Classification in general medicine

Taxonomy is the process of identifying and grouping phenomena (taxa) based on shared characteristics. Nomenclatures are systems for naming those taxa. Medical taxonomies are generally traced back to English physician Sydenham (1624–1689), a friend of empiricist-philosopher Locke (1632–1704). Sydenham insisted on the existence of objective disease types with discernible manifestations. However, he believed that humans are able 'to perceive only the superficies of bodies, not the minute processes in nature's "abyss of cause"' (Sydenham, n.d., quoted in Fischer-Homberger, 1970, p. 397). Syndenham's nosological architecture introduced a novel referential hierarchy, where signs (observed by others) and symptoms (self-reported by the patient[1]) were seen as clues or signifiers for a larger, underlying problem, i.e., disease.

Importation of the medical model

It was this referential hierarchy of an observable signifier (sign or symptom) pointing to an objective but unseen signified (disease) that early psychiatrists imported in order to describe psychological distress and behavioural anomalies in medical terms. Medical discourse, it was hoped, would eventually lead to scientific taxonomies for classifying mental illnesses. Yet as their new medical subdiscipline developed, psychiatrists were quick to disagree on the basic grouping principles that might form the foundation for a formal classification. Indeed, the history of psychiatric taxonomies can be seen as an oscillation between two trends: (1) descriptive classification based on observable signs and symptoms; and (2) disease realism (see Kendell & Jablensky, 2003) based on the theoretical existence of an objective, yet unobservable disease entity or disorder that underlies its perceptible manifestations.

The rise and fall of alienism

Asylum alienists ascribed to a causal version of Sydenhamian disease realism. Although they did not share a standardised taxonomy of mental disorders (Rollin, 2003), asylum doctors believed that the signs and symptoms they observed in their patients were the outward manifestations of underlying disease entities or lesions in the brain (see Bogousslavsky & Moulin, 2011). Asylum medicine started to wane at the turn of the 19th century, when it became clear that custodial institutions did little to improve patients' quality of life and that the incidence of psychiatric disorders was rising rather than falling (Shorter, 1997). According to Shorter (1997), by 1900 asylums were 'mainly warehouses in which any hope of therapy was illusory' (p. 65). With the exception of conditions brought about by alcoholism, at the end of the asylum era alienists ultimately had little empirical evidence to support the idea that 'insanity' (as it was then called) could be attributed to abnormal processes in the brain.

The new biological psychiatry

At the turn of the 20th century, two events led to renewed hopes for the future of alienism, now increasingly referred to as 'psychiatry.' First, the discovery of syphilitic spirochaetes (bacteria) in the brains of patients with general paresis, a disorder that included psychotic experiences, confirmed the theory that syphilis was a neurological disease. Second, advances in research technology were increasingly yielding biological data that supported the causal theories of which Sydenham had been sceptical; perhaps most notably, the previously controversial germ theory of disease had been validated by the discovery of pathogenic bacteria, and medical professionals were no longer persuaded by the theory that diseases were generated spontaneously. Although many illness definitions remained purely descriptive, a growing number of medical diseases were reclassified in line with their underlying biological processes. These developments led to a rekindled fervour in disease-entity theory among psychiatrists despite the fact that, with the exception of neurosyphilis, no specific physiological aetiologies had been discovered for psychiatric disorders. Shorter (1997) has dubbed the ensuing half-century, characterised by 'an absolute craze for studying psychiatry with the microscope' (pp. 78–79), as 'the first biological psychiatry' (p. 69).

The turn of the 20th century also saw early and protean nomenclatures for mental illnesses beginning to appear in various hospitals, clinics, and institutions. In 1891, the International Statistical Institute (ISI) began to develop a classification system for causes of death (see Keeley et al., 2014); though some countries preferred local nomenclatures, the ISI's *International Statistical Classification of Diseases, Injuries, and Causes of Death* (commonly known by its acronym, ICD [see Moriyama et al., 2011; WHO, n.d.])

quickly became the international standard for diagnostic classification in both general medicine and mental health.

In the United States, the classification of mental disorders was born of public policy trends (Grob, 1991). The 1840 census contained a dichotomous category 'idiocy/insanity,' and within 40 years, it expanded to include seven categories (melancholia, monomania, paresis, dementia, dipsomania, and epilepsy [APA, 2000]). In 1918, the American Medico-Psychological Association (alongside the National Committee for Mental Hygiene) published the first standardised nosology in the US: the *Statistical Manual for the Use of Institutions for the Insane*, which contained 22 categories for mental illness (Grob, 1991).

According to Shorter (1997), the first biological psychiatry eventually faded 'because it detached itself too completely from the patients and their world' (p. 79). Due to rise of a new descriptive approach, mental distress was increasingly viewed in the context of environmental and life-historical factors. The first biological psychiatry was laid to rest when the eugenics agenda—which had developed in tandem with biological psychiatry in the United States (see also Dowbiggin, 1997)—was expanded by Nazis in Germany (e.g., Documents on the 'T-4' and '14f13' Programs, 1939–1945/2009). The Nazi exterminations were controversial among American eugenicists; though some enthusiastically supported its sterilisation programme (Mehler, 1987), Nazism ultimately proved an embarrassment for the American 'social hygiene' movement.

The turn to description

The new descriptive approach to psychological distress that emerged in the early 20th century had often two divergent versions, developed concomitantly by 'the two most influential individuals in psychiatry' in Europe at the time (Trede, 2007, p. 237), Kraepelin and Freud. Early in his career, Kraepelin believed that psychological forces were at play in psychiatric illness. In time, however, Kraepelin turned to a predominately biological view of psychopathology, and he developed a classification system that would become the basis of modern psychiatric nosology (see Keeley et al., 2014). Although Kraepelin believed in objective disease entities, he was sceptical about the possibility of classification based on causal substrates. Kraepelin's major innovation was to group symptoms into diagnostic categories on the basis of common course and outcome rather than similarities in clinical presentation or presumed neurological correlates. For example, his two main categories, dementia praecox ('early dementia,' which later evolved into the schizophrenia diagnosis) and manic-depressive illness were distinguished on the basis of prognosis; dementia-praecox patients were supposedly more likely to deteriorate into dementia, whereas patients with manic-depressive illness were expected to recover (Shorter, 1997).

Freud, Kraepelin's contemporary (though the two never met in person [Trede, 2007]), was an Austrian physician who invented the science and practice of psychoanalysis (e.g., Freud, 1909/1963, 1917/1966, 1923/1960; Freud & Breuer, 1895/2000; see also Wertz, 1987). For Freud (e.g., 1917/1966) and later psychoanalysts, most symptoms of mental distress could be directly traced to life-historical experiences of the patient, often their experiences during childhood. Treatment was a verbal form of psychotherapy in which patients relayed their thoughts and feelings to the analyst, who listened and intermittently offered interpretation. Psychoanalysis took the Western world by storm and dominated psychiatric theory for approximately 50 years (until the 1970s), a period that Shorter (1997, p. 145) himself, a biological psychiatrist, would call 'the psychoanalytic hiatus' or psychotherapy period) between two eras of biological psychiatry.

DSMs I and II: The psychotherapy period

During the psychotherapy period, the primary classification system in the United States was the American Medico-Psychological Association's (1918) *Statistical Manual for the Use of Institutions for the Insane.* Medical historian Grob (1991) has noted that the manual was used primarily for institutional data gathering purposes, and it was considered of negligible value to psychiatrists and other therapists. However, during the Second World War, efforts to develop a new diagnostic system were spurred by mounting dissatisfaction with the *Statistical Manual*, as well as a growing desire for a unified taxonomy that would allow for everyday use by both clinical practitioners and researchers (APA, 2000). The American Psychiatric Association (APA[2]) began to develop a local version of the ICD-6 (which contained a section on mental disorders that the APA found 'unsatisfactory' [APA, 1968, p. xii]); their new manual would be called the *Diagnostic and Statistical Manual of Mental Disorders* (DSM-I; APA, 1952).

DSM-I (APA, 1952) was influenced by the two predominant theoretical trends of that time: Kraepelinian disease-entity theory and Freudian psychoanalysis. The manual had two primary sections: 'Disorders Caused by or Associated with Impairment of Brain Tissue Function' (e.g., acute and chronic 'Brain syndromes') and 'Disorders of Psychogenic Origin or without Clearly Defined Physical Cause or Structural Change in the Brain' (e.g., psychotic disorders, psychoneurotic disorders; APA, 1952, pp. 1–8).[3] DSM-II (APA, 1968), which expanded the number of mental disorders from 106 to 182, loosely followed the structure of DSM-I; it contained ten major groupings that distinguished between 'Organic Brain syndromes' and other conditions that were not attributed to a known physical cause. While DSM-I was only loosely influenced by psychoanalysis, DSM-II's focus on non-organic disorder categories reflected the rising popularity of psychoanalytic theory in post-Second World War America. The first two DSMs, then, were theoretically based, and their juxtaposition of biomedical theory and psychoanalytic theory was generally viewed as awkward but palatable (see Grob, 1991).

DSM-III and the second biological psychiatry

In the 1970s, biological psychiatry returned to the limelight in the United States as psychiatrists began to revisit the idea that psychopathology was causally rooted in pathophysiology, and more specifically in neurological disorders (Shorter, 1997). At the time, a convergence of scientific, social, and political developments had planted seeds of doubt about psychoanalysis in the minds of mainstream psychiatrists—most of whom would nevertheless remain psychoanalytically inclined for an additional decade. The advent of chlorpromazine in the mid-1950s had transformed medical conventions for treating schizophrenia. Further, deinstitutionalization had transported many former inpatients to community clinics and the streets. In addition, the growing popularity of behaviourism and the subsequent cognitive revolution in psychology gave rise to a wave of new psychological treatments, including behavioural modification (e.g., Skinner, 1972), cognitive therapy (e.g., Beck, 1976), cognitive-behavioural therapy (e.g., Meichenbaum, 1977), and rational emotive therapy (Ellis, 1989). Although the learning theories of most cognitive-behavioural practitioners stood in contrast to psychiatric disease-entity theories, the changing landscape of clinical psychology further disenfranchised psychoanalysts, paving the way for the emergence of a new era of biological psychiatry.

During the 1970s, a small group of rogue researchers at Washington University in St. Louis made it their goal to revive Kraepelinian theory. The 'neo-Kraepelinians,' as they came to be known, were disgruntled with psychoanalytic psychiatry, which they saw as pseudo-scientific 'baloney' (Guze, 1994, para. 26), and they wanted to bring psychiatric science on a par with the rest of general medicine. Their means of doing so was to create a set of diagnostic criteria that eventually became known as the Feighner Criteria (Feighner et al., 1972; a.k.a. the St. Louis diagnostic criteria; see also Robins & Guze, 1970).

The Feighner Criteria proved influential for the architects of the third DSM (DSM-III; APA, 1980). Robert Spitzer, chair of the DSM-III Task Force, made at least six visits to Washington University in the early 1970s (see Kendler et al., 2009). He worked with Robins to expand the 15 St. Louis categories into 24, forming the now-famed Research Diagnostic Criteria (RDC; e.g., Spitzer et al., 1975). The RDC, in turn, formed the basis of the new diagnostic architecture that became central to American psychiatry with the 1980 publication of DSM-III (APA, 1980), and to international psychiatry with the 1979 introduction of ICD-9 (WHO, 1979).[4]

DSM-III (APA, 1980) was viewed as a revolution in psychiatric diagnosis (e.g., Blashfield et al., 2014). Unlike its two predecessors, which largely reflected the psychodynamic theories of their time, DSM-III diagnoses were defined by observable behaviours and self-reported complaints (i.e., by signs and symptoms; see also Compton & Guze, 1995; Keeley et al., 2014). Though DSM-III architects borrowed the basic blueprint of the St. Louis model (e.g., Feighner et al., 1972), there was one important difference: DSM-III abstained from explicit biomedical theorising and instead took an outwardly agnostic stance regarding the aetiology of mental disorder. This putatively atheoretical approach served a double function: it facilitated the ongoing, behind-the-scenes search for biomarkers while simultaneously allowing for everyday use of the manual by practitioners of diverse orientations.

The modified neo-Kraepelinian model of DSMs III, III-R, IV, and IV-TR (APA, 1980, 1987, 1994, 2000) was a descriptive, multiaxial[5] system with listwise criteria sets for identifying the observable signs and symptoms of what were presumed to be categorical, discrete mental disorders. By basing diagnosis on observable phenomena rather than theoretical speculations about pathogenesis or underlying disease entities, the neo-Kraepelinian model greatly enhanced interrater diagnostic reliability (Spitzer et al., 1979). Enhanced reliability led to hopes for eventually solidifying the validity of diagnostic categories. Throughout the 1980s and 1990s, the DSM-III inspired a surge of research into the biology, epidemiology, and psychosocial correlates of categorically defined mental disorders.

Emergence of the heterogeneity problem

Anomalous findings: The heterogeneity problem

As research based on the new DSM-III system progressed, psychiatric scientists repeatedly came across several unexpected and perplexing empirical findings. The first surprise emerged in the realm of epidemiology; when researchers removed DSM-III exclusion criteria, a set of rules prohibiting the diagnosis of overlapping disorders, they discovered rates of co-occurring (a.k.a. comorbid[6]) disorders that were much higher than would be expected by chance (Boyd et al., 1984; see also Blaney & Millon, 2009). Later epidemiological studies confirmed this finding across multiple disorder categories (Kessler et al., 1994; Kessler et al., 2005). A new catch-phrase held that 'comorbidity is the rule rather than the exception' (e.g., Carlstedt, 2010, p. 87), and terms such as trimorbidity, quadramorbidity, and multimorbidity started to appear (Krueger & Markon, 2006a). Some researchers viewed comorbidity as a statistical artefact or selection bias (e.g., Berkson's bias, which holds that an individual with two disorders has twice the likelihood of seeking treatment and/or being selected by researchers [Berkson, 1946; see also Blaney & Millon, 2009]). Others, however, viewed comorbidity as a threat to the validity of the DSM-III categorical system; if disorders are frequently comorbid, they argued, they may not reflect discrete disease entities or natural kinds, but rather heterogeneous expressions of one or more higher-order process(es) (e.g., Brown et al., 1998; Krueger & Markon, 2006a).

Motivated by the comorbidity studies, psychiatric researchers began to take a closer look at the categorical diagnoses featured in DSM-III and, later, DSMs III-R, IV, IV-TR, and 5 (APA, 1980, 1987, 1994, 2000, 2013); their findings served to increase scepticism about the neo-Kraepelinian taxonomic architecture. Particularly problematic was the discovery of wide empirical heterogeneity characterising the symptom profiles of many DSM- and ICD-defined disorders (e.g., major depressive disorder [e.g., Ghaemi & Vöhringer, 2011; Unick et al., 2009], generalised anxiety disorder [e.g., Unick et al., 2009], panic disorder [Roberson-Nahy & Kendler, 2011], post-traumatic stress disorder [e.g., Nugent et al., 2012], conduct disorder [e.g., Wozniak et al., 2001], bulimia nervosa [e.g., Fairburn, 1991], and borderline personality disorder [e.g., Kopala-Sibley et al., 2012], among others). Heterogeneity was characteristic of symptom profiles within individual diagnoses (within-diagnosis heterogeneity) as well as between two or more disorders or diagnostic sets (between-diagnosis heterogeneity [see Olbert et al., 2012; Olbert et al., 2014]). Within-diagnosis heterogeneity was thought to result from the polythetic structure of most diagnostic criteria sets, where no one criterion is considered necessary or sufficient for a diagnosis. As a result, two individuals can meet criteria for the same diagnosis and yet share few to no symptoms in common (e.g., Krueger & Bezdjian, 2009). Evidence for between-diagnosis heterogeneity came from four findings: (1) high rates of comorbidity (Boyd et al., 1984; Kessler et al., 1994; Kessler et al., 2005); (2) high rates of phenotypic[7] overlap between diagnoses (a.k.a. diagnostic overlap or fuzzy boundaries), such that component symptoms frequently cut across multiple disorders (e.g., Boyd et al., 1984; Frances, 2009b; Krueger & Markon, 2006a; Strauss et al., 1983); (3) neighbouring but putatively discrete diagnoses lack zones of rarity, i.e., clear demarcations for boundaries between them; high rates of 'not otherwise specified' (NOS) diagnoses, where symptoms resemble but do not meet diagnostic criteria for a specific disorder (see APA, 2000); and (4) high genotypic overlap, i.e., non-specific biological deficits spanning multiple disorders (see Regier et al., 2009).

A note on terminology

It is important to note that the term 'heterogeneity' is utilised in discourse on psychopathology in multiple and seemingly inconsistent ways. The term is most frequently used to refer to variation within and between the symptoms and biological correlates of individual disorder categories (e.g., Joyce & Roiser, 2007). In biopsychiatric research, the word heterogeneity is frequently synonymous with multiplicity or multifactorialism, such that multiple genetic or biological correlates are described as heterogeneous. In addition, the term heterogeneity is sometimes used to describe the proliferation of numerous diagnostic categories within the official taxonomic manuals; for example, the DSM-IV-TR (APA, 2000), which contains 365 diagnoses in 17 superordinate groupings, is considered to be a heterogeneous classificatory system (e.g., Zimmerman et al., 2010). Treatment outcomes are also sometimes described as heterogeneous when they vary between individuals who receive comparable interventions. Although inconsistent, these multiple denotations of the term heterogeneity in psychiatric discourse all relate to the same structural problem: without biological markers for discrete patterns found in nature, medical terminology in psychiatry functions as figurative rather than literal, and mental health scholars have become increasingly uncertain as to the conceptual differences between disorder class and disorder species, disorder species and symptom, symptom and sign.

The struggle to 'carve nature at its joints'

To psychiatric taxonomists and other researchers, evidence of rampant within- and between-diagnosis heterogeneity seemed to indicate that DSM-III diagnostic architecture did not 'carve nature at its joints' (Plato, 370 B.C./1952; see Regier et al., 2009, para. 15); i.e., it did not reflect the natural structures of mental disorders as they manifest in actual clinical populations. As a result, the neo-Kraepelinian diagnostic system did not, as expected, facilitate the discovery of measurable biomarkers, nor did it lead to the invention of laboratory tests for diagnosing mental disorder (e.g., Regier et al., 2009). Moreover, evidence of variable phenotypes suggested that symptom clusters had been arbitrarily split (divided) or lumped (grouped) together by psychiatric taxonomists such that DSM- and ICD-defined diagnostic categories might actually correspond to multiple disorders, complex syndromes, and/or empirically unrelated sets of symptoms; similarly, groups of disorder categories might in fact be varied manifestations of one higher-order disorder or process (e.g., Bhugra, 2007; Houts, 2002; Marsella, 2016). As a result of these disappointments, in recent years, researchers have increasingly questioned the 'conceptual cacophony' of the classificatory system on which their work is based (Pies, 2012b, para. 5). In the words of Carpenter (2013), '[t]here is a growing consensus in the field that the current classifications for many disorders are not sufficiently robust for advancing knowledge' (para. 4). Likewise, Insel (2012) stated, 'it is more parsimonious to conclude that nature does not define the disorders designated by our current diagnostic labels, all of which were devised by committees of clinicians who were voting on the symptoms' (para. 4).

Cultural heterogeneity

Some of the most robust, yet enigmatic evidence of phenotypic heterogeneity has emerged from cross-cultural, transcultural, and multicultural research. It is important to note that, in the research literature on cultural variation in mental distress, the word 'culture' is utilised in polysemic and often inconsistent ways. Prior to the civil rights era in the United States, the word, 'diversity' was often used as a euphemism for 'inferiority'; even in the late-20th century the term was intermittently employed as a synonym for 'deficit' or 'disadvantage' (Trickett et al., 1994). Hopper (2004) lamented that in recent, large multi-country psychiatric studies, '"culture" has been a mock-elegant way of referring to "there" as opposed to "here"' (p. 65). Therefore, caution is advisable when interpreting the meaning of 'culture' in the research described below.

This book adopts the American Psychological Association's (2002) definition of 'culture' as 'the belief systems and value orientations that influence customs, norms, practices, and social institutions, including psychological processes [...] and organizations' (p. 8). Culture is a function of race, ethnicity, gender, sexual orientation, political position, subjection to structural violence (Farmer, 2005) or privilege, socioeconomic status, geographic region, national identification, religion, spirituality, and experiences in mental health treatment environments, among other contextual factors (e.g., Sue et al., 1999). Culture is also influenced by institutions, professional affiliations, social class structure, societal individualism versus collectivism, and social embeddedness (e.g., Sue, 2001). Culture influences a person's beliefs, practices, experiences, and general world views; indeed, cultural background may even affect one's very definition of 'culture.' Increasingly, researchers have advocated for attention to both inter- and intra-cultural variation in psychological research endeavours (see, e.g., Corin et al., 2005; Lichtenberg et al., 2003; Marsella & White, 1982; Marsella & Yamada, 2000). Trickett et al. (1994) have proposed a cultural pluralism framework in which cultural identity is affirmed rather than denied, and all people—including white men and other privileged persons—are recognised as having a race, gender, sexual orientation, and social status.

The APA (2002) defines 'multiculturalism,' which is used interchangeably with the word 'diversity,' as 'the broad scope of dimensions of race, ethnicity, language, sexual orientation, gender, age, disability, class status, education, religious/spiritual orientation, and other cultural dimensions' (pp. 9–10). 'Transculturalism' refers to the range of phenomena that occur across heterogeneous cultures without compromising their individual particularity. Recent decades have seen increasing recognition by psychologists of a culturally pluralistic world (see Marsella & Yamada, 2000), as well as the need for culturally pluralistic psychological practices (Hoffman et al., 2015). Research and practice in psychology are increasingly approached from cross-cultural, transcultural, and multicultural frameworks. As a result, there is increasing recognition within the discipline that all human interactions and experiences, including the experience of mental distress, are culturally situated (APA, 2002).

Cultural syndromes

Kraepelin himself was one of the first psychiatrists to observe variation in the experience of distress and the expression of symptoms across cultures (see Marsella & Yamada, 2000). Since that time, numerous multidisciplinary international researchers (including medical anthropologists [e.g., Kleinman, 1987]) have documented the existence of symptoms and other expressions of psychological suffering that seem to be unique to specific cultural contexts (Marsella & White, 1982). 'Culture-specific disorders' are featured in the ICD-10's Annex 2 (WHO, 1992b). DSM-5 (APA, 2013) replaces DSM-IV's (APA, 1994) term, 'culture-bound syndromes,' with a tripartite distinction between 'cultural syndromes,' which are culture-specific symptom clusters; 'cultural idioms of distress,' or culture-specific ways of describing distress; and 'cultural explanation or perceived cause,' which are the culture-specific ways of thinking about aetiology.[8] The rationale given for this change was as follows:

> [...] the term *culture-bound syndrome* ignores the fact that clinically important cultural differences often involve explanations or experience of distress rather than culturally distinctive configurations of symptoms. Furthermore, the term *culture-bound* overemphasizes the local particularity and limited distribution of cultural concepts of distress. The current formulation acknowledges that *all* forms of distress are locally shaped, including the DSM disorders. (APA, 2013, p. 758)

In other words, DSM-5 explicitly recognises that it is not only the particular symptom profile, but also the person's *experience* and explanation for symptoms that differ as a function of culture. An example of a specific cultural syndrome is *Ataque de nervios* (found in Latin American populations), an experience of losing psychological control that may be accompanied by aggressive or affective outbursts and dramatic dissociative episodes.

The idea of cultural syndromes remains controversial among some psychiatric researchers (e.g., Kleinman, 1987). While some have argued that cultural syndromes are not 'real' mental illnesses because they appear to be aetiologically related to sociocultural context rather than (presumably) universal biological mechanisms, others have argued that putative culture-bound phenomena are in fact local variants of the classic categories listed in the DSM and ICD (see Guarnaccia & Rogler, 1999; WHO, 1992b). Watters (2010) has argued that the globalisation of American psychiatric discourse is—by virtue of its rapid dissemination to varied sociocultural contexts across the globe—increasingly transforming local idioms for distress and corresponding treatments into their Western variants (see also Karter, 2018; Mills, 2014). A new intellectual movement called Indigenous Psychology seeks to challenge the increasing globalisation of American and European ideas about mental distress by validating the paradigms and practices of local psychologists (Sundararajan, 2015; see also Desai, 2014a,b). In general, mental health researchers increasingly agree that all phenomena currently labelled as mental disorders, including the official Western versions, are cultural phenomena (e.g., APA, 2013; Flanagan & Blashfield, 2002; Jadhav, 2000; Kleinman, 1987; Lock, 1987; Rahimi, 2015; Sundararajan et al., 2000; see also Prince & Tcheng-Laroche, 1987).

In sum, the global mental health field is nascent and controversial, and there is no consensus on the validity of cultural syndromes nor on the generalisability of Western models to other contexts (see also Karter, 2018, 2021). When the evidence first emerged, cultural heterogeneity within and between mental disorders represented a significant challenge to the doxa that DSM- and ICD-defined diagnostic categories corresponded to universal, biologically based phenomena that were ubiquitous across the globe and throughout time. Together, the new data on heterogeneity in psychiatric diagnosis, cross-cultural heterogeneity in particular, led to calls for a radical change, or paradigm shift (see Kuhn, 1962/1996), in psychiatric classification.

Calls for a paradigm shift

By the turn of the 21st century, there was increasing disenchantment with the neo-Kraepelinian model for classifying mental distress. Chair of the DSM-IV Task Force Allen Frances (2011) prognosticated that '[t]oday's psychiatric labels will one day seem […] quaint' (para. 8). While developing the new manual, the DSM-5 Task Force announced that the extant diagnostic architecture is 'now holding us back because the system has not kept up with current thinking' and that researchers 'are skeptical that the existing DSM categories represent a valid basis for scientific investigations' (Schatzberg et al., 2009, para. 7; see also Barkil-Oteo, 2012; Galatzer-Levy & Galatzer-Levy, 2007; Phillips, 2013). Furthermore, practitioners increasingly complained about the utility of the DSM and ICD manuals for understanding the clinical presentations they encountered in their everyday work (see First, 2010a, 2010b; Reed, 2010).

A research agenda for DSM-V[9] (Kupfer et al., 2002) contained a now-infamous prognostication that in order for psychiatric researchers to succeed in 'uncovering […] underlying etiologies' of mental disorder, 'an as yet unknown paradigm shift may need to occur' (p. xix). The term 'paradigm shift' evoked the work of philosopher of science Kuhn (1962/1996), who proposed that science does not advance by slow incremental advances (e.g., Popper, 1963/2009), but rather by revolutionary shifts in scientific worldview—followed by periods where scientists conduct 'mop-up work' and 'puzzle solving' by conducting studies that attempt to validate the new paradigm (Kuhn called this 'normal science' [pp. 10, 24, 35]; see also Marsella, 2016). When normal science produces anomalies that seem to contradict the status quo, scientists enter a paradigm crisis in which they scramble to resurrect the existing paradigm or erect a new one. Thus, by proposing the possibility of a paradigm shift in psychiatry, DSM-5 architects implied that taxonomies for mental disorder, and thereby the science and practice of psychiatric diagnosis, may soon undergo a radical conceptual upheaval (see also Bracken et al., 2012). Although they did not specify the precise nature and means by which they intended to exact this paradigm shift, DSM-5 authors (e.g., Kupfer et al., 2002a) were interested in achieving a familiar, neo-Kraepelinian goal: the establishment of pathophysiological substrates or biomarkers for the diagnosis of psychopathology. As such, their proposed 'paradigm shift' did not ultimately represent a novel change in scientific worldview, but rather a recalibration of the contemporary biomedical paradigm (Cerullo, 2010; Kamens, 2011; Marsella, 2016).

Leading up to the publication of DSM-5 (2013), calls for a paradigm shift in psychiatry were met with considerable controversy (e.g., Alarcón, 2009; Carlat, 2009; Costello, 2009; Frances, 2009a; Frances & Spitzer, 2009; Lane, 2011), with critics of the idea arguing that, in light of the elusiveness of reliable aetiological evidence, the goal of effecting a revolution in psychiatric science is 'absurdly premature' (Frances, 2009a, para. 7; see also First, 2010c). The DSM-5 Task Force eventually postponed the goal of exacting a radical paradigm shift; the 'Guidelines for making changes to DSM-V' (Kendler et al., 2009), revised in 2009, stated:

> [w]hile DSM-V will not in itself represent a 'paradigm shift,' it is intended to start a process that will lead to more useful ways of classifying and diagnosing mental disorders based on our current knowledge and reasoned predictions of where the science is heading. (p. 1)

Indeed, despite organisational changes to the structure of the manual, the addition of fine-tuned severity scales, and varied changes to specific disorder categories and groupings, DSM-5 did not represent a significant conceptual departure from its immediate predecessors, DSMs III and IV.

Despite the fact that a paradigm shift was not attempted in DSM-5 or ICD-11, various researchers have continued to envision diagnostic models for future editions of the manuals—or new manuals entirely. Some researchers believe that the sixth edition of the DSM (DSM-6) may constitute a paradigm shift in the cross-cultural aspects of diagnosis (e.g., de Jong, 2012). Many have argued that dimensional modelling will eventually replace the current categorical classification featured in DSM and ICD (e.g., Kamphuis & Noordhof, 2009; Strauss, 1973; Widiger & Samuel, 2005; see also Joiner & Schmidt, 2002 and Meehl, 2001); indeed, many disorder groupings are already seen as 'spectra' (e.g., autism-spectrum disorders and schizophrenia-spectrum disorders) containing multiple categories that differ as a matter of degree rather than kind. A recent effort to reconceptualise DSM-defined disorder categories as dimensions can be found in the Hierarchical Taxonomy of Psychopathology (HiTOP), a comprehensive theoretical model that attempts to reduce comorbidity by conceptualising co-occurring syndromes as spectra (Kotov et al., 2017). In addition, prototype-matching approaches to psychiatric classification, in which individuals are rated on their level of similarity to prototypical disorder phenotypes, are gaining popularity as a possible alternative to criterion-based categorical classification (e.g. Pies, 2012a).

Biologically oriented psychiatrists, citing the lack of congruence between the official diagnostic systems and the state of the art in neuroscience, have proposed that any future paradigm shift must be an interdisciplinary movement aimed at aligning psychiatric diagnosis with advances in molecular neuroscience and genetics (e.g., Rubin & Zorumski, 2012). For example, there is rising interest in the idea of accounting for biogenetic and phenotypic heterogeneity via the mapping of multivariate, stable psychometric patterns dubbed endophenotypes. Gottesman and Gould (2003) argue that the problem of aetiological modelling could eventually be solved by identifying disorder-specific endophenotypes, which they define as 'measurable components unseen by the unaided eye along the pathway between disease and distal genotype' (p. 636).

One of the most comprehensive attempts to transform psychiatric classification is the Research Domain Criteria (RDoC[10]) project launched by the National Institute of Mental Health in order to '[d]evelop, for research purposes, new ways of classifying mental disorders based on behavioural dimensions and neurobiological measures' (NIMH, 2015, para. 5; NIMH, 2021). In RDoC, a 'matrix of functional dimensions, grouped into broad domains' (e.g., negative and positive valence systems, cognitive systems, and systems for social processes) for which data will be collected across multiple 'units of analysis' (e.g., genes, molecules, cells, circuits, behaviour, subjective reports, and paradigms). The ultimate goal of RDoC is to discover biogenetic and neurological mechanisms (of mental disorder) that are 'independent' of DSM categorical diagnoses (Morris & Cuthbert, 2012, p. 35; see also Insel, 2013).

Despite high hopes about RDoC, no one newly proposed model has yet gained consensus as the potential future of psychiatric diagnosis. However, there is increasing consensus that change is needed. Hopes for such a shift are exemplified by an oft-cited prognostication that:

> We are at the epicycle stage of psychiatry where astronomy was before Copernicus and biology before Darwin. Our inelegant and complex current descriptive system will undoubtedly be replaced by explanatory knowledge that ties together the loose ends. Disparate observations will crystallise into simpler, more elegant models that will enable us not only to understand psychiatric illness more fully but also to alleviate the suffering of our patients more effectively. (Frances & Egger, 1999, p. 165)

To summarise: while psychiatric research in the two decades following the publication of DSM-III (APA, 1980) attempted to validate and extend the neo-Kraepelinian paradigm, recent uncertainty about the future of the DSM and ICD systems—alongside the theoretical and empirical nascency of newly proposed taxonomic models—has engendered a discourse about psychopathology that is increasingly characterised by theoretical multiplicity, polyvocality (i.e., varied voices and perspectives), and controversy. Central to this new discourse are the major taxonomic dilemmas that have emerged over the course of the last three decades. Any future taxonomy, psychiatric scientists contend, will have to resolve the empirical-conceptual problems present in the current versions of DSM and ICD—and, in particular, the heterogeneity problem.

Notes

1 The term 'patient' is retained in Chapter 1 to reflect the role of the term in psychiatric history; note that the non-medical term 'service user' is utilised in later chapters.
2 In 1921, the American Medico-Psychological Association became the American Psychiatric Association.
3 DSM-1 also contains separate, yet relatively brief sections for 'Mental Deficiency' and 'Nondiagnostic Terms for Hospital Record.'
4 Notably, DSM-III Task Force Chair Robert Spitzer rejected the term 'neo-Kraepelinian' because the manual did not mirror Kraepelin's explicit emphasis on aetiology. However, general consensus among psychiatric historians holds that the manual's predominant influence was the neo-Kraepelinian model of his close colleagues at Washington University, whose ultimate goal was to discover underlying biological aetiologies (Decker, 2007; Spitzer, 2001; see also Feighner et al., 1972; Robins & Guze, 1970).
5 The five diagnostic 'axes' introduced in DSM-III (APA, 1980) were Clinical Disorders, Personality Disorders, General Medical Conditions, Psychosocial and Environmental Problems, and Global Assessment of Functioning.
6 Note that, in contemporary psychiatric literature, there are two common, related denotations of the term 'comorbidity': (1) the co-occurrence of two or more disorders in one individual (Feinstein, 1970) and (2) the co-variation of disorders across individuals (Krueger & Markon, 2006a, b; Lilienfeld, 2003).

7 Contemporary psychiatric discourse has imported the terms 'phenotype' and 'genotype' from genetics to describe the difference between observable characteristics (signs and symptoms) and the presumed genetic substrates of mental disorder, respectively.

8 As a result of these fine-tuned distinctions, the inclusion of a comprehensive cultural formulation interview (Lewis-Fernández et al., 2014), the emphasis on experience and explanatory models, and the recognition that all mental disorders are cultural phenomena, DSM-5 is generally considered to be a vast improvement over DSM-IV in the area of culture (e.g., Cummings, 2013).

9 The DSM-5 Task Force switched the title from Roman to Arabic numerals in 2010.

10 The acronym RDoC is a likely allusion to the Research Diagnostic Criteria (RDC; Spitzer et al., 1975), which formed the basis for DSM-III (APA, 1980).

2

THE 'SCHIZOPHRENIA' DIAGNOSIS: PREDOMINANT, CROSS-CULTURAL, AND ALTERNATIVE APPROACHES

Sarah R. Kamens and Frederick J. Wertz

'Dementia praecox'

The concept of schizophrenia is typically traced back to the German psychiatrist Kraepelin (n.d.), who over a century ago (following Morel [1857]) defined dementia praecox as a special type of dementia with early onset and chronic course. Scholarly consensus on the post-Kraepelinian history of the schizophrenia diagnosis is elusive. Some see its development as a mostly linear, Popperian progression of accumulating evidence and theory refinement; others (e.g., Berrios et al., 2003) have argued that '[t]he history of schizophrenia can be best described as the history of a set of research programmes running in parallel rather than serialism and each based on a different concept of disease, of mental symptom and of mind' (p. 111; see also Marsella, 2016).

According to most accounts, the dementia praecox diagnosis was imported into the United States by Meyer, an influential Swiss psychiatrist who studied with Kraepelin in Heidelberg. In 1908, the Swiss psychiatrist Bleuler (1911)—Freud's contemporary and Kraepelin's student—coined the term 'schizophrenia,' a portmanteau of the Greek words for 'split' (*skhizein*) and 'mind' (*phrenos*). The Bleulerian concept, which quickly became official nomenclature, differed from dementia praecox in four ways: (1) it was not viewed as invariantly chronic and incurable; (2) onset could occur at any point in the lifespan, not only in adolescence; (3) it was presumed to be biologically based but also the result of (and eponymous for) psychological processes such as splitting (e.g., Janet, 1901/1978); (4) experiences were heterogeneous in essence, such that schizophrenia was more properly the *schizophrenias* (see also Kurtz, 2015). In a lecture to the German Psychiatric Association, Bleuler introduced the new term and explained, 'I wish to

DOI: 10.4324/9780429055454-3

emphasise that in Kraepelin's dementia praecox it is neither a question of an essential dementia nor of a necessary precociousness' (Bleuler, 1908, quoted in Fuser-Poli & Politi, 2008, p. 1407).

In the United States, biogenetic theories of schizophrenia predominated throughout the early 1900s. They faded into the background the rise of the psychotherapy period in the mid-20th century. It would be several decades before the neo-Kraepelinians ushered biogenetic theories of schizophrenia and other mental disorders back into the limelight, where they remain today (e.g., NIMH, 2023). The contemporary biogenetic view posits that schizophrenia is a neurobiological illness that has long existed but has been conceptualised by Western physicians as a mental illness only since the 19th century, after the advent of psychiatry. (Youssef & Youssef [1996] have argued that Islamic physicians probably diagnosed persons with a similar concept as early as medieval times.) Indeed, some contemporary accounts have interpreted ancient, medieval, Renaissance, and early modern practices such as prophecy, exorcism, and witch-hunting as evidence of societal misunderstanding and mistreatment of individuals suffering from the disorder (e.g., Cornblatt et al., 2009; Shorter, 1997; Stein, 2008). However, historians of psychiatry caution against uncritical presentism, or use of contemporary scholarship to retroactively understand previous eras. Scull (2015), for example, has argued that '[w]e run enormous risks of misconstruing history when we project contemporary diagnostic categories and psychiatric understandings back on the past' (p. 16; see also Berrios et al., 2003; Kurtz, 2015; Noll, 2011).

Schizophrenia-spectrum diagnoses: Current definitions

The contemporary clinical view sees schizophrenia as a chronic, biologically based disorder characterised by (1) delusions, (2) hallucinations, (3) disorganised speech, (4) disorganised or catatonic behaviour, and (5) 'negative symptoms' such as flat affect, avolition, and alogia. In order to meet criteria for a DSM-5 diagnosis of schizophrenia (APA, 2013, pp. 99–100), two or more of the above symptoms must be present for at least six months, including a minimum of one month in which symptoms are experienced 'for a significant portion of time (or less if successfully treated).' Diagnosis is also contingent on the presence of reduced functioning in work, interpersonal relations, or self-care. The diagnosis of schizophrenia also requires ruling out schizoaffective disorder, depressive or bipolar disorder with psychotic features, psychosis caused by substance use, and autism spectrum or communication disorders.

Psychosis and schizophrenia

The term 'psychosis' has polysemic and overdetermined meanings throughout the psychiatric, psychoanalytic, and empirical-psychological literature. The words 'psychosis' and 'schizophrenia' are sometimes treated as loose synonyms, but this semantic conflation is problematic, as, it is important to differentiate between psychotic experiences, symptoms, syndromes, and disorders (e.g., van Os et al., 2009). An increasing number of scholars (e.g., BPS, 2017) hold that there are only psychotic experiences or states that are not *ipso de facto* symptoms to be treated. Indeed, it is likely that clinicians underestimate the true prevalence of psychotic experiences, as individuals who are not distressed are less likely to report their experiences to mental health professionals (Hill & Linden, 2013).

When psychotic experiences lead to emotional distress or other life problems, they are typically interpreted as symptoms of disorders (APA, 2013). Historically, schizophrenia has been viewed as the most prototypical example of a psychotic disorder (Sass, 1992a, b; Woods, 2011). However, there is no clear differentiation between psychotic-disorder diagnoses and schizophrenia-spectrum diagnoses in the contemporary nomenclatures. The DSM-5 (APA, 2013) groups schizophrenia-spectrum and other psychotic-disorder diagnoses together and lists the key features of both as delusions, hallucinations, disorganised thinking (speech), grossly disorganised or abnormal behaviours (including catatonia), and negative symptoms (pp. 87–88).

Phenotypic heterogeneity in schizophrenia

Historically, the schizophrenia diagnosis has been a centrepiece of psychiatric theory; it has been dubbed 'the most severe' of all mental disorders (Sass, 1992a, p. 13). Woods (2011) has described schizophrenia as 'at once the bedrock of psychiatry's claim to scientificity and the source of its seismic tremors' (p. 37). It is perhaps unsurprising, then, that recent research literature on schizophrenia contains increasing deliberations concerning the taxonomic dilemmas that have recently beset psychiatric science as a whole, including the heterogeneity problem.

Contemporary researchers have documented heterogeneity within and between the symptoms of schizophrenia in multiple studies (e.g., Andreasen, 1985; Carpenter & Kirkpatrick, 2005; Fenton, 2000; Joyce & Roiser, 2007; Raffard & Bayard, 2012; Seaton et al., 1999; Tsuang et al., 1990; Wolitzky et al., 2006; cf. Huber & Gross, 1989). As stipulated by DSM-5 (APA, 2013), '[i]ndividuals with the disorder will vary substantially on most features, as schizophrenia is a heterogeneous clinical syndrome' (p. 100). Between-diagnosis heterogeneity in schizophrenia is evidenced by (1) high rates of comorbidity, (2) phenotypic overlap with other (but not, as in comorbidity proper, co-occurring) disorders (Marsella, 2016; Strauss et al., 1974), and (3) the high prevalence of DSM-defined psychotic disorder NOS (APA, 2000; now known as Unspecified Schizophrenia Spectrum and Other Psychotic Disorder [APA, 2013]) and its ICD-equivalent, other schizophrenia (WHO,

1992a, 1992b), which are diagnosed in individuals with clinically significant psychotic experiences that do not meet criteria for any established disorder category. Like those in most other official diagnostic classes, schizophrenia-spectrum and other psychotic-disorder diagnoses are commonly comorbid with other mental disorder categories, including panic disorder; post-traumatic stress disorder, obsessive compulsive disorder, and major depressive disorder (Buckley et al., 2009). There is also high phenotypic overlap (a.k.a. fuzzy boundaries) between schizophrenia and other mental disorder categories (see Maj & Sartorius, 2003). For example, schizophrenia is often thought to be phenotypically congruous with autistic spectrum disorders, bipolar disorder, dissociative identity disorder, and the other psychotic disorders with which it shares DSM- and ICD-defined superordinate diagnostic groups (APA, 2000; WHO, 1992a, 1992b). In addition, some individuals have psychotic experiences that do not meet criteria for any specific DSM disorder (e.g., Perälä et al., 2007).

While between-diagnosis heterogeneity reflects substantial overlap between schizophrenia and other DSM and ICD disorders, within-diagnosis heterogeneity has led to suggestions among biologically oriented researchers that the diagnosis may itself comprise multiple syndromes, distinct disorders, or experiences of distress that overlap with non-distressing experiences. Variations across the negative symptoms (e.g., anhedonia, avolition, and blunted affect) have long been well documented (e.g., Ahmed et al., 2017; Buchanan, 2007; Buckley et al., 2009; Davidson & McGlashan, 1997). One complicating factor is evidence suggesting an aetiological relationship between putative negative symptoms and treatment for schizophrenia (e.g., neuroleptic medications, which can cause blunted affect and akinesia, or alienating hospital environments, which can induce anhedonia), as well as between negative symptoms and other symptoms of the disorder (e.g., avolition as secondary to a delusion of persecution). As a result, some researchers differentiate between primary and secondary negative symptoms (e.g., Velligan & Alphs, 2008); the former are conceptualised as core 'pathological' processes, whereas the latter arise secondary to either clinical intervention or to the primary symptoms (see also Buswell et al. 2021).

Another area of empirical focus has been the heterogeneity of cognitive abilities in persons diagnosed with schizophrenia; although some individuals have average to high levels of cognitive functioning, heterogeneous challenges with cognition have been documented in various studies (e.g., Joyce & Roiser, 2007; Raffard & Bayard, 2012). However, evidence for specific cognitive profiles in persons diagnosed with schizophrenia remains mixed, and recent research has suggested that cognitive challenges may be unrelated to both the severity of distress and variations in clinical presentation (Seaton et al., 1999).

Heterogeneity is also characteristic of experiences that are labelled as the positive symptoms of schizophrenia (see also Kurtz, 2015). Traditionally, 'hallucinations' and 'delusions,' both classified as positive symptoms, have been viewed as the hallmark features of schizophrenia.[1] A demonstration of the vast heterogeneity in positive symptoms can be found in recent research on hearing voices (in clinical terms, auditory hallucinations). Not only is the content of the voices often unique to the individual, but their sensory qualities are often different from predominant definitions (see Hearing the Voice, 2021). Jones and Luhrmann (2016), for example, conducted qualitative interviews with 80 voice hearers carrying a schizophrenia-spectrum diagnosis and found that only a minority (17.5%) reported that their dominant pattern of voices was literally auditory. Other participants described dominant patterns of voices that were quasi-auditory, thought-like, or a combination of auditory and thought-like.

Following Jaspers 1913/1963, 1912/1968), an influential German psychiatrist and philosopher who is often credited (perhaps mistakenly [Berrios, 1992; Rulf, 2003]) with importing Husserlian phenomenology (e.g., Husserl, 1913/1962, 1939/1970, 1948/1973a, b, c) into psychiatric discourse, it is traditionally the *form* (e.g., symptom type, duration, and severity) rather than the content of hallucinations and delusions that is seen as relevant to diagnostic decision-making (see also Schneider, 1950/1959). Discussions about the potential interactions between form and content (e.g., effects of belief content on their duration) are thus relatively scarce in late-20th-century psychiatric literature from the United States and Europe, where the vast majority of empirical investigations into DSM- and ICD-defined mental disorders have been conducted. It was perhaps inevitable, then, that evidence of within-diagnosis heterogeneity in schizophrenia first emerged from investigations into the generalisability of the diagnosis across cultures.

International evidence: Phenotypic heterogeneity in schizophrenia

Cross-cultural variations in the content of psychotic experiences have been extensively documented (e.g., Bhavsar & Bhugra, 2008; Eghigian, 2010; Luhrmann & Marrow, 2016; Marsella, 2016; Sadowsky, 2004; Siddle et al., 2002), but largely dismissed as superficial fluctuations overlying core pathophysiology. Indeed, contemporary psychiatric textbooks (e.g., Cornblatt et al., 2009; Sadock & Sadock, 2010) have promoted the idea that schizophrenia is a biogenetic enigma found in 1% of populations across cultures and across history. Despite the long-held existence of this hypothesis, it was not until the late-20th century that researchers began to investigate the diagnostic concept at the international level.

Starting in the 1970s, the World Health Organization (WHO) conducted a series of studies that examined whether the classic symptoms of schizophrenia are invariant across cultures. To the astonishment of all involved, these studies revealed prognosis was more favourable in socioeconomically disadvantaged countries than in wealthier nations; researchers decided to repeat the study in ten countries, only to find their original results replicated (see Hopper, 2004; Jablensky, 1987; Jablensky et al., 1992). According to Jablensky et al. (1992), on five of six outcome measures, participants in developing countries had 'markedly better prognosis' than those living in developed countries (p. 93). Even more surprising, acute psychotic 'attacks' followed by recovery were more frequent in developing countries (Nigeria and India), while 'chronic unremitting psychotic illness' was more common in 'first-world' countries (Denmark, the United Kingdom, the United States, and Czechoslovakia; Jablensky, 1987, p. 165).

Recent studies have provided further evidence for the possibility that experiences commonly viewed as symptoms of schizophrenia may differ in prevalence across cultures and locations (Jenkins & Barrett, 2004). A systematic review of 188 studies conducted in 46 countries revealed that the general prevalence of schizophrenia was higher for migrants; prevalence rates were most favourable in 'least developed' nations, as compared to 'emerging' and 'developed' countries (Saha et al., 2005, p. e141). Due to the predominant belief that schizophrenia is a chronic, biologically based disorder that is best treated by allopathic medicine, these findings are controversial. Some have argued that favourable prognoses in developing countries can be attributed to cross-cultural differences in family systems, community rituals, and/or explanatory models for interpreting mental distress. For example, greater value may be placed on community and family relationships in predominantly collectivistic societies, which in turn may alter the person's experiences; conversely, in predominantly individualistic countries, there may be 'something essential to recovery [...] missing in the social fabric' (Jablensky & Sartorius, 2008, para. 7; see also Myers, 2010). Other researchers, in contrast, have suggested that various aspects of the industrialised, 'first-world' mental health system—for example, iatrogenic effects of neuroleptics or confirmation biases upholding longstanding beliefs in the chronicity of the disorder—could be to blame (e.g., Luhrmann, 2007; Whitaker, 2010). Indeed, in developing countries, psychosocial and supernatural theories of mental disorder, which tend to conceptualise mental distress as relatively transient, are often more prevalent than disease realism theories, which posit that the disorder is a chronic biogenetic condition (e.g., Bhikha et al., 2012).

Cross-cultural differences in the prevalence rates of the schizophrenia diagnosis have also been discovered within diverse European and American populations. Robust evidence supports the relationship between psychosis risk and urbanicity, low socioeconomic status, and segregation (e.g., Faris & Dunham, 1939; Marcelis et al., 1999; Spauwen et al., 2004). For example, the risk of being diagnosed with schizophrenia increases as socioeconomic status at birth decreases (e.g., Werner et al., 2007). In a study of 427 participants with first-episode psychosis living in inner-city boroughs of East

London, Kirkbride et al. (2014) found that neighbourhood social composition was associated with the incidence of psychosis. More specifically, for Black-Caribbean participants, psychosis risk was increased in neighbourhoods with high levels of segregation from persons of other ethnicities. For Black African participants, psychosis risk was reduced in neighbourhoods that were more densely populated by other Black Africans. For all participants, the risk of nonaffective psychosis increased as a function of the neighbourhood's increasing population density, multiple deprivation, and income deprivation inequality (i.e., high socioeconomic disparities) after standardising for age, sex, ethnicity, and social class (see also Kirkbride et al., 2014; Veling, 2013). Further evidence has indicated that neighbourhood qualities such as perceived dangerousness and segregation are robust risk factors for psychotic symptoms (see, e.g., Bhavsar et al., 2018; Nager et al., 2006; Wilson et al., 2016).

Some studies have examined potential socioenvironmental factors that may contribute to the urbanicity phenomenon. For example, a recent study by Freeman et al. (2014) examined the experience of psychosis in urban populations; they found that as compared to staying inside, exposure to the street resulted in increased paranoia, voices, anxiety, negative beliefs about the self, and negative beliefs about others. Söderström and colleagues (2016, 2017) followed persons experiencing a first episode of psychosis as they walked on urban streets and reflected on their experiences. They found that most participants preferred countryside to the city due to the density of persons, high sensory stimulation, obstacles to mobility, and uncertainty about role management in urban settings; they also found that participants used tactics such as 'creating bubbles of isolation' to manage their stress in cities.[2]

Another robust finding in the epidemiological literature has been the association between psychotic states and migration (e.g., Hollander et al., 2016; Morgan et al., 2010; Tarricone et al., 2015). Bourque et al. (2011) conducted a meta-analysis of studies examining risk for psychotic disorders among first- and second-generation immigrants. They found that both first-generation immigrants and second-generation children of one or two immigrant parents have increased risk for being diagnosed with schizophrenia-spectrum disorders, with significantly higher risks for immigrants with visible minority status. The authors conclude that post-immigration factors such as social discrimination may play a role in the increased vulnerability of migrant groups.

Some scholars have attributed cross-cultural differences in psychotic symptoms to differing norms, beliefs, traditions, and historical experiences of cultural groups (e.g., Chidarikire et al., 2020; Corin et al., 2005; De et al., 2013; Luhrmann, 2011; Luhrmann & Marrow, 2016). Indeed, Western definitions of psychosis have proved difficult to translate to other settings. For example, on the Indonesian island of Borneo, Barrett (2004) located

50 persons from the Iban culture who were said to be suffering from *sakit gila*, a local illness concept comparable to the Western definition of chronic psychosis. Barrett found that, although these individuals met criteria for various schizophrenia-spectrum disorders; they were completely puzzled by questions about classic forms of thought disorder. Because the Iban concept of thinking involves embodied processes related to the emotions and bodily function, they could not imagine how thoughts might be 'read' by other persons or removed from the head—and they wondered if questions about these experiences were a sort of riddle posed by the investigator.

European and American researchers have often described psychosis in terms of disrupted selfhood, or 'self-disturbances' (e.g., Mishara et al., 2014; Sass & Parnas, 2003; see Chapter 3). However, the 'self' may have different meanings for persons living in societies with different beliefs about the person and selfhood (Fabrega, 1989; Tirupati & Ramachandran, 2020). For example, a tendency towards social self-effacement and deferral to group norms may be relatively more common in societies with high levels of collectivism and sociocentric values (Banerjee, 2012). These cultural differences in self-understanding and social behaviours may correspond to variations in the experience of an altered 'self' in psychosis. For example, in one comparative study of African American, Caucasian, and Latino service users living in the United States (Brekke & Barrio, 1997), non-minority groups were found to display greater severity of symptoms than minority groups, and sociocentric tendencies (high empathy and social competence) were statistical mediators of between-group differences in psychotic symptoms.

In her detailed examination of psychotic experiences in the West and India, Dhar (2020) describes the ways in which postcolonial rural Indian culture allows for multiple subject positions as well as non-binary, contradictory narratives. Whereas a Western perspective might attempt to resolve or explain these contradictions—and potentially view them from a pathological lens if they cannot be resolved or explained—from an Indian perspective, human experience is fundamentally multiple and pluralistic. As Dhar writes,

> the Indian psyche is highly comfortable with paradoxes [...]. These differences cannot be captured by phrases like collectivistic and individualistic, but exist at a more fundamental level – a difference in the discourses that build us, the visibilities that shape us, and the contradictions that structure us. (p. 159)

These differences make room for the types of shifting and oscillating subjectivities that might be seen as self-disturbances from a Western perspective.

Positive symptoms, which were so named to reflect the addition of anomalous elements to normative experience, may have different meanings in cultures and cultural subgroups where extrasensory experience is more commonly experienced as non-distressing. For example, Luhrmann et al. (2015) compared the experiences of voice-hearers in India, Ghana, and the United States and found that while many participants in the Indian and Ghanaian samples reported predominantly positive experiences with their voices, not one of the American participants did so (see also Luhrmann, 2011). Moreover, Indian and Ghanaian participants described social relationships with their voices, which they conceptualised as persons or spirits, even when the voices said mean things or gave them commands. In contrast, American participants described their voices 'as bombardment and symptoms of a brain disease caused by genes or trauma' (p. 42). Similarly, Dhar (2020) came to the conclusion that hearing and seeing things that others do not perceive does not always generate distress in persons living in India.

Luhrmann (2012) also conducted an anthropological investigation of American evangelical culture, within which God is sometimes experienced as a concrete presence. Along with her colleagues, Luhrmann asked 124 Evangelical Christians a series of nine questions about experiences that are commonly reported by persons diagnosed with a psychotic disorder (e.g., 'Have you ever thought that your thoughts are being broadcast so loudly that other people know what you are thinking?' [p. 235]). Only 14 of the 124 subjects endorsed one or more of the questions positively. However, 50 participants who did not endorse any typical psychotic experiences reported that they had heard voices when alone.

Similarly, in a study of Spiritist mediums in São Paulo, Brazil (Moreira-Almeida, 2009), the number of reported psychotic symptoms was not correlated with other markers of mental disorders, nor was it statistically related to history of childhood abuse. Further, the 115 participants in the sample had a relatively high educational level and were well-adjusted to their social context. Moreira-Almeida concluded that the psychotic and dissociative experiences that the mediums reported were not necessarily symptoms of psychopathology.

Additional studies have indicated that positive symptoms may be relatively common outside of clinical settings (e.g., Rains et al., 2012, p. 102), and it is now recognised that many people who have these experiences are not distressed by them, nor is their functioning impaired. For example, in the National Comorbidity Study conducted in the United States, 28.4% of respondents in the general population endorsed at least one question about psychotic symptoms, whereas the lifetime prevalence of psychotic disorders was estimated to be less than one percent of the population (Kendler et al., 1996). In a systematic review and meta-analysis, van Os et al. (2009) examined subclinical psychotic experiences in the general population and found a prevalence rate of approximately 5% and an incidence rate of approximately 3% (see also Verdoux & van Os, 2002). In a more recent survey of representative households in 18 countries, McGrath et al. (2015) found a lifetime prevalence of subclinical psychotic experiences of 5.8%; hallucinations (5.2%)

were more commonly reported than delusions (1.3%). Van Os et al. (2009) also found that approximately 75–90% of developmental psychotic experiences fade over time, but that environmental risk may lead to abnormal persistence of these experiences. Van Os and colleagues concluded that there is a continuum of psychosis ranging from non-distressing experiences to symptoms to disorders (see also Strauss et al., 1983).

In sum, multiple international studies have suggested that sociocultural and other contextual factors may influence the prevalence, content, and form of psychotic symptoms. At present, there is little consensus as to whether the schizophrenia diagnosis varies across time and place (Marsella, 2016; Summerfield, 2013; Watters, 2010), and compelling anthropological and clinical observations have indicated that the form and content of psychosis may differ across cultures in ways that have yet to be systematically investigated. One region in which idiosyncratic forms of psychosis have been documented is Israel-Palestine, which was also one of our data collection sites for the research study described in Chapters 4 through 14 of this book.

Cultural heterogeneity of schizophrenia in Israel-Palestine

Israel-Palestine is a site of wide demographic diversity, longstanding historico-cultural traditions, and intense political conflict. Its population of Palestinians, Jews, and others (e.g., African refugees and Armenians) comprise a plurality of historical, linguistic, and sociocultural communities. Some minority groups in Israel are subject to ethnic and socioeconomic discrimination, among other forms of structural violence (e.g., Khattab, 2003). As a result of demographic diversity, strong in-group identifications, and ongoing political turmoil, Israel-Palestine is an established site for research into cultural differences in mental distress and the psychological sequelae of traumatic events (e.g., Arafat & Boothby, 2003; Chaitin et al., 2009; Friedman-Peleg & Bilu, 2011; Haj-Yahia & Abdo-Kaloti, 2008; Lev-Wiesel et al., 2007).

Schizophrenia has been one topic of investigation in Israel-Palestine, with local research supporting the hypothesis that, alongside genetic risk (e.g., Mirsky et al., 1995), environmental context plays a role in development of psychotic symptoms. For example, risk for meeting schizophrenia criteria is significantly increased among first- and second-generation immigrants to Israel, with particularly high risk in Ethiopian immigrants and their offspring (Weiser et al., 2008). Epidemiological research in Israel has suggested that low socioeconomic status, and in particular economic inequality, is a particularly robust risk factor for the development of psychotic experiences (see Dohrenwend, 1990; Dohrenwend et al., 1992).

The majority of research on the schizophrenia diagnosis from Israel-Palestine has explored its prevalence, incidence, predictors, and psychological correlates as defined by DSM and ICD standards. Though the research on cross-cultural heterogeneity of psychosis is relatively scarce, extant evidence for the existence of distinct forms of psychosis within Israeli and Palestinian populations is dramatic and compelling. For example, Kremer et al. (2008) conducted a comparative study of 174 Palestinians diagnosed with schizophrenia from three demographic subgroups: Bedouins in the Negev, Palestinians living in the Galilee (within Israel), and Palestinians living under the Palestinian Authority in Palestine. Findings revealed between-group differences in reported types of psychotic experiences. Anomalous somatic beliefs were present in 86% of the Palestinian Authority areaparticipants but in only 25% of participants from the Galilee, religious delusions were present in 55% of the Bedouin sample but in only 24% of the Galilee and Palestinian Authority area participants, and anomalous auditory experiences were recorded in 89% of participants from the Galilee but in only 44% of the Bedouin sample. The authors concluded that differences in the social experiences of each group may translate into differences in their psychotic experiences.

In the city of Jerusalem, local psychiatrists identified a cultural syndrome that they termed Jerusalem syndrome (Bar-el et al., 2000), with an estimated incidence of approximately 100 new cases each year. Over the course of 13 years (1980–1993), Bar-el et al. (2000) documented 1,200 tourists with Jerusalem-triggered symptoms. On the basis of clinical experience and observations, Bar-el et al. (2000, p. 87) created a tripartite typology of Jerusalem syndrome: Type I includes people with previous psychiatric history and current 'psychiatric religious ideation' and the 'need to accomplish [a] mission'; it may include identification with a biblical character or magical ideas concerning health and healing connected with Jerusalem. Type II is characterised by 'curiosity plus strange (non-psychotic) thoughts or [need to accomplish a] mission' in individuals with sub-clinical features; this subtype may occur in groups (e.g., missionary groups) and, according to Bar-el et al. (2000), probably describes the majority of persons with Jerusalem syndrome. Type III (a.k.a. Discrete Type) is found predominantly in tourists with no previous psychiatric history and characterised by the belief that they are a religious figure from history (e.g., the Virgin Mary, Prophet Mohammed, or the Jewish Messiah) and symptoms such as '[t]he need to scream, shout, or sing out loud psalms, verses from the bible, religious hymns or spirituals,' 'preparation, often with the aid of hotel bed-linen, of a long, ankle-length, toga-like gown,' and '[d]elivery of a "sermon"' (p. 88; see also Kalian et al., 2008).

Debates surrounding Jerusalem syndrome mirror debates about other cultural syndromes (see Guarnaccia & Rogler, 1999; Kleinman, 1987; Prince & Tcheng-Laroche, 1987; Watters, 2010); psychiatrists disagree as to whether it is a discrete syndrome with a unique form (e.g., Bar-el et al., 2000) or, conversely, an expression of classic schizophrenia with locally inspired content (Fastovsky et al., 2000; Kalian & Witztum, 1999, 2000). Jerusalem syndrome Type III is sometimes compared to other transient psychoses that have been documented in tourist and travelling populations (see Halim, 2008, for a review of city-syndromes). Paris syndrome (e.g., Viala et al., 2004), for example, is an acute form of psychosis that sometimes strikes (primarily Japanese) visitors to Paris. The tourists, who often arrive to the city with romanticised expectations, are reportedly struck by language barriers and 'the quotidian banalities of contemporary Paris' (Halim, 2008, p. 2). Shapiro (1977, 1982) described airport-wandering behaviour in service users with ideations related to abandonment and the reuniting of family; he concluded that the airport has a 'magnetic effect [...] for a particular group of disturbed patients' (Shapiro, 1977, p. 555) who 'may be found wandering in various airports around the world' (Shapiro, 1982, p. 173; see also Hopper, 2003; Jauhar & Weller, 1982).

Despite the promising studies described earlier, the extant research literature on unique forms of psychotic experience in Israel-Palestine is still in its infancy. Notably, cultural heterogeneity in psychotic experiences is observable not only in cross-national research, but also in research conducted within individual nations. Indeed, the United States is one location in which researchers have documented variation in the form and content of psychosis across cultures.

Cultural heterogeneity of schizophrenia in the United States

In the United States, where biomedical models of psychopathology have formed the dominant paradigm for over three decades, evidence of cross-cultural heterogeneity has been particularly controversial. One robust finding from epidemiological research in Western countries is higher prevalence rates of 'severe mental illness,' including schizophrenia, in homeless populations. This finding has been particularly relevant in the United States due to its dramatic rise in homelessness starting in the 1980s. In one systematic review of 33 studies conducted in Western countries (16 in the United States), Folsom and Jeste (2002) found prevalence rates of schizophrenia among homeless populations that ranged from 1% to 45%, with a weighted average (calculated using ten studies) of 11%.

There are two competing theories often used to explain the high prevalence of schizophrenia in homeless and other disadvantaged populations. According to the social defeat hypothesis (Selten & Cantor-Graae, 2005; Selten et al., 2013; see also Hopper, 2003; Luhrmann, 2007; Rosen et al., 2017), social stress, in particular experiences of discrimination and marginalisation from a dominant social group, may result in increased risk for psychosis via sensitisation of the mesolimbic dopamine system (Post, 1992; see also Adler, 2009; Geronimus et al., 2006, cited in Fisher et al., 2012). From this framework, experiences of homelessness and related stressors (e.g., poverty, unemployment, and discrimination) have a cumulative effect, with longer durations and more extreme stressors resulting in weathering or kindling effects (see also Hudson, 2005; Veling et al., 2016; see also Karadzhov et al., 2020). Social defeat theory is supported by extensive evidence from social epidemiological research, animal studies, and neuroimaging studies (Selten et al., 2013). In one study of 6,646 participants in the Netherlands, van Nierop et al. (2014) found that the experience of social defeat mediates the relationship between childhood trauma and psychosis. In another study that examined archival data from 50 countries, Johnson et al. (2015) found that the prevalence of hallucinations, delusions of thought control, and delusional mood was associated with economic inequality, regardless of per capita income or regime type.

A competing theory for explaining the high rates of schizophrenia in homeless populations is the downward social drift (or social selection) hypothesis, which holds that individuals with mental disorders such as schizophrenia will move to lower socioeconomic strata as a result of difficulties associated with their symptoms (e.g., Clark, 1948). Some standard textbooks portray social drift theory as the 'correct' explanation for correlations between schizophrenia and homelessness (see Norquist & Narrow, 2000, cited in Luhrmann, 2007). Indeed, this theory is featured in the DSM-5 (APA, 2013, p. 104) as an explanation for the relatively low educational attainment and high unemployment rates among persons diagnosed with schizophrenia. However, due to evidence that these putative outcomes are actually risk factors for psychosis (e.g., Johnson et al., 2015; Saha et al., 2005; Selten et al., 2013), the social drift hypothesis is losing ground as the dominant explanatory model for psychosocial hardships in schizophrenia.

Another social-epidemiological finding is the greater prevalence of schizophrenia in African American populations in the United States. Indeed, schizophrenia is diagnosed more often in African Americans—and in particular in African American males—than in any other American demographic group[3] (Aponte et al., 2000; Delphin-Rittmon et al., 2015; Metzl, 2009; Neighbors et al., 2003). This finding has been subject to varying interpretations. Some have argued that higher rates of schizophrenia reflect actual differences in levels of psychological distress, perhaps due to greater exposure to racial discrimination and socioeconomic hardship (e.g., Fearon et al., 2006). In contrast, some have proposed that clinicians' psychological processes, including unconscious racism, result in bias during the diagnostic encounter (e.g., Schulman et al., 1999; see also Morawski, 2000). Others have argued that clinical training programmes provide insufficient education in cultural competency, structural competency, and related critical thinking skills, resulting in misinterpretation of cultural differences and structural disadvantage as symptoms (Metzl & Hansen, 2014; Metzl & Roberts, 2014; Neighbors et al., 2003; see also Jones et al., 2021). Clinicians might mistake adaptive suspiciousness—arising from exposure to racism and structural violence (see Farmer, 2005)—as 'paranoia'[4] (Whaley, 2002; Whaley & Hall, 2009; see also Rosen et al., 2017). Ridley (1984) differentiates between *cultural paranoia*, a normative response to discrimination and racism, from *functional paranoia*; this distinction has inspired ongoing research into the cultural meanings of paranoia in African American populations (e.g., Whaley, 1997; Wolny et al., 2021).

Another interpretation holds that the diagnostic architecture is itself a sociocultural repository of racial biases (e.g., Afuape, 2011). Metzl (2009) conducted a historical analysis of trends in the diagnosis of schizophrenia and found that the disorder category, once a popular label for housewives who rebelled against domestic work, came to be seen as a 'Black disease' during the civil rights era. Using the historical example of the Ionia State Hospital outside of Detroit, Metzl demonstrated the transformation of the clinical concept of schizophrenia into a placeholder for 'hostility' and 'aggression' just as the movement for social justice was underway. Metzl presents an advertisement from the 1970s featuring a Black man with his fist up. The caption reads: 'Assaultive and belligerent? Cooperation often begins with Haldol' (p. xiv). As these historical contingencies evolved, the American public, and at times members of the scientific community, increasingly described schizophrenia as a violent social disease (Metzl, 2009, p. xii).

In sum, demographic differences in the prevalence of schizophrenia in the United States are poorly understood, and systematic investigations into the cultural and structural origins of these epidemiological patterns have yet to be conducted. However, within the mental health professions, these disparities have spurred discussion about the social and cultural determinants of psychological suffering. Yet due to the popularity of medico-biological explanations for psychological distress in the latter half of the 20th century, most data documenting phenotypic heterogeneity in schizophrenia—including the international data suggesting substantial variations across cultures—has been largely interpreted as evidence of superficial fluctuations within a singular illness category. It was mounting evidence of heterogeneity in the biological and genetic bases of schizophrenia that ultimately led researchers to consider the possibility that phenotypic variation may signal meaningful variations in disorder structure and type.

Biological heterogeneity in schizophrenia

'A widely accepted view is that schizophrenia is a disease of the brain,' explained MacDonald (2014, p. 343) in the *Oxford Textbook of Psychopathology*. During the latter half of the 20th century, scholars' confidence in the imminent discovery of schizophrenia's biological mechanisms filtered into media discourse and the general public. For example, a 2002 article in the *New York Times* (Wade, 2002) announced that 'researchers hope they are now starting to close in on some of the genes that go awry in schizophrenia, a devastating mental disease that affects two million Americans' (para. 1). Within the last two decades, however, psychiatric researchers have tried to understand the ongoing elusiveness of the biogenetic evidence that seemed, for so long, to be 'just around the corner' (Jablensky, 1999). For biologically oriented psychiatrists, evidence of heterogeneity in the biological and genetic correlates of schizophrenia raised questions about the validity of the diagnostic category as classically defined.

Evidence of biological heterogeneity has emerged from three major research areas: (1) genetics, (2) neurochemistry, and (3) neuroanatomy. These three areas of research have been viewed as potential sites for the eventual discovery of biomarkers and/or aetiological evidence that might retroactively serve as the grouping principles for future taxonomies.

Genetic research on schizophrenia

Genetic research has revealed consistent, solid evidence for the heritability of schizophrenia. Gottesman (1991) gathered family and twin studies conducted on Western European populations between the years 1920 and 1987 and found the following heritability risks for schizophrenia: monozygotic (MZ) twins, 48%; dizygotic (DZ) twins, 17%; children of two parents diagnosed with schizophrenia, 46%; children of one parent diagnosed with schizophrenia, 13%; parent of child diagnosed with schizophrenia, 6%; siblings, 9%; grandparent diagnosed with schizophrenia, 5%; first cousin diagnosed with schizophrenia, 2%. Heritability estimates in more recent studies have been more modest, with one large-scale study (Hilker et al., 2018) indicating 33% concordance in MZ twins and 7% in DZ twins. Aberrations in eye-tracking (the smooth pursuit of moving objects), a phenomenon commonly found in persons diagnosed with schizophrenia, are also found in their first-degree relatives (e.g., Levy et al., 1994). Research has suggested that eye-tracking technology can differentiate persons diagnosed with schizophrenia from controls at greater than 98% accuracy (Benson et al., 2012). However, it is unclear as to whether aberrant eye tracking cuts across other psychiatric disorders, and many studies have not properly controlled for the effect of antipsychotic medication on this potential biomarker (Sweeney et al., 1994). Sekar et al. (2016) identified specific genetic risk factors that might lead to excessive synaptic pruning during late adolescence and early adulthood, leading speculation that psychotic disorders might be autoimmune disorders (cf. Hunter, 2016).

Findings from family, twin, and adoption studies have indicated the possible existence of a schizophrenia genotype that interacts with environmental context (e.g., MacDonald, 2014). In one 18-year longitudinal follow-up study, Gottesman & Bertelsen (1989) found that offspring of MZ twins discordant for schizophrenia developed the condition at rates of 16.8% (symptomatic parent) and 17.4% (healthy parent), whereas children of discordant DZ twins developed the disorder at rates of 17.4% (symptomatic parent) and 2.1% (healthy parent). Similarly, in a 21-year follow-up study of Finnish adoptees conducted by Tienari et al. (2006), only those adoptees with high genetic risk for developing the disorder showed an interaction between the development of symptoms and interpersonal conflict in the adoptive family.

Inspired by these discoveries in behavioural genetics, late-20th-century molecular geneticists set out to discover the precise genetic code that formed the presumed schizophrenia diathesis, and several possible candidate genes have been identified. Some studies suggest that disruptions in the protein structure of the *DISC1* gene lead to increased risk for the development of schizophrenia (e.g., Morris et al., 2003; Wang et al., 2018). Also implicated are genes that encode dysbindin (DTNBP1), neuregulin 1 (NRG1), NRG1's ErbB4 receptor, and complement component factor 4 (C4A); mixed data have also suggested the involvement of D-amino-acid oxidase (DAO), D-amino-acid oxidase activator (DAOA, formerly G72), and regulator of G-protein signalling 4 (RGS4) (Jaaro-Peled et al., 2010; Kim et al., 2021; Owen et al., 2005).

These diverse findings have highlighted the heterogeneity and non-specificity of genetic anomalies in schizophrenia and in other psychiatric diagnoses (e.g., Li et al., 2017; Liang and Greenwood, 2015). The *DISC1* gene (e.g., Lee et al., 2015; Wang et al., 2018), for example, has been implicated not only in schizophrenia, but also in other psychotic spectrum disorders, bipolar disorder, and autism spectrum disorders (e.g., Chubb et al., 2008). In a review of the evidence from molecular genetics, Kukshal et al. (2012) stated that:

> Belying earlier expectations, it is now becoming increasingly clear that the cause of SZ [schizophrenia] does not reside in a single mutation, or even in a single gene. Rather, there are multiple DNA variants, not all of which have been identified. Additional risk may be conferred by interactions between individual DNA variants, as well as 'gene-environment' interactions. (para. 1)

Altogether, wide heterogeneity in the genetic profile of schizophrenia (and other psychiatric disorders) has led some psychiatric geneticists to proposed revising the schizophrenia phenotype or, alternatively, shifting focus to single symptom- or deficit-specific genetic patterns (endophenotypes; Gottesman & Gould, 2003). Still others have proposed that there may, in fact, be no singular, indexical genetic pattern for schizophrenia. Liang and Greenwood (2015) explained that '[t]he clinical heterogeneity associated with schizophrenia has likely frustrated decades of attempts to illuminate the underlying genetic architecture' (p. 490). Complicating the picture of genetic heterogeneity in schizophrenia were findings from another major area of biological research in psychiatry, namely, neuroscience.

Neuroscientific research on schizophrenia

Neurochemical research

Neuroscientific research has unveiled substantial heterogeneity in the neurochemical correlates of schizophrenia. Historically, psychiatric researchers have particularly focused on dopamine, a monoamine neurotransmitter implicated in regulating motor control, reward-seeking behaviour, and judgments of salience, among other basic cognitive-behavioural functions (MacDonald, 2014). The dopamine hypothesis emerged from the discovery that dopamine antagonists tended to subdue some psychotic symptoms (Baumeister & Francis, 2002). Because neuroleptics block dopaminergic receptors in the brain, reducing overall dopaminergic activity, researchers hypothesised that psychotic symptoms were the result of excessive dopaminergic function. The dopamine hypothesis of schizophrenia was a, if not *the* primarily aetiological hypothesis put forth by psychiatric textbooks through the mid-to-late-20th century.

The logical-empirical problem with the dopamine hypothesis of schizophrenia was that it conflated cure with aetiology. 'By this same logic,' Carlat (2010) explained, 'one could argue that the cause of all pain conditions is a deficiency of opiates, since narcotic pain medications activate opiate receptors in the brain' (p. 7). Further, the dopamine hypothesis failed to account for negative symptoms, which were unresponsive to antipsychotic drugs. An additional blow to the hypothesis came from researchers' mounting realisation that, because it was considered unethical to allow service users with psychosis to go untreated for extended periods of time, many studies failed (or never attempted) to disentangle the effects of neuroleptics from the symptoms they were said to treat (Ho et al., 2011; Lieberman et al., 2005; Whitaker, 2002, 2010). According to Kendler and Schaffner (2011), the longevity of the dopamine hypothesis might have resulted from the absence of a viable alternate theory, as well as from sociological factors such as the rise of the (second) biological psychiatry movement.

Today, many researchers believe that psychotic symptoms are related to multiple neurotransmitters, including dopamine, norepinephrine, amino acids (glutamate and GABA), serotonin, and adrenal steroids (e.g., MacDonald, 2014). As a result, contemporary research on the neurochemistry of schizophrenia is increasingly focused on complex neurocircuits and their relationship with multiple neurotransmitters as well as environmental risk factors. Another area of focus for biologically oriented schizophrenia researchers has been neuroanatomy.

Neuroanatomical research

Some researchers hold that neuroanatomical research represents the most promising scientific arena for the development of a future biological theory of schizophrenia. Indeed, there is a vast research literature on the structural neurocharacteristics of individuals diagnosed with schizophrenia, with recent advances in research technology offering myriad methods in brain imaging (e.g., magnetic resonance imaging [MRI], functional magnetic resonance imaging [fMRI], diffusion tensor imaging [DTI], and magnetic resonance spectroscopy [MRS]). Like the evidence from genetic and neurochemical studies, however, research on the neuroanatomy of schizophrenia has yielded a portrait of psychotic experiences as heterogeneous and diffuse phenomena spanning multiple brain regions and networks.

Cornblatt et al. (2009) list eight focal phenomena of interest that are commonly seen in persons diagnosed with schizophrenia: enlarged ventricles, enlarged sulci, hemispheric asymmetry (a.k.a. torque), decreased frontal lobe volume, reduced superior temporal gyrus volume, enlarged basal ganglia, reduced medial temporal lobe volume, and thalamic abnormalities. Three of these neurostructural phenomena (enlarged ventricles, enlarged sulci, and torque [see Cornblatt et al., 2009; Keshavan et al., 2011]) are generally considered to be relatively stable, reliable, and independent of the effects of neuroleptic medication. However, various inconsistencies (e.g., reversal in the direction of torque [Malla & Payne, 2005]), imaging protocol artifacts (e.g., Weinburger et al., 1996), and frequent conflation between pathogenetic abnormalities and the iatrogenic effects of antipsychotic medication (e.g., mass reduction in brain volume [Ho et al., 2011; Lieberman et al., 2005]) have led to empirical uncertainties about neuroanatomical findings. Some studies have tried to link neuroanatomical abnormalities with genetic risk factors (Zhu et al., 2021). Hybrid neuropsychological and imaging studies (e.g., Clementz et al., 2016; Wojcik et al., 2017) have suggested that three multivariate (e.g., cognitive and sensorimotor) 'biotypes' of psychosis that may correspond to clinically heterogeneous dimensional clusters in the schizophrenia spectrum (see also Barch, 2017). However, most neuroimaging studies have failed to differentiate schizophrenia from other psychiatric diagnoses, 'exactly the studies required' to achieve diagnostic specificity (Gur et al., 2010, p. 122).

Other studies of brain structure in first-episode psychosis have challenged the predominant view that unmedicated psychotic conditions are *de facto* risk for deterioration of the brain. For example, Beng-Choon et al. (2003), in a study of 156 participants with untreated psychosis, found no evidence of abnormalities in brain volumetric measures, brain surface anatomical indices, or cognitive functioning. The authors concluded that the data, 'do not provide compelling evidence that long periods of untreated psychosis are associated with greater deficits in neurocognitive functioning or in brain morphology' (p. 145). Technological advances in machine learning and neural network analysis have yielded similarly heterogeneous portraits (e.g., Collin and van den Heuvel, 2016; Honnorat et al., 2019; Wolfers et al., 2021). Due to these empirical challenges, the discovery of neurostructural biomarkers and related taxonomic grouping principles for schizophrenia seems a distant, if not idealistic goal.

Biological research: Conclusion

Together, contemporary genetic and neuroscientific research suggests that the schizophrenia diagnosis is genotypically heterogeneous. Geneticists seeking explanations for the heritability seen in twin studies have lamented that '[d]espite considerable effort to identify susceptibility loci for schizophrenia, none have been localized' (Pulver et al., 2000, para. 1; see also Kukshal et al., 2012; Li et al., 2017; Liang & Greenwood, 2015). Taxonomists developing DSM-5 concluded that new biological research 'throw[s] into doubt the assumption that schizophrenia exists as a discrete disease entity' (Tamminga et al., 2010, p. 3). The *Oxford Textbook of Psychopathology* claims that 'schizophrenia is neither a disease entity nor a group of disease entities [...] For most purposes it is useful to understand schizophrenia as an open concept' (MacDonald, 2014, p. 338). In a presentation that addressed the elusiveness of biomarkers for schizophrenia, Carpenter (2011a), chair of DSM-5's Workgroup on Psychotic Disorders, announced: 'I think we made very serious mistakes in the way we conceptualise schizophrenia currently' (see also Keshavan et al., 2011). With these doubts increasingly becoming consensus, researchers have started to seek a new diagnostic understanding.

Newly proposed and alternative models

Proposals to resolve the heterogeneity problem in schizophrenia reflect the polyvocal and contentious discourse characteristic of contemporary debates about psychopathology in general. At present, there are multiple competing models for reconceptualising schizophrenia through the retaxonomisation or conceptual overhaul of the diagnostic category (see also Chung et al., 2007). Newly proposed and alternative models can be divided into proposals to (1) create new disorder subtypes, (2) 'deconstruct' the diagnostic category into its component parts, (3) rename schizophrenia, and (4) conceptually reframe psychosis.

Proposals to create new disorder subtypes

Proposals to subtype the schizophrenia category have appeared throughout the late-21st-century (e.g., Strauss & Dochtery, 1979). Andreasen and Olsen (1982) proposed a tripartite division of the disorder into positive schizophrenia (with predominantly positive symptoms), negative schizophrenia (dominated by negative symptoms), and mixed schizophrenia (with both positive and negative symptoms; see also Kay et al., 2006). Similarly, some have proposed the concept of a 'deficit' or 'negative' syndrome, characterised by predominantly negative symptoms and more chronic course (e.g., Arango et al., 2000; Kirkpatrick et al., 2001). Others have proposed future taxonomic models based in biotypes (Clementz et al., 2016; Wojcik et al., 2017).

Proposals to 'deconstruct' schizophrenia into component symptoms

Carpenter (2011a, 2011b), chair of the DSM-5 Psychotic Disorders Workgroup, has suggested that schizophrenia should be 'deconstructed,' or disassembled into component symptom domains in order to facilitate future research into putative biomarkers that might underlie them (see also Tamminga et al., 2010). Similarly, van Os and Tamminga (2007) explain:

> Given the fact that we have not yet discovered the natural boundaries of psychosis, but only observe its properties, the only way to achieve progress is to periodically reassess all the evidence in the hope of catching a glimpse of its natural pathology. (para. 2)

Among other proposals in this family of approaches is RDoC (NIMH, 2021), which aims to map dynamic criteria matrices onto genetic and neuroscientific dimensions. However, given that the project is still in its early stages, RDoC architects have not yet made specific proposals for remodelling or 'deconstructing' schizophrenia-spectrum and other psychotic disorders.

Proposals to rename schizophrenia

Proposals to rename schizophrenia generally comprise more than just a nominal change and reflect some alteration to the disorder concept. Lasalvia et al. (2015) explained that:

> The term schizophrenia is increasingly contested by researchers, clinicians, patients, and families. Mental health users and professionals around the world have started calling for a change of the name, seeing it as stigmatizing and harmful. (p. 376)

Lasalvia et al.'s conclusions reflect mounting disenchantment with the schizophrenia diagnosis among multiple interest groups (see also Boyle, 2002; BPS, 2017; Hammersley & McLaughlin, 2012; Inquiry, 2012; Link & Phelan, 1999). For example, an online petition by Koehler (2021) that has received over 9,000 signatures (by July 2021) reads 'the time is now to drop this stigmatizing, hope-disabling, scientifically controversial term [schizophrenia] which is saturated with various myths about non-recoverability and dangerousness.'

One popular proposal for renaming schizophrenia has emerged from the work of van Os, a member of the DSM-5 Psychotic Disorders Workgroup. Van Os's earlier writings (e.g., van Os, 2009) suggested that the term schizophrenia should be replaced with 'salience dysregulation syndrome' or 'salience disorder' to reflect the idiosyncrasies in salience attribution commonly seen in psychosis, such as excessive salience attributed to internal psychological processes, elements of the environment, or stimuli that are interpreted differently by most others. In later work, van Os (2016) and his colleagues launched an online campaign titled 'schizophrenia does not exist' and proposed that the schizophrenia-spectrum diagnoses be replaced with the term 'psychosis spectrum syndrome' (PSS) to reflect the heterogeneity of clinical presentations currently identified by the diagnosis. Similarly, Henderson and Malhi (2014) advocate for 'psychotic spectrum disorder' (Peralta, 1999, cited in Henderson & Malhi, 2014) or 'psychotic syndrome.' Another similar proposal, intended to emphasise periods of remission between active symptoms, is 'psychosis susceptibility syndrome' (PSS; George & Klijn, 2013a, 2013b).

Another well-known proposal to rename schizophrenia has been officially implemented in Japan, where *seishin bunretsu byo* ('mind-split-disease') was officially changed to *togo shitcho sho* ('integration disorder') in order to reduce iatrogenic stigma and improve clinical practice (DeVylder et al., 2020; Sato, 2006). According to Sato (2006), within three years of this formal nomenclatural change, 86% of psychiatrists in Miyagi reported that they preferred the new term. Further, cases where the diagnosis was reported to service users increased from 36.7% to 69.7%.

Keshavan et al. (2013) suggested the term 'youth onset conative, cognitive and reality distortion (CONCORD) syndromes.' Keshavan and colleagues argued that renaming schizophrenia with the acronym CONCORD would be more inclusive of various symptoms, reduce stigma, reflect the heterogeneity of the syndrome, and remain neutral regarding aetiology. Some researchers (e.g., Lasalvia et al., 2015) have argued that a name eponymous with a researcher or psychiatrist might help to reduce social stigma. Proposals along this line include 'Bleuler's syndrome' (George, 2012) and 'Kraepelin–Bleuler disease' (KBD; Kim & Berrios, 2001). Still other proposals highlight the putative biological underpinnings of the disorder. For example, 'neuro-emotional integration disorder' (NEID) was proposed by Levin (2006). Lieberman and First (2007) state that 'dopamine dysregulation disorder' has been suggested as a possible alternative.

Note that proposals to rename the disorder are far from universally supported. Lieberman and First (2007), for example, argue that until underlying pathophysiology is discovered, 'the benefits conferred by the concept of schizophrenia far outweigh any perceived disadvantages' (p. 108). For now, in the United States, this has been the predominant view among researchers and clinicians, and the term remains in use today.

Proposals to conceptually reframe psychosis

A growing number of person-centred movements have emphasised the person's potential to generate meaning and live a self-actualised life while having—and in some cases *because* they are having—psychotic experiences. Among the most prominent is the Recovery Movement, which emphasises meaning-making, personal agency, empowerment, hope, and community. From a recovery-oriented perspective, persons diagnosed with psychotic disorders and other serious mental illnesses have the capacity to lead gratifying and fulfilling lives—even with the experience of ongoing symptoms (see Davidson, 2003, 2008; Davidson et al., 2008; Davidson et al., 2010; Deegan, 1994, 1996a, 1996b). As Davidson et al. (2003) put it,

> the recovery model argues that psychiatric disability is only one aspect of the whole person (Corrigan and Penn, 1998) [...] unlike in most physical illnesses, people may consider themselves to be 'in recovery' from a psychiatric disorder while continuing to have, and to be affected by, the disorder. What recovery seems to entail is that people overcome the effects of being a mental patient—including rejection from society, poverty, substandard housing, social isolation, unemployment, loss of valued social roles and identity, and loss of sense of self and purpose in life—in order to retain, or resume, some degree of control over their lives. (Anthony, 1993; Deegan, 1996a, 1996b, p. 38)

Although the recovery model has been rapidly expanding in both alternative and predominant approaches to psychosis, there is still much work to be done in promoting these understandings.

Alternative models are also gaining popularity in the United Kingdom. For example, the British Psychological Society's (BPS) Division of Clinical Psychology published a report titled *Understanding Psychosis and Schizophrenia* (BPS, 2017). The BPS report represents a growing trend to see medical-model diagnostic jargon as only one of multiple ways to frame or conceptualise experiences commonly labelled as 'psychosis' (see also Read et al., 2004; Schrader et al., 2013). The authors summarise their review of the literature and assert:

> Hearing voices or feeling paranoid are common experiences which can often be a reaction to trauma, abuse or deprivation. Calling them symptoms of mental illness, psychosis or schizophrenia is only one way of thinking about them, with advantages and disadvantages. [...] There is no clear dividing line between 'psychosis' and other thoughts, feelings and beliefs: psychosis can be understood and treated in the same way as other psychological problems such as anxiety or shyness. (p. 6)

Another example is the *Hearing Voices Network* (HVN; e.g., Hearing Voices Network, 2019; Jones et al., 2016; Jones & Shattell, 2013; Schnackenberg & Martin, 2014), a service-user-led movement that conceptualises voice-hearing as an experience that a person can not only come to meaningfully understand, but also to live with during the course of everyday life. From the HVN perspective, the way in which voice-hearing is understood—the meanings that each person makes from the voices' presence and/or content—can fundamentally alter the experience of voice-hearing itself. The HVN website (hearing-voices.org) explains:

> Psychiatry traditionally refers to hearing voices as 'auditory hallucinations' but research shows that there are many explanations for hearing voices. Many people begin to hear voices as a result of extreme stress or trauma. We offer information, support and understanding to people who hear voices and those who support them.

Following the tenets and general ethos of HVN, researchers and other scholars have increasingly looked into the psychological, existential, cultural, structural, and spiritual meanings of hearing voices. Examples include the work of Eleanor Longden (2013; Longden et al., 2012), whose work has emphasised the role of trauma and adversity in the development of voice-hearing, and the work of Nev Jones and colleagues (e.g., Jones & Luhrmann, 2016; Jones & Shattell, 2013), who have extensively documented experiential diversity in both the meanings and psychological qualities of voices (see also Britz, n.d.). In addition, a large interdisciplinary project called *Hearing the Voice* (2021) in the United Kingdom explores 'why it is that some voices (and not others) are experienced as distressing, how they can change across the life course, and the ways in which voices can act as important social, cultural and political forces' (para. 3).

Closely related is the growing Experts by Experience movement, within which service users, consumers, clients, and patients are central to the understanding and redefinition of ideas about mental health, mental disorder, and recovery (e.g., Law & Morrison, 2014; Waddingham, 2012; see also Jones & Kelly, 2015). From this perspective, experiences of mental health challenges and the mental health system—conventionally seen as hardships—are forms of valuable knowledge that should be elevated and respected. In this way, the Expert by Experience movement is aligned with critiques of epistemic injustice (harm to a person's status as a knower [Fricker, 2007])—in mental health services and healthcare more broadly. Various scholars have pointed out that persons experiencing physical or mental illness may be particularly susceptible to epistemic injustice (see Crichton et al., 2017), despite the fact that it is precisely their experience of their own illness that provide a valuable kind of knowledge inaccessible from other epistemic standpoints (see also Forgione, 2019). Some Experts by Experience who have gone on to become psychotherapists and other types of healers have written about the ways in which their personal experiences have enhanced their capacity to help others (e.g., Adame et al., 2017; Cornwall, 2018b; Esima, 2017; Frese, 2009; King, 2007; Russell, 2018; see also Kalweit, 1989). Various researchers and scholars (e.g., Byrne et al., 2018; Flanagan et al., 2010; Kamens et al., 2018; Pavlo et al., 2019) have argued that understandings of lived experience—and in particular understandings based in first-person accounts and expert-by-experience leadership—will be crucial in shaping any future diagnostic system that truly cuts human experience 'at its joints' (Plato, 370 B.C./1952; see Regier et al., 2009, para. 15). Closely linked with the Experts by Experience movement is the global disability rights movement, which encompasses multiple and pluralistic perspectives on rights-based approaches to reframing ideas about psychosocial disability and mental health (see Karter, 2021).

In 2018, a group in the United Kingdom (BPS, 2018) released the *Power Threat Meaning* (PTM) framework, an alternative to the DSM that offers new ways of understanding and conceptualising mental distress. Critiquing pathologising approaches, the PTM locates individual distress and life challenges in the broader structures and social systems within which they occur (see also Elkins, 2016; Robbins et al., 2015). In doing so, PTM advocates for understanding *power* (structural advantage and disadvantage), experiences of *threat*, and the *meanings* that are made from power, threat, and distress. The PTM framework replaces the implicit question 'what's wrong with you?' with the four questions 'What has happened to you?,' 'How did it affect you?,' 'What sense did you make of it?,' and 'What did you have to do to survive?' Applied to psychosis, the PTM framework highlights the role of adversity—including childhood abuse, other forms of trauma, and social isolation—in the development of anomalous beliefs and perceptions.

The recent Mad pride and Mad studies movements (e.g., Russo & Beresford, 2015; Schrader et al., 2013) view alternative ways of being-in-the-world as potential sources of existential meaning and personal agency (e.g., Andersen et al., 2018; Cutler, 2018; Kalathil & Jones, 2016; LeFrançois et al., 2013). As Starkman (2013) put it: 'An important new movement is sweeping through the Western world. The "mad," the oppressed, the ex-inmates of society's asylums are coming together and speaking for themselves' (p. 27). Mad activists have aligned with other social justice movements, including the queer rights movement (Spandler & Barker, 2016), the psychiatric survivors movement (Adame et al., 2017), and broader civil rights movements in order to advocate for recognition of Madness as an identity category and way of being that should garner respect rather than discrimination and stigma.

Last but not least, some existential and spiritual approaches have seen in psychosis not a problem to be cured, but a difficult experience that, once worked through, can become a gift—sometimes a gift that helps one to heal others. In various traditions throughout history, shamans are 'wounded healers' who experience an initiation period characterised by illness and great suffering; it is the shaman's journey to recovery that leads to her, his, or their development into a shaman (see Esima, 2017; Kalweit, 1989). These traditions mirror the more contemporary approach taken by mental health practitioners, researchers, and other experts by experience who draw on their own recovery from mental health challenges to help others (e.g., Cornwall, 2018b; Esima, 2017; Frese, 2009; Jung, 2009; King, 2007; Russell, 2018; see also Romanyshyn, 2007).

As a result of these movements, various stakeholders have suggested non-pathologising, non-diagnostic language to describe psychotic experiences. For example, in 2012, the International Society for Psychological and Social Approaches to Psychosis (ISPS)—formerly the International Society for the Psychological Treatments of the Schizophrenias and Other Psychoses—voted to drop the term schizophrenia from its title (Waddingham, 2012). In an example of non-pathologising scholarship, Cornwall (2018a) edited a special issue on extreme states in the *Journal of Humanistic Psychology* with diverse perspectives on experiences often referred to as schizophrenia or psychosis. The mission statement of the Icarus Project (2019), a mutual support and education network (see DuBrul, 2014), states: 'We envision a new culture that allows the space and freedom for exploring different states of being, and re-cognises that breakdown can be the entrance to breakthrough' (para. 2).

Summary: Newly proposed models

There are currently multiple competing models for the renaming of schizophrenia, and researchers increasingly question not *whether* the schizophrenia diagnosis will be renamed, but *when*. Regardless of whether researchers prefer to revise, deconstruct, reinterpret, or rename the schizophrenia construct, there is growing consensus among contemporary psychiatrists that '[t]he current construct of schizophrenia as a unitary disease is far from satisfactory, and is in need of reconceptualization' (Keshavan et al., 2011, p. 3). Although no one model has yet gained consensus, proposals to rename schizophrenia are gaining familiarity and traction.

The heterogeneity problem in schizophrenia: Conclusion

The need for newly proposed models of schizophrenia arose from both the conceptual dilemmas specific to the diagnosis and the general dilemmas in contemporary psychiatric taxonomising. These dilemmas are not transient flukes or empirical accidents, but rather systemic, historical problems that date back to the importation of classificatory terminology from the general medical sphere. This import led to the adoption, within psychiatry and clinical psychology, of a hierarchical referential system connecting observable signs and symptoms to unobservable disease entities. However, from a contemporary biogenetic perspective, without reliable biological evidence, psychiatric taxonomies lack an empirical grouping principle on which this taxonomic hierarchy can be based. Although the two goals need not be mutually exclusive, the contemporary hunt for biomarkers has often eclipsed the description of psychological meanings on which future nomenclatures might be based. Attempting to reconceptualise schizophrenia on the basis of 'deconstructed' or atomistic signs and symptoms extends the tendency to overlook the subjective dimension of experience (see Strauss, 2011, 2013; Strauss & Carpenter, 1981), which, both presently and historically, remains the primary source of data with which the diagnosis of mental disorder is made. Indeed, in their everyday work, clinicians and researchers continue to rely on verbal reports to identify and evaluate symptom profiles. Thus, in revising, renaming, deconstructing, and/or dividing schizophrenia according to biological hypotheses, contemporary psychiatric taxonomists are effectively disassembling the one source of data on which psychologically valid taxonomic principles could be grounded: lived experience.

Notes

1 However, some proposals have suggested that negative symptoms may be most characteristic of the disorder.
2 See also Davidson et al. (1997) for a study of socioenvironmental experiences contributing to recidivism in urban hospital service users.
3 Similarly, in the United Kingdom, incidence rates of schizophrenia are 'remarkably high' in Black African and African Caribbean populations (Fearon et al., 2006, p. 1549).
4 This argument has also been put forth about 'paranoia' in other cultural groups that have experienced oppression; for example, in a study of persecutory beliefs in postcolonial Nigeria, Sadowsky (2004) concluded that reported experiences of persecutory delusions were inseparable from the historical experience of colonialism itself.

3

PHENOMENOLOGICAL ACCOUNTS

Sarah R. Kamens and Frederick J. Wertz

A method for investigating human experience

A long-standing yet oft-marginalised tradition has offered systematic means for identifying *psychological structures*, or organisations of meaning in lived, subjective experience. The name of this tradition is phenomenology. Phenomenology is a method for the investigation of human consciousness that was initially developed by Austrian mathematician and philosopher Husserl (e.g., 1913/1962, 1939/1970, 1948/1973). Dissatisfied with the narrowness of the scientific methods of his time, Husserl created a new qualitative method that was specifically designed for the study of conscious, lived experience in human beings. Phenomenology acknowledges the *intentional* structure of consciousness, i.e., the fact that human consciousness is consciousness *of something* (Brentano, 1874; Wertz, 2005, 2015). Following Husserl, phenomenology was further developed by Heidegger (e.g., 1927/1962), Merleau-Ponty (e.g., 1945/2012), Sartre (e.g., 1943/1993), and Ricœur (e.g., 1975), among others. More recently, Giorgi (1975, 2009), Wertz (1985, 2005, 2010, 2015), and Wertz et al. (2011) have systematised and modified Husserlian phenomenology for empirical research in the social sciences, psychology in particular.

'Phenomenology' is a term that is often employed loosely and inaccurately in psychiatric discourse, where it is variously used to describe observable disorder phenotypes, measurable symptoms, and/or general clinical presentations (see Rulf, 2003). Indeed, in psychiatric discourse where mental disorders are assumed have a dichotomous structure with observable symptoms overlying biological substrates (e.g., Gottesman & Gould, 2003), 'phenomenology' has become common shorthand for the former (see, e.g., Baron et al., 1984; Berrios, 1989; Carpenter et al., 1981; Gecici et al., 2010). In other words, clinicians often use the term phenomenology to signify any visible behaviours or verbal reports that they believe to be symptoms.

These popularised uses of the term, however, have little to do with the long-standing phenomenological tradition and method of inquiry that originated in Europe at the turn of the 20th century. Following Jaspers

DOI: 10.4324/9780429055454-4

(1913/1963, 1912/1968), Husserl (e.g., 1913/1962, 1939/1970, 1948/1973), Giorgi (1975, 2009), and Wertz (1985, 2005, 2010; Wertz et al., 2011; Wertz et al., 2017), this book employs the term 'phenomenology' to refer to the systematic method for investigations of human experience; the adjective 'phenomenological' is used to describe aspects of this scientific procedure or the findings about lived experience that are derived from its use. As detailed by Parnas and Zahavi (2002), this more restrictive definition of the term is preferable to its current polysemic use in psychiatric literature, as the phenomenological study of experience—which produces detailed portraits of the structures of psychological life—is essential for the scientific advancement of psychiatric classification.

Phenomenology does not start with a deductive hypothesis; instead, it provides a method for the comparative analysis of emergent data in order to determine structural differences or types (Wertz, 2005, 2015; Wertz et al., 2011). In other words, phenomenology begins with experiential data and progresses from the bottom up, as themes and structures emerge within and across narratives. The psychological structures yielded by phenomenology represent meaningful organisations of experiential life that are invariant characteristics of the phenomena under investigation called *essences*. The use of the word 'essences' by phenomenologists is often associated with postmodern critiques of essentialism and thereby misunderstood. As Wertz (e.g., 2010, 2015) has pointed out, phenomenological methods are not dogmatic, deductive, or totalising, but rather methodical, self-correcting, and evidence-based ways of knowing that have open, variable boundaries. Moreover, phenomenological essences are not 'unchanging, eternal, complete, separate from existence' or 'incorrigible' (Wertz, 2015, p. 87), but rather open, flexible, and continuously adapted according to evidence as it is gathered.

Meaningful phenomenological essences are precisely the type of knowledge that is lacking in contemporary psychiatric taxonomies, which earmark the presence of empirically obscure, hypothetical disorder entities using atomistic descriptions of observed behaviours and verbal reports, which are then interpreted as symptoms and signs. Indeed, phenomenologists have long suggested that the meaningful, essential structures of psychological life might provide a reliable and valid basis on which the theory, aetiological understanding, cultural contextualisation, and classification of psychological distress might be based.

Jaspers (1913/1963, 1912/1968) was one of the earliest psychiatrists to import Husserlian phenomenology into psychiatry.[1] Jaspers believed that phenomenology was the method that could delineate 'what the psychiatric patient *really* experiences' through systematic description of first-person verbal reports (Jaspers, 1912/1968, p. 1323; see also Mishara & Schwartz, 2013). Thus, according to Jaspers (1912/1968),

> [...] phenomenology demands that we should account for every psychic phenomenon and every experience that comes to light in the investigation of our patients or in their own self-descriptions. We should in no circumstances be content with a general impression extracted from the total picture, but should get to know, as regards each detail, how it is to be viewed and assessed. (p. 1323)

With notable exceptions (e.g., Minkowski, 1927/1953), Jasperian phenomenology largely disappeared from the psychiatric literature until the latter half of the 20th century. However, over the last 50 years, investigators have begun to revisit the potential contributions of phenomenology to the empirical understanding of psychological distress. Indeed, one of the primary focal topics that contemporary phenomenologists have investigated is the diagnostic category of schizophrenia.

Phenomenology and schizophrenia

Phenomenologists have long suggested that the official psychiatric manuals fail to reflect the meaningful patterns of experiences in the lives of individuals diagnosed with schizophrenia (e.g., Flanagan et al., 2012). As aforementioned, the use of phenomenology in psychiatry dates back to Jaspers, who nevertheless described schizophrenia as intuited through particulars and essentially 'ununderstandable' in universal psychological terms (Jaspers, 1913/1968, p. 308; see also Hoerl, 2012; Mishara & Schwartz, 2013). According to Mishara and Schwartz (2013), Jasperian phenomenology, which may have differed in some ways from Husserlian methods (Berrios, 1992), aimed at understanding the meanings of individual symptoms and life-historical experiences rather than universal phenomena underlying those symptoms. Contemporary phenomenologists vary in the extent to which they utilise phenomenology for understanding the essential meanings of individual symptoms or experiences (e.g., voice-hearing) versus positing core psychological structures that cut across multiple symptoms. Following is a brief overview of previous phenomenological research on psychosis and schizophrenia, starting in the mid-20th century.

One common trend in the past phenomenological literature on schizophrenia are accounts that posit core disturbances in the person's orientation to the world, here referred to as world-disorientation accounts. One of the earliest world-disorientation accounts was put forth by French psychiatrist Minkowski (1927/1953), who believed that the experiential essence of schizophrenia, which he called the 'trouble générateur,' was the loss of 'vital contact with reality' (VCR), or a loss of dynamic limits between interior and exterior which resulted in a kind of autistic stance towards the world (see Urfer, 2001). For Minkowski, the trouble générateur was grasped instantaneously and intuitively as a unified essential structure; in his own words:

> Sitting face to face with my patient, I am meticulously writing down his utterances, and then suddenly, like in a flash, one of his sentences illuminates everything with a particular clarity, and I have a feeling of having seized a complex living whole, of having grasped the 'trouble générateur', which now appears as the touchstone of the whole clinical picture. (Minkowski 1948, p. 145, quoted in Urfer, 2001, p. 282)

Minkowski divided VCR into two types: rich and empty autism. He described rich autism as the conflation of fantasy and reality such that the person often lives an imagined life based predominantly in past experiences; empty autism, in contrast, was said to involve 'morbid rationalism' with a focus on intellectual (especially mathematical and geometrical) concepts (see Urfer, 2001).

In his book *The Divided Self*, the Scottish psychiatrist R. D. Laing (1960) described one life-historical path leading to the development of a mode of being-in-the-world that is sometimes called schizophrenia. According to Laing, a schizoid position arises from ontological insecurity, an existential state in which the self is not experienced as whole, continuous, embodied, and/or 'real'; ontological security, in contrast, is a firm, grounded sense of being-in-the-world as a whole, continuous person. An individual experiencing ontological insecurity may be deeply threatened by activities that ontologically secure people take for granted, and as an attempt at self-protection, they may conceal, hide, or withdraw what they experience as their 'true self.' The self is thus split: the 'true self' develops in quasi-estrangement from the body, which is treated as a protective and performative extension into the threatening world of reality, where the 'false self' engages with the surrounding world. For Laing, the movement from the schizoid to the schizophrenic position occurs when, in the schizoid way of life, a person becomes increasingly detached from the world and begins to experience, with increasing horror, a perceived annihilation of one's being, often paradoxically as a consequence of this very means of self-preservation. One typical transition to schizophrenia occurs when a person decides to shed the façade of false adaptation to the demands of the social world: 'Indeed, what is called psychosis is sometimes simply the sudden removal of the veil of the false self' (p. 99).

Laing and Esterson (1964) demonstrated the meaningfulness of interpersonal interactions in persons diagnosed with schizophrenia through their phenomenological study of families. Through detailed descriptions of interactions between family members, Laing and Esterson demonstrated the intelligibility of psychotic symptoms when viewed from the lens of the specific interpersonal contexts within which they arise. For example, they conducted extensive interviews with the Abbott family, whose daughter Maya had been diagnosed with paranoid schizophrenia; in doing so, they discovered that Maya's symptoms were meaningfully related to her parents' beliefs and behaviours, including their belief that her desire for autonomy was part of her 'illness,' their frequent invalidation of Maya's independent use of her own mind, and the games they played to test what they presumed to be Maya's quasi-psychic powers. Though Maya was still struggling to preserve her sense of self (e.g., in arguing that her parents did not see her 'as the person that I am' [p. 36]), her personality was continuously negated by her environment, and she began to believe her thoughts were controlled by others and to view herself as a machine and not a person. As Laing (1960) wrote, 'it [the self] sought to preserve its identity; but, no longer anchored to fact [...] it loses its possibility of exercising effective freedom of choice in the world' (p. 142).

Binswanger (1956, 1957, 1963), a Swiss contemporary of Laing, described schizophrenia as characterised by exaggerated or extravagant ideals, experiential inconsistencies, dichotomous thinking, the covering (concealing) of negative experiences, the experience of being 'worn away,' and the renunciation of the world [existential retreat]) rather than a withdrawal from it per se (see Kouba, 2006; Noll, 2007, p. 117). Influenced by Heidegger, Binswanger, who worked under Bleuler and Jung at the Burghölzli Hospital in Switzerland, developed a treatment method that he called *Daseinanalyse* for the existential analysis of human experience (see also Boss, 1963, 1975).

After Minkowski (1927/1953), Laing (1960), and Binswanger (1956, 1957, 1963), additional phenomenologists attempted to investigate psychological experiences that are associated with schizophrenia and other psychotic states (e.g., Boss, 1975; Bovet & Parnas, 1993; Broome et al., 2013; Davidson, 2002; Fuchs, 2005, 2007; Jones et al., 2016; Jones & Luhrmann, 2016; Jones et al., 2018; Jones & Shattell, 2016; Keller, 2008; Kimura, 1982; Parnas & Handest, 2003; Parnas et al., 2002; Pienkos, 2014a, 2014b, 2015, 2020; Pienkos et al., 2017; Sass, 1992a, 1992b, 1994a, 1994b; Sass & Parnas, 2003; Sass et al., 2011; Stanghellini, 2011). Late 20th-century and early-21st-century phenomenological investigations into psychotic (and pre-psychotic) states have elaborated on early theories of fundamental self-disturbances (Ichstörungen [e.g., Bleuler, 1911; Jaspers, 1913/1963]; for a historical overview see Mishara et al., 2014) by positing central disturbances in time consciousness (e.g., Denischik, 2015; Fuchs, 2005, 2007) and experiences of the 'self' (Parnas, 2011; Sass, 1992a, 1994a, 1994b; Schneider, 1950/1959; see also Davidson & Strauss, 1992). In addition, late-20th-century world-disorientation accounts have posited core disturbances in the understanding of consensual reality such as loss of 'natural self-evidence' (Selbstverstandlichkeit) or a 'common-sense' orientation towards the world (Blankenburg, 1969/2001, 1971; see also Pienkos, 2014a; Sass, 2003a).

Some phenomenological researchers have posited essential, invariant psychological features as unifying explanations for putative symptoms of schizophrenia that might otherwise appear to be disparate and heterogeneous.

Phenomenological investigation does not preclude establishment of biomarkers or biogenetic correlates of mental distress; instead, phenomenologists have insisted on the systematic description of meaningful psychological processes. From a phenomenological perspective, this systematic description is a precondition to the understanding of aetiology.[2] Thus, according to Parnas et al. (2011), phenomenology is 'indispensable for psychiatry in its praxis of clinician–patient interaction, diagnosis, therapy, theoretical work, formation of pathogenetic hypotheses, and empirical data collection' (p. 36).

One example of a unifying phenomenological account of psychotic experiences is Fuchs's (2005, 2007) work on disturbances in the basic temporal structure of psychological life, i.e., in time consciousness. Drawing on Husserl's (1893–1917/1980) work on time consciousness, Fuchs postulated that symptoms such as delusions, loss of automatic behaviour, and altered self-awareness may be accounted for by a dissolution in the understanding of a normative, causal relationship between past, present, and future. Through Husserl, Fuchs explains that basic psychological functions such as memory and goal-directed behaviour are contingent upon a linear and passively synthetic understanding of the temporal unfolding of events. When this passive synthesis is disrupted, time is experienced as fragmented and discontinuous (see also Denischik, 2015). As a result, events are experienced as isolated or meaningless rather than causally interdependent and meaningful. For example, a person may have difficulty understanding speech because words are experienced as puzzlingly independent from each other; similarly, the plotline of a story or narrative may seem disjointed and incomprehensible. Fuchs (2007) suggested that social withdrawal, avoidance of overstimulation, and catatonic immobilisation may result from this overwhelming experience of temporal fragmentation, which disrupts the experience of meaningful continuity and one's own agency in the world.

Perhaps the most comprehensive account of heterogeneity in schizophrenia from the contemporary phenomenological literature can be found in the writing of Sass (e.g., 1987, 1988, 1992a, 1992b, 1994a, 1994b, 2000, 2001, 2003a, 2003b, 2004, 2007, 2011, 2014a, 2014b; Nelson et al. 2014; Sass & Parnas, 2003, 2007; Sass et al., 2013, 2018), whose extensive body of work has shed light on psychological experiences that were long considered enigmatic and 'un-understandable' (Jaspers, 1913/1968, p. 308). According to Sass and Parnas (e.g., 2003), schizophrenia is a disturbance of *ipseity*. Ipseity ('self' or 'itself' in Latin) is the sense of a unified, centralised self that is experienced as implicit and obvious in everyday experience; ipseity disturbance, in contrast, is a disturbance in typical experiences of selfhood and self-consciousness. Ipseity disturbance affects the 'minimal' (a.k.a. 'core' or 'basic') self (as opposed to the 'narrative' or 'social' self), i.e., the prereflective sense of self that imbues consciousness with a first-person, '*my*' perspective (Nelson et al., 2014, p. 479). Sass and Parnas identify two main facets of ipseity disturbance in schizophrenia: 'hyperreflexivity' and 'diminished self-presence' (a.k.a. diminished self-affection). Hyperreflexivity refers to an exaggerated sense of self-consciousness (reflexivity) in which the individual focuses on features of the self or the environment that are usually overlooked or taken for granted (e.g., heightened attention to one's own fleeting thoughts or minutiae in others' social gestures). The other component of ipseity disturbance, diminished self-presence, is a mitigated sense of being a central subject, agent, or possessor of one's own experiences; in the words of Sass et al. (2011), diminished self-presence is characterised by 'a decline in the (passively or automatically) experienced sense of existing as a living and unified subject of awareness' (p. 7). A third element of ipseity disturbance, 'disturbed hold' or 'grip' on the world, involves a 'disturbance of the field of awareness' and, frequently, a kind of perplexity that is associated with hyperconsciousness (Sass, 2014b, p. 6). Though disturbed hold on the world is grounded in a disturbance of the embodied self, from the ipseity disturbance framework, the former is no less central to experience in schizophrenia than the latter. As Sass (2014b) explained, 'from a strictly phenomenological standpoint, self and world are often seen as complementary or even "equiprimordial" poles of experience' (p. 9).

According to Sass and Parnas (2003), diminished self-presence and hyperreflexivity, as core psychotic processes, represent potential solutions to the heterogeneity problem in the schizophrenia diagnosis; in their words, 'although the major symptoms and signs of schizophrenia are heterogeneous in many respects, they can nevertheless be understood in a fairly unified way' (p. 428; see also Sass et al., 2018). From this perspective, the varied, superficially heterogeneous symptoms of schizophrenia share an underlying disruption in self-experience, i.e., ipseity disturbance. Put differently, the loss of a centralised, singular, and agentic sense of self leads to essential vacillations and inconsistencies in speech and behaviour that may appear vastly incongruent, heterogeneous, or paradoxical to the observer. For example, the experience of omnipotence, grandiosity, and radical solipsism may progress into its apparent opposite: the experience of the self as not-whole, multiple, or fragmented (as in Laing, 1960). A sense of absolute freedom may be undercut by an experience of extreme passivity, in which one's thoughts and actions are controlled by external forces. Similarly, auditory hallucinations and thought broadcasting are classic symptoms that may appear to be conceptually opposed; auditory hallucinations are the perception of voices or sounds that are experienced as external to the self, while thought broadcasting involves the belief that one's own consciousness is transparent and somehow available to the external world. Both symptoms, however, involve diminished self-presence, such that the self is not experienced as the central originator or (in the case of thought broadcasting) addressee of one's own thoughts, as well as hyper-reflexive attentiveness to one's own psychological processes and/or sounds and activities in the external environment.

Within the ipseity disturbance framework, the unmooring of agentic selfhood (diminished self-presence) and attentiveness to seemingly mundane detail (hyper-reflexivity) results in the experience of a kind of conceptual freedom, an opening of interpretative possibilities in which the norms of consensual reality are abandoned or regarded as arbitrary. As Sass (1992a) explains in *Madness and Modernism*, persons diagnosed with schizophrenia often approach situations as if anything is possible, and they often hesitate or vacillate between multiple ideas and interpretations. To the observer, the simultaneous entertainment of multiple possibilities and shifting between discursive frames of reference may result in behaviour or speech that appears as erratic, indecisive, and disorganised—a 'radical kind of heterogeneity,' in Sass' own words (p. 133). Within ipseity disturbance theory, however, these perplexingly discontinuous, heterogeneous symptoms are the produce of the experiential decentralisation and disunification of agentic selfhood, coupled with an exaggerated attentiveness to aspects of one's surroundings that are, in non-psychotic states of consciousness, ignored or taken for granted.

Sass' extensive work (e.g., 1987, 1988, 1992a, 1992b, 1994a, 1994b, 2000, 2001, 2003a, 2003b, 2004, 2007, 2011, 2014a, 2014b) has significantly advanced the scientific understanding of schizophrenia as a psychological phenomenon. As a demonstration of the ways in which the structural unity of psychological processes has been posited to account for empirical variation in psychotic symptoms, the theory of ipseity disturbance represents the most comprehensive solution to the heterogeneity problem to date. However, according to Sass (1992a), the universality of this account of schizophrenia remains an open empirical question. One particular enigma in need of further investigation is the phenomenon of cross-cultural variation in psychotic symptoms.

Cross-, trans-, and multicultural phenomenological research

Phenomenological accounts of ipseity disturbance (e.g., Sass, 1992a; Sass & Parnas, 2003) focus on a construct that varies extensively across cultures: the self. Recall that mounting evidence points towards the possibility that psychosis might not exist in the same form outside of the Western world (see Chapter 2). Indeed, differences in self-experience are one empirically under-investigated explanation for variation in the form of psychotic symptoms across cultures (e.g., Jablensky, 1987). For example, the tension between totalistic solipsism and self-disintegration (e.g., Sass, 1992a; see also Cushman, 1990) may be a dualistic experience that is unique to Western, individualistic conceptualisations of the self and subjectivity. Indeed, some researchers and theorists have suggested that schizophrenia itself is a phenomenon that may be produced or exacerbated by modern, post-industrial, capitalist society (e.g., Deleuze & Guattari, 1972/1983, 1980/1987; Jameson, 1991; Luhrmann, 2011; Sass, 1992a). However, the majority of extant psychiatric investigations into schizophrenia have been conducted in wealthier, Western nations, and there are few systematic phenomenological investigations into the heterogeneity of psychotic experiences in persons living in developing countries and other non-Western regions. It follows that cross-cultural variation in psychotic symptoms is a central dilemma for future phenomenological researchers concerned with the heterogeneity problem. Sass (1992a) reviewed the cross-cultural literature on the epidemiology of schizophrenia and concluded that 'the evidence does seem to indicate that the most clear-cut cases of schizophrenia [...] may well be less common in cultural settings where traditional or premodern forms of social organization prevail' (p. 364).

The extant cross-, trans-, and multicultural phenomenological studies have tended to focus on cultural differences in the content of psychotic symptoms, including differences in the experience of the body and in the experience of religious ideation. For example, Moreira and Junior (2003) found that whereas in Chilean persons diagnosed with schizophrenia attributed their bodily changes to illness mechanisms or the side effects of medication, persons in Brazil attributed bodily changes to both illness or medication effects and to the incorporation of supernatural spirits into the body. Good and Subandi (2004) studied the case of a Javanese woman whose psychotic symptoms were deeply intertwined with themes in Islam. In addition, Luhrmann (2012) and Luhrmann et al. (2015) investigated cross-cultural differences in voice-hearing experiences using anthropological methods and found that cultural communities play a role in the extent to which voices are experienced as pleasant or distressing (see Chapter 2).

As researchers and other taxonomists deliberate the fate of schizophrenia as a diagnostic category, the enigma of cross-cultural heterogeneity in psychotic experiences has become a focal topic. However, mental health researchers have been historically concerned with the validation of diagnostic models developed solely in Western societies. As a result, the potential empirical contributions of transcultural, international phenomenology to the reconceptualisation of the schizophrenia diagnosis have largely been neglected.

Notes

1 However, some scholars have questioned his understanding of Husserlian methods (see Berrios, 1992; Wiggins & Schwartz, 1997).

2 Notably, physicians have historically recognised the central place of descriptive observation in the scientific identification and study of diseases. Exemplifying this tradition is a quote from 19th-century French physiologist Claude Bernard: '"Pathology" should not be subordinated to physiology. Quite the reverse. Set up first the medical problem which arises from the observation of a malady, and afterwards seek for a physiological explanation. To act otherwise would be to risk overlooking the patient, and distorting the malady' (quoted in Charcot, 1889, p. 8).

4

A MULTI-SITE, INTERNATIONAL PROJECT

Sarah R. Kamens, Frederick J. Wertz, Jessica Yisca Baris Ginat, Jacob Kader, David Miller, Lyra Ward, Tal Shachar-Malach, and Pesach Lichtenberg

A transcultural, phenomenological study

When we started developing our research project in 2012, we had not yet identified the psychological structure of urhomelessness, nor did we anticipate its emergence during data analysis. Instead, our goal was to investigate experiential and cross-cultural heterogeneity in the schizophrenia diagnosis using phenomenological research methods (Giorgi, 1975, 2009; Husserl, 1913/1962, 1939/1970, 1948/1973a, b, c; Wertz (1985, 2005, 2010, 2015). A broader goal was to contribute to the resolution of conceptual dilemmas in clinical taxonomisation through the use of experiential description. The phenomenological method is particularly applicable to the heterogeneity problem in the schizophrenia diagnosis—and to classificatory problems in general—as the careful and systematic comparison of verbal reports may point to homogeneous psychological structures; alternatively, it may reveal heterogeneous structures that resist generalisation into superordinate wholes. Therefore, in the present study, this meticulous, participant-centred analytic procedure was employed to investigate experiential heterogeneity in the verbal reports of persons who had been diagnosed with psychotic disorders.

As described in Chapter 3, previous phenomenological studies of schizophrenia have revealed experiential features which have not been included in the diagnostic manuals; they have also yielded crucial insights into the psychological, interpersonal, and contextual situations of persons diagnosed with schizophrenia that may have general bearing on the heterogeneity problem (e.g., Boss, 1975; Davidson, 2002; Flanagan et al., 2012; Fuchs, 2005, 2007; Jones et al., 2016; Keller, 2008; Kimura, 1982; Laing, 1960; MacNab, 1965; Parnas & Handest, 2003; Parnas et al., 2002; Sass, 1992a, 1994a,b; Sass & Parnas, 2003; Sass et al., 2011). However, the phenomenological literature on schizophrenia is, for the most part, not reflected in contemporary psychiatric nomenclature (see Flanagan et al., 2012; Parnas & Zahavi, 2002). Further, the

 DOI: 10.4324/9780429055454-5

extant phenomenological literature on schizophrenia lacks systematic investigation into the central problem of heterogeneous experience at the international level. Therefore, we designed a transcultural, international, phenomenological research project involving interviews with persons carrying a schizophrenia-spectrum or other psychotic-disorder diagnosis.

The objectives of the study were to investigate psychological structure(s) that are diagnosed as psychotic disorders in diverse persons; to examine experiential similarities and differences among diverse persons carrying schizophrenia-spectrum diagnoses; to examine the relationship between the experiences of persons diagnosed with schizophrenia-spectrum disorders and cultural life in Israel-Palestine and the United States; and, finally, to evaluate the potential contribution of phenomenological research methods to the resolution of taxonomic dilemmas in mental health research. More specifically, we posed the following research questions:

1 What general structure or structures are found in the psychological meanings and experiences of diverse persons diagnosed with schizophrenia-spectrum disorders?
2 What are the meaningful similarities and differences among the psychological processes and experiences of diverse individuals diagnosed with schizophrenia-spectrum disorders?
3 How are the experiences of persons diagnosed with schizophrenia-spectrum disorders related to cultural life?

Method

A major challenge for our study was determining which participants to include and how to recruit them. We wanted to investigate heterogeneity in the schizophrenia diagnosis using qualitative research methods. More specifically, we wanted to know what experience or experiences, from a qualitative-phenomenological perspective, were typically labelled as indicative of schizophrenia. It was theoretically possible that our results would indicate differences between the standard diagnostic definition and the essential experiences reported by participants. However, phenomenology is a data-driven process that does not presuppose or hypothesise the findings in advance; therefore, we did not know which experiences might emerge as salient or central. Recruiting participants based on any one experience or specific set of experiences would have limited the scope of our investigation. The only feasible way to identify potential participants was to utilise the very diagnostic categories under question, namely, psychotic disorder categories as defined by the *Diagnostic and Statistical Manual of Mental Disorders* (DSM). The description of our method and procedures below thus reference DSM disorder definitions; it is important to note that our purpose in utilising these definitions was not to reify them, but rather to explore the experiential-existential meanings of the experiences that they are commonly used to label. This approach also had a major limitation: were we to discover an essential experience that differs from standard DSM definitions, it would not be possible to determine whether (and to what extent) it might be present in other populations (see Chapter 13 for a longer discussion of this limitation). We recruited pilot-comparison participants in order to start examining this question, remaining aware that, should unique findings emerge, questions of generalisability would require further examination in future follow-up studies.

Participants

Participants in the present project were 21 culturally diverse hospital service users diagnosed with psychotic disorders and receiving inpatient or outpatient psychiatric care at one of three hospitals in New York City (NYC; ten participants) or Jerusalem (11 participants). There were seven females (including one transgender woman and gender fluid individual[1]), 13 males, and one biologically male participant with unknown gender identification (mean age = 42 years, age range: 23–61 years). Three of the inpatient hospital participants (two in New York and one in Jerusalem) did not describe experiences consistent with their diagnosis during our qualitative interviews (see next). These participants were thus used as ad hoc comparison cases (see next), leaving 18 participants whose interviews formed the primary psychotic-disorder-diagnosis dataset (hereafter referred to as 'primary participants'). In addition, one participant's mother attended the interview with her and was thus consented and interviewed briefly. Four pilot-comparison participants (two females, two males, mean age = 29 years,[2] age range: 24–32 years) who were not psychiatrically hospitalised or presently diagnosed with a psychotic disorder also provided interviews.

Recruitment

Inpatient and outpatient hospital participants

Inpatient and outpatient hospital participants were recruited on-site at each location. Hospital staff were asked to indicate service users diagnosed with schizophrenia-spectrum or other psychotic disorders who might be able and willing to participate in an interview about their life experiences. Hospital staff were also asked to indicate service users whose demographic and symptom profiles matched specific indicators of heterogeneity (see next). Service users with severe symptoms that might prevent them from providing descriptions of their life experiences were excluded from the study. For example, some potential participants declined or were unable to speak verbally. One potential participant spoke to us only in a language unknown to investigators and his treatment team. One participant agreed to participate but then answered all questions, including open-ended questions (e.g., 'Tell me about yourself, starting with your life story'), with only 'yes' or 'no'; this participant was withdrawn from the study. Another participant completed the informed consent process but later, during the interview, indicated that they believed participation was related to their discharge; this participant was also withdrawn from the study, and we reiterated that participation was unrelated to their treatment or eventual release from the hospital.

During recruitment, potential inpatient participants were approached in person by the researchers or hospital staff. Outpatient participants were first telephoned and invited to meet in person to discuss potential participation in a research study. When meeting in person, participants were verbally invited to participate in an interview study about the 'life experiences of hospital patients.' After consenting to and completing the study, participants received approximately $10 in credit at hospital kiosks or, for outpatients, local businesses. (One Jerusalem outpatient who had to take a taxi to reach the hospital was also reimbursed for transportation.)

Inclusion/exclusion criteria

Inpatient and outpatient hospital participants were ages 18 or older, carried a current psychotic-disorder diagnosis (see Table 4.1), were receiving current inpatient or outpatient psychiatric treatment at one of the three data-collection sites, and (for inpatient participants) had the capacity to consent to research according to a psychiatrist's assessment. Primary psychotic-disorder diagnoses were verified through hospital records, hospital staff reports, and additional interview questions as needed. Exclusion criteria for inpatient and outpatient hospital participants were severe traumatic brain injury and (for outpatient participants) active use of substances or alcohol. Participants were not excluded on the basis of comorbidity with personality disorders, substance use disorders, or other psychiatric disorders.

Inpatient and outpatient hospital participants were selected using a purposive sampling procedure (see Patton, 1987) prioritising critical cases based on their potential contribution to the cultural and/or diagnostic diversity of the sample. In other words, participants were selected based on their demographic uniqueness relative to the accumulating sample. More specifically, hospital staff consultations and hospital records were used to identify potential participants, and subsequent participants were selected in consideration of prior recruits, such that the cultural and clinical heterogeneity of the sample was successively enhanced. Using hospital records and staff consultations, potential participants were assessed for the following demographic indicators (identified as jointly constitutive of 'culture' in the cross-cultural literature on psychopathology [see APA, 2003; Sue et al., 1999]): socioeconomic status; age; age of illness onset; assigned sex and gender

Table 4.1 Participant pseudonyms, demographics, and official diagnoses at the time of the interview

Pseudonym	*Participant type, level of treatment (for hospital participants)*	*Location, language(s) of interview/other languages*	*Age, gender, sexual orientation*	*Ethnicity, country of birth, identified religion/other relevant demographic information*	*Diagnosis*
Avery	Primary, inpatient	New York, English	55, Trans F/ gender fluid, B	Latinx, United States, no religion reported	Schizophrenia, paranoid type
Leonard	Primary, inpatient	New York, English	49, M, H	Trinidadian American male, Trinidad, Muslim (medical records) or 'all religions' (interview)/ immigrated to the United States in his late teens or early 20s	Schizophrenia, paranoid type
Charles	Primary, inpatient	New York, English	61, M, H	African American, United States, Muslim (interview) or no religious belief (medical records) (with past identification as Christian and future interest in Buddhism)	Schizophrenia, R/O schizoaffective disorder
Greg	Primary, inpatient	New York, English/ Chinese (mother tongue)	47, M, U	Chinese American, China, thematically Christian (mother Buddhist)/ immigrated to the United States at the age of three	Schizoaffective disorder; heroin dependence and cocaine abuse in remission

Lynn	Primary, inpatient	New York, English	29, F, H	European American, United States, no religion reported	Schizophrenia, disorganised type
Douglas	Primary, inpatient	New York, English	27, M, H	African American, United States, reports appreciating all religions (Christian upbringing)	Schizoaffective disorder, bipolar type
Roger	Primary, outpatient	New York, English/ Tagalog (mother tongue)	50, M, U	Filipino American, Philippines, Catholic/ immigrated to the United States at the age of 19	Schizophrenia, paranoid type
Crystal	Primary, outpatient	New York, English	54, F, H	European American, United States, converted from Judaism to Catholicism as an adult	Schizoaffective disorder [recovered according to interview content]
Rabbi Danny	Primary, inpatient	Jerusalem, English (mother tongue) and Hebrew	51, M, H	European American, United States, Jewish/ immigrated to Israel in his 30s	Schizophrenia
Saleh	Primary, inpatient	Jerusalem, Hebrew and Arabic (mother tongue)	23, M, U	Palestinian, Jerusalem, Muslim	Schizophrenia; suicidal ideation [interview content suggested R/O of OCD]
Eve	Primary, inpatient	Jerusalem, Hebrew/ French (mother tongue), English,	51, F, H	Israeli, Morocco, Jewish/ Sephardic heritage; immigrated to Israel at the age of 8	Schizophrenia, paranoid type

(*Continued*)

Table 4.1 (Continued)

Pseudonym	*Participant type, level of treatment (for hospital participants)*	*Location, language(s) of interview/other languages*	*Age, gender, sexual orientation*	*Ethnicity, country of birth, identified religion/other relevant demographic information*	*Diagnosis*
		some Moroccan Arabic			
Yuval	Primary, inpatient	Jerusalem, Hebrew (mother tongue) and English	46, M, H	Israeli, Israel, Jewish/ Ashkenazi and Sephardic heritage (father immigrated from Romania and maternal grandmother from Turkey)	Schizoaffective disorder
Lior	Primary, inpatient	Jerusalem, Hebrew/ Russian (mother tongue)	26, M, H	Israeli, Israel, Jewish/ second-generation Russian immigrant	'Psychotic state' [sic]
Jean	Primary, inpatient	Jerusalem, English and Hebrew/French (mother tongue)	34, M, H	French-Israeli, France, Jewish/parents are Algerian-Jewish refugees in France; immigrated to Israel in his 30s	Schizoaffective/ schizophrenia [sic]
Asad	Primary, inpatient	Jerusalem, Arabic (mother tongue) and Hebrew	37, M or Trans, U	Palestinian, Jerusalem, Muslim	Schizophrenia, paranoid type
Gilah	Primary, inpatient	Jerusalem, Hebrew (mother tongue)/ some English	61, F, B, or H	Israeli, Israel, Jewish/ Ashkenazi heritage	Schizophrenia, paranoid type

Haseeb	Primary, inpatient	Jerusalem, Arabic (mother tongue) and Hebrew/some English	35, M, H	Palestinian, Jerusalem, Muslim	Schizophrenia; drug abuse
Luma	Primary, outpatient	Jerusalem, Hebrew and Arabic (mother tongue)/some English	32, F, H	Palestinian, Jerusalem, Muslim	Schizoaffective disorder
Amy	Pilot-comparison	New York, Pilot-Comparison, English (mother tongue)/ Spanish and German	28, F, H	European American, United States, secular Christian	OCD (*per participant report*)
Zev	Pilot-comparison	New York, Pilot-Comparison, English/Hebrew (mother tongue)	24, M, H	Israeli, Israel, Jewish/ Ashkenazi heritage; currently living in New York	PTSD, ADHD (*per participant report*)
Claire	Pilot-comparison	New York, Pilot-Comparison, English (mother tongue)/ French	40, F, B	European American, United States, Jewish	N/A
Oliver	Pilot-comparison	New York, Pilot-Comparison, English (mother tongue)/ other languages	31 (estimated), M, G	Australian, Australia, no reported religion	OCD (*per participant report*)
Paula	Ad hoc comparison, inpatient	New York, English	58, F, H	European American, United States, Catholic	Schizoaffective disorder; noncompliance with treatment [V-code] (*potential misdiagnosis*)

(*Continued*)

Table 4.1 (Continued)

Pseudonym	*Participant type, level of treatment (for hospital participants)*	*Location, language(s) of interview/other languages*	*Age, gender, sexual orientation*	*Ethnicity, country of birth, identified religion/other relevant demographic information*	*Diagnosis*
Olufemi	Ad hoc comparison, inpatient	New York, English/five African languages (mother tongue)	28, M, H	African American, Ivory Coast, Muslim/ immigrated to the United States from West Africa at the age of 15	Schizophrenia, paranoid type (*potential misdiagnosis*)
Noam	Ad hoc comparison, inpatient	Jerusalem, Hebrew (mother tongue)/ some English	27, M, H	Israeli, Jerusalem, Jewish/ Ashkenazi heritage	Schizoaffective disorder, manic state (*potential misdiagnosis*)

Note: Sexual orientation is identified as heterosexual (H), gay (G) or lesbian (L), bisexual (B), or unknown (U).

identification; sexual orientation; ethnic and racial identities; relative isolation of rearing environment and/or community residence from the surrounding society; religious affiliation, beliefs, and practices; political orientation and involvement; affiliation and involvement in community or social institutions; and intersectionality (multiple and intersecting social identity categories; e.g., Buchanan & Wiklund, 2021). At each location, participant selection also aimed to maximise diversity in positive, negative, and mixed symptom profiles (see Andreasen & Olsen, 1982). Critical cases of persons with idiosyncratic symptom profiles were also given high priority in order to enhance the diagnostic heterogeneity of the sample.

During reviews of the interview content by members of our research team who are trained in clinical diagnosis, it was determined that three participants (1) did not definitively meet criteria for a DSM-defined psychotic disorder (APA, 2000, 2013) or ICD (WHO, 1992a, 1992b) at the time of the interview and (2) reported experiences that were suggestive of other diagnostic possibilities. It is possible that these three participants experienced a change in their symptoms such they no longer met criteria for a psychotic disorder at the time of the interview; it is also possible that they were initially misdiagnosed.[3] These three participants were thus utilised as ad hoc comparison cases.

Diversity of the sample

Demographic diversity

Both primary and comparison participants were demographically diverse. Table 4.1 presents a list of participants by demographic indicators and diagnoses at the time of the interview. Those interviewed in New York included two African American participants, two European American participants, one Latinx (trans) participant, and three naturalised immigrants from Trinidad, China, and the Philippines. The participants interviewed in Jerusalem included four Palestinian participants, three Israeli-born Jewish participants, and three Jewish immigrants to Israel from Morocco, France, and the United States. Across all 21 inpatient and outpatient hospital participants (i.e., both primary and ad hoc comparison participants), only two New York participants and three Jerusalem participants (respectively) had similar patterns across the four demographic indicators of nationality, ethnicity, native language, and religion. Participants also differed across age, gender, and sexual orientation, among other demographic indices. The ad hoc comparison sample comprised one European American participant, one African American participant who immigrated from West Africa, and one Jewish Israeli participant. In the pilot-comparison sample, two participants were from the United States, one was from Israel, and another was Australian.

Diagnostic diversity

The DSM-5 (APA, 2013) was published concurrent with Phase I and prior to Phase II of data collection; however, our data-collection sites had not systematically switched to DSM-5 at the time the interviews were collected. Therefore, the 18 primary participants carried a DSM-IV-TR (APA, 2000), DSM-5 (APA, 2013), or ICD-10 (WHO, 1992a, 1992b) psychotic-disorder diagnosis. Note that from a standard diagnostic perspective, some DSM-IV and ICD-10 diagnoses were of questionable precision; for example, some New York participants were diagnosed with schizophrenia subtypes that did not consistently match their current presentation, and one Jerusalem participant was diagnosed with 'schizoaffective/schizophrenia.' Altogether, 11 participants (five in New York and six in Jerusalem) were diagnosed with schizophrenia, five participants (three in New York and two in Jerusalem) were diagnosed with schizoaffective disorder, one participant (in Jerusalem) was diagnosed with schizoaffective/schizophrenia [sic], and one participant (in Jerusalem) was diagnosed with 'psychotic state.'

Pilot-comparison participants

Pilot-comparison participants served two purposes: they allowed for the primary investigator (PI; SRK) to practice and refine the scope of the interview, and they served as comparison cases for the inpatient and outpatient hospital sample. Pilot-comparison participants were not psychiatrically hospitalised or diagnosed with a psychotic disorder at the time of the interview. However, three of the four reported other psychiatric diagnoses: two pilot-comparison participants reported having obsessive-compulsive disorder (OCD), and one reported having both posttraumatic stress disorder (PTSD) and attention-deficit hyperactivity disorder (ADHD). Although pilot-comparison participants' subjective descriptions of their symptoms and subjective understandings of these diagnoses were addressed as topics within the interviews, structured diagnostic interviews were not conducted to confirm the accuracy of their reported diagnoses, as these diagnostic categories were not the focus of the present study.

Pilot-comparison participants were recruited through the interviewer's social network utilising convenience sampling. They were contacted in person or by telephone and invited to participate 'as a comparison subject in an interview study about the life experiences of hospital patients diagnosed with schizophrenia.' Pilot-comparison participants were compensated for their time with tea or coffee and a snack of their choice.

Ad hoc comparison participants carried schizophrenia-spectrum diagnoses but did not currently meet full criteria for these diagnoses according to our research team's review of their interview content, which included an established tool for assessing psychotic symptom profiles. However, structured diagnostic assessments were not conducted to determine potential alternative diagnoses. Rule-out diagnoses (other diagnostic options) based on our team's review of their interview content included major depressive disorder, generalised anxiety disorder, PTSD, ADHD, body dysmorphic disorder, and bipolar I disorder. Table 4.2 presents a list of rule-out diagnoses and corresponding symptoms or features as derived from ad hoc comparison participant interviews.

Materials and measures

Informed consent forms

Informed consent forms described the project as a study of the 'life experiences of hospital patients.' This was an accurate description of the project, but it did not mention the diagnostic inclusion criteria described earlier. The decision to leave the participants' diagnoses out of informed consent procedures was threefold: (1) some participants were unaware of their diagnosis, and it was not the role of the researchers to present it to them; (2) avoiding use of diagnostic concepts most authentically reflected the assumptions and goals of this study, which started with questions about the reliability and validity of the schizophrenia diagnosis and categorical diagnoses more broadly; and (3) from a person-centred perspective, the introduction of psychiatric jargon prior to the life-narrative task might have influenced the participants' descriptions of their anomalous experiences, rather than allowing them to describe their experiences in their own words and on their own terms. For these three reasons, technical terms such as psychosis and schizophrenia were not mentioned in the description of the study or in consent procedures.

Measures

Participants completed in-depth first-person interviews of approximately two to four hours in duration. The full interview protocol included the following four components: (1) a semi-structured narrative task, in which participants were asked to describe their life experiences in their own words; (2) select items from both the Examination of Anomalous Self-Experience interview (EASE; Parnas et al., 2005) and the Examination of Anomalous World-Experience (EAWE; Sass et al., 2017); (3) the Positive and Negative Syndrome Scale (PANSS; Kay et al., 2006), a gold-standard tool for assessing positive, negative, and mixed symptom profiles; and (4) debriefing questions.

Semi-structured narrative task

The semi-structured narrative task, designed for the purposes of the present study, contained one open-ended narrative question about the participant's life history and significant events within it:

Table 4.2 Ad hoc comparison participant current diagnoses, reported diagnostic possibilities, perceived misdiagnoses, and rule-out diagnoses as suggested by interview content

Pseudonym	*Current diagnosis according to medical records*	*Past and present diagnoses as reported by participants*	*Perceived misdiagnoses (diagnoses perceived as inaccurate by participants)*	*Other rule-out diagnoses (for current presentation only) as suggested by interview content*	*Features supporting rule-out diagnoses as suggested by interview content, researcher observations, informant reports, and/or medical records*
Paula	Schizoaffective disorder; noncompliance with treatment [V-code]	Major depressive disorder, generalised anxiety disorder, (complex)) PTSD, ADHD, (past) body dysmorphic disorder	Schizoaffective disorder	Major depressive disorder; R/O somatic symptom disorder	Sadness, hopelessness, and frustration, often described as a consequence of involuntary hospitalisation and iatrogenic treatment by mental health professionals; frequent focus on chronic physical pain/disability after unwanted hip replacement surgery (Paula currently uses a wheelchair).
Olufemi	Schizophrenia, paranoid type		Schizophrenia	PTSD	Direct exposure to and witnessing multiple traumatic events (childhood spent in war-torn country); intrusive memories and nightmares; attempts to avoid thoughts and memories of the events.

Noam	Schizoaffective disorder, manic state		Bipolar I disorder	Periods of elevated mood and goal-directed activity, with increased energy and inflated self-esteem; alternating with periods of feeling tired, self-critical, oppressed, and unmotivated (tired and low moods are often described as specific to periods of hospitalisation and during employment).

Note: Rule-out diagnoses and symptoms/features supporting rule-out diagnoses were derived from interview content and not formal diagnostic interviews.

> I want to get to know you. Tell me about yourself, starting with your life story. You can start wherever you like, with your childhood or later, and walk me through the significant events in your life up to now, the present, your being here in this place.

Follow-up questions were comprised of requests for clarification and elaboration, and reflections of the participants' experiences and feelings were offered in order to ensure understanding and evoke more precise clarification and elaboration.

The narrative task also contained a series of possible probe items that reflected topics pertinent to the goals of this study. Probes included specific items about each participant's background and personal identity (e.g., 'can you give me some examples of different situations in which you feel most "like yourself?"'), identification with groups (e.g., 'who are the people you feel most connected with?'), recent history and daily life (e.g., 'tell me what a typical day is like for you'), present context (e.g., 'do you like living here [city of residence]? Would you ever live anywhere else?'), and past and present mental health treatment (e.g., 'tell me about this hospital we're in now. What's it like?'). In order to obtain data on the way in which interviewees describe their own experiences, follow-up questions and reflections of interviewee's spontaneous statements were generally prioritised over probe items. When used, probe items were introduced in a person-centred way as part of the conversation and were integrated into the discursive flow introduced by the participants as much as possible.

Most participants spontaneously addressed or elaborated important topics in major domains of their lives on their own, making probe questions proportionately less frequent than open discussion, follow-up questions, and reflections during the life-historical narrative. Interviewer-generated questions and topics, including probe items, were proportionately more frequent for three interviewees whose style of speech was more minimalistic and sparing. However, even in these three interviewers, follow-up questions that followed the participants' thought and natural flow of conversation were prioritised over probe items that introduced new topics.

EASE and EAWE items

The second component of the interview protocol contained select items from the EASE (Parnas et al., 2005) and the EAWE (Sass et al., 2017). These two measures are semi-structured symptom checklists that reflect anomalies in self-experience (EASE) and world-experience (EAWE) as described in previous phenomenological literature on schizophrenia (e.g., Fuchs, 2007; Laing, 1960; Sass, 1992a, 1994a, b; Sass & Parnas, 2003). In this study, select items from the EASE and the EAWE were used to gather in-depth experiential narratives that reflect participants' experiences and ideas about the self and the world.

The EASE[4] was developed by Parnas et al. (2005) for the assessment of experiential anomalies that may reflect 'a disorder or deficiency in the sense of being a subject, a self-coinciding centre of action, thought, and experience' (p. 236). The interview is comprised of successive descriptions of anomalous self-experiences divided into domains, subdomains, and subtypes (of subdomains). The five primary EASE domains are (1) cognition and stream of consciousness (examples of subdomains include thought interference, silent thought echo, and discontinuous awareness of own action), (2) self-awareness and presence (examples of subdomains: distorted first-person perspective, derealisation, hyperreflectivity), (3) bodily experiences (examples of subdomains: somatic depersonalisation [bodily estrangement], bodily disintegration, and motor disturbances), (4) demarcation/transitivism (examples of subdomains: confusion with one's own specular image, threatening bodily contact and feelings of fusion with another), and (5) existential reorientation (examples of subdomains: feeling of centrality, magical ideas linked to the subject's way of experiencing, solipsistic grandiosity).

The format of the EAWE, recently developed by Sass et al. (2017), is parallel to that of the EASE, with successive descriptions of anomalous world-experiences divided into domains, subdomains, and subtypes of subdomains. The EAWE contains the following six primary domains: (1) objects and space (examples of subdomains: disturbances in reality of visual perceptions, abnormal intensity of visual perception, disturbances in reality of auditory perceptions), (2) events and time (examples of subdomains: time appears to change speed or stop, disturbed awareness of the future, disturbed or diminished anticipation), (3) persons (examples of subdomains: difficulties in interpersonal rapport/communication, anomalous behavioural responses to others, depersonalisation of others), (4) language (examples of subdomains: change in standard meaning or usage of words, disturbances of the abstract and the concrete, anomalous style of speech), (5) atmosphere (examples of subdomains: derealisation, inanimate things seem alive or intentional, déjà vu experiences), (6) existential reorientation (examples of subdomains: disinclination for human society; wilful eccentricity, originality, specialness; sense of loss of freedom or uniqueness).

In the present study, EASE (Parnas et al., 2005) and EAWE (Sass et al., 2017) questionnaire items were selected according to their relevance to the constructs of selfhood (e.g., 'do you ever feel fragmented or split, as if you are not whole?'), interpersonal experience (e.g., 'do other people ever seem dead, unreal, or mechanical to you?'), and culture (e.g., 'would you prefer not to participate in human society?'). In addition, items that reflected experiences that may be unique to psychosis (e.g., 'do you sometimes wonder whether your experiences are reality or a fantasy?') were included. Items reflecting symptoms that overlapped significantly with other non-psychotic DSM- and ICD-defined (APA, 2013; WHO, 1992a, 1992b) diagnoses (e.g., ruminations, social disinhibition) were excluded. Items that overlapped with the PANSS (Kay et al., 2006) were also excluded.

Administration of the EASE and the EAWE followed a semi-structured approach in which the interviewer attempted to engage the participant in a 'patient-doctor mutually interactive reflection' or dialogue about specific questionnaire items and their relationship to the person's experience (Parnas et al., 2005, p. 238). According to Parnas et al., the ideal procedure is an interactive, reflective process in which the interviewer poses questions, requests examples from the participant, then reformulates the participant's statement and offers more examples in order to elicit additional descriptions from the participant. For our purposes, select EASE (Parnas et al., 2005) and EAWE (Sass et al., 2017) items were used as potential probe items, such that not all selected items were used in all interviews. Instead, in-the-moment selection of items during each interview followed a person-centred, flexible gating approach in which the interviewer selected items concerning themes and topics that (1) were not already addressed in the life-historical interview or (2) seemed to require further elaboration after the life-historical interview. When possible, the interviewer offered examples and posed additional questions to confirm understanding of the participants' experiences. If specific topics and themes (e.g., anomalous experiences with time or language) were clearly denied or rejected by the participant, the interviewer did not continue to ask questions about this topic; instead, focus was given to clarification about previously unaddressed themes and questions that resonated with each respective participant.

PANSS

The PANSS[5,6] is often considered to be a gold standard measure for parsing symptoms of schizophrenia into positive, negative, and mixed syndromes. In this study, the PANSS (Kay et al., 2006) was used to gather comprehensive information about participants' symptom profiles and as a post-hoc screening procedure to determine whether participants fell into positive, negative, or mixed syndrome subgroups. The Structured Clinical Interview for the PANSS (SCI-PANSS) is comprised of 179 open-ended questions for the assessment of 33 symptom-items on 7-point scales.[7] It also includes standard items for assessing mental status (including orientation), as well as similarities and proverbs for assessing abstract thinking. The PANSS compiles data from the SCI-PANSS, observer ratings, medical records (when available) and informant reports (when available) to systematically assess symptom functioning within a time-limited period that is determined according to the specific objectives of each research study. Although the typical duration for longitudinal studies is one week, the present study utilised the informal upper-bound of one month (M. Opler, personal communication, October 17, 2012) to obtain a broader portrait of participants' experiences over time. Examples of SCI-PANSS questionnaire items are '[s] ometimes people tell me that they can hear noises or voices inside their head that others can't hear. What about you?' and '[c]an you tell me something about your thoughts on life and its purpose?' (Kay et al., 2006, pp. 3 & 7). The PANSS (Kay et al., 2006) also suggests the use of informant data, when available, to supplement the information provided by participants. PANSS informants can include hospital staff or participants' family members and/or friends.

In this study, the PANSS was scored according to both the Standard and the Pentagonal Models for profile interpretation (White et al., 1997).[8] The PANSS includes a bipolar dimensional assessment, the Composite index, which represents the predominance of positive versus negative symptoms (Kay, 1991). As per the scoring methods specified by Kay et al. (2006), Composite index scores for both the Standard and Pentagonal Models for profile interpretation were calculated by subtracting the negative scale from the positive scale, and Total Scores were calculated by summing the Standard Model Positive, Negative, and General Psychopathology scales. According to Opler et al. (2006), persons receiving an outpatient level of care tend to have total scores that range from 60 to 80, and persons receiving an inpatient level of care have total scores rarely exceed 80 to 150 (see also Leucht et al., 2005).

Kay et al. (2006) outlined two methods for subtyping respondents into positive, negative, and mixed syndrome profiles. For the present study, results of both methods are presented. The first method, which is more stringent and exclusionary, necessitated counting the number of moderate or higher ratings (i.e., ratings of 4 or higher) on both the Positive and Negative scales of the Standard Model.[9] A second and less stringent method for subtyping respondents utilised the 'schizophrenic sample distribution curve for the PANSS Composite index' of the Standard Model for profile interpretation (Kay et al., 2006, p. 13). More specifically, the sample distribution curve of the Composite index was used to subdivide scores into negative, positive, and mixed-syndrome classes comprising the 25th percentile (Composite index score that is less than −7), 75th percentile (Composite index score that is greater than 3), and interquartile range (Composite index score falling between −7 and 3); these scores were used to identify participants with negative, positive, and mixed syndrome subtypes, respectively.

Scoring of our PANSS (Kay et al., 2006) data revealed that primary participants' symptom profiles varied across the standard positive, negative, and mixed syndrome profiles using both methods of subtyping. Table 4.3 presents the PANSS subtypes and Total Scores by participant and diagnosis.

According to both the stringent and interquartile-range methods of subtyping, eight of the 18 primary participants had positive symptom profiles.

Table 4.3 Participant diagnoses and PANSS subtypes

Pseudonym (participant type)	*Diagnosis at time of interview*	*PANSS composite index - pentagonal model*	*PANSS composite index - standard model*	*PANSS subtype—stringent method*	*PANSS subtype—interquartile range method*	*PANSS total score*
Avery (PH)	Schizophrenia, paranoid type	3	14	Mixed syndrome	Positive syndrome	116
Leonard (PH)	Schizophrenia, paranoid type	2	17	Positive syndrome	Positive syndrome	108
Charles (PH)	Schizophrenia, R/O schizoaffective disorder	−1	8	Positive syndrome	Mixed syndrome	64
Greg (PH)	Schizoaffective disorder; heroin dependence and cocaine abuse in remission	−28	−1	Mixed syndrome	Mixed syndrome	152
Lynn (PH)	Schizophrenia, disorganised type	−31	−8	Mixed syndrome	Negative syndrome	124
Paul (PH)	Schizoaffective disorder, bipolar type	15	17	Positive syndrome	Positive syndrome	75
Roger (PH)	Schizophrenia, paranoid type	1	9	Positive syndrome	Positive syndrome	75
Crystal (PH)	Schizoaffective disorder[10]	−7	−3	Neither syndrome	N/A (total score less than 60)	39
Rabbi Danny (PH)	Schizophrenia	4	24	Positive syndrome	Positive syndrome	83

Saleh (PH)	Schizophrenia; suicidal ideation [interview content suggested R/O of OCD]	−11	2	Neither syndrome	Mixed syndrome	84
Eve (PH)	Schizophrenia, paranoid type	−29	−12	Negative syndrome	Negative syndrome	87
Yuval (PH)	Schizoaffective disorder	1	9	Positive syndrome	Positive syndrome	74
Lior (PH)	'Psychotic state' [sic]	−16	1	Neither syndrome	Mixed syndrome	87
Jean (PH)	Schizoaffective/ schizophrenia [sic]	−8	12	Positive syndrome	Positive syndrome	102
Asad (PH)	Schizophrenia, paranoid type	−30	6	Mixed syndrome	Positive syndrome	123
Gilah (PH)	Schizophrenia, paranoid type	8	25	Positive syndrome	Positive syndrome	103
Haseeb (PH)	Schizophrenia; drug abuse	9	17	Positive syndrome	Positive syndrome	105
Luma (PH)	Schizoaffective disorder	0	4	Neither syndrome	Positive syndrome	73
Amy (pC)	Obsessive-compulsive disorder	0	4	Neither syndrome	N/A (total score less than 60)	49
Zev (pC)	Posttraumatic stress disorder; attention deficit hyperactivity disorder	−3	0	Neither syndrome	N/A (total score less than 60)	42
Claire (pC)	None	0	10	Neither syndrome	N/A (total score less than 60)	57
Oliver (pC)	Obsessive-compulsive disorder	−2	3	Neither syndrome	N/A (total Score less than 60)	43

(*Continued*)

Table 4.3 (Continued)

Pseudonym (participant type)	*Diagnosis at time of interview*	*PANSS composite index - pentagonal model*	*PANSS composite index - standard model*	*PANSS subtype—stringent method*	*PANSS subtype—interquartile range method*	*PANSS total score*
Patricia (ahC)	*Potential misdiagnosis;* schizoaffective disorder; noncompliance with treatment [V-code]	−8	−2	Neither syndrome	Mixed syndrome	62
Olufemi (ahC)	*Potential misdiagnosis;* schizophrenia, paranoid type	−4	6	Neither syndrome	N/A (total score less than 60)	51
Noam (ahC)	*Potential misdiagnosis;* schizoaffective disorder, manic state	−11	−3	Neither syndrome	Mixed syndrome	63

Note: Participant type is identified as primary hospital (PH), pilot-comparison (pC), or ad hoc comparison (ahC).

Seven had profiles that were subtyped as mixed using one or both methods. Only two participants received a negative syndrome subtype, one according to both methods and one according to the interquartile-range method. One primary participant was fully recovered at the time of the interview and had no syndrome profile according to both methods of subtyping. Three primary participants had neither syndrome according to the stringent but not the interquartile-range method. Of the three ad hoc comparison participants, one participant had neither syndrome according to both methods, and two had a mixed profile according to the interquartile-range method but neither profile according to stringent method. None of the pilot-comparison participants had PANSS scores higher than 60, and none could be subtyped into PANSS syndrome profiles. Recall that PANSS total scores under 60 indicate questionable pathology.

Because the PANSS is a semi-structured interview that elicits information about the subjective experiences and life histories of respondents, all PANSS interviews were audio recorded, and the data were incorporated into phenomenological data analyses.

Debriefing questions

The four debriefing questions posed to participants were as follows:

- What was it like to answer these questions?
- What do you think of questionnaires like this?
- What has this interview been like for you?
- Is there anything I didn't ask about that you think I should know about you?

These questions, posed to participants after completion of all interview tasks, were designed to assess participants' views of the research study. They also served as a manipulation check to ensure accuracy and understanding of the purposes of the study.

Order of interview components

All interview components were presented to participants successively, in the order of (1) semi-structured narrative task, (2) EASE (Parnas et al., 2005) and EAWE (currently in development by Sass and Pienkos [Sass et al., 2017]) items, (3) PANSS (Kay et al., 2006), and (4) debriefing questions. This order was established in order to elicit participants' descriptions of their experiences in their own words and from their own perspectives prior to introducing the specific terminology, concepts, and structure of the EASE, EAWE, and PANSS. By implementing the semi-structured narrative task first, the researchers also gathered data on whether participants spontaneously used psychiatric jargon without its prior introduction by the researcher. Note that despite the fact that the life narrative task was administered first, the second and third interview components also contained questions that led to discussion of the participant's life history, which generally proceeded throughout the interview in a flexible and open fashion.

Translation of interview protocol

The PANSS has been translated into Hebrew, and we utilised an existing translation for the present study. All other interview protocol items for this study were translated into Arabic and Hebrew, and the translations were verified by Palestinian and Israeli mental health professionals, respectively.

Procedures

The method and all procedures for this study were approved by four institutional review boards (IRBs): the Fordham University IRB and the IRBs at each of the three hospitals where data were collected. Data collection for inpatient and outpatient hospital participants was conducted in three phases: Phase I, in which eight inpatient interviews were conducted at a psychiatric hospital in New York, took place from May to July of 2013. Phase II, in which one outpatient and ten inpatient interviews were collected at a psychiatric hospital in Jerusalem, took place from September to November of 2014. Phase III, in which two outpatient interviews were conducted at another psychiatric hospital in New York, took place from December 2014 through March of 2015.

Consent procedures

Prior to obtaining informed consent for hospital service users, a psychiatrist provided an assessment of each person's capacity to consent. Potential participants without capacity to consent were excluded from the study. For participants whose capacity might have varied on a daily basis, the psychiatrist's reassessment and verbal assent was also obtained for each new interview day.

Before the start of each interview, potential participants were provided with the consent form, and the researcher reviewed the form item-by-item to assess each participant's understanding. At the Jerusalem hospital, informed consent procedures were conducted in the person's language of choice with native speakers of that language; some of the bilingual participants were also given hard copies of the consent forms in more than one language. The principal investigator worked together with an Israeli co-investigator and a Palestinian translator to ensure the participant's full understanding of the study procedures before beginning. When indicated, consent procedures and information were revisited during the course of the interview, and participants' ongoing understanding of the nature of the study was confirmed. For the participant whose mother attended the interview and was consented, standard informed consent procedures were followed in order to inform her of the nature of the research and provide her with an opportunity to voluntarily participate or decline participation.

Interview procedures

Interviews at the New York data-collection sites were conducted in English. Jerusalem interviewees were asked whether they preferred to conduct the interview in Arabic, Hebrew, or English. Some interviews with bilingual participants were conducted in both English and Hebrew or Arabic and Hebrew. The PI conducted all English-language interviews (11 inpatient and outpatient hospital participants and all four pilot-comparison participants). For all but one of the seven interviews conducted fully or partially in Hebrew, an Israeli co-investigator (JYBG; also a psychiatric resident at the data-collection site) was present to assist with translation when needed. At times, the Israeli co-investigator participated in the interview conversation by asking questions or noting potential themes of interest; for the last two interviews conducted in Hebrew, she led the interview with the PI present part of the time. Arabic-speaking participants were given the option to be interviewed by a Palestinian interviewer or by the PI in English or Hebrew. Two of the four Palestinian participants chose to speak in Hebrew. The two interviews in Arabic were conducted through simultaneous translation. Arabic translators were two Palestinian mental health professionals who were also on-site hospital staff.[11] Very brief portions of some interviews were conducted in French to clarify meanings for interviewees who spoke French as their mother tongue. All pilot-comparison interviews were conducted in English.

Comparison-participant interviews were conducted at locations of convenience, such as apartments and cafes. Hospital interviews were conducted on-site in areas of varying sizes provided by the hospitals, often on the participants' wards or treatment malls. Due to hospital staff schedules and participant preferences, it was sometimes necessary to change locations, pause the interview, or conduct the interviews in outside areas.

Hospital-participant interviews were approximately two to four hours in length, with the shortest interview lasting one hour and 36 minutes and the longest interview lasting five hours. They were conducted in one sitting on one day or multiple sittings across up to five consecutive or non-consecutive days, over the course of up to eight weeks, according to the in-the-moment preferences of participants.[12] At times, further questions arose during reviews of the interview data by our research team; when this occurred, participants, if they were available, were invited to provide follow-up interviews after the initial interview to clarify meanings in their original narrative.

Informant procedures

As aforementioned, the PANSS (Kay et al., 2006) suggests the use of informant data when it is available. During Phase I of data collection, one hospital IRB in New York denied permission to contact participants' family and friends. Therefore, for purposes of standardisation across sites—as well as difficulties in securing flexible, immediate on-site translation of informant interviews—no active attempt was made to recruit family and friends in Jerusalem; however, one participant attended the interview with her mother, who then consented to the study and was interviewed briefly.

The researchers often had questions about participants that were not answered in the interviews or medical records. When this happened, participants' treating psychiatrists, psychologists, social workers, and other mental health staff members acted as informal PANSS consultants by providing verbal information about participants' psychiatric histories and behaviour on the ward. Hospital-staff informants were given the opportunity to reflect openly about the participant's history and present circumstances. Often, the researcher asked clarifying questions about specific symptoms or life experiences of participants. Informants were thanked for their time and efforts in providing further information about the participants.

Audio recordings and transcriptions

All interviews were audio recorded.[13] Regardless of the language in which they were conducted, all interviews were transcribed into English. All translations were forward-translations into English only; back-translations were not conducted. English-to-English transcriptions and Hebrew-to-English transcriptions were conducted by research assistants in New York and Jerusalem. Arabic-to-English transcriptions were conducted by a Palestinian mental health professional (also staff at the Jerusalem hospital) who also helped to conduct both Arabic-language interviews. All transcribers were fluent in English; however, due to varying levels of transcription training and English fluency among those conducting translations, transcript quality varied; when necessary, the PI reviewed translations with translators. Transcribers were instructed to prioritise and preserve the meaning of participants' utterances over stylistic qualities of the transcriptions when necessary.

Phenomenological data analysis

The objective of the present study was to investigate the heterogeneity problem in the schizophrenia diagnosis through a descriptive study across a multicultural sample. In order to achieve this objective, this project employed the phenomenological procedures developed by Giorgi (1975,

2009) and Wertz (1985, 2005, 2010, 2015, in press; Wertz et al., 2011), who formalised Husserlian methods (Husserl, 1913/1962, 1939/1970, 1948/1973a, 1973b, 1973c) into a systematic, empirically grounded procedure for the human sciences. This rigorous and descriptive procedure was specifically designed for the analysis of the meaningful, organised, and essential structures of lived experience (see also Morrissey & Barber, 2014). Phenomenological analysis yields both individual and general findings corresponding to core psychological structures that emerge across variations in the data.

Prior to data analysis, phenomenologists engage in a procedure called *bracketing* (a.k.a. the *epoché*). The researcher brackets, or puts aside, previous assumptions or expectations that may arise from personal experience, previous research literature, and/or prior theories (Wertz, 2005, 2015, in press). Most importantly, the researcher turns from a focus on objects of experience to a focus on the meanings of the participant's experiences as they are given—or, as Husserl put it, 'to the things themselves!' (*zu den Sachen selbst!*). In this study, we individually documented our hopes and expectations, then discussed them together during collaborative team meetings. We then put those hopes and expectations aside in order to approach the data for themselves with the intent of understanding the meanings of our participants' experiences without any judgments or concerns about the 'reality' of their situations independent of their experience.

The systematised phenomenological procedures (Giorgi, 1975, 2009; Wertz, 1985, 2005, 2010, 2015, in press; Wertz et al., 2011) begin with open reading of each transcript. The next step[14] is systematically identifying its readily analysable meaning units, i.e., its discrete and meaningful constituents. The following step involves reflecting on the meaning units and assessing what they reveal about the topic under investigation. The researcher considers the ways in which the psychological processes expressed in each meaning unit are relevant to and answer the research questions. Reflections on individual meaning units, after being compared within each participant and across various participants, are synthesised in order to create an individual psychological structure that depicts the interrelations among meaning units, as well as emergent dissimilarities and larger patterns in individual examples of the phenomenon. Throughout each of the above stages, the researcher employs phenomenological procedures such as *intentional analysis*, or reflection on experiential meanings and psychological processes, and *eidetic analysis* (including free imaginative variation), which is the method for grasping the invariant characteristics of a phenomenon in order to distinguish its essential features from incidental facts found in particular examples. In free imaginative variation, the researcher distinguishes the phenomenon's essential features by considering possible variations of the example through which its invariant (essential) constituents and structure can be grasped and conceptualised. Eidetic analysis thus allows the researcher to identify essential constituents of the phenomenon under investigation, and thereby to understand its general contours and boundaries.

Using eidetic analysis, emergent findings are not only imaginatively varied but also compared to data drawn in from external sources, such as, in the present study, nonfictional memoirs, the PI's clinical training experiences, and examples drawn from prior phenomenological research on schizophrenia (see Wertz, 2005, 2010). Throughout this process, general findings emerge and begin to coalesce. In the final phases of phenomenological research, the researcher compares the individual structures and discerns similarities and differences in order to arrive at higher levels of generality, and the general psychological structure(s) of the research topic is(are) presented. These higher-level comparisons may yield a single general psychological structure or several typical psychological structures, depending on whether one or more structures is found in the examples analysed.

Due to the gap of approximately one year between data-collection Phases I and II (see earlier), analyses of the New York hospital inpatient interviews were conducted prior to data collection in Jerusalem (Phase II) and the collection of two outpatient interviews in New York (Phase III). As a result, a tentative general structure based on the Phase I hospital data emerged prior to Phases II and III.

The investigative process in which the general structure emerged is worth noting, as there is a need for methodological scholarship on the precise ways in which phenomenological researchers identify eidetic generalities within and across particular instances in the data. In the present study, the PI performed the steps outlined above by first openly rereading the interviews, then delineating and reflecting on meaning units. Afterwards, the PI created individual psychological structures for each participant, synthesising across them using intentional and eidetic analysis. This was an immersive and meditative experience in which the PI intensely contemplated various aspects of the participants' worlds and ways of understanding their lived experiences. At first, the meanings in the data appeared to be notably varied, inharmonious, and difficult to synthesise and conceptualise as a whole. However, after some time performing these systematic data analytic procedures, the most general essence of the individual structures emerged at once, as a whole, in a moment of realisation. At this moment of realisation, aspects of the data that had previously appeared disparate and unrelated coalesced into the holistic, unifying structure; this coalescing occurred by virtue of a pervasive, but often quite implicit experiential quality that was grasped and conceptualised prior to deciding what word or words best describe it. During a continued process of systematic data analysis, the primary moments and constituents of the general structure slowly came into focus, and technical language descriptive of this highly general characteristic of the experience was formulated.

After Phase II of data collection, this tentative general structure was bracketed as the researcher fully analysed three participants from the

Jerusalem dataset; these three participants were selected on the basis of having the most clearly given qualitative differences from participants the New York dataset. Once saturation was reached (i.e., once it was determined that the Jerusalem data yielded structural insights that were consonant with and could be used to better delineate but not structurally alter the general structure from the New York data), the researcher continued to reflect on the data in order to identify counter-evidence that might contradict the emergent general structure as well as additional variations through idiographic analyses. Each narrative was carefully assessed for potential variations, which were reflected upon, analysed, and used to revise or elaborate the general structure. Notably, these variations clarified the boundaries of the general structure but did not alter it in a fundamental or substantial way. Individual psychological structures were completed for all inpatient and outpatient hospital participants, and as the general structure became increasingly saturated and elaborated, these individual structures became increasingly condensed.

Emergent findings from analyses of the inpatient and outpatient participants' data were then compared to the content of pilot-comparison and ad hoc comparison interviews. Comparisons to the pilot-comparison and ad hoc comparison participants were used to identify the horizons or possible reaches, contours, and boundaries of the emergent structure (for more on the phenomenological concept of 'horizon,' see Kuhn [2013]). Comparison participant interviews also helped to shed light on essential versus incidental constituents of the general structure.

This was a collaborative project in which research assistants and select hospital-based co-investigators participated in the data analytic process intermittently during regular team meetings as part of their training in phenomenological methods. Most research assistants were undergraduates, recent graduates, or graduate students in psychology; one had an M.A. in psychosocial studies. Research assistants and select hospital-based co-investigators provided supplementary reflections on some of the transcripts, data analytic documents, and thematic similarities and differences across the interviews that they transcribed. The PI made decisions concerning when and how to integrate team members' supplementary reflections into data analytic documents. Throughout this process, the PI worked closely with doctoral mentor and research team member FJW. During our work together, the team members reviewed the literature on team science and collaborative phenomenological research; we co-presented our experiences with this collaborative project at an American Psychological Association convention (Minahan et al., 2014).

Notes

1 This participant sometimes referred to her/themselves as a female, and sometimes as both female and male.

2 One pilot participant's exact age was unknown and estimated at 31 years.

3 Uncertainty or ambiguity in diagnoses was communicated verbally (informally) to relevant hospital staff by the researchers. Determinations of potential misdiagnoses were based on evaluation of interview content, including responses to the PANSS (Kay et al., 2006) rather than structured diagnostic interviews. It is possible and likely that participants' clinical presentations varied over time (e.g., between admission and the time of the interviews or over the course of receiving mental health services).

4 Parnas et al. developed the EASE through extensive clinical-phenomenological observations and interviews with over 100 persons diagnosed with schizophrenia-spectrum disorders over a four-year period at the University Department of Psychiatry at Hvidovre Hospital in Denmark. The authors found moderate to excellent interrater reliability estimates (with kappa values for single items ranging from 0.6 to 1.0) based on 14 video-taped interviews with inpatients below the age of 30. More recently, normative data supporting the psychometric properties of the EASE were provided by Raballo and Parnas (2012), who found good to excellent internal consistency (with alphas ranging from 0.85 to 0.90) across diagnostic subgroups of persons diagnosed with schizophrenia, schizotypal disorder, and nonschizophrenia spectrum (affective) disorders and an overall alpha for the whole sample that was greater than 0.90.

5 Prior to data collection and analysis, the PI of this study received official certification in PANSS rating through The PANSS Institute (PANSS Institute, 2012).

6 Normative data for the PANSS were provided by sample of 240 medicated persons diagnosed with DSM-III-defined schizophrenia at an urban psychiatric hospital (Kay, 1991; Kay et al., 1989; Kay et al., 2006). According to the authors (see overview in Kay, 1991), all four scales exhibited normal distribution curves and met requirements for parametric statistical analyses. The standardisation data for 101 service users diagnosed with chronic schizophrenia was studied more closely. Internal reliability analyses for the positive and negative scales yielded alpha coefficients of 0.73 and 0.83, respectively. Both scales correlated with the composite scale ($r = 0.59$ and -0.61, respectively). The general psychopathology scale yielded an alpha coefficient of 0.79, indicating good internal consistency; it also correlated significantly with the positive ($r = 0.68$) and negative ($r = 0.60$) scales but not the composite scale ($r = 0.07$). Kay et al. (2006) further review the literature on the psychometric stability of the PANSS and conclude that the PANSS has adequate psychometric stability as measured by the following reliability indices: internal consistency (with alphas of .72, .81, and .77 for the positive, negative, and general scales, respectively [DeVellis, 1991]); test-retest reliability (with test-retest coefficients in three studies ranging from $r = -.13$ [Negative subscale in a group of acute service users; Lindenmayer et al., 1984] to $r = .80$ [Positive subscale in a group of chronic service users; Kay et al., 1987]); and interrater reliability (with correlations between raters' ranging from .83 to .87 [Kay et al., 1988]). According to Kay et al. (2006), the psychometric stability of the PANSS is further supported by validity data from multiple studies that establish its construct validity (as representing distinct psychotic syndromes and co-exclusive domains of psychopathology [e.g., Kay et al., 1986]); and criterion-related validity (when compared with results from the Scale for the Assessment of Negative Symptoms [SANS; Andreasen, 1984b], the Scale for the Assessment of Positive Symptoms [SAPS; Andreasen, 1984b], the Clinical Global Impressions Scale [CGI; Guy, 1976], and DSM-III diagnostic criteria for schizophrenia [APA, 1980]).

7 The 33 PANSS (Kay et al., 2006) symptom-items are delusions, conceptual disorganisation, hallucinatory behaviour, excitement, grandiosity, suspiciousness/

persecution, hostility, blunted affect, emotional withdrawal, poor rapport, passive/apathetic social withdrawal, difficulty in abstract thinking, lack of spontaneity and flow of conversation, stereotyped thinking, somatic concerns, anxiety, guilt feelings, tension, mannerisms and posturing, depression, motor retardation, uncooperativeness, unusual thought content, disorientation, poor attention, lack of judgement and insight, disturbance of volition, poor impulse control, preoccupation, active social avoidance, anger, difficulty in delaying gratification, and affective lability.

8 The Pentagonal Model was developed to enhance the goodness of fit of the model to a normal distribution using data polling across five treatment centres for individuals diagnosed with schizophrenia. The Pentagonal Model, which is organised into five symptom scales (negative, positive, dysphoric mood, activation, and autistic preoccupation), has enhanced internal reliability relative to the Standard Model and is applicable to individuals who vary in age and symptom severity and duration (Kay et al., 2006; White et al., 1997).

9 Respondents were classified as having a positive subtype if they scored three or more moderate-to-high ratings on the positive scale but less than three on the negative scale. Likewise, respondents with three or more moderate-to-high ratings on the negative scale but fewer than three on the positive scale were classified as having a negative subtype. Service users with three or more moderate-to-high ratings on both scales were classified as having a mixed subtype, and service users with fewer than three moderate-to-high ratings on both scales were classified as having neither type.

10 Crystal was in recovery at the time of the interview.

11 Participants were asked whether they preferred simultaneous translation into Hebrew or English; one participant chose Hebrew so that he could understand the full conversation, and the other did not have a preference. The two interviews that were conducted in Arabic sometimes slipped into Hebrew due to the simultaneous translation, as the participants sometimes spoke directly to the researcher in Hebrew. When this happened, the researcher usually answered directly, then attempted to redirect the conversation to Arabic. On several occasions, the translator was called out of the room, and the interview proceeded in Hebrew until he returned.

12 If a participant appeared to tire or indicated that they would like to pause, they were invited to take a break and given the option to continue the interview at a later time or date. On the rare occasions that participants became emotionally distressed while discussing life experiences, they were invited to take a break and reminded that they do not have to talk about anything that upsets them. After the break, they were asked whether they prefer not to continue with the interview.

13 Minor edits were made to some audio files to redact information for confidentiality and for training purposes. For example, some participants requested the deletion of audio-recorded personal information.

14 In order to analyse what previous phenomenologists have identified as essential inconsistencies, incongruities, paradoxes, and non-linear forms of thinking and expression in psychosis (Fuchs, 2005, 2007; Sass, 1992a, 1994a, b), we did not conduct the intermediate step of constructing a phenomenal description, which reorganises the participant's narrative developmentally or thematically.

5

URHOMELESSNESS AS A WAY OF BEING-IN-THE-WORLD

Sarah R. Kamens, Frederick J. Wertz, Ryan Scanlon, Jessica Yisca Baris Ginat, Jillian Minahan Zucchetto, Faith Forgione, Ileana Driggs, Lia Kamar, Katherine Sullivan, Caroline Silva, Oren Matar, and Mary Beth Quaranta Morrissey

A way of being-in-the-world

This chapter presents a general overview of the findings from our phenomenological data analysis. It will be followed by five chapters that delve into different aspects of the findings in greater detail.

Data analysis revealed that what is sometimes called schizophrenia or schizophrenia-spectrum disorder is a unique mode of being-in-the-world characterised by the twofold experience of feeling (1) profoundly vulnerable and unsafe in an inhospitable world and (2) alienated, invalidated, and unacknowledged, such that the experience of basic belonging to one or more human communities is eclipsed or foreclosed. These experiences are not necessarily pervasive or chronic; for some, they come and go intermittently, and for others, they are omnipresent and indefinite. To those who encounter it, this mode of being-in-the-world—which for many persons remains unactualised in the background of experience—is experienced as a primordial and fundamental existential possibility. Therefore, this mode of being-in-the-world we tentatively name *urhomelessness*. The prefix *ur-* means 'original' or 'out from'[1] and is used to emphasise the fact that this mode of being-in-the-world is experienced as having a timeless or original quality, even when briefly inhabited.

The general structure of urhomelessness was common to all 18 inpatient and outpatient hospital participants who clearly met DSM (APA, 2000) and ICD (WHO, 1992a, 1992b) criteria for a psychotic disorder. Three ad hoc comparison participants experienced partial features of urhomelessness, but the full general structure was not actualised in the past and present experiences they described and demonstrated. In addition, the general structure was not fully given in the narratives of the four pilot-comparison participants, who nevertheless described non-distressing anomalous

 DOI: 10.4324/9780429055454-6

experiences as well as fleeting and partial experiences of urhomelessness during childhood, semi-wakefulness, non-sobriety, and/or times of notable stress or life change. One pilot-comparison participant, 'Oliver,' was terrified to encounter the possibility of urhomelessness during a particularly harrowing and stressful period of his early adulthood.

The general structure of urhomelessness is schematically represented in Figure 5.1. The three component moments of urhomelessness are here named (1) nomadic, (2) settled, and (3) destitute. Each moment represents an experiential style and strategic orientation for withstanding the crisis of urhomelessness. The moments are non-discrete and often impermanent; as such, they may occur successively or simultaneously. Each moment has predominant, essential constituents as well as common, nonessential variations. Moments and constituents that are not actualised in the foreground of experience may remain in the horizon (background) of experience as potentials that are only partially thematised or unthematised. As such, the moments, constituents, and common variations of urhomelessness cannot be dichotomously quantified as present versus absent; therefore, quantitative frequencies of each moment, constituent, and common variation are not presented in the summary of phenomenological findings.

The psychological experiences comprising urhomelessness are to a great degree ineffable and indescribable, and as a result, there are no perfect terms to characterise them. However, the structure is intuitively given in each example, such that it becomes increasingly (though never fully) apparent through multiple demonstrations. Therefore, throughout Chapters 5 through 10, there are brief, exemplary quotations from participants, as well as longer examples from participants' narratives where relevant.

Urhomeness

Persons experiencing urhomelessness lack the experience of basic existential at-homeness in the world of others. 'Urhomeness' is the experiential horizon of what is missing for the person experiencing urhomelessness. Urhomeness is not a material or physical place, but a condition of possibility in which the world is experienced as reliably offering (1) basic acknowledgement of the person's existence as a human with rights to protection, safety, and the fulfilment of basic needs; and (2) a minimal but meaningful role, position, or place *vis-a-vis* other people, i.e., a sense of basic belonging to a human community. Like urhomelessness, urhomeness is experienced as an original and primordial possibility.

Eidetic analysis revealed that the experience of urhomeness is not contingent upon the absence of physical devastation and suffering, nor is it contingent upon the absence of psychological distress. Interpersonal loss, professional or personal failure, and lack of basic resources do not necessarily lead to urhomelessness. Some persons who are involuntarily

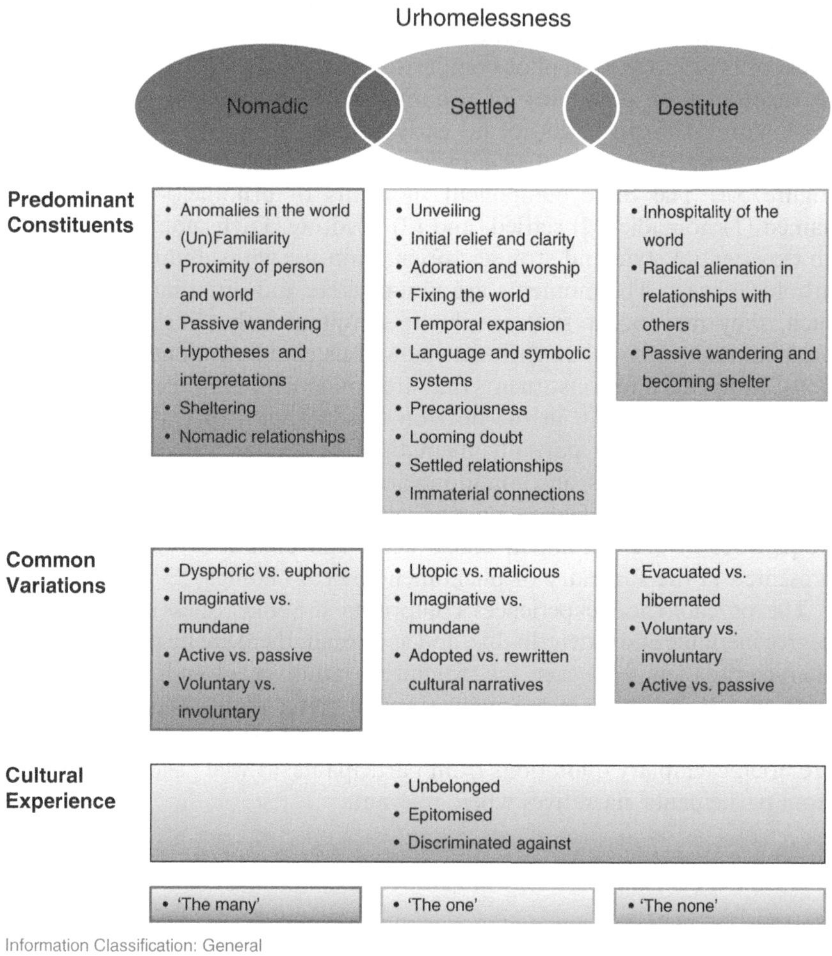

Figure 5.1 An overview of the general structure of urhomelessness, with its three moments and their predominant constituents, common variations, and similarities and differences in cultural experience.

subjected to barely livable ontic[2] conditions such as war, poverty, and other forms of structural violence nevertheless maintain the experience of urhomeness, as they retain the sense of basic (ontological) safety and belonging that has been physically (ontically) infringed upon.

The ontic means of accessing urhomeness vary tremendously between persons and are often multiple and pluralistic. In the present study, eidetic analysis revealed diverse examples of experiences, roles, and activities in which a person might secure urhomeness, including family and community roles, professions, hobbies or leisurely activities, social or group identities, religious activities, wealth or socioeconomic status, spirituality, physical activities, intellectual activities, virtual social networks, and films, art-work, or literature. For example, 'Claire,' a pilot-comparison participant, maintained a sense of urhomeness in part through her love of painting and identity as a painter (see Chapter 9). 'Zev' found a sense of urhomeness through his activities as a peace activist and graduate student. Affordances of the world-as-urhome might also derive from unusual pastimes, such as childhood games, philosophical concepts, relationships with animals, or violent rituals. The experience of urhomeness can be gleaned from past memories, hopes for the future, or imaginative activities such as day-dreaming or artistic production.

The activities and experiential engagements that may serve as a means of becoming urhomed for one person do not necessarily rise to the level of doing so for another. Activities, interests, hobbies, roles, memories, and relationships do not constitute urhomeness unless they provide the afore-mentioned key elements, i.e., a sense of basic, minimal safety and basic existential belonging to one or more human communities.

The 'before' of urhomelessness

There are diverse experiential pathways that can lead to the experiential foregrounding of urhomelessness. Importantly, urhomelessness may or may not be preceded by the experience of urhomeness. In some cases, the person may not remember experiencing urhomeness at all; instead, they may describe life-long experiences of profound vulnerability, lack of protection, alienation, and loneliness. 'Charles,'[3] for example, described a primarily urhomeless existence starting at the age of one. His first statement when answering the life-narrative interview prompt was: 'my childhood, I was given away by my parents. I was one year old. They gave me away.' For other individuals, the process of becoming urhomeless begins with the ex-perience of damage to or loss of a previous urhomed way of being-in-the-world. The person may feel that she[4] was involuntarily exiled, forcefully removed or cleared from former sources of protection and shelter by pow-erful forces or people. For example, one participant, 'Jean,' exclaimed that the people around him 'were taking my life [...] they were hungry and eating my life.' Alternatively, the person may have voluntarily 'jumped ship,' abandoning prior ways of being-in-the-world that were experienced as uninhabitable or simply undesirable. For example, environmental contexts in which the person formerly secured urhomeness may have become violent, alienating, invalidating, and/or 'unreal.' When preceded by urhomeness, urhomelessness is experienced retroactively as *having been* an unactualised, original possibility that nonetheless remained unencountered up until a certain point in the person's life.

Urhomelessness

Urhomelessness is an experience that is uniquely *psychological* and *existential*; as such, it is a way of viewing and experiencing one's existence in the world. The state of being urhomeless is not equivalent to the lack of a material dwelling place, i.e., to ontic houselessness or the lack of a loving family or community—although these structural conditions might lead to the development of urhomelessness. Instead, urhomelessness is a kind of existential and psychological homelessness in which there is a loss of, damage to, or originary lack of a reliable threshold or ontological container that holds and protects the person in the world just as it allows for agentic, grounded participation in it. In the present study, many participants experienced both concrete privations such as houselessness alongside the existential experience of urhomelessness. Further qualifications and distinctions can be found in the Appendix, which outlines the ways in which urhomelessness contrasts with varied privations and human activities that it sometimes resembles, such as ontic houselessness, lack of family and friends, corporeal embodiment, other types of existential crises, other anomalous experiential states, urhomed nomadism, and rebellion and countercultural stances.

The person experiencing urhomelessness is dislodged from familiar, specific bearings and cast into the world-at-large, where personal meanings constantly branch into the collective. The world is paradoxically experienced as distant and unfamiliar just as it becomes all-too-familiar and encroaching. The world is also experienced as inhospitable and profoundly invalidating, such that the person feels unsafe when expressing thoughts, feelings, experiences, and ideas. The person is thus existentially homeless in a lifeworld (*lebenswelt*) experienced as both extremely dangerous and replete with limitless potential. Out of this potential may arise new and strange experiences: voices, images, and feelings that, though radically new and not immediately intelligible, may open up onto new horizons of meaning. These transformations of the person's experiences are grounded in a radical existential displacement in and from an unpredictable world.

Unanchored, cast about, the person loses track of where her surroundings end and where she begins. Paradoxically, she feels both a heightened sense of alienation from and a strong connectedness to humanity. Her social presence takes on ephemeral and strange qualities; she may feel disembodied or omnipresent, invisible or expansive. Everything is acutely familiar and unfamiliar, proximal and distant. Personal meanings branch out and dissipate amid the greater cosmos of collective cultural, historical, even mythological meanings. Familiar contexts are experienced as either unduly fortified and impermeable or porous and insufficient; the person may feel either trapped or uncontained in the universe, the world, her community, her family, and sometimes even her own body and/or mind. Aspects of the experienced world threaten to become existential constituents of the person just as she begins to merge into the world. Being-in-the-world (*In-der-Welt-sein*) risks becoming a symbiotic *worldbeing* (*Weltsein*) or an alienated *world/being* (*Welt/sein*).

Moments of urhomelessness

The data revealed three moments or facets of the general structure, here called (1) nomadic, (2) settled, and (3) destitute. These moments are experiential constellations and strategies for withstanding and surviving the experience of urhomelessness. However, they are imperfect strategies, as they do not fully resolve—and in some cases even exacerbate—the basic crisis of urhomelessness. The three experiential styles are interrelated on the basis of striving, and in particular, the striving of the person to secure a sense of urhomeness, or, at minimum, to mitigate the suffering of urhomelessness. They are also horizons of each other; i.e., each moment is constitutive of the structure as a whole, and each one remains present as a *possibility* in the background of a person's experience regardless of which moment or moments were actualised at any given time. As experiential styles and qualitative constellations of meaning, the moments are non-discrete and often overlap simultaneously in the foreground of experience. In the present study, some participants seemed to experience a single moment indefinitely, whereas others appeared to shift between or experience multiple simultaneous moments. Even while unactualised, moments in the horizon or background of experience were often implicitly given as experiential possibilities. The possibility of experiencing the three moments successively or simultaneously is thus essential to the general structure.

The nomadic moment is characterised by a way of *worldbeing* in which the experience of wandering—or being experientially dislodged and diasporic within the world-at-large—predominates. In the nomadic moment, the person is driven by the strivings to explore and seek safety. The settled moment is characterised by the adoption of an imaginal urhome. The person discovers a new and all-encompassing means of securing basic safety and basic belonging in the world of others. In contrast, the destitute moment is characterised by a relinquishment of the attempt to secure these two elements of urhomeness. In the destitute moment, the person experiences a fundamental hopelessness in which basic safety and basic social belonging are viewed as fully impossible to attain. Each of the three moments of urhomelessness has unique constituents, as well as common variations. In Chapters 6 through 8, each moment is summarised and exemplified with longer idiographic examples. In addition, the predominant constituents and common variations of each moment are outlined and described.

Importantly, urhomelessness is a mode of worldbeing that is infused with the possibility of its own overcoming. Some persons may thus experience urhomelessness as alternating or simultaneous with urhomeness.

Put differently, the possibility of recovery from urhomelessness is a horizon of all three moments. Chapter 9 describes this possibility as part of the continuum or urhomeless experiences.

Notes

1 The connotation 'primitive' does not apply to the present use of the prefix.
2 Heidegger (e.g., 1927/1962) distinguishes between the 'ontic' realm, which pertains to facts and material entities, and the 'ontological' realm, which pertains to the meaning of being. This distinction is dubbed the ontico-ontological difference.
3 All participants' names have been changed to protect their privacy.
4 In order to maintain gender neutrality while avoiding confusion of the pronouns they/them/theirs with the anomalous experience of pluralistic subjectivities, the text alternates between feminine and masculine singular pronouns (she/her/hers and he/him/his).

6

WANDERING IN EXILE: THE NOMADIC MOMENT

Sarah R. Kamens and Frederick J. Wertz

Overview

In the nomadic moment, psychological life is characterised by a fundamentally nomadic and diasporic way of being in which the person is radically exposed to the world-at-large, or the larger world of collective meanings. If the person experiencing the nomadic moment was previously urhomed, he might view the world as newly exposed, inverted, or changed in some way. As Jean put it, the person may feel that an 'other world' has suddenly unconcealed itself.[1] With the unconcealing of this new world, the person might feel that he has gained a new sense of freedom or limitlessness; alternatively, the world may seem more mysterious, dimmer, and less accessible than usual. The world might also seem extraordinarily 'real' or 'unreal.' The person wanders through this newly unconcealed realm, noting its contours, appearances, and meanings, unable to locate and orient himself in familiar territory. He may feel variously surprised, awed, terrified, and mystified by his surroundings.

Wandering is the central experiential constituent of the nomadic moment. There are two primary strivings in the nomadic moment: (1) the exploration of unchartered, expansive (ontological) territory and (2) the procuring of safety and protection. The person in the nomadic moment may experience one or both of these strivings. She might wander in order to explore; for example, 'Leonard' imaginatively explored thousands of years of collective human culture and history:

Leonard:	I migrated to the U.S. in about like the 14th, the early 1400s.
Interviewer:	You migrated to the U.S.?
Leonard:	Yeah I migrated. I, yeah! It /(?:was)[2] crazy [...] I discovered America. [...] And that was the late; the mid, the mid to early 1400s going the other way around the clock.

DOI: 10.4324/9780429055454-7

Or the person might wander to secure shelter in the face of perceived threat and danger:

'Roger':	I keep moving around. [...] Moving, I go to different places.
Interviewer:	Why?
Roger:	Uh because my mind. I'm, I'm escaping something.
Interviewer:	You're escaping.
Roger:	From something but I don't know what or why or who.
Interviewer:	So in each place you feel like you need to escape.
Roger:	Yeah.
Interviewer:	And you don't know what it is?
Roger:	Yeah I don't know what it is.

As the person wanders, the difference between things happening *to* and *around* him begins to fade. 'Container' concepts such as universe, world, nation, society, community, family, body, and mind are experienced as permeable, transcendible. The nomadic moment is a fundamentally exilic mode of worldbeing in which identity, body, and personhood are as temporary tents pitched in an expansive wilderness. As Charles put it, 'Sometimes I can/(?:take) myself out of my body. [...] Go into another universe.'

Persons experiencing the nomadic moment wander in diverse and heterogeneous ways. The person might wander reluctantly and hesitantly, fearful of the strange objects and persons she encounters, frantically searching for something familiar. Or she might wander in euphoric leaps and bounds, thrilled and curious to discover the newly unconcealed world. He might meander in his imagination, travelling to distant and fantastical lands, countries, kingdoms. Wanderings can also be non-imaginal; for example, the person might engage in temporary social activities, jobs, hobbies, pastimes. She might even (ontically) roam on her feet, concretising her existential nomadism by travelling across streets, towns, nations. Often, her wanderings are both imaginal and non-imaginal. In all instances, the person experiencing the nomadic moment lacks the rootedness and sense of safety typical of urhomed modes of being-in-the-world.

Idiographic examples

Below are five brief descriptions of participants within whose narratives the nomadic moment was present in full intuitive clarity, i.e., they were present in the data in a clear and holistic manner.

Charles

Charles was a 61-year-old African American, heterosexual man whose specific mode of being-in-the-world was characterised by wandering between experiences, people, places, and things. His wandering was expressed both concretely and existentially. Charles lived on the streets, accustomed to being involuntarily shuttled from shelter to shelter and from institution to institution by caregivers and, later in his life, by authorities such as police and doctors. While in jail or prison, he wandered in his contemplations and imagination; when free on the outside, he walked the streets, slept on park benches and in shelters. The tendency to wander was also manifest in Charles's communicative style in relation to others. When conversing with interlocutors, he wandered between distally associated thoughts, memories, times, and places. Though his constant wandering was driven by the need for the gathering of resources and survival in the face of great deprivation, it was also basic—existential, ontological, and originary—part of a diasporic and exiled existence without a sense of urhomeness from which the first exile took place. Even the first set of parents who abandoned Charles at the age of one were partially nameless, without faces or personalities in Charles's memory, just the first in a series of nominal quasi-caregivers, sometimes-providers and sometimes-deniers of shelter and sustenance. Charles's wandering was so basic and fundamental that he wandered not to seek urhomeness, but rather in search of minimal sustenance to support the wandering itself.

Lior

'Lior' was a 26-year-old Jewish-Israeli male who was born in Jerusalem. He was diagnosed with 'psychotic state' as a result of his tendency to enter into mystical-divine reveries in which he began to doubt the appearances of the world around him, including the intentions of family members and other persons. Lior was often shy and withdrawn from others, believing that they would not accept his way of being and viewing the world. He felt particularly vulnerable to interpersonal exposure, having once smashed a camera at a yeshiva because cameras both 'intrude on my privacy' and 'don't belong' in a place of bible study.

Lior began to embark on mystical wanderings that led him far from his family and into nature, where he felt proximal to the divine, as well as to a Holy Site in Jerusalem, where he slept for 'some days' instead of returning to his family's house. Throughout his wanderings, Lior attempted to discover and cultivate himself as a righteous servant of God and an ethical human being. As he did so, he increasingly questioned the mundane world and people who seemed increasingly distant from him. He began to see visions of angels and to hear the voice of God, who told him that ultimately, despite his continued wanderings, 'there is nowhere to go.'

Asad

'Asad' was a 37-year-old Muslim Palestinian male from Jerusalem who had been diagnosed with schizophrenia due to a pattern of what others saw as unpredictable and seemingly inconsistent behaviour. At times, Asad appeared to be directly engaged with his interlocutors; at other times, he ignored or rejected them entirely. He often approached others, started a conversation, then abruptly stopped speaking and departed; sometimes, Asad repeated this oscillation between approach and departure multiple times in a matter of minutes. When he did speak, he frequently contradicted previous statements, making it difficult for his interlocutors to determine how he truly thought or felt, or leading them to believe that he held opposing wishes and opinions. For example, he often requested to talk to the interviewers, but then refused to speak when they sat down with him; later that same day or week, he would approach them and request to speak once again. He was often observed gesturing or talking to himself, as if responding to percepts or imaginal events that were not shared by others.

Asad's seeming unpredictability mirrored the unpredictable and volatile world that he experienced as surrounding and sometimes overpowering him. He resented being subjugated to the will and demands of others, including the hospital staff and the military personnel[3] whom he believed to have brought him into the hospital. Asad's inconsistent, sometimes-volatile style was thus a reflection and rendition of the way in which he experienced the world.

Gilah

'Gilah' was a 61-year-old Jewish-Israeli female of Ashkenazi origin. What was viewed as her schizophrenia was an associative, oneiric, dream-like orientation towards the world in which persons, places, events, and objects took on symbolic, often mystical qualities that were often displaced or exchanged for each other in rapid and seemingly irrational succession. Gilah described her life history as series of wanderings through a highly meaningful, symbolic, and mystical world with an attitude of wonder and amazement that sometimes, during negative or tragic events, became confusion, consternation, and/or fear. Gilah's communicative style also meandered; while speaking, she wandered between themes, topics, and memories, following a logic that was alternately phonetic, affective, or otherwise associative. For example, Gilah told us that:

> They gave us peanuts, so I told her 'I want to be a monkey.' That's what one of her friends said. That I'm going to be a monkey and that I have cancer. And I will be in a home, and I will die, and I will suffer indescribable pain. And I will walk without clothes in the streets, God forbid, and will save daughters of the house of Jacob. You know I would look at that, from golden stripes she was dressed; virgin friends would come after her. I would look at it like that, with Holiness. Would I go naked in the streets? Where can you hear such a thing? And with no shower? My sister showered today, she showers every day. What did they do? Our old tub, they made

> corner that she can walk straight into so she doesn't put her feet up because she fell a few times. And they put up a rail.

Gilah's disparate memories and thoughts were intermixed and traversed as if part of the same unbroken experiential plane. She surfed through the mysteries of life, flowing from place to place, encountering people and objects in an enigmatic world that she experienced as pregiven, inevitable, and self-evident.

Haseeb

For 'Haseeb,' a 35-year-old Palestinian male from Jerusalem, it all started at the age of 13. Sitting at his house alone, the violence of the intifada (popular uprising against the Israeli military) raging outside, his parents and siblings away, Haseeb felt an excruciating 'boredom': 'I had nothing to do,' he explained, 'sitting at home most of the time and no school.' The world seemed unbearably barren of meaning and futile, and Haseeb was all alone, vulnerable and bored in his empty, empty house. He began to feel things around him changing. His house was no longer a place of safety, love, and protection, but a porous structure, permeable by frightening *jinn* (Arabic for 'demons') that he could see through the windows. Terrified, Haseeb ran out of his house, roaming everywhere and anywhere: 'because of the *jinn* and I used to wander in the streets,' he explained. Sometimes, Haseeb's worried father would find him roaming the streets and bring him back to the house or to the hospital.

Predominant constituents of the nomadic moment

This subsection describes the predominant experiential constituents of the nomadic moment. They are labelled as follows: anomalies in the world, (un)familiarity, proximity of person and world, passive modes of wandering, hypotheses and interpretations, sheltering, and nomadic relationships with others. After outlining these constituents, common variations of the nomadic moment are explicated.

Anomalies in the world

For the person experiencing urhomelessness in the nomadic moment, the experiential threshold between self and world is compromised or lacking. As a result, the person is radically exposed to the world-at-large. The world, in turn, seems strange, anomalous—newly opened or closed, perhaps even inverted, like in a mirror. People, objects, and events seem somehow different, mysterious, illegible, ineffable. Others around her may seem like they're signalling something to her, winking or passing on secret message. As described by 'Crystal,' a 54-year-old European American female:

Crystal: I would be afraid to go throw the garbage out in the hallway because I thought people were spying on me. So uh if there was a little red uh piece like the garbage bags that have the red or the strings if I saw uh a piece hanging out of the door then it was safe to go outside.

[…]

Interviewer: Okay. So that was kind of a signal to you.

Crystal: Yeah.

Interviewer: And what did you feel like was signalling to you in that?

Crystal: The colour, uh the message.

Interviewer: The colour, the message.

Crystal: Yeah.

Interviewer: Was there a person behind that?

Crystal: No.

The person may feel as if signs are scattered everywhere, signalling something esoteric but vital, warning and guiding her. The contours of the world may seem to exhibit strange mutations that symbolically reflect her urhomelessness; walls might ripple, the ground might shake or weaken, and objects might appear and disappear as if unbounded by physical laws. Alongside her changing environment, she might experience a vast range of differing and transitory emotions, physical sensations, and thoughts. The person's experiences undergo multiple shifts from day to day, moment to moment.

(Un)familiarity

As the person wanders, leaving her familiar bearings behind, a fundamental experiential reversal takes place where that which was previously *familiar* becomes *unfamiliar* and that which was previously *unfamiliar* becomes strangely *familiar.* For example, when Haseeb was alone, the walls of his house seemed to become permeable to *jinn* that looked like once-familiar animals, with slight but uncanny differences in physical appearance from non-demonic animals, such as 'a black dog, a black animal, and a snake that moves straight and not in a zigzag.'[4] In extreme instances of the nomadic moment, the person may feel that elements of the familiar world disappear completely. For example, Haseeb explained that 'once I was walking and saw all the cars disappear. This is what happened. I don't know [how].' Haseeb also reported having witnessed whole persons disappearing:

Interviewer: Previously you mentioned that you saw unreal people. Are they here with us now?

Haseeb: No, they aren't here.

Interviewer: Where did you see them?
Haseeb: In the street.
Interviewer: What are those unreal people?
Haseeb: When I'm sick I imagine things.
Interviewer: What other things happen in your imagination?
Haseeb: People disappear. Is this real or imaginary?
Interviewer: What do you think?
Haseeb: This is an imagination. In reality there is no [such thing]. [...]
Interviewer: Why do you laugh when speaking about this topic?
Haseeb: Because it's strange.

The experience of unfamiliarity is particularly salient when it characterises relationships, objects, and events that were previously personally significant. As the person wanders further away from the people and places he once knew, he may claim that family members, friends, and/or co-workers are not who he once thought they were. Other humans may be experienced as increasingly distant, untrustworthy, illusory, or simply irrelevant in the face of the wider expanse of persons and things. When talking about his sister, for example, Leonard compared her to an extra-terrestrial being: 'I told her what the deal [...] he[5] sent you from Mars.'

Just as the familiar world grows increasingly unfamiliar, previously unfamiliar persons, events, and objects suddenly take on a strange and sometimes frightening familiarity. For example, strangers may seem recognisable, as when Crystal identified passers-by on the street as her family. In another example, 'Saleh' stated:

Interviewer: Have strangers ever looked familiar to you?
Saleh: Strangers looked familiar? Yes.
Interviewer: Where? On the street?
Saleh: Yes, even in college. [...] I see people whom I remember seeing in my dreams when I was little. Is there something like this?[6]

As the world-at-large becomes more proximal, the experience of familiarity may become more and more frequent. In time, the person may feel that wherever she goes, whatever she does, she encounters objects and people who are familiar to her in a meaningful, but perhaps indescribable way. She might believe that she sees meaningful relationships between objects that others do not, and she may report a heightened sense of meaning that is experienced as indescribable but inescapable. Small details of her surroundings like the wallpaper in a restaurant or the sign on a passing truck may seem like highly meaningful clues or signs:

Haseeb:	I used to understand everything people said and I even understood cars, why they use their horns.
Interviewer:	Why do they beep?
Haseeb:	Why do people smoke? Because there is a secret in cigarettes; [that's why] people smoke.
Interviewer:	What is the relationship between smoking and horns?
Haseeb:	Because they talk to each other. Birds talk to each other, and everything is related.
Interviewer:	What is the secret in smoking?
Haseeb:	Something unknown, we can't explain it.

In sum, in the nomadic moment, the person's familiar world is inverted or reversed, such that once-familiar people and things become distant and unfamiliar, and the world-at-large becomes proximal and familiar. Eventually, the familiar and the unfamiliar may seem to overlap and blur together, such that the person feels a sense of confusion coupled with a sense of greater, even special understanding about the world. She may seem to talk in paradoxes, reporting, for example, that she now meaningfully understands the arbitrariness, meaninglessness, and fleetingness of all things—or conversely that she does not understand how the world is so meaningful. The world appears to contradict itself and yet make perfect sense.

Proximity of person and world

Experientially, wandering has become a basic part of the person's *world-being*; his way of being in the world has become a way of being *as* the world, a way of being that constitutes the world just as he is constituted by it. This paradoxically results in both alienation and merging between the person and world. The person may feel that he blends into his surroundings and that his surroundings blend into him. Leonard expressed this experience in claiming to be a 'chameleon,' effectively indistinguishable from his surroundings. The person may report that varied events in the world are happening specifically to or within him; conversely, he may feel that his own thoughts, feelings, and/or actions can causally influence (e.g., physically control) other persons or events in the world. Indeed, the person's own developmental trajectory may be experienced as the *becoming of the world.* For example, Leonard stated, 'I was there from the very first; there was no beginning to my existence,' and he described major events in human history (e.g., the discovery of America, man stepping foot on the moon) as significant events in his personal life story.

Profoundly exposed to new experiences in a ubiquitous, omnipresent way, the person may feel that he is *known*, the epistemological object of a subject he cannot necessarily see or hear. For example, he might report that passers-by performatively mimic his desires or that his thought stream is broadcast on the radio. As Roger, a 50-year-old Filipino American male, put it,

> Sometimes when I hear voices, I look around myself, around me. Nobody's in the, at my back. Nobody is, but I hear the voice. […] I hear them in the radio also. […] As if they talking to me. 'You.' […] They [are] using the word 'you.' […] Sometimes they said on; they said, 'we're talking to you.'

Unable to put her finger on where these experiences are coming from, the person may begin to believe that there's something mysterious unfolding. She may start to suspect that people are watching her, following her, talking about her, plotting against her. As Crystal put it, 'I was thinking people were following me. And um I stopped eating and I was staring at the headlights of the cars.'

Alternatively, the person may feel that he has unusual control over the world and/or others in it. His heightened sense of familiarity may lead him to the conclusion that he understands events before they occur or somehow wills them into existence. He may report the ability to influence natural or supernatural phenomena; Leonard, for example, reported that he was able to control the weather, his own future, and the resurrection of his family members from the dead. In these instances, it is not the world that is experienced as impinging upon the person, but rather the person who is experienced as impinging upon the world. Some persons may report experiencing person-world influence working both ways, such that they control the world just as it exerts control over them.

Passive modes of wandering

At times, the person's existential-psychological wandering is passive, such that he experiences himself as the object and not the subject of wandering. Indeed, the world may seem to wander by the person, around him, within him, through him. Images, words, or beings may appear and disappear mysteriously. For example, Charles described seeing 'print material' with words appearing in front of his eyes:

Interviewer:	What kind of print material?
Charles:	Uh, book // pages on a book. The lines on a book. Words.
Interviewer:	You see that?
Charles:	I see that. // words appear in front of my eyes.
Interviewer:	You see words appear in front of your eyes? What kinds of words?
Charles:	Words, uh, beginning with a a, u, b, t, s, words in /. Strange letters. But they has a meaning to them.

In another example, Roger reported witnessing an autobus appear in thin air:

Roger:	When I ride the bus/suddenly appear in front of me. [...] It suddenly appears.
Interviewer:	Like it drives up?
Roger:	Yeah. [...] It happens, uh last month. When I went to my sister's place. [...] I didn't see the bus, then when I went to the bus stop the bus appeared.
	[...]
Interviewer:	It drove up?
Roger:	No.
Interviewer:	It just appeared.
Roger:	It just appeared.
Interviewer:	Out of air.
Roger:	Yeah. [...] Just like, 'oh, here it is.'
Interviewer:	I'm just gonna; [demonstrating with hands] so here's the street, and here's you, and then instead of driving up, the bus just *poof,* appears. [...]
Roger:	Yeah uh-huh, yeah.

These strange appearances may be accompanied by equally enigmatic disappearances. Haseeb, for example, reported seeing people disappear before his eyes: 'once I saw some people and they disappeared. I don't know if they were *jinn.*'

In the passively nomadic mode, the person's thoughts, feelings, and perceptions are just as nomadic and transient as the people in her life. Experiences take on a vagabond-like quality. They come and go, enter and exit, present themselves and then leave her. She sees, hears, smells, and/or feels the passing presence of unmoored and travelling people, places, and things; those people, places, and things that may pass by her like ships sailing on the horizon. When passively nomadic, she is merely a locus for these varied and transient happenings, observing them as they pass by. People and places are strangely present, absent, present, absent.

In some instances, persons or strange entities may seem to wander not only by, but *through* the person:

'Avery':	Sometimes when I take a shower, after I take a shower and I feel like I have like, a, uh, an extra-terrestrial inside of my skull.
Interviewer:	Like an alien?
Avery:	Yeah, like a, from uh, from the *Independence Day*.
Interviewer:	Inside of your skull?
Avery:	Yeah, inside.

Interviewer: And how long does it stay there?
Avery: It stays there in my brain and then it goes back to normal. It interferes when I get out from my shower. […] Yeah, uh, like that. I felt like it, inside.
Interviewer: What does that feel like?
Avery: Very spooky.

The person may claim that her brain, body, mind, or person is being invaded or possessed. Structures and zones of safety, including physical structures like buildings and social structures like institutions, may also be seen as permeable. In Haseeb's case, both his house and his body were experienced as permeable to demons, such that 'no one can protect me in my house.' Vulnerable and frightened, Haseeb wandered the streets at night: 'when I was alone, the *jinn* [demons] came, and that's why I was wandering. Once I was in a kitchen, and I felt that a woman [female demon] went out from[7] my body.'

In the nomadic moment, these passive wanderings of other beings *through* and *by* the person are generally experienced as temporary and fleeting, much like everything else in the person's quotidian experience. They may be frightening, amusing, or strange, but they are also impermanent. (When passive wanderings become constant and seemingly inescapable, the person is likely to experience the destitute moment; see Chapter 8). Indeed, in the nomadic moment, nothing is permanent; the person's everyday actions, thoughts, and feelings are transient, fleeting, unpredictable, and transitory. There is nothing but ceaseless movement and temporary waystations; when not in motion, she herself becomes a waystation, another site or shelter for world's wandering.

Hypotheses and interpretations

Although it is common for the person experiencing the nomadic moment to lack an explanation for her new and strange experiences, some persons hedge tentative interpretations or hypotheses. For example, the person may posit that the world is an ongoing movie, that extra-terrestrials have transformed the earth's atmosphere, or that God has invented new doors of experience for his servants. In the below example, Gilah proposed an explanation based on her perception that a teacher she knew did not physically age:

Gilah: You know what happened? In school, in kindergarten, we had 'Ms. Richards,' the nursery teacher, who today looks like [she once did] 40 years ago. She looks the same. […] I don't understand, how can this happen?
Interviewer: Strange.
Gilah: Can't believe it. Maybe she's also from that world.
Interviewer: What do you mean, from that world?
Gilah: An angel.

Interviewer:	And who else is from that world?
Gilah:	Angels. I had [names of people] helped me to know when my mother was born, on [date]. Passed away on [date].
Interviewer:	What do you mean, she also is from that world? Who else is from that world?
Gilah:	Lots, lots. I had friends. [Name].
Interviewer:	Everyone you're telling me about now was from that world?
Gilah:	Yes!
Interviewer:	How can you know?
Gilah:	Angels. I feel it.
Interviewer:	From what world is that?
Gilah:	[...] From the next world, from the stars!

At first, these interpretations may be held as tenuous hypotheses; in time, the person may develop a preference for one or more specific interpretations that seems to explain the puzzling events surrounding her. (If a person has a favoured interpretation that holds over the course of time, this interpretation may lead into the settled moment; see Chapter 7).

Sheltering

As the person wanders, she may find zones of transient safety and comfort that, because they are unstable and temporary, do not lead to the experience of urhomeness. For the present purposes, these zones are referred to as *shelters* and the person's act of temporarily inhabiting them is referred to as *sheltering*. Shelters are here defined as unstable and fleeting experiences of perceived safety and basic acknowledgement by other humans. The person may find shelters in real or imaginal social roles, positions, activities, jobs, hobbies, or interpersonal interactions. For example, she might become sheltered during an unexpected encounter with an old friend, in a new community gig, during a visit with a trusted family member, or in a professional project she's taken on. Sometimes, shelters are enjoyable and exciting (e.g., an opportunity to travel, a visit with loved friends); at other times, they're mundane (e.g., a boring part-time job, smoking a cigarette, running errands). Some are even unpleasant (e.g., an involuntary stay in the hospital). These types of activities do not always provide relief from the distress of urhomelessness, but when they do, the relief is only temporary, fleeting; often, the person anticipates its imminent subsiding.

Some persons take on characteristics of shelters, ontologically donning them as a form of further protection. Gilah, for example, had multiple predictions[8] about her future that often changed according to the topic of conversation and objects in her immediate surroundings. For example, when she saw picture of a kangaroo, she stated she was going to Australia, and when she spoke about cutting her hair, she stated that she was going to become a monkey. Often, the person's experiential merging with the world is a sheltering strategy by which she camouflages herself, assuming various roles and activities to evade perceived dangers. For example, Leonard gathered personas from his surroundings, including the psychiatric institution in which he resided: 'In [19]78 I went to England again. I was studying med; I studied um, I studied psychiatry. But I had to/the United States/the Board of Medicine in America.' When donning aspects of shelters, the person may oscillate between feeling like she is 'faking' to throw others off and authentically identifying with the temporary roles she assumes. In other words, she may feel that she is simultaneously performing these new roles as she genuinely—but temporarily—becomes them.

For some, it is rapid movements or meanderings between shelters—and not necessarily the shelters themselves—that serve as the person's strategic means of withstanding urhomelessness. By moving rapidly from place to place, role to role, thought to thought, the person avoids getting stuck in dangerous places or with dangerous others. In this way, she can also 'go with the flow' to evade conflict. Leonard, for example, donned identities even during the interview itself by successively answering the interviewer's questions in the affirmative:

Interviewer:	Is there one country that you feel like you belong to more than others?
Leonard:	Yeah.
Interviewer:	Which one?
Leonard:	England.
Interviewer:	England. So you're British?
Leonard:	[...] British yeah.
Interviewer:	So [...] you're British. And do, do you belong to like a specific race or ethnicity?
Leonard:	No.
Interviewer:	No. So you're all.
Leonard:	All.
Interviewer:	All races?
Leonard:	All races yeah.
Interviewer:	Or no race?
Leonard:	[...] Chinese, Koreans, Russians. Africans.
Interviewer:	So you're everything?
Leonard:	Yeah. I'm a chameleon.

Despite their provision of transient comforts, shelters are merely waystations, briefly lived zones of safety along a treacherous journey. Ultimately, they do not lead to urhomeness because they are transitory and do not provide abiding existential safety or meaningful experiences of belonging for the person in the world. Instead, they are impermanent and interchangeable; the new temporary job is pulled, the friend or lover leaves, the movie ends, the book is closed. Perhaps a fellow service user bursts into the room, ending a midday reverie, and the person is launched into the expanse of the (un) familiar world once again. Thus, even when temporarily sheltered, the person remains fundamentally urhomeless. Acutely familiar with the proximal dangerous of the world, she is aware that the sheltering is a temporary and transient respite, like pausing to stand in the eye of the storm.

Nomadic relationships with others

Just as the person in the nomadic moment experiences the world as wildly vast and unpredictable, interlocutors may experience his behaviour as unpredictable and difficult to follow. Indeed, others often view the person as behaving in unpredictable and erratic ways. For example, at several points during his interview, Asad surprised the researchers by abruptly standing up in the middle of the conversation, saying goodbye, and exiting the room. Below is an excerpt from such occurrence:

Interviewer:	Can you tell about something from the past that relates to your personality?
Asad:	Trance music […] [name of a holy site in Jerusalem]
Interviewer:	What is the relationship between the two?
Asad:	Yes. I heard music from God. I prayed God to get beautiful music. I adore [name of holy site], and it loves me. We both love each other. […] [W]e both pray to each other.
Interviewer:	Were you praying at [name of holy site] as you listened to music?
Asad:	Yes.
Interviewer:	What did you feel when you listened to music?
Asad:	[Slams hands on the table, gets up, and leaves the interview.]

The person experiencing the nomadic moment of urhomelessness often feels radically alone. He might communicate with God or magical, mystical, or immaterial entities, while his interpersonal relationships are experienced as lacking in authentic intimacy. Saleh, for example, was fearful of interactions with others and believed himself to be socially inefficacious: 'every time I speak with someone I have a feeling I'm saying something wrong. I repeat everything to myself back at home and I'm ashamed.'[9] He described a special relationship to God, whom he implored for an empathic companion:

Interviewer:	Which things do you talk to Him [God] about?
Saleh:	Mm. I want to find someone like me.
Interviewer:	Did you get an answer from him?
Saleh:	[Signals 'no']
Interviewer:	He says 'no'? Or there is no answer at all?

Saleh: Both. There is no answer; he tells me there aren't any.
Interviewer: How did you know that he said there aren't any?
Saleh: He told me 'stop being a noodge [*noodnik*[10]].'

Notably, despite his profound loneliness and alienation, Saleh engaged in agentic efforts to establish meaningful connections with others. For example, when initially interviewed by the ward psychiatrist, Saleh stated that his main goal in the hospital was to find someone who could understand him.

Sometimes, in attempting to shelter, the person reaches out to multiple others in her environment with gestures intended to be kind and caring. Persons in the nomadic moment are often keen to seek meaningful human relationships that might lead to urhomeness. For example, some interview participants developed an immediate rapport with the interviewer, and several approached her on the hospital wards for subsequent conversations after the interview was completed. One participant, after meeting the interviewer and completing the brief consent procedure, told the interviewer 'I will miss you' prior to the start of the interview the next day.

Some persons experiencing urhomelessness may report having numerous, even multitudinous acquaintances or admirers from a distance. However, genuine and caring friends, family members, and colleagues are often perceived as generally absent or otherwise inaccessible. For example, Charles reported, 'I never had no long life-long friends.'

The person may feel that her radical distance from other humans precludes her ability to communicate with them. These difficulties may be manifest in various linguistic anomalies in speech, writing, and language comprehension. She might speak in secret languages that only she can understand, or she may describe difficulty expressing herself in a way that others can easily comprehend. For example, Leonard stated:

Leonard: My speech is being blurred and all that, right. And he said, 'what is the problem?' I couldn't mention a thing because my speech is so blurred that I couldn't speak much. But I was able to //, to write and spell. They couldn't take that away from me.

To some persons in the nomadic moment, other humans may be experienced as fascinating and desirable, yet ultimately unreachable and incomprehensible, like objects on display behind a department store window. When in the presence of others, the person might experience feelings of longing that he does not fully understand. People, like the person's environments, seem to be constantly changing, moving, on the go; the person often observes them from a distance of sorts. Others may be conceptualised as distant placeholders for unactualised possibilities. Leonard, for example, did not directly answer a question about his relationships with other service users, but instead expressed his general appreciation for the basic fact of their existence:

Interviewer: Do you like any of the other patients here? Do you have friends here?
Leonard: I like the fact that they exist.

In another example, Avery answered a question about her identification with groups with a statement about viewing her sister as a 'sex object,' highlighting her alienation from meaningful others in her life, including family members:

Interviewer: Is there, um, a people, like a group of people who you, you identify with or who you, who you like more than others?
Avery: What do you mean, like?
Interviewer: A group of people who you feel like they're *your* people.
Avery: My people? No.
Interviewer: No?
Avery: I think of my sister like a sex object.

In another variation of this type of distant, alienated interpersonal experience, the person experiencing urhomelessness in the nomadic moment may view all others in an equally positive manner. He may feel that he understands and relates to all humans with comparable ease. In this case, other persons are superficially liked—or even admired and loved—by default, but no single relationship (or set of relationships) is seen as more intimate or meaningful than any of the others that pass him by. As Charles put it:

Interviewer: [Do] you have any people you don't like?
Charles: I like everybody.
Interviewer: You like everybody? Ok.
Charles: Even you.
Interviewer: Even me?
Charles: I understand you.

Similarly, when asked to whom he feels closest, Asad stated: 'I love all people.'

The person's exposure to the-world-at-large often generates a radical sensitivity to the suffering of other humans. Indeed, urhomelessness is often accompanied by an acute awareness of pain and hardships in global humanity. The person may claim that she will attempt to alleviate this suffering, or that she is emotionally tortured by the thought of what happens to kindred souls. In some cases, the person may demonstrate extreme generosity in everyday situations. Charles, for example, was highly attentive to other service users' wishes and needs. While taking the elevator to an interview room on a different floor, he stepped back so that all other service users could enter the elevator before he stepped on; he also planned to spend the $10 in hospital funds that he received for completing the interview on snacks for other service users. However, the person experiencing urhomelessness expresses her care for and sensitivity towards other humans generally, without intimate connections to one or more people in particular. The person is attuned to the needs of others who are nevertheless experienced as emotionally distant.

Communicative style

In the nomadic moment, spoken, written, and other forms of symbolic communication are roaming, winding, and associative. Interlocutors may have difficulty deciphering the person's meanings and intentions. Below is an example of wandering, nomadic speech from Leonard's interview:

Leonard: What I'm trying to do like, uh it's hard for me to explain but, // I ///// and he //// some-something that, that deteriorated; defeated. Cause I had been /// which would've ///. Still is. And they, they found it; they found the pills. They put them together. They, they formulated something like; but my name is 'Budu' too. In the street they call me 'Buddha.' Anyway they pu-; they made something up that; de-de deteriorated the um, the cerebral palsy and bring me; bring me back to, neutrally right. Bring me back to neutral state where I could, function an-and; as a normal person. But what I did was, I-I went back to; so 1967; I forgot the name of; I was carrying, back in those days, what they call it it, but I have books on it. In my; my la; in my room. And I wrote on it about/personalities and disorders and stuff.

The person may explicitly recognise that others have trouble following her communications:

Gilah: How I jump from one topic to another.
Interviewer: That's true.

In addition to being circumlocutious, the person may purposely avoid speaking to others about her unusual experiences. She may remember prior experiences being ridiculed, rejected, or medicated when attempting to communicate. Indeed, speech itself is often viewed as an additional source of vulnerability to the world-at-large:

Charles: God talks to me like once or twice a week. […] I hear him often.
Interviewer: Did it-, did it happen this week?
Charles: It's happened.

Interviewer:	What'd you hear?
Charles:	I'm not telling.

Some participants demonstrated this hesitance and sense of vulnerability through minimalistic speech, pauses, and even silence at points during the interview.

In some cases, the person may hold superstitious beliefs about the nature of language itself. Some participants alluded to certain discussion topics being 'forbidden' or dangerous to mention. For example, Charles stated that he would 'lose myself' if he spoke about the new universes to which he believed that he could travel:

Interviewer:	What's that universe like?
Charles:	Well kind of personal. I don't want to tell you about that.
Interviewer:	You don't want to tell me about that.
Charles:	I don't want to talk about it.
Interviewer:	Is it not; okay, you don't want to talk about that.
Charles:	[...] I would lose if I told you about it. I would lose if I told you about that.
Interviewer:	You would lose. What would you lose?
Charles:	I would lose [...] watch me all the time. I would lose it. That's what I'm talking about.

Similarly, Gilah refused to talk about specific topics and even requested that the interviewers to delete several sections of her transcript because 'I'm not allowed to talk [...] it's forbidden to talk about it.' Spoken language is thus viewed as something that can increase the person's vulnerability and exposure to an uninhabitable and dangerous world.

Common variations of the nomadic moment

The nomadic moment is experientially diverse in its essence. Because the person wanders through the previously unfamiliar and vast world-at-large, constituent experiences have an inherently novel, inconsistent, contradictory, and unpredictable quality. Some common experiential variations within the nomadic moment include dysphoric versus euphoric, imaginative versus mundane, active versus passive, and voluntary versus involuntary. These variations are not necessarily static or characterological, but rather varied expressions of the nomadic experience that arise over the course of the person's existential-psychological wanderings, as she enters into and interacts with the multitudinous contexts and situations to which she is exposed. Thus, the person experiencing urhomelessness may oscillate between these common variations or even experience them simultaneously.

Imaginative versus mundane variations

The wandering that is essential to the nomadic moment may be imaginative or mundane. In the imaginative variations, the person might travel to extraordinary and faraway places, to empires in the sky, or to utopic, cosmic kingdoms. The predominantly imaginative variation is exemplified in this oneric excerpt from the narrative of Gilah:

> Are you listening? They said my house will burn down from the candles, from burning candles. So, I remembered that in the spaceship, in the spaceship there was this one Jewish guy. In a spaceship to the moon. It is forbidden for Jews to go onto astronomical-objects,[11] it is forbidden by the laws of the Torah. And he went on it, and lit candles, and the spaceship fell into the sea, and it was completely fell apart, all the parts were scattered everywhere [...] and they told me too that my house will burn down.

In other cases, wandering has a more quotidian, mundane experiential quality. Note that these mundane wanderings may be *imaginal,* but not necessarily *imaginative*; i.e., they may be relatively mundane, common activities that occur solely in the person's imagination. The person may simply roam from street to street, house to house, friend to friend, family to family, or profession to profession. She might never adopt one particular hobby, job, social role, or relationship long enough to make it a viable shelter. Mundane meanderings might be *imagined*, but not necessarily *imaginative*; in some cases, they are expressed concretely through extensive engagement in activities such as street-wandering, serial dating, and job-hopping.

For some persons, wandering is *both* imaginative and mundane. The person might meander about cooking ideas, websites, television channels, or other daily activities just as he wanders the galaxies. Haseeb, for example, wandered the streets of his neighbourhood as he collected others' prayers to deliver to Allah. To the onlooker or interlocutor, the person may appear to be erratic, unpredictable, or even mysteriously immobile. To the person, his wanderings are part and parcel of an equally meandering, unpredictable world.

Dysphoric versus euphoric variations

In the dysphoric version of the nomadic moment, the person is beset by emotional distress as a result of his wanderings. As he moves from place to place and shelter to shelter, he may describe feeling variously downcast, saddened, helpless, hopeless, aimless, despondent, angry, desperate, confused, and even apathetic about his day-to-day prospects. Jean, for example, complained of being utterly 'miserable,' such that 'I am next to death. And everything, all my soul.' If she exerts agency, it is in order to find the next temporary refuge, to evade or attack dangerous or threatening others, or to evacuate—in Jean's words, to 'only survive.'

In contrast, in the euphoric variation of the nomadic moment, the person is joyous and excited about the seeming expanse of imaginative opportunities opened up by her wanderings. She jumps or swims from one place to the next, trying on this hobby here, that one there, this shelter here, that castle there. She's an explorer, a navigator. She may report that her wanderings are unconstrained by the laws of physics. For example, Leonard experienced the nomadic moment as an opportunity to transcend borders, space, and time:

> Like in a minute in a flash, I can be in another world. I could disappear in another world. But with a body that is, that is great, like um, like Odysseus. I don't know if you've ever heard of him.

Similarly, Lior described enjoying his nomadic wanderings, which he experienced as divine reveries in which he saw 'angels [...] sometimes I see also the nature. That God changes nature for me. Special things in nature.'

Voluntary versus involuntary variations

Nomadic wanderings can be voluntarily or involuntarily. The person might voluntarily wander with the aim of obtaining shelter, or with the aim of exploring new relationships, places, or social roles. Conversely, the person might feel involuntarily cast or coerced into a state of nomadism. He might feel that there is no safe place other than the open expanse, the streets, the forest, the beyond. In some cases, the person might report being tossed between institutions such as hospitals and jails. Charles, for example, stated:

> I don't got a place [...] to stay, they take me to the nutty house. /// he takes me there. /// live there. [...] that's what happens to me. jail, the nuthouse, it happens to me. /// (laughs) //// What the hell happened to me? Look what's happening to me? Look what's happened to me. You're in the nuthouse. //// I can't help it.

Charles's nomadic movement exemplified both the voluntary and involuntary variations of the nomadic moment. Sometimes, he was involuntarily bounced between jail and the hospital, where he felt that he had been robbed of his freedom:

> I can't go outside. I can't eat what I wanted to eat. I can't go the places I want to go. I can't get / friend. I can't make no / friend. I

> can't do a lot of things // when I walk without my freedom. [...] I'm trapped. [...] he takes me to jail.

At other times, Charles wandered on his own, voluntarily. Free on the outside, he walked the streets, slept on park benches and in shelters. He travelled long distances to find work, food, a roof over his head.

> I [was] just trying to survive. [...] After school I was in the air force. It's a // my family went back, then got an apartment in and stayed there, then go back to family. Then I left for awhile. //// stayed there //// and sold magazines door to door //// stayed there for a year and a half. [...] a job, I said I'll go. // What do you say? Head me down south to a farm in um, North Carolina.

Experiences that wander *through* or *before* the person (e.g., voices, images, or smells that seem to originate in the world) are typically experienced as involuntary. For example, Avery reported that she saw 'a lot of ghosts,[12] flying, // from the wall' of her apartment. She elaborated about the strange experiences she endured involuntarily in his house: 'there's a lot more things, strange things that happened in there. [...] They poked things in my body. They played with my feet. They, uh; it was a spooky time for me.'

Voluntary and involuntary wandering are not respectively equivalent to active and passive wandering as described above. Voluntary wandering is often active, and involuntary wandering is often passive. However, voluntary wandering may be passive when, for example, the person voluntarily becomes the receptor or host for strange voices and visions, thereby allowing himself to serve as a shelter for wanderings. Involuntary wandering may be active when the person agentically evacuates a situation that is experienced as unlivable, oppressive, treacherous, and/or coercive.

Prolonged wandering

In time, the person may give up on finding shelter or urhomeness, and he may wander for wandering's sake, i.e., for the sake of having no choice but to wander. He might believe the nomadic life is his only future. For example, at one point in her interview, Gilah stated that her long-lost romantic interest, 'Solomon,'[13] once told her, 'you will move from one place to another to another to another, until you die.'

For some, wandering eventually becomes more than a mere means of seeking shelter or an urhome; the person may view himself *as* transient, and urhomelessness as his shelter. In other words, wandering may be viewed as ontologically originary, primary, and fundamental. Often, in these cases, even the state of wandering fluctuates and oscillates with an apparently stable, grounded way of being. People, places, and things are temporarily fixed, then ephemeral, then stable, then transient again. The wandering itself wanders; even the person's wandering is impermanent, and shelters are experienced as merely transitory.

Notes

1 This 'other world' may be vaguely sensed prior to full-blown urhomelessness. For example, 'Noam,' an ad hoc comparison participant, stated that he knew of the existence of this other world but did not know it personally. When asked if there was more than one world of meaning, Noam stated 'yes [...] it's like there is one room and another one next to it. Same with the one world and a world next to it.'
2 Where possible in the transcriptions, slashes are followed by parenthetical notations with transcribers' speculations about undecipherable utterances.
3 The Israeli police (who, for Asad, may be indistinguishable from the military) brought Asad to the hospital.
4 Put differently, 'black color and straight-line movement are signs of demons.' Note that snakes and dogs, especially black dogs, are common manifestations of *jinn* in certain Islamic traditions.
5 The subject of the male pronoun is unclear in the transcript.
6 This is a literal translation from the Hebrew; Saleh means, 'do other people have this experience?'
7 In other words, emerged from his body after being inside of it.
8 Gilah's descriptions of her nomadic movements were often in the future tense. Her narrative was thematically unique within the dataset for being predominantly driven by predictions and prophecies.
9 Saleh's ruminations and time-consuming compulsive attempts to imaginatively repair conversations also constituted symptoms that would be considered to meet criteria for DSM-defined OCD (APA, 2000, 2013).
10 Contemporary Hebraic declension of the Yiddish word for 'pest.'
11 Gilah uses very high, literary-biblical Hebrew to describe this supposed prohibition.
12 Avery pronounced the word like 'goat.' Upon review of the audio recording and transcript, research team members came to a consensus that she likely meant 'ghost,' given the fact that she described them as 'like a fog.'
13 Also the name of a biblical prophet in the original, but he is likely also a real person in her life, so the name has been changed for purposes of de-identification.

7

IMAGINAL AND IDEAL HOME: THE SETTLED MOMENT

Sarah R. Kamens and Frederick J. Wertz

Overview

Sometimes, during her wanderings, the person stumbles upon a surprising discovery. It may begin with something as miniscule as an ant on the ground, or as commonplace as a traffic light. Or it may be enormous and momentous, like an announcement on the front page of a newspaper, lottery winnings, eschatological thunder, or fanfare from heaven in the sky. Regardless of how mundane or extraordinary its commencement may seem to others, the discovery signals something incredibly meaningful and momentous for the person experiencing urhomelessness. Often, the person is the only one who knows what it signifies—namely, that she is now settled.

The term *settled* (and its grammatical variations, including the noun *settlement* and the verb *settling*) is here reserved for a specific moment of urhomelessness in which the person becomes imaginally urhomed. Often, the settled moment appears as a dawning discovery, a revelation. The settlement can be defined as a special meaning afforded to a site or location, activity or talent, or a new narrative identity. For example, the person may discover that he is a member of an elite and hidden race or royal family, a brilliant rocket scientist, or an invisible angel. He might settle in a hobby apprehending terrorists or designing secret robots, in a holy site or an ornate palace, or in the position of Ultimate Queen or Famous Diplomat. He might claim to inhabit another planet or to exist within a network of invisible electronic waves called "The System":

"Douglas": There was a System that I told you about where they can hear everything and see everything. They can read the thoughts of anyone and they can also [...] control an animal's brain. [...] I shouldn't call it a thing; it's called a "world blessing." [...] They don't tell me how old it is.

The settlement is constructed from familiar worldly elements, such as sociocultural roles, themes, or narratives that the person might have encountered

DOI: 10.4324/9780429055454-8

prior to experiencing the settled moment; however, in the settlement, these aspects take on novel and revolutionary meanings.

In stark contrast to the experience of the nomadic or destitute moments, the settled person feels contained rather than porous; indeed, she may feel so contained that she begins to view herself as completely unitary, singular, and unparalleled.

Leonard: I was prince in England. And then uh I went to the; I came; I went to Vatican. And I became the; The First uh, First One.
Interviewer: The First One in the Vatican?
Leonard: First One in the Vatican.

In some cases, the settlement might even be the imaginal restoration or reparation of a former means of being urhomed; for example, the person may believe that she has returned to inhabit a previous job or relationship.

Across its myriad moments, the settlement provides the person with a sense of (1) ultimate safety, protection, provision of basic needs, and acknowledgement of her basic existence, and (2) an extraordinarily meaningful role and place in human society. However, in contrast to the relatively mundane, everyday experience of being urhomed, the settlement often provides an exquisitely special and important—and sometimes painful or lonely—position in relation to other humans. In contrast to the brevity and fleetingness of shelters, settlements are often (but not always) experienced as permanent and abiding. The settlement functions as a central point around which seemingly disparate meanings constellate. Moreover, the person often feels central to and/or implicated in the settlement's very existence.

Other persons tend to deny or reject the veridicality of the settlement, and the person may hypothesise that those who do believe in it conceal those very beliefs from others in order to avoid invalidation and rejection.

Interviewer: Your dad doesn't really believe you? Or he doesn't want to?
Douglas: He's scared. If he even knew, he's scared to admit to it. Same as my mom's fiancé-husband.

As a result of its invalidation by others, the settlement's seeming provision of protection and social belonging is ultimately incomplete relative to the experience of urhomeness. Any reflection on the settlement's imaginal, constructed, and non-consensual nature threatens its very existence and may lead to further feelings of frustration, anger, sadness, and alienation. For example, Leonard complained that his sister did not believe he was a "supreme being": "She wants me to prove myself to her and I'm not gonna do that. I did it before, but I'm not gonna do it no more. [...] She, she knows better than that!" When the person experiencing urhomelessness feels forced to defend its existence, the settlement becomes a source of great vulnerability. Settlements are tremendously fragile and precarious, as they ultimately magnify and amplify the very alienation that they were designed to negate.

Idiographic examples

Below are five examples of participants for whom the settled moment was given in full intuitive clarity.

Douglas

Douglas was a 27-year-old African American, heterosexual male from the North-Eastern U.S. "The System" was Douglas's name—albeit an imperfect name ("I call it the system because it's easy words" [laughs])—for a complex network of intimate, immaterial connections between special, chosen human beings. These select others, according to Douglas, ranged in social and economic status from celebrities to houseless persons. For Douglas, immaterial interpersonal connections took priority over concrete, physical interactions within an everyday world that was experienced as relatively disappointing, unsafe, alienating, and meaningless. These immaterial connections formed a new sense of safety, security, existential grounding, and locatability—an explanation and end goal for experiences of hardship and suffering. Although Douglas claimed to be its Chief or Head, The System was the great equaliser. For those on the inside, it did not discriminate by class, race, economic status, or religion; according to Douglas, all those in its grasps universally enjoyed its benefits, and they suffered for the same cause. The System was a place of familiarity and protection; it was also, conversely, a source of tremendous distress. However, unlike inexplicable suffering, the suffering perpetrated by The System was always—no matter how seemingly unbearable—experienced as existentially meaningful and exacted for a greater purpose.

Yuval

"Yuval" was a 46-year-old Jewish-Israeli male of both Ashkenazi and Sephardic origin. What had been called Yuval's schizophrenia was a radical passion for a specific holy site in Jerusalem where he prayed to God for hours on end, often neglecting to care for his basic needs, like eating and sleeping. Yuval remained at the holy site day after day, night after night, priding himself on his ability to withstand long hours, inclement weather, and other difficult conditions to continue standing and praying to God, whose voice he heard telling him that this is his work,[1] his role in life. Yuval mentioned the holy site at the beginning of the interview:

Yuval: I go every day to the [holy site]. [...] You know the [holy site]?
Interviewer: Yes, yes. You go every day. What do you do there?

Yuval:	I'm praying.
Interviewer:	Praying.
Yuval:	This is my house.[2]

Throughout Yuval's life, he intermittently found himself in the hospital, because, in his own words, "my life is *very* difficult." These life difficulties are often related to his striving to be stronger and more righteous than the average human by humbly serving others (e.g., God and his ailing mother) while denying himself the fulfilment of his own needs and wishes. He viewed his endurance as a testament to his strength, a divine gift from God: "it's more difficult for me, but I do it with love. And I get, with this work, strong and feeling good, and I have eh something from God that makes me very, very strong."

Haseeb

Haseeb, the 35-year-old Palestinian male introduced in Chapter 6, began to experience the settled moment during his nomadic wanderings. Just as he began to see the *jinn* that led him to wander in the streets, Haseeb also began to feel a tremendous sense of moral responsibility. There was terrible violence outside; people were injured and dying, caught up in the ongoing intifada. Haseeb believed that he could hear the prayers of others—not only those of his fellow Palestinians, but people of all other nationalities concerned with the violence, including Israelis, Europeans, and Americans. According to Haseeb, people would pray for the occurrence of certain political events (e.g., the start or end to a skirmish, the success or failure of a particular political party), and they would communicate these prayers to Haseeb, who would in turn transmit them to Allah [God], because Allah privileged Haseeb's prayers. In this way, Haseeb became a kingly, divine intermediary between God and humans. As Haseeb explained, "I'm responsible for the wars in Iraq, Syria, Libya, and the Intifada—and peace."

Avery

Avery was a 55-year-old Latinx transgender woman and gender-fluid individual[3] who identified as bisexual. Avery was diagnosed with schizophrenia due to a persistent and emphatic insistence on spending the majority of her time in an imaginative world that was largely inaccessible to most others, with the exception of those invited and willing to share it. In this imaginative realm, Avery was an expert technological designer of spaceships, her central passion. Avery's imaginative world also contained certain horrors, like ghosts that fly through walls, brain-invading aliens, and painful bodily experiments that Avery exacted upon herself compulsively. Avery's focus on her spaceships constituted a particular mode of being-in-the-world in which dreariness, horror, uncertainty, and suffering were avoided by becoming and embodying that which was experienced as exciting, joyful, beautiful and feminine, comforting, familiar, predictable, and powerful. To Avery, the spaceships were not merely drawings or works of art, but blueprints for devices that could be used by the government to advance the future of humankind. Avery's spaceships were her passion, her hope for making a contribution to human society, and her *raison d'être.*

Rabbi Danny

"Rabbi Danny" was a 51-year-old American-Jewish male who was raised in a predominantly secular household in the U.S. and immigrated to Israel in his 30s. What had been called Rabbi Danny's schizophrenia was an intricately developed belief system in which, according to Rabbi Danny, he took on the spiritual obligation of suffering for the Jewish people as the King of Israel and potential candidate for the position of Messiah. When asked at the beginning of the interview about the meaningful events in his life, Rabbi Danny responded,

> Okay at one point in my life I took on myself—or before I was put in this world—to suffer on behalf of the Jewish people. I felt that in order to move forward we had to [...] atone for the sins of Jewish people. I accepted that myself, consciously, when I was about, when I was about twenty years old.

Rabbi Danny's everyday experiences, actions, and feelings were intimately tied to this worldview. His prior strivings—becoming a musician, finding a girlfriend—were, upon experiencing the settled moment, integrated into the larger narrative of his Kingship, which functioned as an interpretive lens through which he understood his present, past, and future. For example, he viewed his psychiatric hospitalisation as part of his sociopolitical persecution at the hands of persons who were against his ascendancy to the throne. To Rabbi Danny, his identification as the King of Israel and the potential Messiah affected not only his personal history, but the collective history of the Jewish people as a whole.

Predominant constituents of the settled moment

The predominant experiential constituents of the settled moment are presented below. They are labelled as follows: unveiling, initial relief and clarity, adoration and worship, fixing the world, temporal expansion of the settlement, language and symbolic systems, precariousness, looming doubt, settled relationships with others, and immaterial connections. Below is a description of the common variations of the settled moment.

Unveiling

The settlement's very existence is a dawning, sometimes sudden realisation, and its discovery has a starkly revelatory quality. The person may begin to feel that she has changed, or that the world has changed in some subtle way that she can sense but cannot articulate. Experiences that once seemed irrelevant or upsetting suddenly take on meaningful, vivid, and familiar qualities. She feels a rising sense of validation, even self-importance, though she may not initially know why. In the midst of these confusing, exciting, perhaps even frightening, changes, the settlement unveils itself. The unveiling may be experienced as a miracle or epiphany; in other cases, it might be given as a serendipitous accident, like winning the lottery. Often, it is retroactively seen as a hidden truth, concealed during the person's early years and waiting to reveal itself at the right time. For example, Douglas was working at Walmart as a cashier when he heard the voice of his "mom or dad" on The System for the first time. When he noticed their voices, they said "oh shit, he heard us." For Douglas, it was a moment of recognition, joy, surprise, and awe during which the existence of The System—which supposedly preceded his knowledge of it—was revealed to him.

Similarly, Rabbi Danny's discovery of his settlement was experienced as a revelation:

> I did not know that there was a state of Israel around [the age of] sixteen. I knew war, I knew music, I knew sports, I knew math, science. I did not know the state of Israel and
> I didn't even know what the Bible was. I heard about the Bible. So when [Name] sat me
>
> down said, "listen, this is the Bible. This is the word of God. Okay, it says here in Isaiah […] that the Jewish people […] will return to the land of Israel after being in exile for thousands of years. This has happened. There's now this thing called 'the state of Israel.'" […] He showed me on the map, "this is the state of Israel. There's a prophecy that we come back." And I said, "okay [if] that's true, then this Bible's true. It's from God." Very simple connection for me. And that this Bible prophesised that.

To Rabbi Danny, learning about the existence of the state of Israel indicated that the prophecies in the Bible were accurate and, further, divinely ordained. In his early 20s, Rabbi Danny travelled to Israel to live on a kibbutz, then study in a yeshiva.[4] There, he happened upon another biblical prophecy that radically changed his worldview; in Rabbi Danny's words: "[in] Isaiah 60 He [the Messiah] accepts on himself the suffering of the Jewish people and he does imprisonment, derision, battle, attacked constantly. That is the story of my life and so it kind of matches." Suddenly and retroactively, Rabbi Danny understood the reason for his sufferings:

> I've been basically accepted by Heaven as King of Israel. [...] It's like King David's life basically. King David was alone with the sheep in the field. I feel that that's very similar to my life. [...] I think I'm the reincarnation of King David.

With the unconcealing of his role as King David, Rabbi Danny experienced a coherence and an overarching, greater sense of meaning among the disparate and painful experiences of his previous life.

Initial relief and clarity

After the settlement is discovered, feelings of relief, clarity, calm, and/or excitement flood in as the person discovers that she has been the princess of England, a famous television actress, or the Virgin Mary all along. The person gains a new sense of her place or role in human society. As Danny put it, "I felt that it was one of the reasons I was brought into the world to do and that and I [...] discovered myself, who I'm supposed to be."

Without the settlement, the world is a confusing place:

Interviewer: Does the world ever seem [...] puzzling? Or meaningless?
Yuval: If I don't go to the [holy site] I feel like that.

The settlement provides a ubiquitous, omniscient interpretive sphere:

Interviewer: Have you ever wondered if your experiences are real-; realistic or are they imaginary?
Yuval: They are real. [...] Everything is clear, everything is clear/ of God.

The person feels protected, and the existential meanings of her existence are stark and bright as day.

Interviewer: And what's it like to have that huge family in the system? How do you keep them straight?
Douglas: Oh *man* it's awesome! They're the best. They'd kill for me.

The settlement provides an explanation for any present or past suffering. The person often reinterprets all previous life experiences, though unbeknownst to her at the time, as leading up to its discovery. In Rabbi Danny's case, for example, painful experiences were interpreted as part of his ordainment as redeemer of the Jewish people. Thus, this new sense of purpose and meaning retroactively explained his difficult experiences prior to the discovery of his settlement. As Rabbi Danny put it, "I discovered my personal job is [that] I'm supposed to suffer."

The settlement often appears as enticing and habitable—at least initially. At first glance, the settlement is typically a relief, a safe haven from the world's dangers. It allows for the experience of safety and security rather than wandering and exile. Experientially, it protects the person from danger, sometimes in seemingly magical ways:

Douglas: Like if there was a lion [that] attacked me they [the System] could change, how quickly they could change the lion to sleep, to fall asleep to protect me.

When first discovering the settlement, the person is typically so comfortable that she decides she'll never leave. The settlement seems to offer precisely those feelings of safety and security that are lacking in urhomelessness, and the person often experiences a sense of tremendous relief: she finally feels "at home."

Adoration and worship

To the person, the settlement garners not only acknowledgement and validation, but also reverence, adoration, and/or fame. As a king, divine ruler, or world-famous actor, the person commands the ultimate respect and admiration of others. For example, Douglas spoke about walking into the hospital and being saluted by those who recognised his role on The System: "they would call me chief or champ. Some people bow or salute." Likewise, Rabbi Danny described people who believed in his message: "they're people who just said, 'he's the king' and then followed me. [...] It's the opposite of a cult; it's just the most natural, down-to-earth people, normal people." In another example, Yuval described being adored and admired by visitors to the holy site where he prayed all day long:

> People love me in the [holy site]. [...] People very love me, respect me and love me, and bring me food and money. [...] Two hundred, when I pray, two hundred Shekels.[5] [...] They see me, "how he praying." [...] And I don't want money. I take the money and put it into the Chabad[6] charity box.

Fixing the world

The settlement is often seen as having healing properties, not only for the person, but for humankind as a whole. Often, it is conceptualised as a means of restoring the world to a kind of unspoiled, undamaged, or prelapsarian state:

Avery: They [hospital staff] want me to go to the program they got up there to teach people. What I need that for? If I work on these things [points to his drawings of spaceships], that [can or will] change the whole world.

In this way, the settlement transforms the horrors of the world in which the person became urhomeless. As Douglas put it:

> The System can heal almost anything. They can, I think they said they can make organs. And I said "take care" because I saw / yesterday about Nelson Mandela that touched me. And even, um, certain people. Osama Bin Laden, I said keep him alive. [...] And him saying certain things like "peace around the world."

The settlement may also be seen as healing and redeeming personal, life-historical troubles and relationships. For example, Douglas reported an experience of reconciliation with his father that occurred shortly after he discovered his role as President of The System:

> This is a special moment/; excuse me; I went around the stores to look for food to eat. [...] I saw my brother's friend [...] he asked me what I do, and I said, "this is where I live." And I was sitting on a bench. I sat on a bench, and my dad walked up behind me. [...] [It] was such a special moment. I didn't have my cell phone. I had no way of communicating. No money. [...] I don't know what made him come. But my dad said before that, "how come you're not living with me?" And um, and that was the end of it.

Douglas explained that after his dad approached him on the park bench, he stopped abusing Douglas and provided him with a place to live. Douglas's experiences of basic safety and familial belonging were restored; he reported subsequently living in an apartment where, though he did not know it at the time, he was protected by a "bodyguard on The System."

Temporal expanse of the settlement

The settlement expands through and beyond time. It is experienced as always having been there, waiting for the person to recognise it. It capsizes prior events that seem to change meaning in its wake, such that the details and suffering of life prior to its appearance may take on the settlement's meanings, or they may be seen as relatively unimportant in comparison. Alternatively, previous life-historical experiences may be completely forgotten or recalled as fragmentary scenes from an unremarkable or distressing past:

Interviewer: Do you remember anything about your early childhood? [...]
Douglas: I know I used to cry when I would see pictures of when I was a baby. I don't know why. I would just cry.

If the person's past is completely foreclosed, she may believe that she has always been settled.

Often, it is the experience of the settled moment that clarifies previous experiences as characterised by wandering and the nomadic life. The settled person often feels to be *more urhomed* than she ever did previously, even in prior urhomed states before the beginning of urhomelessness.

Interviewer: And are there any people who you would consider to be your people more than others?
Douglas: My family in The System. They even more than, in ways, even more than my immediate family outside the system, are awesome. They're awesome.

Language and symbolic systems

In the settled moment, the person may view symbolic systems as a means of identifying and decoding the mysteries of the world. Language, once confusing and mystifying, becomes a source of revelation as the person learns that it is more than a mere arbitrarily designed and imperfect means of personal expression, but rather a highly structured symbolic system capable of delivering prophecies and mystical messages about the settlement. For example, Gilah interpreted people's names as signifying their particular roles within the literary and biblical realm that she inhabited as future mother of the Messiah. Persons bearing biblical names may be treated as those very characters from the bible; if not, they may act as or bear similarities to their namesake. Gilah also assumed that a friend who was named after a planet[7] was *from* that planet. In another example, Rabbi Danny viewed people's names, as well as the names of events, as signifying their role precisely for him, in his settlement as the King of Israel and potential Messiah:

Danny: [Hurricane] Sandy equals *shen die*.[8] And *die:* enough, *shen*: enough of damaging other people's properties and things and getting benefit from them. Enough of this damaging other people and getting benefit from it, enough!
Interviewer: That's interesting, so that *shen die* is "Sandy." It's the sound of the words. Do you often kind of figure out what's happening in

your life are signs that God is giving you through this, through the language in this way?

Danny: All the time.

[...]

Interviewer: So that's the way God gives you signs in a way.

Danny: Yeah, like one thing I just liked about you when I met you [is that] your name was Sarah, and I thought that, wow, Sar-, I get to speak with Sarah whose I mean I believe that you *are* your name. I believe that you have Sarai[9]; I feel Sarah ///. I feel, I feel soothed and calm being in your presence. I feel like I'm sitting with one of the *emot* [mothers] right now."

Similarly, when looking at the interviewer's hospital name tag, Leonard abruptly stated "oh *now* I know who you are." When asked what he meant, he elaborated, "Yeah. [...] it came to me. Sarah. It's a biblical name." For both Danny and Leonard, names indicate meaningful identities of others beyond their existence as mere time-bound, perceived individuals; they imaginally map others' potential relevance within or for the atemporal settlement.

For some persons experiencing the settled moment, language is a realm in which immaterial beings and forces communicate their presence:

Rabbi Danny: The world is coded with letters, like the whole world. The world is filled with Hebrew letters, so if you can look at the connections between the letters and words, you see how the world is built. It's a code that if you can um decode the code you see what's going on.

Words function as signs of archetypal, mystical meanings, or signposts for the person in navigating her settled experiences. Note that persons experiencing urhomelessness also utilise language in ordinary, consensual ways; however, there is often a kind of elevation or special, preferential status given to the imaginal use of language—to its ability to signify, herald, and lead the way to the settlement.

Precariousness

The person often gains a sense of relief—and often joy, euphoria, or ecstatic experience—from the settlement's provision of imaginal acceptance, validation, and even love and respect. However, settlements are implicitly flimsy and precarious, for two related reasons. First, the settlement acts as a kind of totalling lens through which objects, persons, and events—including those that are experienced as alienating or upsetting—are interpreted or otherwise understood. However, other persons and objects are often nuanced, non-binary, and non-totalising, and thus not always readily integrated into the settlement. As such, they may be experienced as stubbornly opposing, rejecting, or resistant to it. The second and related reason that the settlement is ultimately precarious is that, as aforementioned, its non-shared and non-consensual nature may exacerbate the very alienation that its existence was thought to negate. Indeed, for most non-imaginal others in the person's life, the settlement is fundamentally chimerical, and the person's belief in it often increases interpersonal distance and/or conflict rather than enhancing her social world. Thus, although it appears to bring systematic order to the world, including but not limited to the world of others, the settlement also intrinsically includes loneliness, isolation, rejection, conflict, and a kind of social invisibility, as the settlement's existence is often denied or rejected by other persons. The settled person may speak about being profoundly misunderstood or rejected, even by those closest to her.

Looming doubt

Doubt looms large in the horizon of the settled moment. The person gives it her all to ignore this doubt, push it aside. Within the settlement's enormous, magical walls, the person feels safe and protected, meaningfully acknowledged and validated—even revered or worshipped by others. Negative, distressing, and torturous elements of the settlement have the quality of staving off a more horrific thought: that the settlement might not exist. The person avoids thinking about the settlement's precariousness, often giving off an attitude of utter conviction, even proselytising to herself and/or others about its wonders. As a result, to interlocutors and observers, the person may seem utterly convinced that her beliefs correspond to a kind of irreducible truth.

Settled relationships with others

In the settled moment, the person's experiences are often divided dichotomously. There is life "before" and the "after" the discovery of the settlement. There is ultimate comfort and pleasure—and then there are dreadful flickers of horror, torture, and despair. The settled person's interpersonal relationships are often experienced in a dichotomous fashion, with two types of others: those who believe in the settlement, and those who do not (or, similarly, those who cohabitate with the settlement and foreigners). When he meets new people, the settled person often categorises them into believers or nonbelievers, insiders or outsiders, and/or those "for" or "against" him. Some persons may try to convert others from nonbelievers to believers:

Interviewer: Did you tell your father about The System? Your father here, [the one] who is out of The System.

Douglas: Yes. [...] He laughed and said things. I don't know if he means it, but he says, I don't know, he speaks like he's scared to find out the truth. I see him. He hears things that The System does and he gets scared. [...] If they [people outside of The System] hear it [The System] and they admit to it, it's an uncomfortable feeling. Um what are they going to say to me after I've been saying this for how many years? Not too many people have that heart to say "I'm sorry." That's the hardest thing about this. I'm trying to tell you that I forgive you I just need someone to back me up. To believe in me and if I go in the hospital you'll get me out. Um to cry to hug me when I need to be held. Because I've been through a lot.

Anticipating rejection or lack of understanding, the person might keep his settlement relatively hidden and unverbalised; when this happens, the idiosyncrasy and solitude of his settled position is experienced as taken-for-granted and, though disappointing, part and parcel of the settlement. The person might develop fear, frustration, and anger towards others for denying the existence of settlement. He might feel that his settlement is disregarded and ignored, that it is envied by others, or that it is under constant attack. Avery, for example, often complained that the hospital staff prevented her from creating spaceships by forcing her to attend treatment groups or turning off the lights in her room.

Communicative style

Those communicating with the person might find themselves quickly placed into one of the two camps: believers and non-believers, or those inside versus outside of the settlement. They may feel pressured to profess agreement or disagreement with the person's statements about the settlement. They may experience authentic being-with as contingent upon entertaining or adopting the idea of the settlement or, at minimum, offering one's own presence as an example of the dismal, mundane, unenlightened life outside of settlement. To the person, conversations with those who are not on the side of the settlement, the remote others, may take on a robotic, flat, empty, or even angry and distrustful tone.

During the research interviews with persons experiencing the settled moment, the interviewer often found it difficult to remain "neutral" with regard to her beliefs about the settlement. She found that when she listened to the participants with genuine interest in their lives, they often automatically placed her on the side of the "believers." For example, Douglas stated, "It's hard when your family doesn't believe you and everyone else; well not everyone. You were the biggest; well let's see, um, you were the biggest listener." At times, participants seemed to probe for the interviewer's beliefs in order to assess her potential allegiance. Thus, conviction versus doubt in the settlement was a theme that affected—and potentially threatened—the rapport between interviewee and interviewer. In the example below, Douglas asks the interviewer to help him "spread the news" about existence of The System so that he can meet his "family" (on The System):

Douglas: Well I was wondering if, um, you could find me some help.
Interviewer: What kind of help are you looking for?
Douglas: I don't know. Just to spread the news [about The System].
Interviewer: You want to get out of here, huh?
Douglas: Not only that. I just want to meet my family. My family on The System.

Immaterial connections

The settlement facilitates what the person sees as a new possibility for special, immaterial connections with others. These immaterial connections not only restore the absent sense of belonging in urhomelessness, but also seem to surpass any interpersonal acknowledgement, validation, and love in urhomed ways of being-in-the-world. For example, Douglas described having a loving family, a future wife, and famous friends in The System, which also employed a secret organisation called "Qi Org" that assured his safety and happiness: "They're the hearts of the world I feel. The best, best minds. [...] I don't know how Qi Org works. But they watch over me."

The settlement often seems to allow for immaterial relational epistemologies, ways of understanding other persons that are unmediated by speech, behavioural gestures, and other symbolic systems. For example, the person may believe that she can magically hear and respond to the thoughts of others. Reflecting on his experiences hearing voices, Greg stated, "there was a point when I was glad I heard the voice. Because I thought that meant I was going to be a telepath." In some cases, the person may feel that she is able to influence others' behaviours and feelings at the tap of a button, or with a single thought. She may believe that she can simply feel the presence of loved ones, magical or mystical beings, extra-terrestrials, or the divine.

The settled person may locate self at the centre of these immaterial connections, as in the following example from Haseeb's interview:

Haseeb: I feel that people ask for things, for my help through telepathy.
Interviewer: Who asked?
Haseeb: All the people, the Arabs, America, Europe and the Jews.
Interviewer: How can you help them?
Haseeb: I pray and ask God. Sometimes they ask me to stop the

Intifada. I pray and ask from God to give them what they asked for.

Interviewer: Does God always answer your prayers?

Haseeb: Yes he always does. I am responsible for Netanyahu's Government, Hamas and the Palestinian Authority and Abu Mazen[10] [...] I feel like a king who is responsible for all Muslims, Jews, Arabs, America, Europe, all the Arab countries. I'm in charge.

Haseeb also described an immaterial network binding him to the voices he heard: "It's a very complicated thing. They connect to each other. I'm connected to them. And they are connected to me. I affect them when they think and walk and talk."

Often, a powerful sense of community, togetherness, and unmediated knowledge is a dominant feature of the settlement, even when the settlement is conceptualised as a concrete site, place, or social role rather than a set of immaterial relational connections. For example, Rabbi Danny described a unique ability to identify and relate to others who, like him, also believe themselves to be the Messiah; he believed that the book he was writing on the Messiah would be of particular interest to this group, which he described with affectionate humour:

Rabbi Danny: I'm selling it for a very high price too, a really high price.

Interviewer: Oh yeah? How much?

Rabbi Danny: $135 [...] that's what someone who has interest will have to pay [for the book]. They may not, [because] mostly screwballs want to know the Messiah. Most people who want to know the Messiah are screwballs.

Interviewer: Why is that?

Rabbi Danny: 'Cuz they think they're the Messiah. [...] Most people who want to live like the Messiah think they're the Messiah, the screwballs. [...] I should say that in my book, [that] most people who want to buy this book are, most people who think they are their Messiah are screwballs and this proves that you're a screwball.

Interviewer: [laughs] If you're buying the book?

Rabbi Danny: You're a screwball. [...] The Rabbinate is filled with them. The people in the Mossad[11] [...] Every second manager in the Mossad thinks he's a Messiah. The Rabbinate is filled with Messiahs. I'm not in the Mossad but I know, I can smell them. [...] I can sniff; I can feel their tentacles.

Rabbi Danny described a special, ineffable ability to identify others who also believe they might be the Messiah; his jocular, affectionate tone when describing them as "screwballs" seemed to indicate an empathic understanding with their position as social outsiders, despite his belief in the veridicality of his own settlement. In another example, Greg portrayed his fellow psychiatric service users as part of a "matrix" of people who hear voices:

Greg:	They [the voices] can read thoughts. I can't.
Interviewer:	Okay. And they can read anybody's thoughts?
Greg:	Well they could, connect to it.
	[...]
Interviewer:	Can anybody read your thoughts aside from the voices?
Greg:	I don't know. Maybe some of the people who are connected to me can hear them.
Interviewer:	So the voices can connect two people together?
Greg:	Yeah it's not easy to connect two people [...] They're considered God; I guess you could say that.
Interviewer:	They're like God? Or they are God?
Greg:	Yeah you could say; I don't know. They're considered like God. [...]
Interviewer:	So once two people are connected to the voices they're also connected to each other? It's kind of like a network?
Greg:	Yeah a matrix.
Interviewer:	A matrix. Like some people are in it and some people are not?
Greg:	Yeah.

In this way, some settlements (e.g., a "matrix," a "network," or a "system" of telepathic or otherwise intimate connections between persons) are an imagined reification of meaningful interpersonal relationships—interpersonal relationships that may be experientially lacking in urhomelessness.

Common variations of the settled moment

Persons in the settled moment often experience dichotomous, opposing extremes. As a result, persons in the settled moment typically experience not one, but both poles of each common variation presented below. These variations are labelled as follows: utopic versus malicious variations, imaginative versus mundane variations, and adopted versus rewritten cultural narratives.

Utopic versus malicious variations

The settlement constitutes an interpretive framework through which the person understands both her past and her future experiences, be they positive or negative. Some settlements take on both positive and negative experiential qualities, oscillating between idyllic refuge and terrifying, lonely prison. The settlement can be a utopia and a wasteland, a source of pleasure and a site of despair. For example, Yuval felt both close to God and unbearably distant from him.

Yuval:	I will continue to go to the [holy site] and pray with all my might day and night. That's the truth.
Interviewer:	So this is something that God wants you to do?
Yuval [on verge of tears]:	Yes. And me too. God and I. I miss God a lot, a lot.
Interviewer:	You miss [him]? What does that mean?
Yuval:	He told me secrets. He told me there is sorrow in the world.

The settlement may be predominantly characterised by the very dangers, threats, and horrors that the person experienced during the unsettled life, prior to the settled moment. However, the settled person believes that these negative experiences must be endured in order to enjoy the perceived benefits of being settled. Douglas, for example, described being maliciously tortured by persons within the very System that selected him as its Boss and The International President of the United States:

Douglas:	[I'm] afraid of being tortured. […]
Interviewer:	[…] Why were they [The System] torturing you again?
Douglas:	I haven't really gotten the details, but I believe it was because there is a lot of racism. Actually it's hard to believe this but the KKK wanted me to be a part of their leadership. // on The System. The KKK is on The System. […]
Interviewer:	So it was kind of like torture through The System?
Douglas:	Yes. Because people, when they get into The System, they kind of forgive the stuff in the System. So if they're in The System they hurt me and take whatever frustrations out they have inside through The System.

Suffering becomes meaningful and, for that reason, more bearable in the settlement; further, there is generally a sense of meaningful *purpose*, often related to justice or redemption, that accompanies emotional distress for the person in the settled moment.

Extraordinary versus mundane variations

For some persons experiencing the settled moment, the settlement is like nothing ever encountered before. It may be experienced as idiosyncratic, wondrous, or unparalleled. The settlement might bring with it a sense of omnipotence and rarity. For example, Leonard said, "I'm a supreme being [...] the most powerful." For others, the settlement is not necessarily novel; it may be utterly familiar. For example, the person may settle in a known profession or previous relationship. She might state that she is an expert chef at a restaurant or a professor at a local college, or she might settle into a life as a married person, or as a member of a well-regarded family. In these latter cases, the settlement is a given social role, activity, or position that mirrors common, relatively mundane ways of securing urhomeness.

Adopted versus rewritten cultural narratives

As aforementioned, settlements are assembled from familiar elements of the world, such as social roles, cultural ideas, or mythological narratives. In the settled moment, the person takes on a new role in these narratives, or she pieces them together in new ways. For this reason, settlements typically have a strangely familiar, even uncanny quality—not only for the person experiencing urhomelessness, but also for others to whom the idea of the settlement is introduced.

Some persons experiencing urhomelessness in the settled moment adopt a specific role in a preexisting cultural narrative that otherwise remains intact or is altered in minor ways to fit the person's life. Rabbi Danny, for example, donned the position of the Jewish Messiah, and he retroactively interpreted various events in his life as fitting pre-existing narratives and prophecies about the Messiah, including traditional-biblical and obscure-Kabalistic sources that he adopted as his own. Similarly, Yuval's settlement was a known holy site where others also pray and fast; although he remained at the site for longer durations than most others and took the standard rituals to an extreme, he did not imaginatively transform the settlement. For other persons, the settlement may comprise cultural narratives that are patched together in novel, imaginative ways. Douglas, for example, stated that he is the "International President of the United States," a new position that he believed to be created just for him. Haseeb's position as Divine Intermediary between human prayers and Allah is another example of a creative, patchwork settlement.

When settlements fail

Despite their seeming impermanence, settlements do not always last. They are built at the site of rupture between person and world—at the critical junctures where urhomelessness occurs. The opportunity to settle appears as a solution to this crisis, but it is a pseudo-solution, as it retains and sometimes exacerbates the person's alienation from the world of others. Because the settlement is a totalizing endeavour that is not founded on consensual ideas about the person's role in the world, it is ultimately precarious, and the person feels compelled to guard against its potential failure. The essential precariousness and brittleness of the settlement risks being exacerbated if acknowledged by the person; the more precariousness it seems, the more precarious it becomes. For this reason, the person's belief in the settlement's existence may quickly unravel. It is the dawning understanding of the *imaginal* nature of the settlement that causes its walls to crumble. Thus, the settlement's potential failure is ultimately not a result of its difference from the horrific, alienating world outside, but rather a result of the fact that, ultimately, it is one and the same.

Notes

1 It is common in Orthodox religious communities to see prayer and study as a man's work [translator's note].
2 In Hebrew, the words for "house" and "home" are the same. Here, he is speaking in English, but may be translating directly from Hebrew. (Yuval's interview took place in both Hebrew and English.)
3 Avery sometimes identified as female, and sometimes as both female and male.
4 He first travelled to Israel in his 20s; he later returned to the U.S. and then immigrated to Israel in his 30s.
5 Approximately 50 U.S. dollars.
6 An Orthodox Jewish religious movement.
7 The name is relatively common in Israel.
8 Rabbi Danny phonetically parses the name "Sandy" into "San" and "Die," which he interprets as *shen*, a Talmudic reference to the collateral damage that animals can cause when grazing, and *die,* an imperative meaning "enough" or "stop."
9 According to the bible, Sarai's name was changed to Sarah. In Judaism, the name is frequently associated with motherhood.
10 Israeli and Palestinian government leadership at the time of the interview.
11 Israeli international secret service (similar to the CIA).

8

IMPOSSIBILITY OF SHELTER: THE DESTITUTE MOMENT

Sarah R. Kamens and Frederick J. Wertz

Overview

To the person experiencing the destitute moment, the world has become an utterly dangerous, rejecting, and often torturous and nightmarish place. She is attuned to the utter inhospitality of her surroundings, and as a result, the person in the destitute moment no longer strives to attain either one or both provisions of urhomeness, namely the potential to obtain safety and protection in the world and a sense of basic belonging and acknowledgement in a community of other humans. The person believes the experience of urhomeness to be inaccessible or illusory, and she also views sheltering (the nomadic moment) and settling (the settled moment) as impossible or inadequate for alleviating the experience of urhomelessness. Hopeless and relinquished to danger and rejection, the person in the destitute moment experiences the utmost extremes of vulnerability and alienation.

In destitution, the person often attempts to radically distance himself from other persons and the world as a whole. In some cases, the person may feel that he dwells nowhere, that he does not exist, that he has been possessed or overtaken by invasive forces, that he has evacuated the world, or that he has buried himself out of sight, in a wasteland of sorts. Time seems to close in on itself. The person's suffering is experienced as endless and inexorable, and he believes that he cannot escape from grave danger or intolerable distress. He may report that his existence is meaningless or empty, that other persons have given up on him, or that he inhabits a wasteland, a void, an uninhabitable place—sheer uninhabitability itself. Jean, for example, reported being robbed of a vital life force by other persons:

Interviewer:	Do you sometimes feel that your thoughts disappear?
Jean:	That they took all my soul? Yes.
Interviewer:	That they took what?
Jean:	My soul.
Interviewer:	Who took all your soul?

 DOI: 10.4324/9780429055454-9

Jean: All types of places. Everything is hard. And everything left. [...] Suddenly I am next to death. And everything. All my soul.

In the destitute moment, the person's primary striving is to reduce his suffering as much as possible, even though it means that he may withdraw and diminish himself in order to do so.

In the destitute moment, wandering is thematised, but only passively, as a kind of being-wandered. The person may describe herself as a mere receptor or site for other persons, forces, or objects in the world, which wholly overtake her. The world has moved in, and the person experiences herself as nothing more than another shelter for the world. She may fantasise about a distant, peaceful void, the utopia of silence, and perhaps about death.

The person's attempt at total withdrawal forges a radical relational distance from others. To the interlocutor, he may appear frozen, stiff, mute, or unresponsive; he may attempt to stop moving or breathing. He may describe himself as empty, nothing, inhuman, or invisible. Alternatively, the person might behave in unpredictable or bizarre ways in order to conceal his true feelings from what he sees as a highly threatening, unbearable, and/or persecutory world.

Destitution is the most austere and devastating moment of urhomelessness. The person is not an active wanderer, nor the key player in a new world of ultimate safety, but rather a passive receptor of meandering experiences—or a human barrier who tries to shut them out. She has given up, or at best, entered into what Jean called "survival mode," attempting salvage a means to bare life, without any hope of attaining urhomeness.

Idiographic examples

Below are four examples of participants with particularly stark experiences of the destitute moment:

Greg

"Greg" was a 47-year-old Chinese American male who immigrated to the US with his family at the age of three. What has been viewed as Greg's schizophrenia was his belief that torturous, evil forces constantly endangered his basic safety and agency in the world. More specifically, Greg reported that his psychological independence and integrity were compromised by malicious (and at rarer times, benevolent) forces that he called "voices." According to Greg, the voices controlled his thoughts, feelings, and behaviours. "They [the voices] play tricks on me," Greg explained, "like hyperventilating, anxiety attacks. And uh they can move, the muscles in my body [...] move different parts of my body. They make me want to commit suicide." As the voices barked commands at Greg, there was no fortress or shelter strong enough to hold them back. Greg's primary goal was to survive under constant threat and to free his mind from forces that he believed sought to appropriate, instrumentalise, and harm him. "I'm just living right now, surviving," he said. Greg's primary survival strategy was withdrawing as much as possible from both the external world and the voices. At various points in his life, he attempted to escape to zones of relative safety (e.g., the woods, the hospital) but these places proved ineffective respites from the omnipresent, invading forces that seemed to endlessly haunt him. His only solace was the community of fellow sufferers at the hospital whom, he imagined, struggled against these sadistic and powerful forces alongside him.

Jean

Jean was a 34-year-old French-Algerian male born to Jewish refugees from Algeria who immigrated to France. What had been called Jean's schizophrenia was a pattern of feeling utterly miserable, desperate, alienated, and alone.

Jean:	[I am] miserable
Interviewer:	Miserable.
Jean:	In misery. [...] Misery, misery.

Jean experienced camaraderie and enjoyment during his adolescent and young adult years in Paris, but he also described lifelong emotional distress. Moreover, he felt unloved, unsupported, unsafe, and generally "hated" by his family and everyone around him. "[I]n this reality, there is[1] only the signs of [...] the death or the bad," he said, "we are living in a world where there always some people wants to kill you. They wants to kill you! They don't want you to exist." Jean was wholly resigned to a life of misery, loneliness, and despair—a non-life, no way to live. He believed that there was no place for him in this world, and he often contemplated escaping the world through death.

Luma

"Luma" was a 32-year-old Palestinian female who was born to a Muslim family in Jerusalem. What had been called Luma's schizophrenia was an extreme alienation from other persons coupled with anomalous perceptual experiences and beliefs, such as hearing commanding voices and believing that she killed her father with poison. In general, Luma's urhomelessness involved a sense of inescapable loneliness and alienation. "I am alone with myself," she explained. Luma was defenceless against other persons who misunderstood her, confined her, and disallowed her self-actualisation.

Prohibited from leaving her house, as well as from using the internet or telephone, Luma lived in a kind of domestic prison. According to Luma, it all began when she met a boy over the telephone. She invited him to meet the family in the hopes of gaining her mother's approval. "I thought he would take me out of the house, and I would have more freedom with him. [...] I wanted to marry and to have a family." Her mother and brothers, however, rejected the idea and concluded that Luma was acting in promiscuous ways. Afterwards, she was not allowed out of the house, or out of her family's sight. She was never physically alone; her mother, brother, or another family member was present at all times, on guard. At the time of the interview, Luma had been discharged to an outpatient level of care, and she arrived to the interview with her mother, who was hesitant to leave Luma alone with one interviewer when invited to speak privately with the other. Once her mother agreed to briefly leave the room, Luma felt more relaxed.

Luma experienced a deep sense of loneliness and alienation: "I do not belong to this family," she stated. She daydreamed about obtaining an education, creating her own family, and exploring the world. She dreamt of freedom, and it was forbidden to her; she often longed to escape through death, and she had attempted suicide several times.

Interviewer: You thought about jumping from the porch?
Luma: Yes. I wanted to be free.
[...]
Interviewer: Free from what?
Luma: From *all of this*. All of this that I am living in. I like feel jailed. All the time. Everything I do, they look. And they want to know what I am doing. And if I take out my telephone, my sister always runs and says to mother "she is taking out her telephone, she is doing something bad, she ... " Like what? I want some freedom. A little. For myself.

Crystal

In the first of four incidents that led to her hospitalisation, Crystal, a 54-year-old Caucasian female from the US, stopped talking to her family and locked them out of her room; she then gazed out of her window at strangers on the street, pretending that they were her "real" family members: "I was making a whole scenario, like [with] the people in the street carrying packages, and I would say 'that's my grandmother,' 'that's my mother,' 'all my family members.' I would make like a little story." Crystal did not interact with these imaginal family members, nor would she answer the new "strangers" (her former family members, and eventually the police) when they banged on her door. Her food was poisoned, she believed, and everyone was trying to follow her; the only way to stay safe would be to shut herself off from the world of others and imaginatively live through the stories that voices told her, stories about humiliation and heartbreak. Anyone who tried to break through the stillness—including the hospital staff who tried to converse with her and move her from her bed—would be met with stone-cold motionlessness, a fortress exterior. It would be several months before Crystal "woke up [...] like out of a dream."

Predominant constituents of the destitute moment

The predominant experiential constituents of the destitute moment are presented below. They are labelled as follows: inhospitality of the world, radical alienation in relationships with others, and passive wandering and becoming-shelter.

Inhospitality of the world

The central characteristic of the destitute moment is relinquishment of the attempt to secure shelters, a settlement, or urhomeness. The world is experienced as an impossible, rejecting place. Active wandering is viewed as ineffective and fruitless. Unlike in the nomadic moment, in which the person seeks shelters within the proximal world-at-large, the person experiencing the destitute moment experiences an ontological chasm between herself and the world:

Interviewer: Did you ever feel that you are one with the world?
Luma: One with the world? No.
Interviewer: No. What yes?
Luma: I am different from the world.

For the person experiencing the destitute moment, the world comprises inhospitable environments and unwelcoming people. If she does venture out, she feels ignored and/or mistreated. New places, people, and events are experienced as rejecting and inhospitable. Jean, for example, reflected on his experiences in Jerusalem after immigrating from France:

Jean: Suddenly [for] five days the city dies. It fits[2] to Satan. Fits to death.
Interviewer: [You mean] that on the holiday and on the Sabbath everything is closed there. There is no shopping. The regular life of the city.
Jean: There is nothing. Nothing. [...]. There is wall in the city. [...] It is not an open city. It's a dead city. A dead city. [...] And either, either you have family and you are with family. Or you have friends or something and you stay home. But eh -, it cannot be like this. To be closed. And to go out and there is nothing. No one, no bus. No one. No one. No car. Everything is dead. Dead.

To Jean, the slowing of Jerusalem for the Sabbath was an expression of nothingness and death; he experienced the city as utterly closed to life, to hospitality and vitality.

For persons in the destitute moment, the hospital itself may be experienced as a reflection of the inhospitable world. Jean reported that "my soul goes out of the body" because "this [the hospital] is not the right place." At best, the hospital is viewed as a minimalistic space that allows for the prolongation of bare life. Greg, for example, felt that the hospital was the only thing preventing his suicide, despite the fact that the hospital's walls were permeable by the voices that continued to haunt and torture him.

In the destitute moment, the person typically believes that she has no viable means of reprieve other than exiting the world of others. She may have forgotten how to shelter, or she may feel too helpless and hopeless to try. For example, Roger, who had attained partial recovery, described his fear of re-entering the destitute moment:

Roger:	And I feel sometimes um it's scared about what might happen to me in the future you know? [...] Maybe I might get uh [become a] bum. People in the street, you know what I mean? [...]
Interviewer:	Why are you scared of that?
Roger:	[...] I can't predict when my illness will uh come back. [...]
Interviewer:	What is the connection between if your illness gets worse? Why would you become a bum? What is the connection?
Roger:	Because if I'm ill I; the first time when I get ill, I don't know what I'm doing. I don't eat, I don't drink, I don't sleep, I don't take a bath, I'm not, I'm not taking I'm not I'm not uh taking my old clothes. [...] I get worried. It's confused.
Interviewer:	You get worried and confused, and you don't take care of yourself.
Roger:	Yeah yeah. I don't take care of myself anymore.

In the destitute moment, the world is inhospitable to the person, and the person eventually ceases to extend hospitality to herself.

Radical alienation in relationships with others

The person experiencing the destitute moment has largely resigned herself to radical loneliness and alienation. Even when others are present, she feels tremendously isolated, misunderstood, and mistreated by others. For example, Saleh reported being profoundly alone despite his family's attempts to reach out:

Interviewer: What do you do when you think about these things [mechanical objects like telescopes and cars]? You are in the room [when thinking about them]?
Saleh: I am in my room, pacing back and forth.
Interviewer: And if someone tries to talk with you? You don't hear him?
Saleh: Who wants to talk to me? I am alone.
Interviewer: No one? You don't have any friend in the world? Someone from your family?
Saleh: The family talks to me. If I hear them, I answer.
Interviewer: I hear that you are very lonely.
Saleh: That's right.
Interviewer: Is there any person in the world whom you feel close to?
Saleh: No.

In time, the person may begin to forget what it is like to engage with the world and other humans. He may even forget what the world looks like; peeking outside, he might see strange and unintelligible shapes, movements, silhouettes. Indeed, as he progressively withdraws from the world, it may take on a frightening unfamiliarity. The person experiencing the destitute moment may claim that he dwells in a faraway and unknown realm or land, a place he inhabits all to himself—in no place known at all.

Communicative style

Some persons experiencing the destitute moment will readily express their suffering, as in the examples above. Sometimes, however, the interlocutor trying to communicate with the person experiencing the destitute moment encounters a non-response, a kind of blankness or quasi-absence of expression that might be accompanied by long pauses in speech or silence. Distant from the world of others, the person may find the experience of destitution difficult or impossible to describe. She might attempt to conceal her destitution from others by putting on a false "front," a seemingly urhomed facade. She might move about frantically, attempting to blend into the chaos and detract attention from herself. She might speak in parables, neologisms, or nonsense languages that her interlocutors do not understand. Or she might go perfectly still and silent in an attempt to become undetectable. Typically, she communicates little beyond the fact of her interpersonal distance from other persons; for example, when the opening interview question was posed to Greg, his first statement was:

Greg: I consider myself a quiet person.
Interviewer: You're a quiet person?

Greg: I'm also withdrawn. I notice /(?: in) my life I alienate myself from others.
Interviewer: You alienate yourself?
Greg: Yeah.

At times, the person may be so far removed from her interlocutors that he does not recognise or acknowledge their attempts to communicate with him. Interlocutors may be completely ignored or, alternatively, experienced as remote, shadowy threats to be avoided. For the above reasons, the present dataset contained more demonstrations of the destitute moment than articulated reflections about it. For example, one participant sometimes dropped into silence or stillness for minutes on end. During her interview, "Lynn," a 29-year-old European American female, sat still in her seat, moving only when absolutely necessary; and breathing as quietly and slowly as she could manage. She appeared to be trying to conceal herself, to disappear, to expend energy only when necessary for her survival. She spoke softly and laconically, and sometimes not at all, answering the interviewers' questions with a "yeah" or other brief response. When she did speak, Lynn provided bare, frequently disconnected, and unembellished facts. At the beginning of the interview, Lynn told the interviewer that she had no memories to share:

Interviewer: First of all, I just want to get to know you. I'm hoping that you can tell me about yourself, um and about any significant events in your life. […]
Lynn: Okay. Um, I don't remember too much.
Interviewer: From your childhood?
Lynn: Nah.
Interviewer: […] what's your earliest memory?
Lynn: I really don't have any.
Interviewer: You don't have any early memories. Do you remember, well, why don't, start wherever you like then.
Lynn: Okay um. [six-second pause] I really don't have too much to talk about.
[…]
Interviewer: Can you tell me, um, a story about one of your siblings or something you did with them?
Lynn: Um [seven-second pause], something I did with them, you said?
Interviewer: Anything to kind of help me get to know you and what it was like for you growing up. If there's […] an example of something you did with them. […]
Lynn: Um [six-second pause], we used to go walking.

Interviewer:	Where'd you go?
Lynn:	Mm, a bunch of places.

For Lynn, this minimalistic style of communicating was both a means of self-protection and a form of resistance against the seemingly unfair demands of others, especially mental health professionals like the interviewer. Lynn acknowledged that she often answered the interviewers' questions with "I don't know" because she did not want to answer the questions, not because she truly did not know the answers. Lynn also acknowledged that she might provide longer answers to similar questions if posed by family members, but that it was difficult for her to trust mental health professionals because they "think they're above you." In the hospital, Lynn abandoned her own agentic engagement with other persons in favour of a safer, tranquil, hidden world in which her thoughts and feelings were surrounded by an impenetrable fortress of near-stillness and near-silence.

Some participants experiencing the destitute moment painted a rosy portrait of a utopian life that was devoid of troubles or difficulties. For example, "Eve," a 51-year-old Jewish-Israeli female from Morocco, reported that her only difficulty was an ongoing disagreement with siblings who unfairly hospitalised her—an experience to which she alluded but chose not to describe in detail. In general, Eve depicted a perfectly tranquil, uneventful, even idyllic, or blissful existence:

Interviewer:	Can you tell me a story about a significant event from childhood?
Eve:	A significant event from childhood? When I was a girl?
Interviewer:	Yes. What do you remember?
Eve:	I remember a very good childhood. I am a twin. [...] and I have a nephew. [...] went on Sunday to the movie theater. [...] It is really nice in Morocco. And that is it.
Interviewer:	What was it like with the twin brother?
Eve:	Fine.
Interviewer:	You are also um, also still in contact with him?
Eve:	Yes. A good boy. We have an excellent relationship. A good boy.
Interviewer:	A good boy.
	[...]
Eve:	With the rest of the brothers and sisters, the relationship is not good.
Interviewer:	Why is this? What happened?
Eve:	It is a long story. I cannot tell it.

When participants in the destitute moment did make an attempt to communicate their distress to the interviewer, they often stated that it was ultimately indescribable, or that they did not have anything worthwhile to talk about. For example, in responding to the first interview question about significant or meaningful events in his life, Saleh stated, "I don't have anything significant in my life." In another example, Jean stated,

Jean:	I am in a different life. I am in a different life. I am not in a regular life.
Interviewer:	What does it mean, a different life?
Jean:	Eh, no. Impossible to explain. [...]
Interviewer:	That you want to be in another life? Or that you are? [...]
Jean:	No. I, I am in another life.
Interviewer:	Different from what?
Jean:	It was like, like a game with the soul.

In some cases, the person may demonstrate their destitution via performative or other unusual behaviours. In one example from the present study, Haseeb, who was generally responsive and engaged with the researchers, abruptly stopped talking in the middle of the interview. His eyes suddenly rolled back, his body went stiff, and he fell backwards from the bench onto the concrete ground (the interview was being conducted outside). Hospital staff rushed over, and it was quickly determined that Haseeb was conscious and breathing normally. Later, he stated that he regretted falling, and that he did so because "I was bored. I was talking about my boredom."

Withdrawal as a means of protection

Persons in the destitute moment withdraw from a world experienced as unduly dangerous and threatening. For this reason, participants who were experiencing the destitute moment at the time of the interview often spoke laconically and did not comprehensively articulate their thoughts and feelings. Because the destitute moment comprises a withdrawal from typical ways of communicating with others, it is possible that some potential participants who declined the interview or did not respond to the interviewers' attempts to engage them might have been experiencing it. For example, some participants brusquely waved the interviewer away when she approached, then returned to a near-immobile posture leaning against a wall or sitting on a couch.

One participant, Crystal, had recovered from destitution and was not experiencing urhomelessness during the interview. Crystal was able to reflectively articulate her past experiences with destitution in a way that she might not have during those same experiences. Because it is a rare and particularly illustrative example, her description is worth quoting at length:

Crystal: It took two months for me to get out of this catatonic state that I was in.

Interviewer: What was that state like?

Crystal: It was like I wasn't talking to anybody. I wasn't moving. They had to lift me up out of the bed, put me in a chair, feed me, bring the food in my room instead of me you know intermingling with the people and going to the dining room and stuff like that. [...]

Interviewer: Do you remember what you were feeling at the time? Why you weren't talking or moving?

Crystal: Uh yes I was feeling very hurt, I was very mad at my family this time. What happened was I was abused when I was a child uh by my grandfather. He used to fondle my breast and everything. And I used to hide from him [...]

Interviewer: And did you feel that; when you were feeling hurt and you didn't talk to people, did you feel that shutting down in that way would protect you?

Crystal: Yeah it was my means of protecting myself, like freezing myself so I wouldn't feel.

Interviewer: So you wouldn't feel hurt anymore.

Crystal: Yeah.

Interviewer: And each time that you were hospitalised you were also in this way very quiet and withdrawn?

Crystal: Yeah and catatonic.

When retroactively reflecting on her childhood experiences, Crystal recalled her emotional pain when hiding from her grandfather in order to escape his abuse. Thus, at a very young age, Crystal learned that distancing herself from other humans was an effective, purposeful means of protecting herself from danger. As Crystal's quote demonstrates, in the destitute moment, previous emotional pain and suffering is often passively synthesised and experientially relived in the present. In this way, the person may feel that she is withdrawing and protecting herself not only from a threatening world in the present, but also from unbearable memories of the past.

Passive wandering and becoming-shelter

In the destitute moment, wandering, nomadism, and exile are sometimes thematised passively. Voices, figures, sounds, or smells wander through, by, and around the person, punctuating her radical alienation with their strange and threatening presence. The person may report that these fleeting voices, persons, or forces have the potential to instrumentalise, become a part of, and/or transform her. When this happens, the person does not experience herself as the originator of her own experiences, but rather a secondary, supportive instrument, coincidental spectator, or objectified victim. For example, Greg's primary goal was to survive and regain the sense of having "independent thoughts" despite the voices "trapped in my mind, my consciousness. They're stuck in my mind." The person may report that her body, mind, and/or very being are no longer her own. Luma stated that "When she [the voice] speaks to me, I feel like I don't have any thoughts. At all." In another example, Greg described the ability of voices to wander through and "attach" themselves to "consciousness":

Greg:	They [the voices] don't want to be attached to anybody when they die. Because they're afraid he might leap into the consciousness of another person. [...]
Interviewer:	The voices can leap into the consciousness of any person?
Greg:	// a special way because // not everybody can do it.

Experientially, the person becomes a site through which other beings speak or act. The person might rigidly guard his own psychological experiences, monitoring for signs of invasion. Charles, for example, stated that he was watched over by an "evil angel" that was trying to possess him. Charles seemed to believe that merely talking about this experience might put him at risk: "I don't want to talk about that."

Passive wandering is usually founded on the implicit or explicit assumption that minds or bodies are permeable, such that they can be entered into, wandered through, and inhabited by other persons or beings. For example, Haseeb complained of *waswas* ("the whispers of Satan")[3] entering into him and causing inordinate anxiety, insomnia, and unease; "Wuswus follows me and comes through thoughts," he complained. In another example, Roger described feeling as if he was followed by a (presumably supernatural) person who could leap between the minds of other people; varied persons whom Roger encountered were experienced as the same threatening, persecutory figure: "Someone's following me. Not by a person but by leaping [...] from person to person. [...] But it's possible also for me because minds can be transferred to another, one to another."

In some cases, the person may ultimately feel that she herself has become a shelter or "home" for other beings who become embodied through her. For example, Roger stated that his voices "play my emotions. They make some; they make me laugh, they make me cry, they make me think." Greg said, "you had to have independent thoughts to know that you're alive. And to prove that [...] I'm this, a living shell, ya know. And I don't have any more independent thoughts." He explained that the voices had the power to assume control over his own consciousness, such that at any given moment, he was unsure whether his thoughts and speech were his or the voices:

Greg: And uh the way that I'm speaking is not really me. It's them.
Interviewer: I was going to ask you that.
Greg: Mm-hm, it's them.
Interviewer: So sometimes the way you're speaking is not even; how would I know if it is really you?
Greg: I don't know.
Interviewer: How would you know if it is really you?
Greg: I don't. That's the hard part. There's so many that, that got absorbed by me.

The experience of becoming-shelter is often inordinately distressing and disorienting:

Interviewer: What do you mean "stuck in your mind?" You said the voices are stuck in your mind.
Greg: Yes. They /. They go into the person. But me // / but I don't know how. They can go into your mind. And through your memories and thoughts. But it would hurt your mind.

Similarly, when speaking about his belief that someone was possessing the minds of others around him, Roger stated, "it's confusing me, scaring me, destroying me." The person may report that parts of her are fading away and crumbling as the world moves in. Indeed, the destitute moment is often accompanied by fantasies of finding a kind of final relief in death. Gilah, for example, stated, "they said that I'm the last scream of the world [...] that I was decreed to die more than everyone. A brutal death."

Passive wandering in the nomadic moment versus the destitute moment

As described in Chapter 6, the experience of being passively wandered *through* also occurs intermittently during the nomadic moment. In both the nomadic and destitute moments, voices, images, or persons might seem to appear in front of, behind, or within the person. Although these experiences are similar, the moments differ on the basis of whether active nomadism is also present. In the nomadic moment, the person actively wanders, seeking shelter or permanent urhomeness; she might freely wander while the world wanders through her. Indeed, at times, she might feel that she herself is the voice, image, or thought wandering through another person or persons. In contrast, the person in the destitute moment does not experience the kind of freedom and world-openness that is characteristic of the nomadic moment, and she does not make an active attempt to locate shelter. She is resigned to feeling static, frozen, withdrawn, emptied—a mere host for other minds, thoughts, forces. Indeed, she finds herself slipping into the background as worldly voices, thoughts, and images take over.

Common variations of the destitute moment

The common variations of the destitute moment are evacuated versus hibernated, voluntary versus involuntary, and active versus passive.

Evacuated versus hibernated

The destitute moment has two primary variations, here named "hibernation" and "evacuation." Often, the person oscillates between both variations, though she may have a proclivity for one or the other. In hibernation, the person gives up on the possibility of securing social belonging and citizenship, but he maintains his striving for basic protection and safety. As a means of securing safety and protection, he evacuates and hibernates in a no-person's-land, a state of solitude and barrenness. The person hibernates in a wasteland where he attempts to void himself of all impinging thoughts and feelings, what Greg called "the conscious mind, clear and free of all other minds."

Anything that enters the person's perception is perceived as having broken through the protective walls she desperately tries to erect. In some cases, hibernation can be just as cacophonous and chaotic as the world that the person has attempted to evacuate. As Crystal put it:

> I would make all this stuff up and it would be the voices that are telling me these things, and it would be auditory, and I would be hearing it and visualising it like a dream but I was awake. I would be hospitalised so I would be in this catatonic state. No one could talk to me, or I wouldn't respond to do anything because all these stories were going on in my mind all these voices at the same time. It was too much for me to break out of it.

In contrast, during evacuation, the person completely gives up on the attempt to attain both essential constituents of urhomeness, the striving for basic safety and basic acknowledgement as part of one or more human communities. Instead, she allows the world to overtake and overrun her. She may believe that evacuation is only hope for maintaining her bare existence; in some cases, she may have also given up on survival itself. Experientially, the person is utterly vulnerable to the world; both person and world are emptied of existential meanings.

Evacuation and hibernation are typically unattainable ideals towards which the person experiencing the destitute moment strives. Due to the incessantly present world, a state completely devoid of thoughts and feelings is unachievable. Ultimately, neither hibernation nor evacuation successfully protects the person from the threatening world of others and the excruciating impingement of passive wanderings.

Voluntary versus involuntary variations

The destitute moment may be experienced as voluntary or involuntary. In the voluntary version, the person decides to shut himself off, finding it increasingly futile to wander and seek safety in the dangerous and oppressive world. He voluntarily decides he has no hope of becoming sheltered, settled, or urhomed. He may feel exhausted, worn down by his urhomelessness. Haseeb, for example, sometimes fantasised about escaping this excruciating boredom via death, "to get rid of life so that I can get rid of this boredom."

In the involuntary variation, the person may experience the destitute moment for reasons that are out of his control. He may report experiences of unjust and unbearable oppression or deprivation. Jean, for example, reported having nothing that might provide temporary reprieve from his all-encompassing misery:

Jean:	[I am] miserable. [...] I don't have money, I don't have a wife. I don't have children. I don't have a life. I don't have. I don't have. I don't have a family. I don't have parents. I don't have. I don't have.
Interviewer:	You don't have parents?
Jean:	My parents are not okay at all.

Similarly, when describing her reasons for attempting suicide, Luma stated, "I have no work. I don't have anything to learn. I don't have anything. Only sit in the house by the television. So what can I do?" The person experiencing involuntary destitution feels altogether helpless and hopeless, compelled to adopt a passive, acquiescent attitude towards a dangerous and threatening world.

Active versus passive variations

While involuntary versus voluntary variations correspond to the experiential *choice* (or lack thereof) that a person has to enter or exit the destitute moment, active versus passive variations correspond to continuous qualities with which this moment is experienced. In the active variation, the destitute moment is characterised by an ongoing rejection of all things interpersonal and worldly. For some persons, a great deal of active energy is required to maintain the destitute moment, viewed as his last and only option for psychological survival. He desperately empties himself of thoughts and feelings, which he experiences as burdensome and painful, and he wilfully quashes his own desire for human and worldly connections.

Persons in the settled moment might also experience pervasive passivity, which can be accompanied by feelings of helplessness, hopelessness, and loss of agency. The person might feel that he is a passive victim of other persons, forces, or his own mental and neurological processes. Roger, for example, stated, "my brain is torturing me." He might feel completely vulnerable to the world and emptied of all existential meanings of his own. As Jean put it, "I am not in life at all."

Extreme destitution

The person in the destitute moment, at its extreme, might report that elements of her person are slowly fading and decaying as she fades into the world. The world, in turn, moves in, wandering through and ultimately as her. In this way, the experience of the destitute moment can eventually jeopardise the person's basic sense of being and presence in the world. She might describe herself as an automaton, slab of meat, or puppet. Her very *being* is instrumentalised by the worldly forces that wander through her, become her, abandon her, wander through her again. Indeed, the person may be just an arbitrary pit-stop for other urhomeless forms of consciousness. In order to evade them, she might contemplate escaping through death. In destitution's starkest form, the world is all that is left.

Notes

1 During the interview, Jean primarily spoke in English and Hebrew, both of which were second languages for him. Some grammatical idiosyncrasies are thus preserved in the transcript.
2 Hebrew was a new language for Jean. He used the word "tasty" but probably meant "fits," which is phonetically similar in Hebrew.
3 In secular Levantine Arabic, *waswas* can also mean "paranoia" and/or "obsession."

9

A CONTINUUM OF EXPERIENCE: URHOMELESSNESS AND RECOVERY

Sarah R. Kamens, Jessica Yisca Baris Ginat, Ryan Scanlon, Faith Forgione, Ileana Driggs, Jillian Minahan Zucchetto, Lia Kamar, and Pesach Lichtenberg

Urhomeness as horizon

The possibility of becoming urhomed is an ever-present horizon of urhomelessness in all three moments. Just as a person might experience more than one moment of urhomelessness simultaneously or in succession, some persons cycle between urhomelessness and urhomeness, or experience elements of both simultaneously. Others fully exit the experience of urhomelessness by (re)gaining (1) a sense of basic safety and protection in the world and (2) the experience of basic acknowledgement and belonging to a human community. While some persons enter a state of urhomeness by readopting previous ways of being-in-the-world, others create or discover new means of becoming urhomed. Others might start to experience urhomeness for the first time. When the person has previously experienced urhomeness, the experience of regaining it might also be called *recovery*.

In all three moments of urhomelessness, even when unactualised, the possibility of urhomeness was implicitly present as a horizon, or a possibility that is both distant and immanent to the experience itself. One example common to most inpatient participants was their desire to leave the hospital for a more welcoming environment. In another example of urhomeness-as-horizon, Leonard expressed his desire to obtain help with his difficulties in communicating effectively with others:

> I wanna get the help that I need [...] I need to be able to [...] be responsible. [...] be able to; I don't know. to /(?:assert, accept) myself humanely [...] without um, making a fool of myself. [...]

 DOI: 10.4324/9780429055454-10

I have to be able to um, assert myself in a human, I mean humanely right?

Urhomeness was given in Leonard's striving towards effective communicative strategies that might enhance his interactions with others, and thereby his sense of agency and belonging in the social world.

Even in the destitute moment, participants reflected upon past or imagined states of urhomeness (e.g., in previous relationships or roles, a world beyond, or an afterlife) despite believing these states might be difficult or impossible to attain. For example, Jean, who complained about being "miserable" and a "prisoner" in the hospital, fantasised about being discharged so that he could work in a rehabilitative cafeteria. Thus, the possibility of urhomeness was a given horizon even for those participants who felt utterly hopeless and disempowered. Indeed, the very experience of urhomelessness, as state of privation, paradoxically implies the possibility of being urhomed.

For most participants in the present dataset, the fully actualised state of urhomeness remained on the horizon of experience. Two of the three participants who were receiving an outpatient level of care reported experiences in which they regained the experience of urhomeness. For example, Roger oscillated between urhomeness and urhomelessness in the destitute and nomadic moments. For Roger, urhomeness was constituted by his perceived ability to wrest control of his mind away from immaterial, persecutory forces (e.g., voices). He attributed his ability to do so to the help of his psychiatric medication, which "makes me stronger" such that "they can't control my mind," and to his freedom to return daily to his apartment, which he experienced as a place of safety that was impermeable to the voices: "I feel very safe in my place. You know, […] all the troubles in my mind's gone."

In addition, Crystal was in recovery at the time of the research interview. Crystal's episodes of urhomelessness were temporary experiences in which her psychosocial world was completely inverted: trust became distrust, safety became danger, and comfort became fear. She locked family, friends, and acquaintances out of her room, believing them to be dangerous. Yet on all four occasions, Crystal abruptly emerged from this "place where I didn't know who to trust" and "woke up […] like out of a dream. What happened to me? I didn't know what happened to me. and I called my husband and he was crying and happy and he, we took me home." Upon being discharged from the hospital, Crystal immediately regained feelings of safety and meaningful social belonging by re-engaging with her family, friends, hobbies, and work; in addition, her sense of existential gratitude was profoundly renewed and enhanced:

I take time out in the day to be thankful and grateful for things and to see the sunrise and sunset. I always make sure I look at nature and find peaceful time and thankful; you know to see god in all situations, even small situations.

Even in urhomeness, the person may retain residual elements or memories of urhomeless experiences. For example, he may still experience intermittent active or passive wandering,[1] or settlement-like reveries. So long as the person has (re)gained a sense of basic safety and protection, as well as acknowledgement and meaningful belonging in the world of other humans, these experiences are not part of the general structure of urhomelessness.

Ad hoc comparison participants

The full general structure of urhomelessness was not actualised in the narratives of the three inpatient hospital participants who did not meet criteria for a psychotic-disorder diagnosis at the time of the interview. However, features or resonances of the general structure were discernible in their narratives. For example, one participant, "Noam," a 27-year-old Jewish-Israeli male of Ashkenazi origin, suspected that as the only redhead in the family, he might have been adopted, suggesting some distrust in his family origins; Noam's potential adoption was the first thing that he mentioned in the interview as a response to the life-historical narrative prompt. When talking about his parents, Noam said, "for some time I have not wanted to be in contact with them. They did not help me in anything in my life. And beyond that, they destroyed everything I want to do." However, Noam experienced urhomeness in his daily life; for example, when travelling or eating with friends, when passionately promoting healthy eating habits, and when selling his favourite herbal supplement. When describing how he felt when taking the supplement, Noam said, "I felt really healthy. Whoah. […] You really feel the / within the mind.[2] You really feel the thoughts balanced. […] They do not run from place to place."

"Paula," a 58-year-old European American female, was lonely and estranged from both family and friends after years of houselessness and multiple hospitalisations. However, Paula experienced urhomeness while dwelling in positive memories of past relationships and when able to engage in her favourite activities in the community, such as walking near the beach, taking a dip in the sea, and seeing familiar faces in her neighbourhood. As Paula put it,

Interviewer:	Do you ever feel like you're empty or void inside?
Paula:	Um, no. Well, these days yeah.
	[…]
Interviewer:	When you say these days you mean …
Paula:	Well, when I'm in this kind of [inpatient hospital] setting, it's kind of alienating.

> [...] It's sort of like you're surrounded by people but you're alone. Because there's not much interaction like this, like I'm having with you, you know. And um, you're not-, you're not relating to anyone. Like, as I said when I-, when I'm on the outside, I go out and do things, and I relate. I go to places where people know me so I can feel like I'm relating to people to some extent. And I get-, I get out of myself more.

The third ad hoc comparison participant, "Olufemi," was an immigrant from a war-torn country in West Africa who wanted to study political science in the US in order to return to his home country and work for a peace-building NGO. Describing his childhood, Olufemi said:

> My country was going through some trial and tribulations. and there's some war. I kinda; I kinda you know, was exposed in a lot of war crime. [...] There's a lot of damage. A lot of death. A lot, a lot of, a lot of you know, you know, a lot of [...] destruction in family, and populations, in-in-in- installed something in you, that make you wanna, try, that make you wanna strive for equality and liberty for everybody.

After immigrating, he found himself imprisoned and then involuntarily hospitalised for reasons that he did not understand. In Olufemi's words,

Interviewer: How did you end up here in the hospital?
Olufemi: Uh, oh I did my time in [name of prison]. And they told me I was going home. And they just throw me here.
Interviewer: They told you you were going home and then they put you here?
Olufemi: Yeah. They sent me here.
Interviewer: And, you don't know why they did that?
Olufemi: I don't know. The night before my release, I cooked, I worked out, I ///(?: ate meal before 9 o'clock). Oh; so for some reason he sent me to be, he sent me here. I was like "oh no." They said "oh he was ill. He was ill." I'm standing there; I wasn't ill. "Man, you guys trying to railroad me. Ain't nothing wrong with me." I was legally. Incompe-, competent to-to carry myself in a ver-, in a very normal manner. "So how come you don't tell me I'm ot, I-I don't know what I'm doing." And they tell me "No. You know you start a fight." I said "you started; you still /(?:know) I started a fight. I did my bed man. Let me go home."

Despite his present institutionalisation, Olufemi maintained a strong sense of communal belonging and validation when thinking about his spirituality and sense of morality, as well as when thinking about his future plans to return to school, then back to his country in Africa so that he can contribute to the political betterment of his society. As Olufemi put it,

Interviewer: Do you have any other plans for when you get out?
Olufemi: Well yeah, well. I-I-I'm trying to go back to school.
Interviewer: Ok. What do you wanna study?
Olufemi: I thought about psy, political psy, and constitution reformations. [...] So political science, fundamental constitutions. [...] How can we can, you know, study a country, and come up with a constitution. [...] Because in my country [...] I wanna be able to, for the former constitution, which should be intact. [...] I wanna add to, build to it, with the information from here. You know that I cou; you know the U.N., you know what I'm saying. UNICEF, you know. Ar-ar; FEMA. you know those the things that I'm looking to, turn in to-to- t, to-to have an internship over it. [...] To help me internship over there.

This hope of studying and returning to his country in the future was one way in which Olufemi maintained a sense of urhomeness. He experienced features of urhomeless experiences; most notably, his psychiatric hospitalisation was experienced as alienating and confusing. However, he maintained a sense of the temporariness of these present injustices, and the general structure of urhomelessness was not fully given in his interview narrative.

Pilot-comparison participants

As with the three ad hoc comparison participants, the four pilot-comparison participants did not experience the full general structure of urhomelessness. However, these participants described brief and non-distressing anomalous experiences as well as fleeting encounters with urhomelessness. Pilot-comparison participants seemed to understand urhomelessness as a horizon of experience or fundamental possibility. One pilot-comparison participant, "Oliver," an Australian male in his 30s, was excruciatingly terrified of urhomelessness as an existential potential. Another pilot-comparison participant, "Claire," a 40-year-old Jewish American painter, struggled with feelings of helplessness when encountering her mother's urhomelessness. However, all pilot-comparison participants maintained a sense of being minimally safe and protected, as well as basic feelings of social belonging and acknowledgement by other persons. This subsection briefly describes pilot-comparison participants' experiences with urhomeness before describing their non-distressing anomalous experiences and their fleeting encounters with urhomelessness.

Urhomeness

Each of the pilot-comparison participants had multiple (ontic) means of sustaining urhomed ways of being-in-the-world. Examples of activities and relationships that functioned as means of attaining urhomeness included travelling, sociopolitical activism, intellectual activities, artistic creation, professional roles and achievements, favoured leisure activities, friendships, romantic relationships, and family relationships. When reflecting on experiences of familiarity and comfort, pilot-comparison participants often described physical places with affordances of basic safety as well as intimate and meaningful social relationships. For example, "Zev," a 24-year-old Israeli male who had moved to New York for graduate school, described feeling at-home in his country of origin despite the fact that he experienced social discrimination and violence there as a peace activist and political minority:

> [My home city] feels like home in a way that I think that is hard to explain, and I, and I think in a way that a home feels like a home […] irrespective of what you think politically or experienced personally, uh, there's real familiarity […] A certain way in which things don't need to be explained, or uttered even. […] There's a certain, um, proximity, emotional proximity to other people in Israel [that] I think I don't have here.

In another example, "Amy," a 28-year-old Caucasian graduate student, stated that despite the fact that she viewed herself as "sort of a loner," she felt existentially at-home in a specific city due to its social, creative, and professional affordances:

> I fit in in [name of city]. […] I had good friends […] these really great friends, and we would like write poetry together […]. We like did this magazine together, and it was really fun. I also like you know meditated a lot, and I was learning how to play the guitar, and, you know, it was just like it was, that was kind of a fun time.

In this city, Amy experienced a basic sense of social belonging that transcended her feelings of being a "loner"; she also experienced a given sense of safety and security that allowed her to pursue her creative goals and passions.

Fleeting anomalous and urhomeless experiences

Pilot-comparison and ad hoc comparison participants described varied anomalous or unusual experiences. Examples included unusual thoughts about death, afterlife, abstract mathematics, and human existence, as well as idiosyncratic perceptual and emotional experiences such as feeling dead inside or seeing strange shadow-shapes. Some were fleeting anomalous experiences that were not accompanied by feelings of distress, and others were transient encounters with urhomelessness without the full actualisation of the general structure. In other words, some anomalous experiences that participants reported did not involve both feelings of being profoundly vulnerable in an inhospitable world and feelings of profound alienation among other humans.

Both non-distressing anomalous and transient urhomeless experiences were often described as occurring during exceptional occasions such as during childhood reveries, states of non-sobriety or semi-wakefulness (e.g., when falling asleep or waking up), and/or during times of notable stress or life change. However, they also occurred during everyday contemplative moments, during extensive physical activity (e.g., backpacking long distances in a foreign country), and during artistic production (e.g., painting). Below, examples of non-distressing anomalous experiences in pilot-comparison participants are provided before examples of their fleeting but distressing encounters with urhomelessness.

Non-distressing anomalous experiences

Pilot-comparison participants reported infrequent anomalous experiences that they described as strange or unusual, but not necessarily upsetting. Sometimes, they even described these experiences as "fascinating" or "mesmerising." In one example, Oliver described unusual experiences during hypnopompic and hypnagogic states:

> I know it has happened before I was going to bed or when I was waking up. […] I just heard like whispers and things like that. […] And I also feel sometimes, um, very small? […] like Alice in Wonderland, like old school, like. Really little […] Like my body was little.

Similarly, when asked if she ever felt that her body was too small or too big, Amy stated,

> Every once in a while, like very very rarely, I have this sort of weird feeling when I'm going to sleep, that like, things are sort of spreading out in this weird way that I can't explain. I think maybe it only happens when I'm stoned, but maybe not. No, I think it happened when I was a kid too. Um, it's a very hard to explain.

In another example, when reflecting on feelings of being "empty" inside, Claire, said:

> When I was really young like maybe three, I remember having this like really vertiginous experience where, I felt like everything inside

> my, my body and my mind was moving so quickly, that, saying a word or like moving my body felt really clumsy. [...] I remember like saying a word like trying to say a word with my mouth and it felt so weird. It was almost like a robot was saying it.

In addition, Zev reported the non-distressing anomalous experience of feeling as if present situations have already occurred in the past (déjà-vu):

Interviewer: Do you ever have experiences that seem to have happened before?

Zev: Yep. [...] It used to be way more often when I was a kid. I remember I was like, really mesmerised by it. And it would drive me nuts. I would actually try to make that happen [...] I know the excitement of understanding in a couple-second delay that you've already thought something, you've already felt something.

Amy reported anomalous experiences while meditating on the nature of life and death when she was approximately seven or eight years old. For example, she described inducing a "sort of weird altered state" when contemplating the nature of her existence:

> When I was a kid I use to play this game with myself where I would like, um, [...] I would like sit on my bed and I would sort of; I would say like "I am me" [...] and it would freak me out. Well it wouldn't freak me out it; would put me in this really really interesting space where it was so bizarre that I was me. [...] it's impossible to explain. [...] And it was like this really fascinating, [...] it was really interesting. And I can't do it. I've tried to do it like in my adult life. I can't do it.

In the above examples, pilot-comparison participants reported unusual, imaginative experiences that were thematically characterised by wandering and exploration. However, during and after these experiences, pilot-comparison participants maintained a sense of basic, minimal safety, and social belonging. As such, these anomalous experiences were unrelated to the general structure of urhomelessness.

Fleeting encounters with the horizon of urhomelessness

Pilot-comparison participants also described fleeting encounters with the horizon of urhomelessness during times of notable stress or life change. In these instances, anomalous experiences were accompanied by distress related to a sense of potentially compromised safety and/or social belonging. The full general structure of urhomelessness remained in the horizon of experience, but it moved from being an indiscernible experiential possibility to a noticeable yet unactualised possibility. Below are examples from three interviews.

Amy: Amy described fleeting anomalous experiences in her childhood and adolescent years. In adulthood, she began to view these experiences as symptoms of OCD. She described one such instance in which the presence of a particular physical object grounded her very sense of being-in-the-world:

> I was unable to hold a coherent image in my head a lot of the time. [...] It was especially the ground. It would be like the ground would fall away, um, in my fantasy world. [...] One day I went to this antique shop [...] and there was this tiny little vase thing. [...] I had this very strange attraction to it, and yet was really terrified of it. [...] When I was at my house that night, like trying to go to sleep, like its presence, like, on the shelf was just [laughs] like, so overwhelming. And that was like, when it started, like this thing, I mean so it was like, it was like centered around this tiny little object. [laughs] [...] The object was just, like, a really coherent, like, starting point and it always sat there on the fucking shelf.

Amy reported that she was "too afraid of what might happen" if she got rid of the object and was only able to do so "after the OCD went away." Though not a direct encounter with the full general structure of urhomelessness, in this example, Amy's anomalous experience momentarily threatened her sense of urhomed grounding in the world.

Claire: Claire described brief but distressing anomalous experiences with what she called "the dead feeling":

> It's an awful, also really weird, unnatural feeling. But it's more awful. It's the kind of feeling; it's related to depression. I mean it's related to despair. [...] It's like when you feel, like being human is disgusting. But not just disgusting because that's almost too fascinating. When it's just gross and dead and it's like almost machine-like in its disgustingness.

Claire starkly experienced the horizon of urhomelessness during certain encounters with her mother, a former physician and second-generation Holocaust survivor who was intermittently houseless and, according to

Claire, "mentally ill" and potentially "paranoid schizophrenic." Reflecting on her mother, Claire explained:

> She was always trying to get a loan so she could reopen her medical practice and these like, just *absolute* delusions of grandeur mixed with *real* grandeur. Ya know because she's my mother and there's ways that I think she's beautiful and amazing and talented and misunderstood mixed with, uh a complete inability, to, like have like a productively good, relationship with her own gifts and talents [...] Um an *absolute absolute* incapacity on her part to listen to reason. [...] I used to think when I was younger, like if I were more intelligent if I were more articulate, I would be able to make sense to her. [...] like I can talk to anyone right. Like I should be able to get through to her.

To Claire, her mother simultaneously embodied multiple polarities: she was at once talented and incapable, amazing and unreachable. Her intermittent houselessness haunted Claire as a "lurking possibility" even when she was domiciled. Throughout her adult years, she attempted to avoid being completely overwhelmed—both emotionally and physically—by her mother's presence. Claire's art, in particular, provided her with a means of feeling minimally protected and validated in the world. However, when her mother knocked on her door seeking shelter, Claire's sense of urhomeness was put at risk:

> For me the nightmare, the way I can best describe it; [...] is like my mother's on top of me, um, psychically. [...] it's like I'm falling through, any hole that could possibly open at the bottom of my life, like I'm falling through all of them at the same time. And [...] those periods when that has happened have been nightmarish not only because any joy, any like beginning to thrive that has ever happened is almost always, she almost always shows up. [...] I guess I could say I had a real fear of success because I was afraid if I got any that I would just go mad because I wouldn't know how to keep her out, but at the same time the guilt of feeling like I wasn't helping her was also so nightmarish. [...] [W]hat was I supposed to do with my- with my *physical* mother? You know it's like did I have the money to support her? No. Could I afford the physical space to live in myself? Barely. I could barely pay for four walls and a door in which to contain my own person. Barely.

To Claire, her mother's (ontic) houselessness and physical presence thematically paralleled the psychological (ontological) experience of her homeless mother "on top of me," an experience that unmoored and destabilised her very sense of groundedness in the world of others. Throughout her life, Claire attempted to support her mother without being epistemologically overcome by her presence, by the "breakdown in meaning, that I experienced by confronting her, or trying to confront her."

Ultimately, Claire realised "that I was not going to be able to get through to her [my mother]" and paradoxically secured a means of attaining an urhomed way of being-in-the-world through a creative reversal of the threat of urhomelessness itself. More specifically, Claire began to paint about her experiences with her mother, and she resiliently utilised these paintings to grasp what she viewed as the puzzling incomprehensibility of the world-at-large:

> I used this [experience with her]. I just used it. I just turned it outward. And I used it to try to in a way to read, um, the world as I saw it. Which was like the world in terrorism during the Bush years, in the post-Holocaust world, um in which not only, not only had meaning in language been broken down and, and turned into hamburger, but then the possibility, that the possibility of locating meaning anywhere or trying to figure how to locate meaning, became more and more impossible.

Claire ultimately transformed her fleeting encounters with urhomelessness into a means of securing existential groundedness in her art, as well as a broadened understanding of the world-at-large, which allowed her to integrate new experiences, even potentially destabilising and highly distressing experiences, into her experience of urhomeness.

Oliver: Oliver reported a series of frightening experiences in which he briefly encountered urhomelessness, but nonetheless did not fully experience the general structure. Of all four pilot-comparison participants, Oliver's encounter with urhomelessness was the most proximal and distressing. However, for Oliver, it was the fear of experiencing urhomelessness, but not urhomeless experience itself, that proved the most distressing.

It all started during his twenties, when Oliver began to experience panic attacks. The first occurred while Oliver was at a party using drugs:

> I'm like, "this music is really; became very loud," and [...] my friend turned around. And when I was pretty much turned around, I saw her face and she laughed. And as she laughed, she receded into the background, like that scene in uh, what's that/movie, the UK? *Trainspotting*. [...] I started to get kind of panicky. [...] And they all

> came out and were like, "are you okay?" And when you're kind of having a bit of a panicky freak out, the more people the worse.

According to Oliver, his distress "snowballed" after that experience, in large part because he became increasingly terrified of the possibility of having more panic attacks. During the attacks, Oliver felt that he was losing his sense of stability and agentic control over his emotional and physical states. Even when not experiencing acute panic, a vague and looming sense of fear seemed to encroach upon him, signifying the possibility of an unknown disaster in the horizon. Oliver felt like the universe itself was at risk:

> Nothing felt real [...] Almost like life was like a/layer on top of like weird dark void that [...] I was scared of being sucked in to. And that was what was so terrifying, like it felt so, everything had felt so fragile and everything I suppose at risk. It was like scary in some way. It literally felt like the world could, it was almost like it could like tear. [...] Almost like ripping a poster.

Oliver encountered the possibility of urhomelessness as a definitive horizon of human experience. Though he managed not to fall into the "weird dark void," he stood on its brink, terrified by the vertiginous experience. Oliver approached his mother for help: "I'm going through some stuff," he told her, "I don't know what's going on but I feel very unsafe." Eventually, his mother took him to a psychiatric hospital.

At first, Oliver "was *super* happy [to be hospitalised] because I just felt like, oh finally some action is going to be taken." But Oliver's initial enthusiasm was quickly dampened. He was paired with a psychiatrist who "was like so clearly depressed [...] like if you had a dictionary definition of 'morose' it would be him." Moreover, despite his new treatment, he continued to have frightening experiences, especially the fear that his panic might return—this time for good: "I was so scared of going crazy again [...] I was scared I was going to have one of those, an attack like the one that kind of started it all, but have it never stop." Oliver ruminated on the fear of losing his memory or forgetting how to speak; for example, he described the following experience on a day trip from the hospital:

> I was driving along. [...] I would mentally go like road signs go like, 'sign,' 'lights,' 'dog,' 'house.' In my mind, to remind myself that I knew what those things were. So ridiculous. But um, I was just afraid of forgetting I guess.

His doubt and dissatisfaction with the treatment at the hospital growing, Oliver requested literature on his "drug psychosis" diagnosis and received "some check list of like seven signs you were psychotic. And I had maybe take like two out of seven when I was like, eh, this isn't convincing." Eventually, he was sent to a neurologist who told him,

> Look, it's not my job to tell you this, but I don't think you're psychotic. Like you seem to have like a form of OCD. Um, which/again I shouldn't even be saying this to you, but maybe you could bring it up to your psychiatrist.

When Oliver's psychiatrist disagreed with the neurologist and instead suggested that he try ECT, Oliver called his mother and asked her to sign his discharge forms.

Oliver's phone call to his mother and request that she retrieve him from the hospital demonstrates the fact that his encounter with urhomelessness was experienced as ultimately evadable, escapable, and fleeting. Oliver fleetingly encountered urhomelessness, as his sense of basic safety was compromised, and he feared social stigma, and thus compromised social belonging, due to his status as a mental patient. However, Oliver ultimately suffered more from the fear of urhomelessness than urhomelessness itself. Eventually, he concluded that a great deal of his suffering stemmed from the experience of misdiagnosis, the iatrogenic suggestion that he was psychotic, and the harmful effects of the treatment and medications that followed. After a new outpatient therapist concurred that he had OCD, he came to believe that his intrusive thoughts were compulsive symptoms that were triggered and exacerbated by his drug use, then misinterpreted by psychologists. Eventually, Oliver returned to his self-actualised life and urhomeness among family, friends, relationship, studying, and working.

Urhomelessness as universal horizon

The fact that the ad hoc comparison participants experienced partial features of urhomelessness—alongside the fact that the general structure was fleetingly encountered on the horizons of the pilot-comparison participants' experiences—suggests that urhomelessness is a fundamental potential of human experience that, for some persons, is not fully actualised in the foreground of experience. Moreover, recovery is a horizon of urhomelessness in all of its moments, and urhomelessness is a horizon of the urhomed way of being-in-the-world. Just as the three moments of urhomelessness are horizons of each other that can be overlapping or simultaneous, urhomelessness and urhomeness are qualitatively unique ways of experiencing that can occur in succession, or even simultaneously. Even when unactualised, urhomelessness is given as an experiential potential in the lives of those who have not fully experienced it, and urhomeness is given as a potential in the lives of those experiencing urhomelessness.

Notes

1 These passive wanderings may be transformed from residual elements or memories of urhomelessness into aspects of a new kind of urhomeness. For example, some recovered persons report finding a new sense of comfort and solidarity in the experience of hearing voices. Though not exemplified in the present dataset, these transformations of residual elements and memories of urhomelessness have been reported in recovery-oriented, peer-specialist communities (e.g., Hearing Voices Network, 2019; Icarus Project, 2019), where Experts by Experience utilise their past experiences to assist others in recovery.

2 The Hebrew word that Noam uses for "mind" (נְשִׁימָה) can also mean breath, soul, or psyche.

10

CULTURAL DIVERSITY AND SAMENESS

Sarah R. Kamens, Frederick J. Wertz, Lia Kamar, Oren Matar, Ileana Driggs, Jillian Minahan Zucchetto, Faith Forgione, Ryan Scanlon, and Jessica Yisca Baris Ginat

Cultural heterogeneity

Demographic differences

The participants in the present study were demographically diverse at both the New York and Jerusalem data-collection sites. Only two participants from New York and three participants from Jerusalem had similar patterns across the demographic indicators of nationality, ethnicity, native language, and religion. Chapter 4 contained a detailed description of demographic differences across the samples.

Among participants who did share demographic similarities, the experience of urhomelessness was not static or unified, as the specific moments of experiencing differed between participants with similar cultural backgrounds. For example, both Crystal and Rabbi Danny had grown up in secular Jewish households in the north-eastern US. Whereas Rabbi Danny eventually immigrated to Israel and settled in the belief that he might be the Messiah, Crystal converted to Catholicism and drew upon her faith as a source of resilience while recovering from the destitute moment. Likewise, Saleh and Asad had both grown up in Muslim-Palestinian households in Jerusalem. Whereas Saleh wandered imaginatively in search of someone who might be able to empathically understand him, Asad was generally evasive of other persons, whom he experienced as dangerous and threatening.

Due to the size and diversity of the present sample, our demographic groups were not large enough for cross-cultural comparison. However, the data revealed trends among participants with demographic similarities that may or may not have been coincidental, and thus should be subject to further research. More specifically, the destitute moment: destitute was given in full intuitive clarity for all four Palestinian participants (Luma, Haseeb, Asad, and Saleh). In contrast, not all of the Israeli and American

DOI: 10.4324/9780429055454-11

participants described or demonstrated the destitute moment as fully actualised, despite the fact that it was thematised as a potential or horizon of their experience. In addition, one common variation of the settled moment was characteristic of both Jewish-Israeli participants for whom the settlement was given in full intuitive clarity; Yuval and Rabbi Danny adopted pre-existing cultural narratives as their settlements, rather than piecing their settlements together from related but different cultural constructs, as some American and Palestinian participants did (see Chapter 7). More specifically, Rabbi Danny adopted varied pre-existing cultural narratives about the coming of the Messiah, and Yuval adopted the longstanding practice of praying at a specific holy site in Jerusalem. Both participants attempted to perfect and epitomise these pre-existing cultural roles, but they did not substantially alter them. In contrast, American and Palestinian participants created new roles by patching together multiple existing cultural ideas; these new roles included Designer of Spaceships for Area 51, the Head of The System, and the Divine Intermediary between Allah and Man.

Cultural heterogeneity across the moments of urhomelessness

Each moment of urhomelessness is a way of being in person-world configurations that include sociocultural roles, practices, and institutions. For this reason, each moment is characterised by a distinct pattern of cultural experience based in identifications with specific cultural roles and activities. Data analysis revealed unique patterns of cultural experience corresponding to the nomadic, settled, and destitute moments of urhomelessness that we (respectively) termed *the many*, *the one*, and *the none*.

In the nomadic moment, the person's experience spans *the many*, i.e., vast, multiple, and pluralistic cultural constructs, narratives, roles, practices, and traditions. Although the person may preferentially wander through specific cultural narratives (e.g., Judeo-Christian narratives or North American narratives), she typically incorporates diverse and wide-ranging aspects of the cultural practices she encounters into her existential meanderings. Through her nomadism, she may report travels near and far, to distant lands and times—even to faraway worlds and universes. She might engage in a local activity before imaginatively traversing time and space to participate in a tale unfolding in a remote land or era. Leonard, for example, described being born in a specific time and place (1960s Trinidad) but also witnessing the beginning of the world in Jerusalem, as well as discovering America in the 1400s. Gilah, likewise, imaginatively travelled between places and holidays:

> [...] in London. I forgot. The town. The town that was there was decorated on their holidays. And on Hannukah they had a

> Menorah, next to the Christmas, how I loved it. I'm a little not Jewish today, from how much I love these holidays. It's my right; it's my right. What, it's fun. To see the pine tree with all of the gifts. And a gentle menorah next to it, a menorah on the side. [...] And Solomon said one day that he will come to my home. [...] He said one day he will come to my home. So what that I did not buy all of the goods of Egypt in the market.

In this way, the person experiencing the nomadic moment traverses multiple and pluralistic cultural histories, narratives, traditions, and practices.

In contrast, cultural experience in the settled moment can be referred to as *the one*. For the person, the settlement acts as a homogenising lens through which diverse cultural experiences are filtered and interpreted. As a result, the person tends to view most cultural experiences, no matter how heterogeneous, as unified under the settlement, which functions as its own monolithic cultural frame. In other words, cultural differences are subsumed and rendered irrelevant under the unifying power of the settlement, which provides a vast and all-encompassing explanatory network for heterogeneous experiences, no matter how disparate or atomistic. As a result, the person's own personal history is viewed as equivalent to and undifferentiated from the broader, collective history of which it is a part. For example, Rabbi Danny viewed events in other countries, such as hurricane Sandy and 9/11 in the US, as God's intervention to assist his rise to power as the King of Israel. Similarly, Haseeb described hearing and integrating the prayers of all persons across the globe in order to report them to God who, in turn, reportedly heeded Haseeb's communications when deciding how to control world events: "I feel like a king who is responsible for all Moslems, Jews, Arabs, America, Europe, all the Arab countries. I'm in charge," Haseeb said.

In the destitute moment, cultural experience can be referred to as *the none*. The person attempts to distance herself from other persons, creating a kind of relational void that is, at its essence, also a vacuum of culture and sociality. She may describe herself as fundamentally different from all persons or inhabiting a no-man's land. As Jean stated when reflecting on his life in Jerusalem, "There is nothing here. There is nothing here. And so this life is absent to me. [...] Jerusalem? No life. None." The person experiencing the destitute moment generally avoids activities with others. She does not explicitly identify with specific social or institutional groups (e.g., family, local community, or nation), nor does she have many relationships that she feels she can count on. Insofar as it represents collective memory, traditions, and relational spheres, cultural life in the destitute moment is antithetical to the person's efforts to create radical social distance. Thus, in attempting to evacuate the world of others and to hibernate, the person makes explicit attempts to rebuff cultural practices and ideas, to keep them at a far distance.

Similarities in cultural experience across participants

Urhomelessness occurs in a world comprised of multiple cultural contexts. As such, feelings of vulnerability and alienation in urhomelessness are also feelings of vulnerability and alienation within and from particular cultural milieus, including families, social communities, professions, nation-states, or even human society as such. What culturally diverse participants diagnosed with schizophrenia-spectrum disorders in this study shared was the experience of being dislodged and alienated within and from the world of familiarity and other persons. Moreover, in the present dataset, the three moments of urhomelessness were transcultural experiences that were thematised across the narratives of participants from varied demographic groups, including female, male, and trans participants; North American and Middle Eastern participants; Palestinian, Israeli, and American participants; Muslim, Christian, and Jewish participants; and immigrant and non-immigrant participants. Data analyses also revealed three primary patterns of cultural experience in urhomelessness that we termed *unbelonged*, *epitomised*, and *discriminated against*.

Unbelonged

Participants often described feeling radically different from persons surrounding them, including their own families and cultural groups. The person experiencing urhomeless feels *unbelonged*—belonging both everywhere and nowhere. Isolated and rejected, he may continue to withdraw, exacerbating his experiential distance from other persons. For example, Jean, a French-Israeli participant living in Jerusalem, stated,

> I'm living out of the community of Israelis. I am not Israeli. [...] I'm an outsider, if I am anything. I'm not Christian. I'm not Muslim. I'm not Jewish. Maybe a Hebrew.[1] [...] The loneliness will kill me here, and the people will kill me here.

Although some persons may identify a particular culture or set of cultures as alienating, it is common for all cultural traditions, practices, and groups to be perceived as equally unwelcoming, unfamiliar, or undesirable. For example, Saleh, a Palestinian participant, reported that he felt closer to Jewish than Arab cultures because "they [Jews] are more accepting of the other"; however, he felt like an unfamiliar stranger or, in his words, "the other" in all cultural groups he encountered, including both the Jewish-Israeli and Arab-Palestinian cultural contexts in which he was ontically immersed:

Saleh:	I also do not feel I belong to my culture. [...] There are things in my parents' culture which are wrong, I do not accept it. I started to feel that I was different from them and not one of them. So I'm looking for a different culture. But it has disadvantages too, so I'm really starting to feel lonely.
Interviewer:	You feel that your culture does not belong to you? What does that feel like?
Saleh:	What does that feel like? I feel isolated, as if there is no one to talk to. But even their dress is the same. Jeans and t-shirt same, same hair, same pants, same glasses. Like robots replicating each other, only I am not [one of them].
Interviewer:	Do you feel that way in every culture?
Saleh:	Yes, every culture has different robots.

To Saleh, other people seemed like "robots" who look and act like one another in superficial ways, creating communities of automaton-like humans from which he was completely excluded, or unbelonged.

Epitomised

In contrast to the experience of radical cultural difference, some participants described an ability to perfect or epitomise cultural mores, traditions, beliefs, ideas, artistic productions, and/or values in unique and often imaginative ways. However, their claim to perfection and epitomisation of these aspects of culture led to alienation from other persons, who did not have the same epitomising beliefs. Although epitomisation can be expressed in all three moments of urhomelessness, it is most common for persons experiencing the settled moment.

Yuval, an Israeli Jew, spent his days praying at a holy site in Jerusalem that is also frequented by other observant Jews. Yet Yuval stood and prayed for much longer than most others, believing that he lived at the holy site and that he had "surpassed the greatest of the righteous," but "*without* being proud." Although Yuval reported that he was admired and appreciated by all those who visited the holy site, including tourists and Muslims, his attempt to perfect and outdo the other pious visitors ultimately exacerbated his feelings of alienation, such that he did not experience intimate relationships and friendships, but only perceived admiration from a distance.

Similarly, through his belief that he was the King of Israel and the potential Messiah, Rabbi Danny assumed a role in which he epitomised a specific cultural belief that was central to diverse Jewish theological traditions. Rabbi Danny saw himself as fulfilling the prophecies concerning the coming of the Messiah and the eschatological redemption of the Jewish people. Despite the fact that this cultural belief was derived from collective cultural narratives that were not invented by Rabbi Danny, others did not share his belief that he embodied the role, which contributed to Rabbi Danny's feelings of loneliness.

In epitomisation, the attempt to perfect cultural roles and practices—rather than garnering admiration or appreciation—often increases feelings of isolation, as others may disagree with or even resent the person's attempts. For this reason, the attempt to epitomise ultimately exacerbates rather than alleviates the urhomeless experience of profound alienation and invalidation.

Discriminated against

Some participants reported feeling discriminated against, neglected, and/or mistreated as a result of cultural differences against which others held biases. For example, Avery was berated by her parents, especially her father, for her identification as a woman and desire to wear women's clothing:

Avery: Both of them [both parents] didn't like me to be a female.
Interviewer: Oh, they didn't want you to be a female?
Avery: Yeah. But I was in my apartment putting lipsticks, and I bought female shoes.
[...]
Interviewer: Are there any people you don't like?
Avery: I don't like my father.
Interviewer: Okay. Because he was mean to you?
Avery: [...] It's because he didn't want me to wear the female shoes.

In another example, Rabbi Danny described being repeatedly attacked by xenophobic persons: "I was attacked by anti-Semites. From age five I had to learn how to fight. I was constantly being attacked by anti-Semites." Similarly, Charles, an older African American man, described a preference for living in the "free states" in the north, where he presumably encountered less racial discrimination and oppression than in southern states. Another African American participant, Douglas, reported being tortured by the Ku Klux Klan (KKK). Some participants demonstrated feeling discriminated against during the interview itself; for example, Asad sometimes suspected that the interviewers might be members of the Israeli secret service,[2] whom he believed had arrested and institutionalised him under false pretences because of his Palestinian identity. For many participants experiencing urhomelessness, experiences of discrimination on the basis of cultural differences were part and parcel of feeling consistently and profoundly unsafe, as well as alienated by other humans in the world.

Notes

1 A reference to Jews who lived in Biblical times. Jean does not feel a sense of kinship with the present-day Israelis and Palestinians among whom he lives.

2 When this occurred, Asad was reminded that the researchers were not Israeli secret service. Due to his expressed suspicion, his interviews were temporarily stopped. When he requested to resume the interviews, his understanding of the nature of the research and comfort in participating in the interviews were confirmed before continuing.

11

DIAGNOSTIC HETEROGENEITIES

Sarah R. Kamens

Overview

How can we understand the findings of our research study—and in particular the general structure of urhomelessness—in the context of contemporary debates about diagnostic and cultural heterogeneity in schizophrenia? This chapter discusses the relationship of the present findings to schizophrenia-spectrum and other psychotic-disorder diagnoses as defined by the DSM (APA, 1994, 2000, 2013) and ICD (1992a, 1992b, 2015), with particular focus on evidence for a psychosis continuum and the problem of experiential heterogeneity across categorical diagnoses. The present results are also considered in the context of literature on cultural experience and cultural heterogeneity. This chapter concludes with a discussion of the present findings in the context of newly proposed models for reconceptualising and/or renaming schizophrenia.

The heterogeneity problem

As described in Chapter 1, the heterogeneity problem has come into the limelight in recent decades due to the fact that neuroscientific, genetic, and other biopsychiatric research has not yielded the expected biological substrates (a.k.a. biomarkers), for DSM- and ICD-defined disorder categories (e.g., MacDonald, 2014; Morris et al., 2003; Tienari et al., 2006). At the same time, mounting evidence, particularly from the realm of cross-cultural psychology, has indicated that the phenotypes (i.e., the observable profiles) of mental disorders are likewise heterogeneous, with wide variation both within and across diagnostic categories (e.g., Bhugra, 2007; Houts, 2002; Regier et al., 2009; Zimmerman, et al., 2010). Biologically oriented psychiatrists have increasingly asserted that psychiatric disorders, as currently defined, are heterogeneous and multifactorial on both the phenotypic and genotypic levels, leading some to propose that official disorder categories may have been "lumped" into or "split" from undiscovered disorder types as they may exist in nature (Bhugra, 2007; Houts, 2002). As a result, in recent years, researchers

DOI: 10.4324/9780429055454-12

have increasingly proposed new models for reconceptualising the taxonomic infrastructure of diagnostic psychiatry and clinical psychology (e.g., Insel, 2013; Kamphuis & Noordhof, 2009; Kincaid & Sullivan, 2014). Schizophrenia-spectrum and psychotic disorders have been categories of particular focus, with ample and mounting research documenting both phenotypic and genotypic heterogeneity (e.g., Andreasen, 1985; Carpenter & Kirkpatrick, 2005; Jones & Shattell, 2016; Joyce & Roiser, 2007; Kendler, 2011; Kirkpatrick, 2011; Kremen et al., 2004; Seaton et al., 1999; Tsuang et al., 1990), as well as wide cultural variation (e.g., Good & Subandi, 2004; Jablensky, 1987; Luhrmann, 2015). Moreover, the past decade has seen a flurry of newly proposed models for subtyping, "deconstructing," reframing, or renaming the disorder category (e.g., BPS, 2017; Buchanan, 2007; Carpenter, 2011a, 2011b; Lasalvia et al., 2015).

Urhomelessness in the context of DSM- and ICD-defined schizophrenia-spectrum disorders

The general psychological structure, invariant constituents, and common variations of urhomelessness differ starkly from the clinical-diagnostic definitions of schizophrenia-spectrum and other psychotic disorders in the DSM and ICD in four important ways. First, general structure differs from established nomenclatures on the basis of the presumed sensitivity and specificity (accuracy in identifying true positives and true negatives, respectively) attributed to specific signs and symptoms when they meet a certain threshold or criteria set. DSM and ICD criteria for schizophrenia are met when a person has exhibited a specific number of symptoms for a specific duration of time. More specifically, in DSM-5 (APA, 2013), the person must meet two or more symptom criteria for a significant portion of a one-month duration (or less if successfully treated), with continuous signs for at least six months. Functionally, in DSM-5, schizophrenia and related diagnoses are polythetic diagnostic categories, meaning that no single criterion is necessary or sufficient for a diagnosis.[1] However, polythetic symptom criteria are assumed to have diagnostic sensitivity and specificity in combination, i.e., by virtue of their cumulative quantities rather than their qualitative meanings or contents. As a result, two people whose symptoms do not overlap in form or thematic content can nonetheless both carry a diagnosis of schizophrenia.

Urhomelessness, in contrast, is not a diagnosis or diagnostic criterion. It is identified when the general psychological structure is clearly given in a person's experience, regardless of the number or type of DSM or ICD criteria for schizophrenia-spectrum and other psychotic disorders that are present. The general structure of urhomelessness comprises the twofold experience of feeling profoundly vulnerable and alienated within the world; the actualisation of this general structure is not monothetically (e.g., pathognomonically) contingent upon the presence of any one symptom of psychosis, such as delusions or disorganised speech, nor is it necessarily present when two or more of these experiences occur in combination. In other words, DSM or ICD symptom criteria are neither necessary nor sufficient for the identification of urhomelessness. Hallucinations, idiosyncratic beliefs, disorganised thought or speech, and other unusual experiences or behaviours can be present in the *absence* of the general structure (see van Os et al., 2009) and are thus not essential constituents of it.

Second, in urhomelessness, the essence of the general structure is given, even if partially, in each constituent, common variation, and example.[2] The general structure is thus meaningfully reflected in each of its essential constituents, which are in turn interrelated through their meaningful relationship to the general structure as a whole. In contrast, in DSM- and ICD-defined schizophrenia-spectrum disorders—as in other DSM- and ICD-defined disorder categories, there is no specified (i.e., an "agnostic") relationship between symptoms other than (a) their factical co-occurrence and (b) the implicit presumption that they signify as-yet-undiscovered biological and/or psychological substrates (or "natural kinds"; Haslam, 2002, 2014) that theoretically might, once scientifically discovered, assume the status of taxonomic grouping principles grounded in empirical evidence (Compton & Guze, 1995; Robins & Guze, 1970).

The third major difference between the present findings and established nomenclatures concerns the conceptual or thematic definitions of schizophrenia-spectrum and other psychotic disorders. Urhomelessness does not coincide with the common historical view that "the patient has lost reality contact" (Shean, 2010, p. x). (For example, DSM-IV defined psychosis as "a loss of ego boundaries or a gross impairment in reality testing" [APA, 1994, p. 273; see also APA, 2000, p. 297].) Instead, feelings of being profoundly unsafe and unacknowledged by others occur in urhomelessness irrespective of the veridicality of these experiences according to social consensus. Note that although the settled moment involves imaginal constructions, imagination does not always eclipse orientation to consensual meanings (see also Jones et al., 2016; Sass, 1994b).

Recent iterations of the DSM (APA, 2000, 2013) define psychotic disorders by the mere presence of component symptoms rather than by any overarching theoretical concept or pathognomonic symptom. The DSM-5 (APA, 2013) lists the following possible symptoms of schizophrenia: (1) delusions, (2) hallucinations, (3) disorganised speech, (4) disorganised or catatonic behaviour, and (5) negative symptoms such as flat affect, avolition, and alogia. A diagnosis of schizophrenia requires two or more of these symptoms (and at least one of these must be delusions, hallucinations, or disorganised speech [Criterion A]). As aforementioned, no one symptom or combination of symptoms from the DSM-5 criteria for schizophrenia-spectrum disorders is necessary or sufficient for the identification of urhomelessness.

Thematically, the similarities between urhomelessness and DSM-5 symptom criteria are partial at best. For example, DSM-5 defines delusions as "fixed beliefs that are not amenable to change in light of conflicting evidence" (p. 87). Such beliefs are not essential to or always present in urhomelessness; while some persons may demonstrate relatively fixed beliefs (particularly in the settled moment), others may have fluid and flexible belief systems (especially in the nomadic moment). Likewise, while some persons experiencing urhomelessness report sensing the wandering of external beings, DSM-defined hallucinations, or "perception-like experiences that occur without an external stimulus" (APA, 2013, p. 87), are not essential to or always present in urhomelessness.

As exemplified in the narratives of the pilot-comparison participants, anomalous beliefs and perceptual experiences often occur in persons for whom the general structure of urhomelessness is not actualised. Similarly, disorganised speech and behaviour may be characteristic of some urhomeless experiences (e.g., nomadic thought), but disorganisation also occurs in numerous common situations that do not involve urhomelessness. Moreover, some persons experiencing urhomelessness exhibit highly structured and organised ways of thinking and behaving; indeed, maintaining order and structure may be particularly important for persons experiencing the settled moment. "Negative symptoms" and catatonia,[3] although common in the destitute moment, are likewise non-essential to urhomelessness and can occur in an array of other conditions and situations (e.g., major loss, violent oppression). In sum, the existential-psychological meanings of urhomelessness do not directly correspond to any one symptom or combination of symptoms in this class of disorders as currently defined by the DSM.

A fourth difference between the present findings and conventional diagnostic definitions concerns the DSM and ICD duration criteria specifying the amount of time that symptoms must be present in order to qualify for a diagnosis. In some cases, duration criteria are contingency specifiers for differential diagnosis. For example, in DSM-5 (APA, 2013), brief psychotic disorder lasts between one day and one month, schizophreniform disorder has a duration of between one and six months, and schizophrenia is diagnosed when symptoms persist for six or more months, including one month of active symptoms. In the present study, we found that while some urhomeless experiences last indefinitely, others can be brief or transient,[4] such that no specific duration is necessary for identification of the full actualisation of the general structure. The present findings also indicated that experiences of urhomelessness alternate and even occur simultaneously with experiences of recovery. These findings support previous research suggesting that the course of most mental disorders is nonlinear, not necessarily chronic, and often leads to recovery (e.g., Davidson, 2003; Davidson et al., 2008; Strauss, 1989; Strauss et al., 1985).

Comorbidity

Most participants in the present sample were not dually diagnosed with psychotic disorders and other non-psychotic disorders or syndromes. Therefore, it was not possible to analyse whether the general structure can be present in diagnostic comorbidity presentations. However, two primary participants experiencing urhomelessness were diagnosed with both psychotic disorders and substance-use disorders (with one in remission), and one participant's diagnosis specified concomitant suicidal ideation. In addition, Saleh's interview suggested a rule-out of OCD, which he did not carry as an official diagnosis; his symptoms included lengthy ruminations about what he might have said "wrong" during social interactions and mental attempts to revise the conversations. These experiences were implicated in his experience of urhomelessness, and more specifically in his broader alienation from the world of others. Thus, urhomeless experiences may overlap with symptoms commonly associated with other DSM and ICD diagnoses such as substance-use disorders and OCD. These observations, though non-comprehensive, reflect growing consensus that psychosis is an "open concept" with boundaries that seem to bridge onto related psychological phenomena (MacDonald, 2014, p. 338; Tamminga et al., 2010).

Experiential heterogeneity

The present findings reveal that extensive experiential variation, i.e., experiential heterogeneity, is an essential quality of urhomelessness, which involves an existential dislodging from familiar worldly coordinates, such that the person feels cast into the unfamiliar and unpredictable world-at-large. More specifically, there was experiential heterogeneity both between and within the three moments of urhomelessness, as well as between the common variations of each moment. Experiential variation was characteristic of all three moments but particularly immanent to the nomadic moment, which involves exposure to the vicissitudes of the world-at-large and a thematic reversal of the familiar and the unfamiliar. Moreover, there is wide individual variation in the duration and actualisation of the moments, such that while some persons may remain in one moment indefinitely, others move between them in relatively slow or rapid succession. Still others experience more than one moment simultaneously. Others, like Crystal, cycle between episodes of urhomelessness and urhomeness (recovery). In addition, some persons emerge indefinitely or fully from urhomelessness, such that they are fully recovered or, alternatively, experiencing urhomeness for the first time.

The present findings suggest that the diagnostic heterogeneity of the schizophrenia spectrum is not an artefact of inaccurate taxonomising (e.g., Buchanan & Carpenter, 1994; Carpenter, 2013), but rather fully consistent with the general structure, which encompasses vast possibilities of responding to the basic crisis state. In other words, there are extensive possible responses to the experience of feeling profoundly unsafe and alienated; even the three moments of urhomelessness have numerous common variations. Due to this essential experiential heterogeneity within and between its moments—as well as its potential simultaneity with the horizon of urhomeness or recovery—urhomelessness may be largely resistant to discrete categorical taxonomising. In other words, any attempt to parse its diverse moments or constituents into discrete categories is likely to result in the heterogeneity problem, i.e., the cluster of taxonomic dilemmas characterised by phenotypic overlap or fuzzy boundaries (e.g., Boyd et al., 1984; Frances, 2009b; Krueger & Markon, 2006), absent zones of rarity (Kendell & Jablensky, 2003), and/or comorbid disorder categories (Boyd et al., 1994; Kessler et al., 1994; Kessler et al., 2005).

Support for a psychosis continuum

As described in Chapter 2, previous literature suggests that psychosis lies on a continuum from non-distressing anomalous experiences to psychotic symptoms and disorders (see Strauss et al., 1983). More specifically, increasing evidence suggests that psychotic experiences commonly occur in non-clinical populations—and in non-distressing forms. For example, van Os et al. (e.g., 2009) and McGrath et al. (2015) have collected extensive epidemiological evidence supporting a continuum of psychosis ranging from non-distressing experiences, which occur in approximately 6 to 8% of non-clinical populations, to psychotic symptoms and, at the other end of the spectrum, psychotic disorders (Jackson, 2007; Verdoux & van Os, 2002).

Importantly, service-user and other grassroots movements (e.g., Hearing Voices Network, 2019; Icarus Project, 2019; Jones & Shattell, 2013; Schnackenberg & Martin, 2014) have emphasised the fact that anomalous experiences are not always distressing or disruptive, can be experienced as a meaningful part of everyday life, and can be understood in the context of present and past experiences. Moreover, some persons may view anomalous experiences as a key to securing authentic spiritual, professional, and communal lives (e.g., evangelistic Christians [Luhrmann, 2012], spiritist mediums [Moreira-Almeida, 2009], and emerging service-user groups [e.g., ICP, 2015]). Expertise by experience is increasingly valued as unique and crucial knowledge about the varieties of human experience; some Experts by Experience use their knowledge to support and heal others (see Cornwall, 2018b; Esima, 2017; Frese, 2009; King, 2007; Russell, 2018; see also Kalweit, 1989). These growing movements, first-person accounts, and alternative approaches support the need for recognition of a psychosis continuum that includes non-pathological conceptualisations of non-distressing experiences.

There are four aspects of our research findings that support previous evidence for a psychosis continuum. First, even among hospital participants receiving an inpatient level of care, the experience of urhomelessness was not necessarily pervasive or omnipresent, such that while some participants described indefinite urhomeless experiences, others described or demonstrated intermittent experiences interspersed with partial or full experiences of urhomeness. Second, features or thematic reflections of urhomelessness, but not the fully actualised structure, were discernible in the narratives of the three ad hoc comparison participants. Third, although the general structure of urhomelessness was not fully actualised for pilot-comparison participants, they nonetheless described non-distressing (and sometimes even emotionally or intellectually stimulating) anomalous experiences, as well as distressing but transient encounters with urhomelessness that occurred during non-sobriety, semi-wakefulness, childhood reveries, and/or times of notable stress or life change. The fact that the general structure was fleetingly encountered on the horizons of pilot-comparison participants' experiences indicated that urhomelessness may be a fundamental potentiality of the human condition that is only sometimes actualised in the foreground of experience. Fourth, one pilot-comparison participant, Claire, transformed her fleeting, partial encounters with urhomelessness into a means of securing urhomeness through her art. These findings indicate that urhomelessness is not a pervasive, chronic condition, but rather a type of experience that can be partial and brief.

Research on the psychosis continuum (e.g., McGrath et al., 2015; van Os et al., 2009; Verdoux & van Os, 2002) points to the possibility that symptom-tallying approaches may not have sufficient diagnostic specificity to exclude non-pathological or non-distressing forms of psychosis. In addition, some have suggested that the very presence of certain types of experiences in a diagnostic manual for mental disorders may iatrogenically generate distress, for example in the form of fear that one is going "mad" or via the generation of social stigma (e.g., Link & Phelan, 1999; Ungar & Knaak, 2013; Yang et al., 2015; see also BPS, 2017); this possibility was reflected in the narrative of Oliver, who became increasingly afraid of losing his memory and his command of language while in the hospital, where he was diagnosed with a psychotic disorder. In order to obviate this risk, symptom tallying approaches might be replaced with an alternative means of identifying the relationship between distress and lived experiences along the continuum of psychosis. The project presented in this book was intended to contribute towards the development of one such alternative (see "The Contribution of Phenomenology," below).

Cultural experiences in urhomelessness

Cultural heterogeneity

As described in Chapter 10, analyses revealed wide experiential variation within the overarching, transcultural general structure. Some participants with similar demographic backgrounds described divergent types of urhomeless experiences (i.e., different moments and variations), while some participants with different demographic backgrounds described similar moments or common variations of urhomelessness. Cross-cultural comparisons were not conducted due to the demographic diversity of the sample; however, thematic trends among participants with demographic similarities revealed potential areas for further investigation. These thematic trends reflect a growing body of research indicating that cultural themes and differences may be meaningfully reflected in the form and content of psychotic experiences (e.g., Barrett, 2004; Brekke & Barrio, 1997; Corin et al., 2005; De et al., 2013; Luhrmann et al., 2015).

The first demographic trend was the full intuitive clarity with which the destitute moment was given for all four Palestinian participants. In contrast, not all Israeli and American participants experienced this moment as actualised, despite the fact that it was thematised as a horizon for all participants. Although this trend may be coincidental, previous research suggests several explanatory possibilities. First, compared to their Israeli peers, Palestinian children are more hopeless and pessimistic about the sociopolitical future of the region, and as a group, they become less optimistic and angrier with age (Sagy et al., 2002). In other words, the common experiences of discrimination and sociopolitical oppression in Palestinian populations may generate hopelessness and pessimism with regard to their future. It may be the case that this sociocultural hopelessness is related to the prominence of the destitute moment for Palestinian participants. Within this context, it is also notable that the hospital at which data were collected has an ethnically mixed group of staff and service users but is located in a predominantly Jewish neighbourhood of West Jerusalem; although staff are multilingual, Hebrew is its primary and official language. Therefore, the hospital context may have highlighted or generated feelings of social exclusion in Palestinian participants, some of whom had also experienced political violence at the hands of the Israeli military; notably, one Palestinian participant (Asad) intermittently suspected that the researchers might be members of the Israeli secret service (see Chapter 10). Second, because the Palestinian participants were subject to segregation and discrimination due to governmental sociopolitical practices in Jerusalem, this finding may reflect previous research demonstrating that neighbourhood ethnic segregation, discrimination, and deprivation are associated with increased risk of psychosis in general (e.g., Bhavsar et al., 2018; Kirkbride et al., 2014) and the normative, adaptive response of cultural paranoia in particular (Whaley, 1997, 2002; Whaley & Hall, 2009).

The second demographic trend was a particular variation of the settlement that was revealed as characteristic of both Jewish-Israeli participants in the settled moment. In becoming the Jewish Messiah (Rabbi Danny) and the most righteous of all pious persons at a holy site (Yuval), these two participants adopted preexisting cultural narratives or practices more or less in whole, exaggerating and extending them without any idiosyncratic alterations. In contrast, for most Palestinian and American participants in the settled moment, the settlement was an idiosyncratic, patchwork creation involving varied cultural ideas that were substantially modified in an unusual way, such as Douglas's belief that multiple celebrities were connected through an ethereal network called The System. Future interdisciplinary (sociological and psychological) research is necessary to determine whether certain cultural ideas are, once encountered, more readily available to function as settlements, and whether other cultural ideas carry tendencies towards integration into nomadic and destitute moments (e.g., Haseeb's experience of destitution while complaining about *waswas* or the whispers of Satan, which is one theological explanation of temptation in Islam). From this perspective, Jerusalem Syndrome (Bar-el et al., 2000) may be a particular variation of the settled moment that is meaningfully related to cultural beliefs about the eschatological restoration of safety and community life (or lost heritages; see Butler, 2016)—i.e., the restoration of the very experiences that are lacking in urhomelessness.

The current findings suggest that Jerusalem syndrome (in which symptoms reflect the historical and religious meanings of the city [Bar-el et al., 2000]), other city syndromes (Halim, 2008; Viala et al., 2004), and other context-specific phenomena like psychotic airport wandering (Jauhar & Weller, 1982; Shapiro, 1977, 1982) may represent ways in which the experience of urhomelessness is shaped by specific cultural, contextual factors (see also Hopper, 2003). Thus, debates concerning whether Jerusalem syndrome and other city syndromes are an independent or classic expression of psychosis (e.g., Guarnaccia & Rogler, 1999; Fastovsky et al., 2000; Kalian & Witztum, 1999, 2000; Kleinman, 1987; Lock, 1987; Marsella, 1993; Prince & Tcheng-Laroche, 1987; Watters, 2010) may reflect an exaggerated and false dichotomy. It is possible that Jerusalem syndrome is neither an independent form of psychosis nor identical to schizophrenia as classically defined. In the context of the present findings, it can be seen as a unique, non-essential variation of the settled moment of urhomelessness that arises in the specific cultural context of Jerusalem.

Cultural heterogeneity across the moments

The three moments of urhomelessness were each characterised by a unique pattern of cultural experience that we termed *the many*, *the one*, and *the none* (see Chapter 10). The three patterns corresponded to relative degrees of engagement with other persons and worldly surroundings, reflecting the multiplicity and fluctuations of cultural experience in the nomadic moment (the many), the relatively fixed focus on a unitary cultural theme in the settled moment (the one), and the person's attempt to remain distant from the cultural world in the destitute moment (the none). In other words, these experiential variations represent three distinct ways in which cultural life is integrated into urhomeless experiences. These findings reflect previous literature on the cultural heterogeneity of psychotic experiences (e.g., Corin et al., 2005; Jablensky, 1987; Jenkins & Barrett, 2004; Luhrmann et al., 2015; Marsella, 2016) and suggest that cultural diversity in psychotic experiences may be due to both the uniqueness of specific cultural contexts and to the person's general orientation towards the cultural world.

Similarities in cultural experience

In the present findings, all 18 inpatient and outpatient hospital participants who experienced the fully actualised general structure of urhomelessness experienced feeling unsafe, unacknowledged, vulnerable, and alienated from their particular cultural contexts, such that they did not have a sense of stable (non-imagined) belonging in any particular sociocultural context. Participants' cultural experiences were generally characterised by three themes: *unbelonged* (belonging both everywhere and nowhere), *epitomised* (epitomising cultural ideas and values), and *discriminated against* (mistreated as a result of cultural differences; see Chapter 10 for more information). These findings reflect mounting research suggesting that persons diagnosed with schizophrenia and other psychotic disorders often experience feelings of stigma, alienation, and lack of belonging *vis-a-vis* dominant social groups (e.g., Bourque et al., 2011; Lasalvia et al., 2015; van Nierop et al., 2014). They also reflect recent research and scholarship suggesting that the experiences of social marginalisation and discrimination are a central social determinant (rather than secondary symptom) and risk factor for schizophrenia and other psychotic disorders (see, e.g., Durgan, 2013; Kirkbride et al., 2014; Luhrmann, 2007; Jablensky & Sartorius, 2008; Selten & Cantor-Graae, 2005; Selten et al., 2013).

Present findings compared to newly proposed models

Proposals to subtype or revise the existing phenotype

As described in Chapter 2, recent calls to reconceptualise the schizophrenia diagnosis include proposals for subtyping the category into subtaxa or subclasses of component symptoms (e.g., Arango et al., 2007; Kirkpatrick et al., 2001). One popular subtyping proposal is the tripartite division of schizophrenia into positive, negative, and mixed syndrome subtypes (e.g., Andreasen & Olsen, 1982). As a post-hoc screening tool to verify the heterogeneity in the sample of participants across symptom profiles, the present study utilised the PANSS (Kay et al., 2006), a gold-standard measure for identifying positive, negative, and mixed psychotic-syndrome subtypes.

Comparisons between these qualitative findings and the PANSS data revealed that participants for whom the settled moment was given in full intuitive clarity had a positive syndrome profile according to at least one method of subtyping (Kay et al., 2006). This relationship is most likely due to the common interpretation of imaginal worlds—and in this case imaginal urhomes, or settlements—as delusions, or false beliefs. However, some participants experiencing the nomadic or destitute moments also had positive syndrome subtypes according to one or both subtyping methods. Moreover, there was no discernible relationship between the nomadic and destitute moments and the positive, negative, or mixed PANSS subtypes. The findings of the present study thus suggest that the moments of urhomelessness can occur across PANSS symptom profiles, and that proposals to divide the schizophrenia diagnosis into symptom classes might not "carve nature" (Plato, 370 B.C./1952; Regier et al., 2009, para. 15) at the joints of urhomeless experiences.

At a theoretical level, the PANSS (Key et al., 2006) system shares two overarching structural assumptions with the present findings. First, the PANSS, which is often used for longitudinal assessment of symptom variation, was constructed for focused assessments of symptom type and severity during time-limited periods, often the previous week (the present study utilised the informal upper-bound of one month [M. Opler, personal communication, October 17, 2012]). In other words, the PANSS was constructed with the assumption that psychotic experiences, like the moments of urhomelessness, typically fluctuate such that it is common to observe substantial and documentable variation—including both mitigations and exacerbations in symptoms—over a relatively short period of time. Secondly, the PANSS assumes that positive and negative symptoms may occur in isolation or concurrently, and that the degree to which they do so varies between individuals as well as within individuals over the course of time. There is a strong resonance between these two structural assumptions and the findings of the present study, which, though cross-sectional, revealed great variation in the experience of urhomelessness between and across the participants' life-historical narratives. Moreover, for some participants, the expression of the moments varied between interview sessions and/or during a singular interview session; some participants even experienced more than one moment of urhomelessness simultaneously.

Proposals to "deconstruct" schizophrenia

Another popular proposal for remodelling the schizophrenia diagnosis is to "deconstruct" the category into its component symptoms and/or domains in the hopes of finding underlying substrates that will eventually allow for its "reconstruction" around putative biomarkers (e.g., Carpenter, 2011a, 2011b; Tamminga et al., 2010; van Os & Tamminga, 2007). NIMH's (2019)

RDoC project is an example of an attempt to deconstruct categorical diagnoses into domains such as cognitive and social systems, which will be further divided into genetic, molecular, neurocircuit, behavioural, and self-report units of analysis. Presently, it is unclear whether RDoC and other proposals to deconstruct psychosis will result in future disorder constructs that involve atomistic lists and symptom tallies comparable to the DSM and ICD or, conversely, an as-yet-unknown alternative approach. Due to the fact that RDoC is still nascent and incomplete, the relationship of the present findings to its eventual content and structure cannot yet be evaluated.

In general, the present findings demonstrate one way in which phenomenological methods can be used to clarify the relevance of taxonomic constructs to subjective, lived experience. If biological substrates are eventually discovered, their clinical and ecological relevance will be contingent upon correspondence to meaningful aspects of lived experience. It may be the case that a relationship exists between the biological substrates of psychological distress and the constituents or moments of urhomelessness. In the words of Sass & Parnas (2007), "[i]t would, after all, hardly make sense to articulate biological hypotheses that clearly contradict human experience" (p. 73).

Proposals to rename schizophrenia

As detailed by Lasalvia et al. (2015), various interest groups—including mental health service users, families, and professionals—view the schizophrenia label as stigmatising and potentially harmful to those who are "living under the description" of the diagnosis (Martin, 2009, p. 88). At present, there are numerous competing proposals to rename schizophrenia; notably, the official diagnostic title has already been changed in Japan (Sato, 2006). The present findings are conceptually divergent from neo-Kraepelinian, atomistic, criteria-based diagnostic models (e.g., APA, 2013; Compton & Guze, 1995; Robins & Guze, 1970), suggesting the need for more than a mere nominal change to the schizophrenia label. As described in Chapter 2, most newly proposed models for renaming schizophrenia represent both a nominal and a conceptual change.

Recently proposed diagnostic labels include "salience disorder" (van Os, 2009), "dysfunctional perception syndrome" (DPS; George, 2012), "youth onset conative, cognitive and reality distortion" (CONCORD) syndromes (Keshavan et al., 2011), "integration disorder" (Sato, 2006), "psychotic spectrum disorder" (Peralta, 1999, cited in Henderson & Malhi, 2014), "neuro-emotional integration disorder" (NEID; Levin, 2006), "dopamine dysregulation disorder" (see Lieberman & First, 2007), "Bleuler's syndrome" (George, 2012), "Kraepelin–Bleuler disease" (KBD; Kim & Berrios, 2003), and "psychosis susceptibility syndrome" (PSS; George & Klijn, 2013a, 2013b). Because PSS is a title that describes the intermittent and non-chronic nature of psychotic episodes, it reflects the present finding that urhomeness (e.g., recovery) and urhomelessness are both potentials of the human condition and horizons of each other. However, none of these newly proposed labels capture the psychological meanings inherent to urhomelessness, including feelings of being profoundly unsafe and alienated from one or more human communities (see Chapter 5).

Proposals to reframe psychosis

The present findings support previous calls to reframe psychotic disorders from a person-centred, recovery-oriented perspective and praxis (e.g., BPS, 2017; Davidson, 2008; Davidson et al., 2008; Deegan, 1996; Jones & Shattell, 2013; Law & Morrison, 2014; Read et al., 2004; Schnackenberg & Martin, 2014; Tirupati & Ramachandran, 2020). More specifically, our findings highlight the discrepancies between person-centred, subjective descriptions of lived experience and the criterion-based lists of clinical symptoms presented in the DSM. In addition, our findings highlight the possibility of recovery in and from experiences of psychosis. The possibility of living a self-actualised and fulfilling life—with or without ongoing anomalous experiences—was a horizon of urhomelessness for all participants. Even those experiencing the destitute moment demonstrated implicit knowledge of this horizon in a paradoxical way by relinquishing all attempts to search for it. Some participants receiving an outpatient level of care had already secured ways of experiencing urhomeness in their everyday lives. For example, one participant, Crystal, was fully recovered from the destitute moment at the time of the interview; she described meaningful and enjoyable experiences among family, friends, and peers. In addition, Roger oscillated between urhomeness and urhomelessness, and he felt especially in control of his own mind when in his own apartment and taking medications. These findings suggest that urhomeness is an omnipresent, immanent horizon of urhomelessness that is potentially actualisable for all persons experiencing any moment of the general structure.

Our findings also support efforts to reconceptualise psychotic experiences in ways that are non-pathologising and account for the diversity of experiences. The BPS (2017) report *Understanding psychosis and schizophrenia* represents one such effort, as does the BPS (2018) PTM framework, which conceptualises mental distress more broadly as it relates to power, threat, and the meanings that persons make from their experiences (see also Rahimi, 2015). The general structure of urhomelessness is particularly consonant with the PTM framework's emphasis on the relationship between contextual hardships, social disadvantage, and emotional distress. The present findings also resonate with the Hearing Voices Network's (2019) emphasis on the diversity of explanations—including psychological, existential, cultural, structural, and spiritual explanations for voice-hearing experiences.

Last but not least, the present findings resonate with growing movements to understand first-person experiences of psychosis as uniquely meaningful and valuable. The Experts by Experience movement, for example, puts service users at the front and centre of understanding, studying, and re-conceptualising mental distress (e.g., Law & Morrison, 2014; Waddingham, 2012; see also Jones & Kelly, 2015). Some Experts by Experience (e.g., Cornwall, 2018b; Esima, 2017; Frese, 2009; King, 2007; Russell, 2018; see also Jung, 2009) have drawn upon their own personal challenges and recovery to support others going through difficult periods. Likewise, the Mad pride and Mad studies movements (e.g., Schrader et al., 2013; Russo & Beresford, 2015) have viewed the experience of altered states as a unique way-of-being and identity that forms the basis of alternative communities and frameworks for understanding the world. While the experiences of ur-homelessness are distressing and difficult, those who have secured new ways—or resecured old ways—of achieving urhomeness might be in a unique position to help and support others.

The contribution of phenomenology

One objective of the present study was to evaluate the potential contribution of the findings of systematic phenomenological description to the resolution of taxonomic dilemmas such as the heterogeneity problem. It might seem unlikely, given the current predominance of biobehavioural approaches, that phenomenological understandings of lived experience will be incorporated into future diagnostic nomenclatures. However, phenomenological approaches should be viewed as complimentary, not contradictory, to any authentically biopsychosocial model. Parnas & Zahavi (2002) proposed that the description of lived experience "must be considered as a necessary first step in any taxonomic effort, including attempts of reducing abnormal experience to its potential biological substrate" (p. 137; see also Sass & Parnas, 2007). Similarly, Flanagan et al. (2010) have emphasised the need for and potential ease of incorporating service user-subjective data into the DSM (APA, 1994, 2000, 2013) and ICD (1992a, 1992b, 2015). The present results support the work of these and other previous scholars who have suggested that phenomenological research methods offer rich and unique contributions that may enhance the subjective relevance—and thus the face and ecological validity—of diagnostic taxonomising (see Strauss, 2011, 2013; Strauss & Carpenter, 1981).

Categorical models

The DSM (APA, 1994, 2000, 2013) and ICD (1992a, 1992b, 2015) are categorical diagnostic systems with supplementary dimensional ratings for severity of symptoms. Categorical taxonomies treat each category as distinct and discrete, such that persons are sorted dichotomously as either members or non-members of each class, with no possibilities for partial or graded membership (see Krueger & Markon, 2006b). As described in Chapter 1, robust evidence for vast between- and within-diagnosis heterogeneity (e.g., fuzzy boundaries and comorbidity) has been interpreted as a threat to the validity of categorical diagnostic models (see Buchanan & Carpenter, 1994; Carpenter, 2013), especially the neo-Kraepelinian system for criteria-based diagnosis (Guze, 1994; Feighner et al., 1972; Robins & Guze, 1970), as it suggests that diagnostic categories may not be empirically dichotomous, discrete, or unitary.

Phenomenological description allows for delineation of kinds as they are given in experience, even if they are characterised by fuzzy boundaries, unclear thresholds, continua, and overlap with related experiences—in short, vast heterogeneity. Indeed, the present results suggest that experiential heterogeneity is not merely "noise in the system," but rather inherent to the experiences commonly labelled as schizophrenia-spectrum disorders, such that any attempt to sort or parse signs and symptoms into discrete or quasi-discrete categories is likely to reproduce the group of taxonomic dilemmas collectively known as the heterogeneity problem (e.g., Boyd et al., 1984; Frances, 2009b; Kendell & Jablensky, 2003; Kessler et al., 2005; Kessler et al., 1994; Krueger & Markon, 2006; see also Sass, 1992a, 2007). Urhomelessness is not a dichotomous category that is either wholly present or absent, but a kind of experience that can be partial, temporary, and non-pervasive; while some persons encounter it fleetingly, others enter into it indefinitely. The heterogeneity of urhomelessness is essential to the general structure, i.e., part and parcel of its coherence as a whole. More specifically, there is wide between-person variation in the constellation of moments and common variations of urhomelessness. In addition, its constituent moments are not discrete, but rather overlapping and flexible, such that they may occur concurrently. These findings demonstrate the ways in which phenomenological description can identify non-discrete and heterogeneous kinds, holistically accounting for both structural sameness and difference. In addition, phenomenological understandings can change over time. As Wertz (2015) put it,

> Phenomenology is not a doctrine or fixed body of knowledge, but a core method of investigation that may be flexibly adapted and remains open to new findings, terminology, and modification of practices [...] [t]he antithesis of dogma. (p. 85)

Dimensional models

One of the most pressing questions regarding the future of clinical diagnosis concerns whether diagnostic constructs should be conceptualised as categories or dimensions (see Strauss, 1973). Indeed, many recently proposed dimensional models of psychopathology include rating scales for the frequency or severity of specific symptoms, personality traits, or diagnostic constructs as a whole (e.g., Kamphuis & Noordhof, 2009; Lopez et al., 2007; Widiger & Samuel, 2005). DSM-5's (APA, 2013) proposed cross-cutting assessment measures are one example of this type of dimensional approach. Notably, most newly proposed dimensional models include a zero-point for the (dichotomous) absence of each symptom or construct; as such, these models are also categorical, i.e., they represent a specific kind that is dimensionalised as a matter of degree. Thus, most newly proposed dimensional models are not alternatives to categorical taxonomising, but rather de facto hybrids that might be called "dimensional kinds" (cf. Haslam, 2002, 2014).

The present findings indicated that urhomelessness is a single general structure with considerable variation within it, and more specifically that urhomelessness varies between persons and within the same person over time, such that it may be fleetingly or partially encountered, as well as intermittently or permanently exited for an urhomed way of being-in-the-world. The quantitative features of these variations and gradations were beyond the scope of the present study. However, theoretically, these variations of urhomeless experience indicated the potential for future dimensionalisation of the general structure, for example through the development of a quantitative scale measuring the duration and/or intensity with which urhomeless experience is given in a person's experience at any particular point in time.

Prototype models

In recent years, prototype models (e.g., Westen, 2012) have gained popularity as a potential alternative to purely categorical diagnostic models. Prototype models incorporate dimensional approach into categorical judgements, such that the diagnostician determines whether and the extent (i.e., quantitative degree) to which a given person's experiences match a brief description of a clinical presentation or prototype (i.e., qualitative kind). Prototypes are flexible structures that can be based on known natural types or, conversely, family resemblance[5] approaches (Wittgenstein, 1953/2001; see also Rosch & Mervis, 2015). Previous research has suggested that a prototype-matching approach might facilitate rapid clinical decision-making and enhance clinical utility due to its resonance with typical cognitive processes for attending to and classifying novel stimuli (Westen, 2012). In a study comparing the utility of criteria-counting, prototype, five-factor, and psychobiological diagnostic models, Spitzer et al. (2008) found that practitioners judged prototype-matching models as the most clinically useful.

The general psychological structures elicited by phenomenology might be incorporated into a prototype-matching approach; despite the lengthy descriptive process that is characteristic of phenomenology as a research method, the findings of phenomenological research can be summarised and apprehended parsimoniously. Moreover, phenomenological research elicits qualitative kinds that could serve as the basis for heuristic prototypes. Like prototype models, phenomenological description can map similarities across experiences that might otherwise be viewed as disparate or even unrelated, such that general psychological structures could, like theoretical types, be used pragmatically to facilitate decision-making. However, phenomenological description often differs from standard prototype models in that the former characterises individuals by personality or diagnostic type, whereas phenomenological methods often describe psychological structures of *lived experience* that may occur across persons or only intermittently for one person. As such, judgements about the degree to which the general structure is present or absent may not signify where a *person* lies on a continuum, but rather the extent to which the continuum of *lived experience* is present for that person. By identifying types of experience that are potentially transient and fleeting, phenomenological prototype models might avoid the risk of increasing stigma and stereotypes resulting from the categorisation of people. In other words, the phenomenological portrait of urhomelessness represents a potentially fluctuating and temporary experience, whereas prototypes—especially those prototypes corresponding to personality types and traits (e.g., Westen, Shedler, & Bradley, 2006)—are often assumed to represent psychological characteristics or experiences that endure over time.

Phenomenological kinds

Chapter 1 presented Haslam's (2002, 2014) conceptual taxonomy of psychiatric categories, or "kinds of kinds." The general structure of urhomelessness, as revealed in the present findings, did not fit neatly into any one of Haslam's five types: non-kinds, practical kinds, fuzzy kinds, discrete kinds, or natural kinds. First, as a general psychological structure, urhomelessness does not fit the profile of a non-kind; although it can be conceptualised dimensionally, its differences from other modes of being-in-the-world are more than merely a matter of degree. Second, it is not a practical kind, as its boundaries are not purely pragmatic, but rather experiential demarcations that are given in the way that the structure presents itself. Further, despite the fact that it overlaps with other ways of being-in-the-world, it is not a fuzzy kind, as it also involves qualitative discontinuities from other experiences (e.g., urhomeness). However, it is also not a discrete or dichotomous kind, as urhomelessness can be experienced partially or fleetingly; as revealed in the comparison data, the general structure is a horizon of experience for all humans, regardless of whether it is actualised in the experiential foreground during any one person's lifetime. Finally, the present findings have no bearing on whether urhomelessness is a natural kind, i.e., whether it corresponds to specific (albeit as-yet-unknown) organic etiological mechanisms or substrates.

It follows that in the context of the present findings, an additional, sixth "kind of kind" (Haslam, 2002, 2014) may be more appropriate for the classification of urhomelessness and the findings of phenomenological research more generally. *Phenomenological kinds*,[6] which might also be called *existential kinds*, are descriptions of subjective, lived experiences that have been derived from systematic phenomenological research. Phenomenological kinds have characteristics that may be at once invariant and corrigible, essential and non-fixed, unified and heterogeneous. Put differently, rather than imposing arbitrary boundaries, phenomenology allows for the identification of psychological "essences" as they are given, even when given as heterogeneous, fluctuating, fuzzy, non-discrete, pluralistic, paradoxical, socially constructed, and/or variable over time. For this reason, as Wertz (2015) has explained, some phenomenologists eschew the word "essence" because of its "misleading connotations, from Plato, of ideas that are unchanging, eternal, complete, separate from existence, and incorrigible" (p. 87). In other words, the use of the Husserlian term "essences" by contemporary social scientists differs from the types of rigid essentialist thought that presume the immutability, solidity, universality, and/or homogeny of any particular experience, entity, or group (Wertz, 2010; see also Husserl, 1913/62, 1939/1970). Instead, phenomenology seeks knowledge about lived experience as it is given, also called eidetic knowledge (Wertz, 2015).

Phenomenological kinds are experiential descriptions that are derived from systematic and sometimes lengthy phenomenological research, as demonstrated in the present study; however, they can be concisely and efficiently summarised for use in research and practice. Because phenomenological kinds can accommodate the essential complexity, interrelatedness, and multi-determined nature of human experiences, they are not beset by the taxonomic problems of diagnostic heterogeneity such as fuzzy boundaries (e.g., Boyd et al., 1984; Frances, 2009b; Krueger & Markon, 2006), absent zones of rarity (Kendell & Jablensky, 2003), or comorbidity (Boyd et al., 1994; Kessler et al., 2005; Kessler et al., 1994). Instead, phenomenological description allows for delineation of the meaningful ways in which invariant psychological essences overlap and are interrelated with related phenomena. For example, in the present study, three ad hoc comparison participants who did not meet criteria for a psychotic-disorder diagnosis at the time of the interview nevertheless demonstrated partial features of the general structure of urhomelessness. In addition, pilot comparisons experienced fleeting and transient encounters with the possibility of urhomelessness. Finally, there was substantial idiographic variation between the participants, such that no two participants experienced urhomelessness in exactly the same way. Because phenomenology does not presume the categorical discreteness or immutability of its kinds, the discovery of these partial and transient experiences serve as fine-tuned delineations, corrections, and elaborations of empirical boundaries rather than perplexing anomalies that may engender a scientific paradigm crisis (cf. Kupfer et al., 2002). In addition, phenomenological kinds might be transient or fleeting and can thus describe psychological phenomena that are not necessarily chronic or pervasive such as urhomelessness.

Most importantly, phenomenological kinds represent a type of *lived experience* rather than a type of person. People may experience or encounter urhomelessness to varying degrees and for varying durations, but they are not, as whole persons, essentially urhomeless, nor can the totality of their experiences be reduced to urhomelessness. As such, phenomenological kinds, when derived from systematic phenomenological research, represent a viable person-centred alternative and taxonomic solution to the heterogeneity problem generated by categorical diagnostic models.

Notes

1 DSM-IV (APA, 1994, 2000) and ICD-10 (1992a, 1992b) are not purely polythetic due to the fact that Schneiderian first-rank symptoms (Schneider, 1959) were considered sufficient if duration and exclusion (and in DSM-IV, social/occupational dysfunction) criteria were also met (see Chapter 1).

2 Note, however, that the presence of the general structure does not necessarily mean that every anomalous experience is a constituent of the general structure (see Chapter 9).

3 In DSM-5 (APA, 2013), catatonia is an independent diagnostic category, as well as a specifier for both mood and psychotic disorders.

4 Recall that pilot-comparison participants experienced fleeting encounters with urhomelessness. The ephemerality of these encounters was not a matter of a specific duration, but an experiential, existential quality of urhomelessness, which was (either initially or eventually) recognised as a temporary and not necessarily permanent for the person, despite the fact that it remained an original or fundamental possibility of human experience. One outpatient hospital participant, Crystal, was fully recovered at the time of the interview and recognised her urhomeless experiences (predominantly in the destitute moment) as fleeting and impermanent. These findings do not reflect objective duration criteria, but rather the subjective chronicity versus acuteness of participants' experiences of urhomelessness.

5 Phenomenological methods share affinities with family resemblance models but, unlike these models, phenomenology aims at the differentiation of meaningful from arbitrary or accidental co-occurrences through eidetic analysis (Wertz, 2005, 2015).

6 Phenomenological kinds share some but not all features with each of Haslam's (2002, 2014) five kinds of psychiatric categories; for this reason, Haslam's "kinds of kinds" may itself be viewed as a heterogeneous taxonomy beset by fuzzy boundaries and absent zones of rarity.

12

PRESENT FINDINGS IN THE CONTEXT OF PHENOMENOLOGICAL AND INTERDISCIPLINARY LITERATURES

Sarah R. Kamens

Phenomenological literatures

As noted in Chapter 4, this study is part of a longstanding tradition of utilising phenomenological methods to understand the meaningful lived experiences of persons diagnosed with schizophrenia and other psychotic disorders. The present findings support the work of previous phenomenologists who have suggested that phenomenological description may provide the foundation for an ecologically valid diagnostic nomenclature that incorporates the *lived experience* of the phenomena that it classifies (Flanagan et al., 2010; Mishara & Schwartz, 2013; Parnas & Zahavi, 2002; see also Wertz et al., 2017). This chapter briefly addresses the explanatory relevance of the present findings before reviewing the relationship of the findings to previous phenomenological accounts of schizophrenia.

Explanatory relevance

Phenomenology is a scientific method for the descriptive delineation of lived experience. Historically, researchers have varied in the extent to which they view phenomenology as useful for the generation, development, and validation of explanatory models, i.e., models for understanding the causal substrates of the phenomena under investigation. Sass & Parnas (2007) reviewed the question of whether phenomenological literature has explanatory relevance for schizophrenia. In doing so, they demonstrated that previous phenomenologists (e.g., Husserl, Merleau-Ponty, Blankenburg, and Minkowski) lacked consensus concerning the question of explanation and often varied in positions not only from each other, but also in their own personal work over

 DOI: 10.4324/9780429055454-13

time. The authors noted that Binswanger (cited in Sass & Parnas, 2007), for example, tried to explain the genetic development of delusional worlds using Husserlian methods. In contrast, Blankenburg (1971) saw phenomenology as a purely descriptive procedure and, according to Sass and Parnas, explicitly denied the possibility of its significance for the aetiology of schizophrenia. Following from our method, which did not include analyses of the aetiology of urhomeless experience, the findings of the present study can be considered as *descriptive*; in other words, the production of an explanatory model was not an aim of the present investigation, and future research is needed to determine the aetiological significance of urhomelessness as a general structure.

Un-understandability

As described in Chapter 3, Jaspers (1913/1968) viewed the core feature of schizophrenia as a resistance to psychological understanding, which he called its "un-understandable" quality (p. 308). More specifically, for Jaspers, schizophrenia is fundamentally foreclosed to intelligibility and empathy, can be described only in particulars (i.e., individual symptoms and experiences) instead of through universals, and can be intuited only through multiple clinical encounters (Mishara et al., 2014). The present results resonate with but also differ from Jaspers' claims. More specifically, the notion of un-understandability, or an empathic failure to understand psychosis, may reflect (from the clinician's perspective) the radical alienation and invalidation described by persons experiencing urhomelessness. Indeed, persons experiencing urhomelessness sometimes feel as if others fail to understand them at a most basic, fundamental level, suggesting that interpersonal impasses may be common to or even constitutive of urhomeless experience. In addition, as in Jaspers, urhomelessness is not a totalising theory that necessarily applies to every psychotic experience or symptom, but rather a general psychological structure that can be grasped intuitively through encounters with its heterogeneous instances. Further, Jaspers' claims are reflected in the fact that urhomelessness, as a phenomenological kind, cannot be explained by an underlying causal mechanism but only grasped through particular examples, through which the structure is intuitively grasped (Mishara & Schwartz, 2014).

However, the present findings differ from Jaspers' theory in demonstrating that the heterogeneity of what has been called schizophrenia *can*, in fact, be meaningfully understood. Moreover, and importantly, Jasperian empathic failures are not in and of themselves the most basic characteristics of the general structure, but rather founded on urhomeless experience (see also Pienkos & Sass, 2012; Sass, 1992a). In other words, un-understandability is not a core feature of urhomelessness; rather, it arises from the failure of others, including clinicians, to understand this unique way of being-in-the-world.

Ontological insecurity

The present findings resonate and partially overlap with the work of Laing (1960), who posited ontological insecurity as an existential state that can, in some cases, lead to schizophrenia (see also Wertz & Alcee, 2003). As described in Chapter 3, for Laing, one way of responding to ontological insecurity is entry into a schizoid way of being in which a "true" or "secret" self is concealed and protected, while a "false self" is extended as a surrogate to contend with a social world seen as deeply threatening and overwhelming. Yet this way of being-in-the-world can eventually endanger the very "true self" it was designed to protect. Estranged from the social world and the body, the "secret self" may become increasingly remote and impoverished. "In the escape from the risk of being killed, it [the 'true self'] becomes dead" (p. 142). One path to schizophrenia, according to Laing, occurs when the "false self" system is removed, revealing a "true self" that has developed in isolation from others and eschews the conformist behaviours of the "false self," viewed as oppressive and inauthentic.

Laing's (1960) account of ontological insecurity overlaps with urhomelessness in four important ways. First, in both existential ways of being, the world of other humans is experienced as potentially threatening, dangerous, and impinging on the person's very being-in-the-world. Second, in both modes, the person attempts to secure minimal protection and basic safety from a world perceived as inordinately threatening and dangerous. For example, the performative strategies of the "false self" can be seen in variations of the nomadic moment in which the person attempts to find existential shelter in sociocultural roles, activities, and contexts that were previously unfamiliar. Leonard, for example, constantly donned new performative identities and described himself as a "chameleon" in relation to his surroundings. As Laing (1960) put it, the person may use "simply nonsense, red-herring speech, prolonged filibustering to throw dangerous people off the scent" (p. 164). The third similarity between ontological insecurity and urhomelessness is the mutual role that both person and world play in the basic crisis state. Just as the person feels dislodged or distanced from the world, the world is experienced as rejecting, threatening, and/or otherwise dangerous and oppressive. Last but not least, "[t]o turn oneself into a stone becomes a way of not being turned into a stone by someone else" (Laing, 1960, p. 51) is a strategy that can be found in the hibernation-attempts and totalistic shunning of worldly experiences in the destitute moment. In these ways, urhomelessness as a general structure reflects and extends Laing's account of ontological insecurity in persons who develop psychosis from a schizoid way of being-in-the-world.

World-disorientation accounts

The present findings have a particularly strong resonance with phenomenological world-disorientation accounts. As described in Chapter 3, among these accounts are Minkowski's (1927/1953) "trouble générateur" or loss of "vital contact with reality" (VCR; see also Urfer, 2001), Laing's description of ontological insecurity (see above), and Blankenburg's (1969/2001, 1971) description of the loss of "natural self-evidence" or a "common-sense" orientation towards consensual reality (*Selbstverstandlichkeit*). A more recent account can be found in Pienkos (2014a), who compared the experiences of participants diagnosed with schizophrenia-spectrum disorders and major depression using the EAWE (Sass et al., 2017) and found that the lived experience of schizophrenia-spectrum disorders was uniquely characterised by the "unmooring of the world" (p. 1), a shift in lived experience such that "the world comes to lose its common-sense anchoring, so that the typical moments of the world, its physical attributes, meanings, relationships, and general reality-sense, are disorganized and dismantled" (p. 25). Pienkos described five themes in the unmooring of the world: distorted appearances, erosion of self-world boundaries, shifting relevancies, precarious reality, and remoteness of the world (see also Pienkos, 2020; Pienkos et al., 2017).

The above-listed accounts vary in the extent to which they posit world-disorientation in schizophrenia as a grounding feature of psychotic experience versus a secondary outcome of a different core process (be it biological, psychological, or other). The present findings revealed that disoriented, newly configured, and/or distant relationships with the world are not a consequence or secondary feature of urhomeless experience, but rather part of *what the experience is*, i.e., its eidos. The experience of being disembedded from familiar worldly persons, events, and objects was characteristic of all moments of urhomelessness but given in particular clarity and vividness in the nomadic moment, where the person is cast from familiar moorings and into the unfamiliar, experientially unpredictable world-at-large. It was also given in the imaginal, other-worldly nature of settlement and the quasi-void in destitution. The present findings thus emphasise that the cognitive-perceptual experience of derealisation and what Pienkos (2014a) called the "unmooring of the world" (p. 1)—including its subcomponent of eroding self-world boundaries—are also existential, sociocultural experiences in which person and world are mutually unmoored, such that the person wanders through the world just as the world wanders through the person (see also Pienkos, 2020). The existential and sociocultural dimensions of this experience are also captured by Hu & Wertz (2019), who recently likened experiences of attenuated psychosis syndrome to the experience of living in exile from one's own country or land.

Binswanger's (1956, 1957, 1963) descriptions of experiential inconsistencies in schizophrenia share affinities with specific constituents of the moments of urhomelessness. For example, the settled moment often involves what Binswanger described as exaggerated or extravagant ideals and dichotomous thinking. In addition, the destitute moment is consistent with the experience of being "worn away" and the renunciation of the world, which Binswanger called the "existential retreat." As described by Saks (2008) in her well-known memoir, *The Center Cannot Hold*, the person may feel like a "sand castle with all the sand sliding away in the receding surf" (pp. 12–13).

Some world-disorientation accounts of schizophrenia have described "atmospheric" disturbances in one's sense of subjectivity; among these atmospheric disruptions is derealisation, a feeling of distance from worldly surroundings or feeling of difference from normal reality (e.g., Blankenburg, 1969/2001, 1971; Minkowski, 1927/1953; Sass & Ratcliffe, 2017). The present results support Sass's (e.g., 2003b, 2007; Sass et al., 2011) arguments that in contrast to being "divorced from reality," or the ordinary world of persons and objects, some persons with psychosis may be excessively attuned to it (or, in Sass's terms, "hyperreflexive")—a kind of hyperrealisation rather than derealisation. More specifically, the person experiencing urhomelessness, dislodged from familiar worldly bearings and radically exposed to the world-at-large, may simultaneously feel proximal to and alienated from the world of other persons. In the nomadic moment, in particular, they may feel excessively exposed to an expanded world of pluralistic and fluctuating meanings.

In all moments, persons experiencing urhomelessness often maintained a basic understanding of the way in which others perceive the world, i.e., consensual reality, even if they were simultaneously oriented towards nomadism, a settlement, or destitution—and even if, in the settled moment, the specifics of personal history before the unveiling of the settlement were foreclosed. The clearest example of this can be found in participants' frequent attempts to convince the interviewer—whose unfamiliarity with their settlement was taken as a given—of the settlement's existence and/or merit. One participant, Rabbi Danny, even made jokes indicating that he understood the ways in which others might view his conviction that he was a potential Messiah ("most people who want to live like the Messiah think they're the Messiah, the screwballs"). Likewise, persons who refrain from attempting to convince others about the settlement may be acting in accordance with an understanding that most others reject or deny the settlement's existence (L. Sass, personal communication, July 16, 2015).

The present findings align with the work of Bleuler (Bleuler & Brill, 1924/1988), Jones et al. (2016), and Sass (1992b, 1994b), who have documented the phenomenon of "double orientation" or "double bookkeeping," i.e., the seemingly simultaneous orientation towards reality and anomalous beliefs (or in clinical terms, delusion). Sass (1992b) has argued that the notion of "poor reality testing" in persons diagnosed with schizophrenia ignores the fact that psychotic symptoms are often experienced as occurring on an imaginary plane from which the person often maintains a sense of irony or distance (see also Kamens, 2018). For this reason, some persons do not act on their anomalous beliefs, which are given as a fundamentally different kind of "reality." As a result, although the person may be convinced of its ontological preferability to consensual reality, the settlement can remain undetectable to others. As Sass (1992b) put it, "the hallucinations and delusions of schizophrenic patients usually seem to be embedded in a context—a clearing or horizon, if you will—that is quite distinct from the common-sense world of everyday pragmatic understanding" (p. 129). Jones et al. (2016) have extended this account by empirically demonstrating ways in which blended explanatory models (e.g., simultaneous clinical and spiritual explanations) for psychosis are present not only in the first-person experiences of service users, but also in broader postsecular society. In Jones et al.'s words,

> Across our interviews, participants frequently emphasized both personal uncertainties and awareness of broader societal doubts concerning the ontological and/or epistemological status of their psychotic experiences. [...] [P]articipants assert the supernatural reality of their experiences at the same time that they frame these same experiences as clinical symptoms of an illness. (p. 7)

Likewise, in the present study, urhomelessness did not foreclose participants' understanding of the consensual realm of others, including their understandings of the way in which others might understand or conceptualise their urhomeless experiences. For example, participants' awareness of others' differing perspectives were reflected in their attempts to invite the interviewer into their settlements, or imaginal worlds.

The concepts of losing VCR (Minkowski, 1927/1953) and "natural self-evidence" (Blankenburg, 1969/2001, 1971) may bear the closest affinity to the destitute moment of urhomelessness, particularly in its hibernated variation, where the person attempts to radically withdraw from the world in order to mitigate feelings of danger, vulnerability, and invalidation—and thereby establish a novel zone of safety and protection. However, even in the hibernated variation of the destitute moment, persons reacted *to* the world by withdrawing from or giving in to it; however painful and antagonistic, their relationship with the world was never fully severed, nor was it successfully rendered innocuous.

Self-disturbance accounts

Chapter 3 presented examples of phenomenological self-disturbance accounts of schizophrenia (*Ichstörungen*; e.g., Mishara et al., 2014), which arose as early as the early 20th century and gained traction in the later 20th and early 21st century. Although these accounts share a focus on disruptions in the "self," they vary in their focus on different aspects or experiences of the self—as well as the extent to which respective self-disturbances are posited as holding explanatory versus purely descriptive relevance for the understanding of schizophrenia (see Sass & Parnas, 2007). Examples of self-disturbance accounts include Jasper's (1923/1963) account of alteration in awareness of one's own existence ("Descartes' 'cogito ergo sum' ['I think therefore I am'] may still be superficially cogitated but it is no longer a valid experience" [Jaspers, 1923/1963, p. 122]); Schneider's (1950/1959, p.58) account of disruptions in "first-personal-givenness" (*Ichheit*) or "mineness" (*Meinhaftigkeit*); and Fuch's (2005, 2007) theory of disturbances in time consciousness, and more specifically in the experienced first-person linkages between past, present, and future. A related atmospheric disturbance is depersonalisation, or feelings of distance from one's self or personal elements such as one's thoughts, feelings, or body (see Sass & Ratcliffe, 2017); in a number of studies (e.g., Perona-Garcelán et al., 2016), depersonalisation has been implicated in the experiential process of psychosis.

Our findings descriptively elaborate and build upon the experiential elements of self-disturbance accounts (including "atmospheric" disturbances such as depersonalisation) by indicating that these disruptions are part of a broader existential and contextual constellation, alteration, or privation in the experiential intersection between person and world. Urhomelessness, when distressing, is not an example of an *Ichstörung* (self-disturbance), but rather more accurately characterised as a type of existential *Heimstörung* (existential-home disturbance). In other words, urhomelessness concerns not only the narrative (or social) self (e.g., Nelson et al., 2014), but also a pre-reflective and social experience of being-in-the-world—what Mensch (1998) calls the passively constituted basis of intersubjective harmony. From a Husserlian perspective, this person-world relationship, as a founding existential configuration, is more fundamental or basic than the self as such. Mensch quotes Husserl in affirming that "[o]n the lowest level [of constitution], we do not yet have an ego, a person, a physical thing" (quoted in Mensch, 1998, p. 180). For Husserl, then, this level is more primary than *both* the prereflective (or "basic") self and the narrative self. As Steinbock (1995) put it, "[w]hat Husserl is sometimes wont to call the 'lowest level' is not the ego at all, but the home to which the 'ego' belongs" (p. 188).

Thus, in urhomelessness, the "home" that is decentralised, disembedded, or lacking includes but transcends the person as such; it is a transcendental constitution of basic, reliable, and familiar worldly coordinates—contextual embeddings, relational belongings, and ways of being-with and being-in-the-world—that protect the person from the world while simultaneously facilitating agentic participation in it. In other words, urhomelessness occurs at the experiential intersection between person and world, which is also the seat or the dwelling place in which the person experiences placement into the world—part of the Dasein's *thrownness* (*Geworfenheit*), in Heideggerian terms (1927/1962). Urhomelessness is experienced by and through the person, but the world participates, constitutes, and registers the habitable and hospitable realms from which the person is experientially excluded—as well as the very fact of the person's exclusion from them. Thus, urhomelessness is an existential-psychological disruption in embeddedness—not only of the person or self as such, but of the *person-in-the-world.*

Ipseity disturbance

Ipseity disturbance is an example of a phenomenological concept that has been suggested as a potential solution to the heterogeneity problem (e.g., Sass & Parnas, 2003). As described in Chapter 3, Sass and colleagues (e.g., Sass, 1987, 1988, 1992a, 1992b, 1994a, 1994b, 2000, 2001, 2003a, 2003b, 2004, 2007, 2011, 2014a, 2014b; Sass et al., 2018; Sass & Parnas, 2003, 2010; Nelson et al., 2014) have proposed that the experiences commonly known as symptoms of schizophrenia are founded upon two core disturbances of the self: hyperreflexivity, an exaggerated consciousness of otherwise taken-for-granted features of the self and/or environment, and diminished self-presence, or a mitigated sense of being the central agent of one's own experiences and actions. A third element, disturbed hold or grip on the world, is grounded in but no less experientially central to these two core components (Sass, 2014b).

Ipseity disturbance is thus a unique model that explicitly accounts for anomalies in the experience of both self and world. The general structure of urhomelessness shares a strong affinity with the ipseity disturbance model in that both reflect a decentralization of familiar anchors of person-world experience, as well as an oscillation between experiences of distance from and extreme proximity to the world-at-large (hyperreflexivity). In the ipseity disturbance model, the fundamental decentralization is thought to occur at the level of the (minimal or basic) self, but this self-disturbance manifests in anomalous experiences of both self and world (Sass et al., 2011), such that "disturbed self-experience or selfhood may underlie and generate many 'surface-level' psychotic symptoms" (Nelson et al., 2014, p. 479). The present study did not investigate causal explanations for the emergence of urhomelessness; thus, it is theoretically possible that ipseity disturbance (or another as-yet unknown factor) underlies urhomeless experience.

As aforementioned, urhomelessness occurs in the experiential intersection between person and world. Similarly, from a purely descriptive standpoint, the ipseity disturbance model holds both self-disturbance and disturbed hold or grip on the world to be central to the experience of persons diagnosed with schizophrenia. For example, Sass (2014b) has pointed out that phenomenologically speaking, disturbed hold or grip on the world and disruptions in self-experience may be "equiprimordial" (p. 9). In Sass's words:

> [...] it may well be that schizophrenia would more accurately be described as a presence-disturbance, in accord with philosopher

> Merleau-Ponty's (2012) statement: "subject and object [are] two abstract 'moments' of a unique structure, namely, presence." Certainly there is no a priori reason to assume that self-related aspects are necessarily superior to more world-related ones [...], either in distinguishing or predicting schizophrenia-spectrum conditions. (p. 9)

Sass's description of "presence-disturbance" aligns with the urhomeless experience of being dislodged or alienated from familiar bearings, such that the person feels cast into the world-at-large, creating an ongoing reversal between the familiar and the unfamiliar. In urhomelessness, it is indeed the person's dislodging (or originary alienation) from the world-as-urhome, as well as the registration of the person's presence by the world-at-large, that constitute an urhomeless way of *worldbeing*. Sass's notion of presence-disturbance is also reflected in urhomeless experiences of passive wandering, in which the world makes itself present *to the person*, who becomes a shelter or site for the expression of disparate voices, images, and other fragmentary urhomeless elements of the world (see Chapters 6 and 8). Urhomelessness thus shares the ipseity disturbance model's emphasis on the disruption of person/world and self/other boundaries (e.g., Nelson et al., 2014), as well as an emphasis on anomalous alterations in the person's experience of being-in-the-world (see Sass, 2014b).

Intersubjectivity and social lives

The present findings have a particularly strong resonance with previous literature on the intersubjective and social lives of persons diagnosed with schizophrenia-spectrum and other psychotic disorders. The experience of social alienation, a component of urhomelessness, has appeared in previous phenomenological studies on psychosis and schizophrenia (e.g., Hu & Wertz, 2019; Pienkos & Sass, 2016; Yen et al., 2020). Pienkos (2015) described various "paradoxes of intersubjectivity" in the experiences of persons diagnosed with schizophrenia (p. 206), such as feelings that other persons are distant objects yet excruciatingly close, as well as the perception that others' motives are both opaque and utterly transparent. Drawing on the theoretical literature on intersubjectivity, Pienkos attributed these variations to a breakdown in the intersubjective experiences of expressive unity, empathy, and the otherness of the other (cf. Bateson et al., 1956). Pienkos concluded that "perhaps the most important insight is that, like all people, individuals with schizophrenia may desire the ability to relate to others but [...] find this extremely difficult to achieve" (p. 207). These fluctuations in interpersonal experience, as well as exasperating difficulties in establishing relationships with others, are part and parcel of urhomeless experience. More specifically, the world from which the person feels dislodged and alienated—and to which they ultimately feel radically exposed—is a world comprised of other persons. In the context of the present findings, Pienkos's "paradoxes of intersubjectivity" corresponded to the ongoing thematic reversal of the familiar and unfamiliar, which occurs when the person is ejected from familiar surroundings and exposed to the vicissitudes of the world-at-large. In addition, the present findings suggest that difficulties relating to others, including alienation and invalidation experiences, may not be a secondary characteristic of experiences associated with schizophrenia, but rather one of its essential components.

The present findings also support the findings of Davidson and colleagues (Davidson & Stayner, 1997; Davidson et al., 1998; see also Strauss, 2011, 2013), who demonstrated that far from renouncing the social world completely, persons diagnosed with schizophrenia often have a subjective sense of sociality and make agentic attempts to reengage with the social domain—and that they do so despite frequent experiences of rejection, including perceived rejection by mental health professionals themselves (see also Işık & Ergün, 2020). These attempts often lead to feelings of hopelessness and intermittent periods of giving up on the interpersonal world, such that the person oscillates between withdrawal and disappointing efforts to reengage (see also Sass [1992b] on act versus affliction interpretations of early psychosis). Davidson & Stayner (1997) quoted Deegan (1994), a leader in the recovery movement, in pointing out that attempts to withdraw and "give up" are agentic and goal-oriented behaviours, or meaningful responses to social experiences in themselves. Outsiders often misunderstand the person's agentic efforts, leading to increased feelings of loneliness, rejection, and alienation (see LaFace, 2014). For example, from the traditional clinical perspective, the person is often viewed as an "empty shell" such that "the person as a person—as a feeling, thinking, and intending subject—is thought no longer to be home" (p. 4). Put in the terminology of the present findings, the traditional clinical perspective ignores the *person* who is experiencing urhomelessness. Davidson and Stayner compare the experience of repeated social rejection in persons diagnosed with schizophrenia to Rilke's poem "The Panther," in which the caged animal perceives the world as only bars (quoted in Davidson & Stayner, 1997, p. 10).

The present study revealed that among the heterogeneous experiences of diverse persons diagnosed with schizophrenia-spectrum disorders, shared general structure comprised strategies for withstanding a crisis state that was worldly and social in nature. More specifically, participants experiencing urhomelessness were engaged in efforts to survive the basic crisis of living within a world experienced as profoundly inhospitable, unsafe, and alienating. The three moments of urhomelessness, as detailed in Chapters 6 through 8, are experiential styles and agentic strategies for re-establishing feelings of safety and validation by others. More specifically, the nomadic moment involves repeated attempts to secure a minimal sense of safety and belonging through sheltering, the settled moment involves an effort to imaginatively establish the experience of urhomeness, and the destitute moment comprises a renunciation of efforts to attain safety and acknowledgement. Even in the destitute moment, the person attempts to salvage a means of existential survival by hibernating or evacuating in the face of perceived danger. These findings reflect Davidson and Stayner's (1997) assertions that the person diagnosed with schizophrenia is engaged in the world as a whole person agentically striving towards recovery (see also Chapter 9).

Previous interdisciplinary literature

Historically, the study of schizophrenia has been interdisciplinary, extending beyond the disciplines of clinical psychology and psychiatry and into other fields such as the humanities and the arts. Woods (2011) has documented how the concept of schizophrenia, which she termed the "sublime object of psychiatry," has been utilised by critical theorists as a conceptual lens through which to interpret historical and cultural experience, and in particular 20th-century modern and postmodern experience in Western countries. Though a comprehensive review of the interdisciplinary literature is beyond the scope of any one book, this section briefly reviews several nonfictional, theoretical, and philosophical accounts that contextualise the present findings and their potential sociocultural extensions.

Nonfictional literature on schizophrenia

The notion that schizophrenia entails a kind of psychological or existential homelessness is both implicitly and explicitly woven throughout the nonfictional literature on psychosis, including the first-person memoirs of persons diagnosed with schizophrenia and the reflective, nonfictional writings of psychotherapists, anthropologists, journalists, and other third-person authors. For example, Morgan (2013) titled her memoir of schizophrenia *A mind without a home*. In another memoir, Edwards (2007) proposed a connection between houselessness and alienation in psychosis; more specifically, houselessness exacerbated his feelings of vulnerability and isolation from other people:

> [S]elf-induced isolation gets to the point where the person sounds crazy to other people; so that they do not respond to him as a human being, as really a member of society. […] Because of this other-induced isolation the psychosis escalates and the person gets further and further removed from society. (p. 134)

In another example, "Joan" stated that meeting her therapist "made me feel like a traveler who's been lost in a land where no one speaks his language" (Hayward & Taylor, 1956, 221). LaFace (2014) spoke about psychosis as a kind of "lostness" that contains an immanent "hope of being found" (p. 2).

Sheehan's (1982) journalistic account of a young woman diagnosed with schizophrenia was *Is there no place on earth for me?* Lovell's (1997) anthropological documentation of the experiences of individuals diagnosed with schizophrenia who were experiencing houselessness was titled "'The city is my mother': Narratives of schizophrenia and homelessness." Writing about a service user experiencing psychosis, psychotherapist Anthony Yeo explained, "He had been living with the ignominy of feeling he probably did not belong in society; having a home, yet feeling homeless in the larger world that considers him an oddball" (p. 107). These accounts reflect the ways in which urhomelessness has been intuitively thematised throughout the extant nonfictional literature.

Theoretical and philosophical literature on schizophrenia

Themes of wandering, societal alienation, and homelessness are reflected in Foucault's (1965/1988) theoretico-historical tome *Madness and Civilization*. Foucault famously detailed the marginalised position that madness held for the Western imaginary after the disappearance of leprosaria—which had presumably once held a similar position—at the end of the Middle Ages. Later, during the Renaissance, madmen were often driven outside of towns and left to wander the countryside; according to some accounts, they were placed on boats as migrants, mirroring the then-popular literary and cultural trope of the "ship of fools" (*Stultifera Navis* [Foucault, 1965/1988, p. 5])[1]. In Foucault's words, "[t]he existence of the mad at that time could easily be a wandering [or errant] one" (p. 8).[2] Starting in the 17th century, the mad would be locked up in a series of institutions such as prisons, hospitals such as the *hôpital général* (which Foucault identified as a semi-judicial and administrative institution, not a medical one), workhouses, and eventually, in the 19th century, asylums. After the Renaissance, the formation of a new "community of labour" resulted in the mad being socially ejected "as into another world" for purported idleness and "social uselessness" (Foucault, 1965/1988, p. 58). This sociohistorically liminal space of madness in society is reflected in the urhomeless experience of feeling excluded from one or more human communities—or human society entirely. In addition, Foucault's description of the historical oscillation between wandering and confinement (and the thematic simultaneity of the two in the "ship of fools" [p. 5]) mirrors the theme of wandering—including, as a common variation, involuntary wandering between institutions like hospitals and jails—that is essential to the nomadic mode of urhomelessness.

Several theorists have drawn parallels between psychotic experience and modern or postmodern culture, highlighting the ways in which urhomelessness is not isolated from but rather reflects contextual experience, including the broader cultural experiences of contemporary society. For example, Baudrillard (1983) described mid-to-late-20th-century existence as generally psychotic and alienated due to the inversion of interiority and exteriority by digital technology. In his own words:

> [W]e are now in [...] this state of terror proper to the schizophrenic: too great a proximity of everything [...] with no halo of private protection [...] open to everything in spite of himself, living in the greatest confusion [...] the overexposure and transparence of the world which traverses him without obstacle. He can no longer produce the limits of his own being. (pp. 132–133)

This description echoes the experience of urhomelessness in the nomadic and destitute moments, in which experiential thresholds between person and world fade, often resulting in profound trepidation, despair, and/or confusion. On an individual level, the impingement described by Baudrillard mirrors the impingement of the world's wanderings upon the person experiencing urhomelessness, such that, in the destitute moment, the person is experienced as a site for the dynamisms of the world. It may be the case that urhomelessness is a specifically postindustrial experience—or one that is exacerbated by the mass technologisation or making-public of formerly private spheres of life.

In his magnum opus *Madness and Modernism*, Sass (1992a) scrupulously delineated the ways in which disturbances in self-experience are expressions of conceptual oppositions (e.g., omnipotence and radical solipsism versus the dissolution or fragmentation of the self) that, though ostensibly paradoxical, form the very epistemological basis of Western culture, especially Western intellectual and artistic traditions (see also Jones et al., 2016; Sass, 1994b). The extreme experiential variations in urhomeless experience reflect these conceptual tensions, particularly in the nomadic moment, where the person is radically exposed to the vicissitudes of the world-at-large, but also in the settled and destitute moments, where oppositional divides are erected between the person's world and the world of others. Sass's work highlights the fact that these extreme polarities of experience are not obstacles to or aberrations from sociocultural history, but rather mirror the very structures of thought—as well as their reification through "high art" and intellectual production—through which modernism has developed and transformed.

Jameson (1991) famously argued that late-capitalist, postmodern culture is characterised by a "schizophrenic present" (p. xi) that he described as an "eclipse of subjectivity in a new anonymity" (p. 174). Distinguishing between the modernist themes of alienation, anomie, and isolation on the one hand and, on the other, the postmodern themes of depthlessness, emotionlessness, and fragmentation, Jameson associated the latter set of themes with schizophrenia. In contrast, the present findings suggest that urhomelessness predominantly comprises the characteristically modernist experiences of alienation and isolation; however, the experiences that Jameson identifies as postmodern[3] may reflect urhomeless experiences such as the voiding or flattening of emotions that is sometimes characteristic of destitute moment. In general, Jameson's theory highlights the ways in which experiences commonly associated with psychosis are not devoid of historical and cultural extensions, but rather situated in particular sociocultural eras and their distinct experiential, temporo-cultural constellations (see also Rahimi, 2015).

Like Jameson, (1991) Deleuze & Guattari (1983, 1987) viewed schizophrenia as a condition that is produced by sociocultural experiences, and in particular the very sociocultural formations that it arises to resist. More specifically, Deleuze and Guattari see in the person with schizophrenia an active agent of struggle against the typical social structures of capitalism (see also Durgan, 2013). From this perspective, although persons with schizophrenia suffer, they are also creative, productive, and relational agents that—contrary to conventional clinical theory—engage with and agentically respond to the world around them. In their (in)famous words, "[a] schizophrenic out for a walk is a better model than a neurotic lying on the analyst's couch. A breath of fresh air, a relationship with the outside world" (Deleuze & Guattari, 1983, p. 2).

Davidson & Shahar (2007) have noted how the work of Deleuze and Guattari represents an alternative to the deficit approach to psychopathology and reflects emerging ideas about the ways in which individuals diagnosed with SMIs are active agents within their social environment, shaping both their risk factors and their own trajectory towards recovery. The present findings support the notion that persons diagnosed with schizophrenia-spectrum disorders are active agents who desire social belonging, freedom from oppressive structures, and imaginative and creative freedom (e.g., in living a settled way of being, as exemplified in Avery's love for creating spaceships). More specifically, the present findings suggest that the heterogeneous variations of urhomelessness, as reflected in its moments and common variations, are strategic attempts aimed at agentically resolving its basic crisis state.

An additional resonance between the work of Deleuze & Guattari (1983, 1987) and the present findings is an emphasis on nomadic thought, which Deleuze and Guattari called "nomadology," a praxis that they differentiated from physical migration as such. Deleuze and Guattari saw "nomadism" as a type of thought and activity that is open and not closed, heterogeneous and not homogeneous, horizontal and not hierarchical, in movement rather than static, and "rhizomatic" rather than "arborescent." Nomads, in other words, carry out the productive and creative work associated with schizophrenia, and they actively resist social danger and oppression (see also Ronell, 1989/1991). In the present findings, persons experiencing urhomelessness in the nomadic moment are likewise in movement and open to varied, heterogeneous experiences in the world-at-large. The ongoing thematic reversal of the familiar and unfamiliar and successive assumption of shelters parallels what Deleuze and Guattari called "deterritorialisation" and "reterritorialisation," or the uprooting from worldly or cultural bearings and relocating, albeit briefly, to new ones before the iterative process begins again.

Theoretical and philosophical literature on not-at-homeness

The interdisciplinary literature is rife with accounts of existential at-homeness and not-at-homeness, which provide a broader theoretical and sociocultural context for understanding urhomelessness and its horizon of urhomeness. A comprehensive review of this literature is beyond the scope of this book; instead, this section will provide an overview of two theories that are particularly relevant to the present findings. These theories are Heidegger's (1927/1962) discussion of the "at-home" and the "not-at-home" and Bhabha's (1992) discussion of the "unhomed" and "unhomely."[4] Both accounts address the experience of the unfamiliar, the "alien," and the not-at-home, which can be directly compared to the general structure of urhomelessness.

For the purposes of brevity and parsimony, this chapter does not address the numerous philosophical accounts of being at-home and at-homeness (e.g., Buckley, 1971; Levinas, 1961), which, though potentially useful, concern a horizon of the general structure.

Heidegger (1927/1962) described a foundational kind of existential homelessness that he called the "not-at-home" (*un-zuhause*) and equated it to the uncanny (the German word for "uncanny," *unheimlich,* literally means "un-home-like"). Notably, Jaspers (1913/1963) used the same word in his description of the *Wahnstimmung* or "delusional atmosphere" that precedes some psychotic experiences (see also Freud, 1919/2003). For Heidegger, the not-at-home did not concern the factical (ontic) existence of a home or material house, but rather the (ontological) nature of being, a word that he wrote with a capital "B." Heidegger associated what he called "Being at-home" (*zuhause sein*) with "tranquillized self-assurance," "lostness," and the "average everydayness of Dasein"[5]—for Heidegger, this was the conformist, unremarkable world of the "they" (pp. 233–234). In contrast, he saw being not-at-home (*Nicht zuhause sein*) as the most basic or primordial way of (ontological) Being. For Heidegger, the experiences of angst or existential anxiety can wrest Dasein back from dwelling in the tranquillised familiarity of feeling at-home in the public, social, consensual world:

> When [...] we flee into the 'at-home' of publicness, we flee in the face of the 'not-at-home'; that is, we flee in the face of the uncanniness [*unheimlichkeit*, or 'un-home-like-ness'] which lies in Dasein—in Dasein as thrown Being-in-the-world, which has been delivered over to itself its Being. This uncanniness pursues Dasein constantly, and is a threat to its everyday lostness in the "they," though not explicitly. (p. 234)

Likewise, the present results support the notion that being not-urhomed, or urhomeless, is a fundamental horizon of the human condition that is nevertheless not always actualised; indeed, some persons never experience it as fully actualised. This mode of being-in-the-world or worldbeing, as a horizon or potential of human experience, is ultimately just as *familiar* as it is unfamiliar (see also Freud, 1919/2003; Ronell, 1989/1991). As Watts (2011) put it, for Heidegger, "this sense of homelessness and alienation is more primordial than our normal feeling of familiarity with the world [...] Homelessness is thus the basic condition of mankind (p. 74). In Heidegger's own words:

> [t]hat kind of Being-in-the-world which is tranquillized and familiar is a mode of Dasein's uncanniness, not the reverse. *From an existential-ontological point of view, the 'not-at-home' must be conceived as the more primordial phenomenon.* (p. 234; italics in the original)

In other words, from an ontologico-existential perspective, the experience of being comfortably urhomed in the public realm of consensus is ultimately less familiar to Dasein than the fundamental uncanniness, or urhomelessness, from which it often flees (see also Heidegger, 1951/1993; cf. Levinas, 1961). As Maron (2010) explained,

> Heidegger stresses the manner in which anxiety (Angst) wrenches us out of our familiarity with the world and makes the 'uncanniness' (*Unheimlichheit*) of the world visible and hence *brings home to us our own essential homelessness.* (p. 172, emphasis added)

Bhabha (1992) wrote about the sometimes "unhomely"[6] effects of dislocation, forced relocation, migration, and forced social accommodation in colonial and postcolonial subjects[7] (p. 14). More specifically, "unhomeliness"—which Bhabha carefully differentiated from homelessness—happens when "suddenly the home turns into another world" (p. 143). Uprooting and displacement result in a blending of the public and private, the personal and the political, such that, in Bhabha's words,

> [T]he border between home and world becomes confused; and, uncannily, the private and the public become part of each other, forcing upon us a vision that is as divided as it is disorienting. [...] [A] nother world becomes visible. [...] The unhomely is the shock of recognition of the world-in-the home, the home-in-the-world. (p. 141)

Bhabha's theories bear a close resemblance to the experience of urhomelessness, in which the boundaries between person and world fade away in moments that are experienced with a sense of astonishment: "[t]he unhomely creeps up on you stealthily as your own shadow" (p. 141). As in urhomelessness, the unhomely involves exposure to the world-at-large and a reversal or transposition of that which was previously familiar and unfamiliar. However, not all unhomely experiences constitute urhomelessness, as the former sometimes, but do not necessarily, involve feelings of radical vulnerability, lack of basic safety, and profound social invalidation and alienation. Thus, while all urhomeless experiences might be seen as unhomely, not all unhomely experiences are sufficient to constitute urhomelessness. These resonances with Bhabha's account provide a tentative basis on which urhomelessness resonates with global postcolonial theory and the subaltern experience of social oppression, subjugation, and structural violence. From a purely experiential perspective, the person experiencing urhomelessness may manifest certain elements of subaltern experience, especially the experience of feeling invalidated and marginalised by hegemonic social structures (Spivak, 1988).

In sum, the interdisciplinary literature on psychosis, schizophrenia, and the not-at-home contains notable thematic intersections with the present findings that help to elucidate their potential extensions in larger spheres of sociocultural life. These interdisciplinary literatures and corresponding broader spheres will be crucial to future investigations of urhomelessness, which, as a fundamental potential of human experience, is thematically reflected in the cultural artefacts and documentations that humans produce.

Notes

1 Note, however, that the historicity of the ship of fools is debated (see Merquior, 1985).
2 Gordon (1990) has suggested that the usual translation of the sentence ("*Les fous alors avaient une existence facilement errante*") as "Madmen then led an easy wandering existence" (e.g., Foucault, 1965/1988, p. 8) is inaccurate.
3 It may be the case that these "postmodern" experiences are founded upon and ultimately undifferentiated from modernist alienation, reflecting Schirmacher's (1984) claim that postmodernity is simply the last phase of a historical process that started with modernity.
4 Also potentially relevant are Husserl's (1921–1928/1973b, 1929–1935/1973c) writings about the intersubjective, dialectical relationship between "homeworld" and "alienworld" (see Steinbock, 1994, 1995, 1996).
5 *Dasein* is a German word that literally means "being there" or "presence," and, more colloquially, "existence." Writing from an existential perspective, Heidegger uses it to mean the experience of existence—or the Being that experiences existence.
6 A retranslation of the German *unheimlich*, with reference to the common English translation of Freud's (1919/2003) article, "The uncanny."
7 Bhabha (1992) noted that although the experience of the "unhomely" is paradigmatically postcolonial, it can be found, perhaps less often or intensely, in other sociohistorical conditions.

13

FUTURE DIRECTIONS

Sarah R. Kamens, Jessica Yisca Baris Ginat, Mary Beth Quaranta Morrissey, Faith Forgione, Ileana Driggs, Jillian Minahan Zucchetto, Ryan Scanlon, Lia Kamar, and Pesach Lichtenberg

Our research project had various limitations, many of which were unavoidable or unexpected. Consideration of these limitations inherently leads to potential directions for future research that might utilise different approaches. Thus, this chapter presents limitations and suggestions for future research in tandem.

Research design

Participatory-action research

Recent recovery-oriented, social-justice, and participatory-action research has emphasised the importance of actively involving persons diagnosed with mental disorders in research about them, not only as participants, but as full researchers and collaborators (e.g., Davidson et al., 1997; see also Morawski, 1998). Service users, consumers, clients, patients, and other Experts by Experience have historically been denied a voice in defining their own experiences (see BPS, 2017; Law & Morrison, 2014; Noorani, 2013; Waddingham, 2012). In 2013, the Hearing Voices Network (HVN, 2013) released a position statement on DSM-5 and diagnosis that stated, "[w]e believe that people with lived experience of diagnosis must be at the heart of any discussions about alternatives to the current system" (para. 3). The project presented in this book took a person-centred, phenomenological approach that attempted to faithfully describe participants' experiences from their own perspectives; however, it lacked the crucial component of a participatory-action approach, which is key to determining the validity of urhomelessness as a conceptual framework for understanding the lived experiences of service users. Thus, participatory-action and social-justice research with persons who identify as having lived experiences of urhomelessness is a vital next step. It is ethically and scientifically crucial that any

DOI: 10.4324/9780429055454-14

attempt to rename or reconceptualise psychotic-disorder diagnoses includes first-person Expert-by-Experience perspectives as a priority.

Research sample

Limits to generalisability

Phenomenological research aims at a special kind of generality that is not comparable to empirical generalisation (Wertz, 2015). Instead of quantitative inferences, phenomenology aims at describing lived experience and the structures of consciousness, as well as typical or common variations based on individual examples of those structures (Wertz, 2005, 2010, 2015; Wertz et al., 2011). As mentioned in Chapter 4, in order to achieve qualitative generalities, our data analysis utilised empirically collected instances of the phenomenon under investigation and then, using imaginative variation, went beyond the dataset by drawing on other empirical sources such as examples from previous literature, nonfictional accounts, and clinical experience. Therefore, the present findings offer eidetic generalities, i.e., descriptions of general kinds of experience, but do not offer empirical quantifications of these phenomena such as their prevalence or frequencies. As a result, the extent to which a given individual or population might be likely to experience urhomelessness remains a matter for future research. Quantitative generalisability was also limited by the purposive sampling procedure, which allowed us to maximise diversity in demographic and symptom profiles.

Recruitment challenges

Approximately 15 potential participants who were invited to participate in the present study declined to participate. Potential participants gave various reasons for not wanting to participate, including being fatigued (one potential participant), polite statements such as "I'm good" or "that's okay" (two potential participants), complaints about having "too many problems" (one potential participant), wish not to be audio-recorded (two potential participants), no reason given (six potential participants), and interest in participating only if it would help secure discharge from the hospital (one potential participant). Others did not respond at all or walked away when approached. In addition, two potential participants were deemed by psychiatrists to lack capacity to consent despite their desire to participate. Therefore, the present sample may have excluded potential participants with severe challenges, apathy, suspicion, and/or a high level of dissatisfaction with the hospital environment. In addition, participants with (in clinical terms) predominantly negative symptoms may have been particularly uninterested or unable to participate; this possibility is supported by the lower frequency of participants with negative than positive or mixed PANSS (Kay et al., 2006) syndrome profiles. While these underrepresented experiences were considered during eidetic (phenomenological) analysis (see Chapter 4), our immediate sample might have not fully represented of the spectrum of psychotic experiences. Future research should specifically seek to include participants with these underrepresented psychological and clinical characteristics.

Comparison participants

Future research on urhomelessness would benefit from a larger and more diverse comparison sample. In the present study, there were only four pilot-comparison participants, and they were selected using convenience sampling. Comparison with the inpatient and outpatient hospital participants should be interpreted with caution due to demographic differences between the two samples; the average age of the four pilot-comparison participants (29 years) was less than the average age of the 21 inpatient and outpatient hospital participants (42 years). In addition, psychiatric diagnoses reported by pilot-comparison participants were not verified via structured diagnostic interviews; similarly, although ad hoc comparison participants were added unexpectedly (due to potential diagnostic error), their rule-out diagnoses were not formally confirmed.

Future researchers might also consider conducting a comprehensive phenomenological analysis of comparison narratives to learn more about the general structure of urhomeness. In the present study, reflections on meaning units and full individual structures were not created for each of the pilot-comparison narratives, which were instead used to systematically assess for differences from the general structure that emerged from the hospital-participants data. Therefore, our portrait of the experience of urhomeless is limited and predominantly focused on differences from the general structure of urhomelessness.

Use of DSM and ICD diagnoses as sampling criteria

A major limitation to the present study was the use of DSM (APA, 2000) and ICD (1992a, 1992b) diagnoses as a basis for identifying potential participants. All but one of the inpatient and outpatient hospital participants in the present study were diagnosed with schizophrenia or schizoaffective disorder; the other participant carried a current psychotic-disorder diagnosis ("psychotic state") that was not a schizophrenia-spectrum-disorder diagnosis. Therefore, the present findings may have limited generalisability to other psychotic disorders such as delusional disorders. However, as described in Chapter 2, due to the de-emphasis of Schneiderian first-rank symptoms (Schneider, 1950/1959) in DSM-5 (APA, 2013) and the ICD-11 (World Health Organisation, 2018), there is no clear standard or threshold delineating schizophrenia-spectrum from other psychotic disorders at present (Tandon, 2014; Tandon et al., 2013). Future research is therefore needed to determine whether urhomelessness is present in persons diagnosed with psychotic disorders that are not classified on the schizophrenia spectrum. The presence of urhomeless experiences in the one participant diagnosed with "psychotic state" suggests that this might at times occur.

Our study also did not include participants who were hospitalised for other, non-psychotic disorders. Although sampling procedures allowed for the inclusion of persons with comorbid conditions, most participants in the present sample were not dually diagnosed with psychotic disorders and non-psychotic disorders or syndromes. Exceptions were two participants with substance use disorders (including one in remission) and another participant whose formal diagnosis also specified suicidal ideation. Another participant appeared to meet criteria for OCD but did not carry a formal diagnosis. Therefore, the present study did not comprehensively investigate the presence of urhomelessness in comorbid conditions, one important type of between-diagnosis heterogeneity (see Boyd et al., 1994; Kessler et al., 2005; Kessler et al., 1994). Future phenomenological research might delineate whether and how urhomelessness is experienced by persons with other comorbid diagnoses, as well as whether the co-occurrence of urhomeless experiences and non-psychotic syndromes is due to a meaningful structural relationship between these experiences or, alternatively, coincidental or arbitrary. More specifically, future research might examine whether components of urhomeless experience are essential to other disorder categories; an example might be feeling that the world is inhospitable or unsafe in posttraumatic stress disorder (PTSD).

The present study did not include persons who were recruited on the basis of having anomalous experiences but did not carry a psychotic-disorder diagnosis and/or had never received mental health care. As described in Chapter 2, mounting research suggests that not all psychotic experiences are distressing and that subclinical psychotic experiences can be found in 5 to 8 per cent of the general population (McGrath et al., 2015; van Os et al., 2009). Indeed, comparison-participant narratives revealed that not all anomalous experiences are distressing, and not all were related to the general structure of urhomelessness. These findings indicated that strange or unusual perceptual and emotional experiences should not be assumed to be *ipso de facto* indicative of urhomelessness. Future research should investigate whether urhomelessness might be fully actualised in persons who explicitly endorse anomalous experiences or subclinical psychosis but do not meet official diagnostic criteria for psychotic disorders. More research is also needed in order to investigate whether the phenomenological kind approach might have enhanced ecological validity and utility for the differentiation of psychotic symptoms from non-clinical experiences (e.g., in the DSM [APA, 2000, 2015] and ICD [WHO, 1992a, 1992b]).

Service-user movements have begun to emphasise the possibility of living full, self-actualised lives with active anomalous experiences—which some find edifying or enhancing for understanding the psychological or existential meanings of their thoughts and feelings (e.g., ICP, 2015; Jones & Shattell, 2013; Longden, 2013). Although some participants enjoyed aspects of their urhomeless experiences or activities—for example, Avery enjoyed creating spaceships, and Lior enjoyed wandering in nature—in the present sample, these experiences were also accompanied by feelings of tremendous vulnerability and eclipsed social belonging. Therefore, future research should investigate whether urhomelessness is present in participants whose anomalous experiences are non-distressing and/or positively valued. Future research should also investigate situations in which anomalous and/or fleeting urhomeless experiences are transformed into a means of experiencing urhomeness, as was exemplified in the comparison narrative of Claire and in previous literature on religious subcultures (Luhrmann, 2012), spiritist mediums and shamans (Esima, 2017; Kalweit, 1989; Lambrecht, 2014; Moreira-Almeida, 2009), and emerging service-user groups (e.g., ICP, 2015).

Inpatient and outpatient hospital participants

Hospitals and outpatient treatment sites are cultural environments that reflect broader psychiatric cultures. The present study did not include persons who met criteria for psychotic disorders but had never been exposed to the mental health system. It is possible that some experiences of urhomelessness could be exacerbated by feelings of compromised safety, vulnerability, and alienation that might arise from the clinical encounter and/or experiences of being diagnosed and hospitalised (see, e.g., BPS, 2017; Link & Phelan, 1999; Ungar & Knaak, 2013; Watters, 2010). Indeed, most inpatient hospital participants described the experience of hospitalisation and institutionalisation as a distinct, and sometimes even primary source of suffering (see also Ginat, 2017). Although most participants described hardships prior to their diagnosis and hospitalisation, it is possible that the experience of mental health treatment further influenced the experienced meanings and emotions associated with these experiences.

Borg et al. (2005) have pointed out that for many persons diagnosed with SMIs, the psychiatric hospital may become a surrogate "home" that might be experienced as a "total institution" (Goffman, 1961) in which their lives are rigidly controlled (see also Ginat, 2017). Oliver's narrative, in particular, demonstrates that alienating aspects of hospitalisation may be experienced by service users as a potential exacerbating or risk factor for urhomelessness. At times, the hospital experience can reflect broader social structures, including discriminatory and unjust structures, with which the person has had negative experiences. The potential for the hospital to be experienced as discriminating, harmful, and alienating—as well as resonant with personal and collective oppression—was expressed by King (2007):

> I also wanted to know if there was a relationship between what happened 400 years ago when black men like me were chained,

> lynched, and brutalized to the way I was overtly medicated, locked up, and injected by white men who replaced their white sheets with white medical coats. (p. 13)

Future research should continue to investigate the relationship between urhomelessness and the experience of cultural oppression, racism, and xenophobia.

Some researchers have pointed out that specific interpretations of psychotic experiences may influence their quality and degree (BPS, 2017). Indeed, one focus of cognitive-behavioural approaches to psychosis is often the person's attributions and interpretations of their symptoms (e.g., Kingdon & Turkington, 2005). Differences in interpretations of psychotic experiences have also been a focus of the cross-cultural literature. For example, Luhrmann et al. (2015) found that in contrast to Indian and Ghanaian voice-hearers, who developed interpersonal relationships with their voices, American participants viewed their voices as bombarding symptoms of disease—reflecting the broader psychiatric discourses and cultures to which the American participants had been exposed. Thus, it is crucial for future researchers to recruit participants who have not been exposed to hospitalisation or mental health services—ideally participants with varying degrees of exposure to mental health discourse in the broader culture—in order to investigate whether urhomelessness might be exacerbated by iatrogenesis, or distressing experiences that may occur as a result of exposure to mental health treatment itself.

Psychiatric medications

All inpatient and outpatient hospital participants were taking psychiatric medications at the time of the interview (one participant received psychiatric medications on the day of the interview, after a period of not taking them in the community). Participants' medications may have affected the symptoms and experiences they reported, their general engagement with the interviews, and/or their ability to focus on and share their experiential reflections. Future research should explore the experience of urhomelessness in persons who are taking medications as compared to those who are not.

Interviews and transcriptions

Interviews were not longitudinal, which would have allowed for analysis of urhomeless experiences as they developed over time. Longitudinal interviews would have also allowed for real-time rather than retrospective reporting of earlier experiences. Future researchers should also consider involving family members and friends; although we were able to interview one mother in the present study, all other participants were interviewed individually.

Aspects of the interviews, such as the number and identity of interviewers, were not standardised across all participants. More specifically, two researchers, the primary investigator (PI) and an Israeli co-investigator, were present for most of the interviews conducted in Hebrew. The Israeli co-investigator conducted two interviews in Hebrew with the PI present part of the time. In contrast, a simultaneous translator was present for the Arabic-language interviews, alongside one or two researchers. Therefore, content of the interviews may have contained variation attributable to the specific interpersonal configuration of the interview setting.

Language barriers also created some minor obstacles during the interviews. The PI's Hebrew was conversational, but far from perfect; therefore, the Israeli co-investigator assisted when translation difficulties or misunderstandings were apparent. In addition, translations were forward-translations from Arabic and Hebrew into English; back-translations were not conducted. Moreover, some interview items—especially items about anomalous experiences, as well as the similarities and proverbs on the mental status examination portion of the PANSS (Kay et al., 2006; see Unsworth et al., 2005)—were particularly difficult to translate from English; therefore, negative responses on these items may have reflected language or cultural barriers rather than the absence of those experiences.

Cross-cultural comparisons

The project presented in this book is most accurately described as a transcultural or multicultural rather than a cross-cultural study. More specifically, due to the diversity of the sample, the current dataset was suitable for eliciting global similarities and transcultural differences, but it did not provide an empirical basis for fine-tuned cross-cultural comparisons. For example, the Jewish-Israeli participants came from diverse cultural and national backgrounds (e.g., French-European, Sephardic, and American), which did not facilitate direct cross-cultural comparisons with the Palestinian participants, who were similarly diverse in terms of their heritages and experiences within present-day Israel-Palestine.

It is also important to note that participants were recruited in only two cities, New York City and Jerusalem. New York and Jerusalem are multicultural centres with rich cultural diversity, histories, and traditions. However, both are considered to be part of the developed world—despite markedly disparate economic, societal, and sociopolitical conditions for Palestinians as compared to Jewish Israelis living in Jerusalem (e.g., Khattab, 2003). Therefore, this study did not contribute to the cross-cultural literature comparing prognostic outcomes and phenotypic differences in psychosis in developing versus developed countries (e.g., Hopper, 2004; Jablensky, 1987; Jablensky et al., 1992), nor was there comparison data to evaluate the popular theory that schizophrenia is a phenomenon particular to postindustrial, late capitalist society (e.g., Deleuze & Guattari, 1983, 1987; Jameson, 1991).

As a result of these limitations, future cross-cultural research is needed to identify and parse out potential cross-cultural differences that were not identified in the present study. More specifically, further research is necessary in order to replicate and elaborate the relationship of heterogeneous cultural experience to the three moments and common variations of urhomelessness. In addition, the inconclusive demographic trends in the present study—i.e., the adoption of pre-existing cultural narratives by Jewish-Israeli participants in the settled moment and the prominence of the destitute moment among Palestinian participants—should be further investigated for replicability and generalisability.

Gap between data analysis phases

As described in Chapter 4, data collection was conducted in three phases that occurred from May to July of 2013 (Phase I, New York), September to November of 2014 (Phase II, Jerusalem), and December 2014 through March of 2015 (Phase III, New York). Data analysis, which started after Phase I, was initially (prior to the emergence of structural unities) more exploratory and detailed; therefore, the reflections on meaning units and individual psychological structures for Phase I were more extensive than they were in Phase II, by which point emergent generalities were clearer, crisper, and immediately recognised. Despite safeguards to ensure that Phase I results were bracketed (see Wertz, 2005) during analyses of the initial Jerusalem participants, it was not possible to fully ensure non-contamination of Phase II by Phase I analyses. Future phenomenological researchers conducting international work should consider analysing data from different locations simultaneously.

Explanatory possibilities

The present study was predominantly descriptive and did not examine potential causal or etiological explanations for urhomelessness. Future investigators might consider genetic-phenomenological, longitudinal-quantitative, or other methodological approaches to the investigation of potential causal or risk factors. Theoretically, potential determinants of and risk factors for urhomelessness could be examined independent of standard diagnostic criteria. Given the ways in which urhomelessness thematises known structural risk factors for psychosis (e.g., houselessness [e.g., Folsom & Jeste, 2002] and migration [e.g., Bourque et al., 2011]), it is critical to investigate the potential contribution of sociopolitical, structural, and economic conditions to the development of urhomeless experiences (see also Kamens, 2018). The social determinants of urhomelessness should be explored using a variety of research methods and approaches, including longitudinal, socio-epidemiological, participatory, and social-justice approaches.

Recovery

Importantly, our findings revealed that urhomeness is a horizon of urhomelessness in all three moments. Thus, a crucial area for further investigation is the experience of urhomeness as it precedes, alternates, or overlaps with urhomelessness. In other words, future social justice research might address resiliency factors that facilitate the overcoming of urhomelessness and the process of recovery. In line with the Experts by Experience movement (e.g., Law & Morrison, 2014; Waddingham, 2012; see also Jones & Kelly, 2015), future research might also examine whether lived experiences of overcoming urhomelessness can be drawn upon to support and guide others. Research on the possibility of recovery in persons experiencing urhomelessness is particularly crucial given ongoing misunderstandings (despite extensive empirical evidence) about the possibility of recovery from schizophrenia (see, e.g., Davidson, 2003, 2008; Strauss, 2013; Strauss et al., 1985). Ultimately, urhomelessness is delineated by the horizon of urhomeness, or existential at-homeness in the world with others.

14

IMPLICATIONS FOR CULTURAL AND STRUCTURAL WORLDS

Sarah R. Kamens and Pesach Lichtenberg

Apples and oranges

This book is a book that compared apples and oranges. The historical and conventional definitions of schizophrenia, a diagnosis that is now over a century old, are vastly different from the urhomeless experiences that we discovered through phenomenological data analysis—so different, in fact, that they may seem incommensurable, divided by a conceptual chasm that would be impossible to bridge.

In general, there are two basic strategies to approaching this chasm. One strategy might be to acknowledge the difference without necessarily grappling with it. Some might say, in fact, that the general structure of urhomelessness is merely the psychological and existential side of schizophrenia-spectrum (and perhaps other psychotic) disorders, and that it has little to do with the everyday clinical treatment of mental health service users. Indeed, some previous qualitative research has been conceptualised as merely an illumination of the lived experiences of psychiatric conditions that the research thereby serves to reify. Another direction would be to grapple with this difference in order to reconceptualise and improve the way in which we diagnose anomalous mental states and emotional distress more broadly.

The approach in this book has been the latter. In other words, the findings of our study represent a contribution to recent movements to reconceptualise the schizophrenia diagnosis. We took this approach for several reasons. One is that the scientific and conceptual status of the conventional approach to schizophrenia, and to mental disorders in general, has recently come under question among mainstream researchers (see Chapters 1 and 2). It is thus crucial for any study of the lives of persons diagnosed with schizophrenia to take this mounting professional uncertainty about the diagnosis itself into consideration. Second, few studies have examined the potential contribution of qualitative research methods to the resolution of taxonomic debates about psychiatric diagnosis. Although phenomenological scholars (e.g., Parnas & Zahavi, 2002) have emphasised the value of the method, its potential has rarely but demonstrated in

 DOI: 10.4324/9780429055454-15

empirical studies. Last but not least, throughout the history, many service users have been dissatisfied with the way in which schizophrenia is defined and treated. Estimates of those who disagree with their diagnosis—what conventional terminology has dubbed 'lacking insight into mental illness'—range from 50 to 80% of those who meet criteria for schizophrenia (e.g., Melle & Barrett, 2012). In other words, at least half—if not the majority—of persons who might receive a diagnosis of schizophrenia do not identify with the diagnosis. This, in itself, prevents conventional practitioners from taking a person-centred approach to working with service users. In a close phenomenological study of three participants from our sample, Forgione (2019) dubbed the experience of actively rejecting a diagnostic label 'diagnostic dissent' and described it as a way of reclaiming agency in the face of perceived invalidation. In Forgione's own words:

> For the three participants in the present study, perceived misdiagnosis was an experience in which the persons act to experientially reclaim agency when they have been labeled with what they believe is an inaccurate and invalidating diagnosis. Perceived misdiagnosis, for these participants, was thus a revalidation of the individual's self-experience prior to the diagnosis. Because it is an act of reclaiming agency that may not be present in all instances of perceived misdiagnosis, this specific form of perceived misdiagnosis is here titled "Diagnostic Dissent." There are three essential constituents of diagnostic dissent: the clinician's loss of legitimacy, privileging self-knowledge, and psychosocial consequences of diagnostic labeling and stigma. (pp. 11–12)

Mirroring the high percentages of individual service users who reject the schizophrenia label are service-user and professional movements that have sought to change it. Chapters 2 and 11 described proposals to reframe psychosis from person-centred, recovery-oriented, and culturally/structurally relevant perspectives. Among those who have advocated for conceptually reframing the schizophrenia diagnosis are leaders of the Recovery Movement (Davidson, 2003, 2008; Davidson et al., 2008, Davidson et al., 2010; Deegan, 1994, 1996a, 1996b), who have advocated for emphasis on the whole person, meaning-making, and agency regardless of whether or not challenges (in clinical terms, symptoms) are ongoing. The British Psychological Society (BPS) has produced several task force reports that have been central in advancing alternative, scientifically grounded perspectives, including *Guidelines on language in relation to functional psychiatric diagnosis* (BPS, 2015), *Understanding psychosis and schizophrenia* (BPS, 2017), and the *Power Threat Meaning* (PTM) framework. As mentioned in Chapter 11, the general structure of urhomelessness is particularly resonant with the PTM framework, which emphasises the person's experience in the world—what *happened* to the person—rather than locating 'disturbances' or 'deficits' within the person. In addition, Mad pride and Mad studies scholars have argued for the reconceptualisation of anomalous and extreme states as different ways of being that, while often distressing and confusing, also have value—in and of themselves as well as in their overcoming—for the individual as well as broader society (see, e.g., Andersen et al., 2018; Culter 2017, 2018; Kalathil & Jones, 2016; LeFrançois et al., 2013). In addition, various existential, cultural, and spiritual approaches have offered ways in which learning to overcome unusual experiences can be a special form of knowledge acquisition that leads to the ability to help others (e.g., Cornwall, 2018b; Esima, 2017; Frese, 2009; Jung, 2009; Kalweit, 1989; King, 2007; Russell, 2018).

Our goal in this book has been to describe and demonstrate the vast differences between the ways in which schizophrenia has been conventionally described and the ways in which some people carrying the diagnosis experience their distress. This understanding, at the very least, should lead to a reconsideration of whether our current diagnostic practices are truly empirically and ethically grounded. A better understanding of urhomelessness might also lead to alternative, non-diagnostic approaches to mental distress and unusual experiences, such as formulation (Johnstone, 2017), recovery-oriented frameworks (Pavlo et al., 2019), and social-justice approaches (Robbins et al., 2015). Understanding urhomelessness might also lead to enhancements in the standard diagnostic paradigm, if that paradigm were to be modified in such a way as to adequately incorporate the subjective, lived experiences of service users (Flanagan et al., 2010). Indeed, our findings have substantial implications for approaching the heterogeneity problem in diagnostic psychiatry.

Implications for the heterogeneity problem and reconceptualising the schizophrenia diagnosis

This book took as its starting point the transformations currently taking place in diagnostic research and practice. The present findings suggest that the current diagnostic definition of schizophrenia-spectrum and psychotic disorders in the DSM (APA 1994, 2000, 2013) and ICD (WHO 1992a, 1992b, 2015) may reflect heterogeneous and incidental variations of a general structure that diverges from the way in which these disorders are classically defined. Therefore, our findings support previous literature suggesting that the prioritisation of subjective experience would require a reconceptualisation of the schizophrenia-spectrum diagnoses, and more specifically a departure from classic categorical and criterion-based definitions (see also BPS, 2017; Chung et al., 2007; Keshavan et al., 2011; NIMH, 2015). Further, our findings revealed that experiential heterogeneity is not a result of taxonomic or measurement error, but rather inherent to the experiences that have been commonly seen as schizophrenia and psychotic disorders. Thus, attempts to parse these experiences into discrete categories have resulted in unstable and fuzzy boundaries as well as substantial overlap with putatively unrelated disorder types. In light of these findings, efforts to conceptually resolve the heterogeneity problem might benefit from approaches that focus on the meaningful structures of lived experience rather than on the dominant Neo-Kraepelinian paradigm, which involves atomistic lists of symptoms with arbitrary boundaries and thresholds (e.g., APA, 2013; Compton & Guze, 1995; Robins & Guze, 1970).

At this point in history, it seems unlikely that standard diagnostic systems like the DSM (APA, 2013) and future RDoC (NIMH, 2021) will integrate findings from qualitative-phenomenological research into diagnostic definitions. Despite this unlikeliness, the present findings highlight the need for consideration of subjective experience in future taxonomies and nomenclatures. Focusing on lived experience may facilitate the development of nomenclatures based on the qualitative delineation of psychological meanings rather than estimations of categorical presence based on rote-frequency contingencies. The present project demonstrated that the identification of phenomenological kinds may contribute to future diagnostic alternatives—alternatives to the current diagnostic system—by providing descriptive, subjective experiential portraits that have flexible boundaries and are open to empirical correction by ongoing research.

The present results represent a first step in delineating the boundaries of a psychological structure that is meaningfully coherent in itself, but thematically and structurally divergent from conventional diagnostic definitions (APA, 1994, 2000, 2013; WHO, 1992a, 1992b, 2015). The extent to which the boundaries of urhomelessness correspond to the epidemiological boundaries of official schizophrenia-spectrum and psychotic disorders remains unknown. Theoretically, the present results may reflect an increased incidence and prevalence of urhomelessness in persons who (1) meet criteria for a DSM- or ICD-defined psychotic disorders and (2) have been previously hospitalised for treatment of a psychotic disorder. However, the present study did not include participants carrying the full spectrum of psychotic-disorder diagnoses, nor did we explicitly recruit participants who were diagnosed with subclinical (e.g., 'prodromal') psychosis or who reported non-clinical anomalous experiences. Our study also did not include participants reporting psychosis who were naïve to mental health treatment (see McGrath et al., 2015; van Os et al., 2009; Verdoux & van Os, 2002). Therefore, the overlap between urhomelessness and DSM/ICD symptom criteria may be merely partial. For example, it might be the case that urhomelessness is present both in schizophrenia-spectrum disorders and in other types of anomalous experiences, non-psychotic symptoms, symptom clusters, or disorders; moreover, it might also be absent in some persons with psychotic experiences, psychotic symptoms, or psychotic disorders. As described in Chapter 1, mounting evidence suggests that DSM and ICD symptom criteria may not reflect the natural epidemiological clustering of these symptoms in a way that 'carve[s] nature at its joints' (Plato, 370 B.C./ 1952; Regier et al., 2009, para. 15). The impact and extent of this mounting evidence is reflected by the recent decision of NIMH to redirect funding for clinical research away from DSM disorder categories because they are 'based on a consensus about clusters of clinical symptoms' rather than empirical evidence about how symptoms naturally co-occur (Insel, 2013, para. 2; NIMH, 2019). As expressed by van Os & Tamminga (2010), 'we have not yet discovered the natural boundaries of psychosis, but only observe its properties' (p. xxi).

Our findings also revealed that urhomeless experience is characterised by a profound sense of invalidation and alienation, suggesting that the effort to rename and redefine schizophrenia in order to reduce the stigma associated with the disorder category (see Lasalvia et al., 2015) may be crucial for reducing the risk of iatrogenesis associated with diagnostic practice. However, given the risk that any new diagnostic label, no matter how neutral, might become imbued with social stigma, newly proposed terms should reflect deeper reconceptualisations that are authentic to lived experience, evaluated in an ongoing way for potential impact on structural stigma, and acceptable from a service-user perspective (L. Sass, personal communication, July 16, 2015).

Implications for approaches and interventions

The present findings have implications for psychological, psychosocial, and community-based approaches and interventions aimed at supporting persons who are experiencing psychosis. Recall that the two main components of urhomelessness are feeling (1) profoundly vulnerable and unsafe and (2) alienated, invalidated, and unacknowledged by other persons. In general, our findings suggest that future preventative and treatment efforts might aim at directly targeting one or both of these distressing experiences.

For example, given the fact that some service users experience psychiatric hospitals and institutions as frightening and alienating (e.g., Ginat, 2017; Goffman, 1961; Lilja & Hellzén, 2008), hospital staff and other providers might consider modifying treatment environments and approaches to minimise experiences of rejection and invalidation. For example, mental health professionals might attempt to create and foster treatment environments characterised by hospitality. Efforts might be made to enhance and create welcoming, supportive relationships between mental health workers and service users, among peer service-user communities, and among mental health professionals themselves. The employment and direct involvement of Experts by Experience, or persons who have themselves been diagnosed with a mental illness and/or experienced the mental health system, might be a part of such a welcoming treatment environment (e.g., Pinfold et al., 2005).

One example of such an effort is the creation of Home Groups, or weekly groups that are co-led by a peer and a clinician (Styron et al., 2017, 2018).

Home Groups, which were designed for service users in community mental health settings, draw on both expertise by experience and clinical services in order to provide a weekly 'home base' for persons experiencing social isolation and structural disadvantage. Home Group members support each other not only when experiencing emotional distress, but also with concrete 'case management' needs, such as grappling with an eviction or caring for the pets of a fellow member who is in the hospital. Importantly, Home Groups provide a space for members to come together on a regular basis; members are encouraged to support each other outside of group sessions as well. In this way, Home Groups offer a place of safety, hospitality, acknowledgement, and validation – the very affordances that are experienced as lacking in urhomelessness.

The provision or improvement of physical dwelling environments and home-based services may also generate experiences of hospitality and welcoming, non-alienating, and non-threatening treatment environments. Borg et al. (2005) found that persons diagnosed with serious mental illness (SMI) viewed having a material home as an important part of recovery, as these abodes were experienced as secure bases. More specifically, they saw their physical home as a place for growth, development, and control; a means with which to balance socialization with privacy; and (when absent) a place that one could long for and dream about. The authors made suggestions for home-based interventions that respect persons' strengths and uphold the values of citizenship and deinstitutionalization.

Some alternatives to psychiatric hospitalisation provide safe and hospitable dwelling environments that might be helpful for the person experiencing urhomelessness. Soteria Houses, in particular, were developed for the creation of a supportive community life within a welcoming, home-like atmosphere (see Calton et al., 2008; Mosher et al., 2004). Soteria Houses offer a democratic setting in which all residents engage in activities and decisions that affect the household. Staff members participate in everyday activities with resident—from household chores, to playing cards, to sitting and talking about one's troubles. For these reasons, one of the co-investigators on the present project (P. L.) spent a decade working to establish a Soteria House in Jerusalem. Lichtenberg (2017) described the experience of advocating for and eventually opening Soteria Jerusalem in a recent article published in *Psychosis:*

> The central therapeutic principle at Soteria was what Mosher termed "interpersonal phenomenology", or, in simpler language, "being with" (Mosher et al., 2004). This meant that whatever was happening with a resident, we would try to be there, sharing the experience with him in a non-judgmental way. If, for example, a resident was disturbing others with a late night ecstatic dance celebrating the imminent coming of the messiah, we would join in

> the dance, which ultimately proved more effective in calming the excitement and getting closer to the resident. (p. 372)

This therapeutic principle had remarkable effects on the experience of residents at Soteria Jerusalem. As Lichtenberg (2017) explained:

> Soteria is first of all a home. It *feels* like a home. People enter and leave, look for food in the refrigerator, invite friends, gossip on the living room couch. A visitor is hard pressed to distinguish those providing from those receiving care. The resident needn't suffer the stigma of being institutionalized. (p. 373)

The type of caring, communal dwelling described by Lichtenberg provides precisely the experiences that are lacking for the person in urhomelessness, namely, a place of basic safety, acknowledgment, validation, and belonging-with other humans.

A number of recent efforts have sought to enhance the community experiences and participation of persons diagnosed with SMIs. For example, Patterson et al. (2013) found that homeless adults diagnosed with SMI who were assigned to independent apartments (as opposed to treatment-as-usual) were more likely to endorse items related to the emotional aspects of community belonging, suggesting that the provision of a physical living space positively enhanced their experiences. A large-scale, community-based, ongoing initiative called Project Citizenship aims at including persons with disabilities, including those diagnosed with SMI, as full citizens by enhancing the five Rs: rights, responsibilities, roles, resources, and relationships (Ponce et al., 2012; Project Citizenship, 2019; Rowe, 2015). Citizenship-oriented care recognises and enhances the rich, ongoing, empowering relationships between people diagnosed with SMIs and the societies in which they live. Future research might address whether efforts such as the Citizenship Project provide a means for experiencing urhomeness by enhancing social acknowledgement and personal agency within local communities and broader society.

In addition, our present findings hold implications for interventions that take action-oriented as opposed to deficit approaches to empowerment (e.g., Davidson & Shahar, 2007; see also Elkins, 2016). While it may be clinically useful to address what is lacking in urhomelessness, interventions might also focus on and emphasise the fact that the moments of urhomelessness represent strategies for overcoming and surviving, demonstrating that individuals with urhomelessness strive towards mitigating their distress. Even in the destitute moment, the person relinquishes attempts to secure shelter and urhomeness in order to survive a world experienced as completely unbearable and uninhabitable. Future interventions might focus on empowering the person through supporting their agentic efforts to create habitable zones of existential safety.

Implications for cultural epidemiology

One central focus in contemporary debates about the future of psychiatric diagnosis centres on unexpected findings that have emerged from the multicultural epidemiological literature. Chapter 2 detailed the mounting epidemiological evidence indicating that the phenotypic profile of schizophrenia varies across cultural contexts. For example, multiple studies have indicated that prognosis for persons diagnosed with psychotic disorders is more favourable in developing as opposed to developed countries (e.g., Hopper, 2004; Jablensky, 1987; Jablensky et al., 1992), and international research suggests that prevalence rates vary across cultures and locations (e.g., Jenkins & Barrett, 2004; Saha et al., 2005). Scholars (e.g., Jablensky & Sartorius, 2008; Luhrmann, 2007; Whitaker, 2010) have debated whether the more favourable prognosis in developing countries is due to differences in family and community systems or, alternatively, the iatrogenic effects of Western mental health care itself, including the iatrogenic effects of some psychotropic medications, institutionalisation, and the potential psychological effects of 'psychoeducation' about the putative chronicity of psychosis (see also Robbins et al., 2015). Some have suggested that for marginalised groups, experiences of discrimination and oppression may be effectively replicated in hospital and other clinical settings (e.g., Metzl, 2009). In consideration of the present findings, which revealed that profoundly alienating experiences are central to urhomelessness, it may be the case that *both* explanations for favourable prognosis in developing countries—the role of community systems and the alienating effects of Western mental health treatment—play a role in this empirical trend (Hopper, 2004; Jablensky, 1987; Jablensky et al., 1992).

As described in Chapter 2, one of the most robust findings in Western epidemiological research has been the higher prevalence of SMIs, including schizophrenia, in homeless (i.e., houseless) populations (e.g., Folsom & Jeste, 2002). Two competing explanations, the social drift and social defeat hypotheses, have been put forward by scholars to suggest that the sequelae of psychosis may lead to homelessness (e.g., Clark, 1948; Norquist & Narrow, 2000, cited in Luhrmann, 2007), and that the stressors of homelessness and deprivation may lead to psychosis (e.g., Post, 1992; Selten & Cantor-Graae, 2005; Selten et al., 2013; Werner et al., 2007). Recently, mounting evidence has supported the latter hypothesis. A study of over 6,000 European participants revealed that social defeat mediates the relationship between childhood trauma and psychosis (van Nierop et al., 2014). A related finding in the epidemiological literature is the relationship between psychosis risk and urbanicity (e.g., Freeman et al., 2014; Marcelis et al., 1999; Spauwen et al., 2004), and in particular, urban neighbourhoods that are high in segregation, population density, deprivation, and income inequality (Kirkbride et al., 2014; see also Davidson et al., 1997). In addition, there is robust evidence documenting an association between migrant status and psychosis risk (e.g., Bourque et al.,

2011; Morgan et al., 2010), as well as socioeconomic status at birth and the later development of psychosis (Werner et al., 2007). Future research might address whether these epidemiological relationships are enhanced when psychosis is defined as urhomelessness.

Given the thematic parallels between urhomelessness and the extant literature on the relationship between psychosis and deprivation, segregation, and houselessness (e.g., Folsom & Jeste, 2002), one of the most important directions for future epidemiological research might be the investigation of potential causal, epidemiological relationships between urhomelessness and structurally violent conditions such as ontic homelessness (houselessness), migration, income deprivation, childhood trauma, and ethnic segregation (see Farmer, 2005; Hopper, 2003; Jones et al., 2017; Metzl & Hansen, 2014; Metzl & Roberts, 2014). In addition, future phenomenological, mixed-methods, and participatory action research might elaborate on the subjective relationships between poverty, deprivation, and houselessness on the one hand and urhomelessness on the other. One hypothesis might be that experiences of deprivation and disparity generate or act as a diathesis for urhomeless experience. Any epidemiological relationship between urhomelessness, houselessness, and other forms of structural violence would have wide-reaching implications for prevention, practice, and research. This is also a crucial area for future mental health and social justice activism that is authentically focused on elevating the voices of Experts by Experience.

This book opened with a consideration of the unseen-elephant theme that has appeared in the recent schizophrenia research literature. For example, Keshavan et al. (2011) compared extant interpretative models of the schizophrenia to the Indian parable of six blind men who touch different parts of an elephant and disagree as to whether it is a fan, a rope, a tree trunk, a wall, a snake, or spears. Our phenomenological approach, grounded in a science created specifically for the understanding human experience, provided a different means of touching and describing that elephant.

Yet there are other aspects of the elephant that remain poorly understood, including how, when, and why it came into existence. If future research indicates that urhomelessness is actualised by the very psychosocial situations into which schizophrenia was conventionally thought to lead—homelessness, socioeconomic inequality, migration, ethnic segregation, and deprivation (e.g., BPS, 2017; Kirkbride et al., 2014; Morgan et al., 2010; Veling, 2013; Werner et al., 2007)—we might eventually investigate not the nature of the elephant, but rather the perplexity and disagreement that it has historically provoked in humans.

REFERENCES

Adame, A., Morsey, M., Bassman, R., & Yates, K. (2017). *Exploring identities of psychiatric survivor therapists: Beyond us and them*. Springer.

Adler, N. E. (2009). Health disparities through a psychological lens. *American Psychologist*, *64*(8), 663–673.

Afuape, T. (2011). *Power, resistance and liberation in therapy with survivors of trauma: To have our hearts broken*. New York, NY: Routledge.

Ahmed, A. O., Strauss, G. P., Buchanan, R. W., Kirkpatrick, B., & Carpenter, W. T. (2017). Schizophrenia heterogeneity revisited: Clinical, cognitive, and psychosocial correlates of statistically-derived negative symptoms subgroups. *Journal of Psychiatric Research*, *97*, 8–15.

Alarcón, R. D. (2009). DSM5–the "we know better/holier than thou" crusade: A response to Drs Frances and Spitzer's comments. *Psychiatric Times*. Retrieved from http://www.psychiatrictimes.com/dsm-5/content/article/10168/1427545

Allen, G. E. (1997). The social and economic origins of genetic determinism: A case history of the American Eugenics Movement, 1900-1940 and its lessons for today. *Genetica*, *99*, 77–88.

American Medico-Psychological Association (American Psychiatric Association). (1918). *Statistical manual for the use of institutions for the insane*. New York, NY: National Committee for Mental Hygiene of the American Medico-Psychological Association.

American Psychiatric Association (APA). (1952). *Diagnostic and statistical manual of mental disorders* (1st ed.). Washington, DC: Author.

American Psychiatric Association (APA). (1968). *Diagnostic and statistical manual of mental disorders* (2nd ed.). Washington, DC: Author.

American Psychiatric Association (APA). (1980). *Diagnostic and statistical manual of mental disorders* (3rd ed.). Washington, DC: Author.

American Psychiatric Association (APA). (1987). *Diagnostic and statistical manual of mental disorders* (3rd ed. text revision). Washington, DC: Author.

American Psychiatric Association (APA). (1994). *Diagnostic and statistical manual of mental disorders* (4th ed.). Washington, DC: Author.

American Psychiatric Association (APA). (2000). *Diagnostic and statistical manual of mental disorders* (4th ed. text revision). Washington, DC: Author.

American Psychiatric Association (APA). (2011). *Schizophrenia rationale: DSM-5 development*. Retrieved December 18, 2011 from http://www.dsm5.org/ProposedRevision/Pages/proposedrevision.aspx?rid=411#

American Psychiatric Association (APA). (2013). *Diagnostic and statistical manual of mental disorders* (5th ed.). Washington, DC: Author.

American Psychological Association. (2002). *Guidelines on multicultural education, training, research, practice, and organizational change for psychologists*. Retrieved from https://www.apa.org/pi/oema/resources/policy/multicultural-guideline.pdf

Andersen, J., Altwies, E., Bossewitch, J., Brown, C., Cole, K., Davidow, S., … & Weber, C. L. (2018). Mad resistance/mad alternatives: Democratizing mental health care. In S. J. Rosenberg & J. Rosenberg (Eds.), *Community mental health: Challenges for the 21st century* (3rd ed., pp. 19–36). New York, NY: Routledge.

Andreasen, N. C. (1984a). *The scale for the assessment of negative symptoms (SANS)*. Iowa City, IA: University of Iowa.

Andreasen, N. C. (1984b). *The scale for the assessment of positive symptoms (SAPS)*. Iowa City, IA: University of Iowa.

Andreasen, N. C. (1985). Positive vs. negative schizophrenia: A critical evaluation. *Schizophrenia Bulletin, 11*, 380–389.

Andreasen, N. C. (2003). Untreated initial psychosis: Relation to cognitive deficits and brain morphology in first-episode schizophrenia. *American Journal of Psychiatry, 160*, 142–148. Retrieved from http://ajp.psychiatryonline.org/data/Journals/AJP/3744/142.pdf

Andreasen, N. C., & Olsen, S. (1982). Negative v positive schizophrenia: Definition and validation. *Archives of General Psychiatry, 39*, 789–794.

Aponte, J. F., Rivers, R.Y., & Wohl, J. (Eds.) (2000). *Psychological interventions and cultural diversity* (2nd ed.). Boston: Allyn & Baco.

Arafat, C., & Boothby, N. (2003). Psychosocial assessment of Palestinian children. Retrieved from http://unispal.un.org/unispal.nsf/59c118f065c4465b852572a500625fea/6bb117b13425504685256ea90055c8ab/$FILE/assessment.pdf

Arango, C., Kirkpatrick, B., & Buchanan, R. W. (2000). Neurological signs and the heterogeneity of schizophrenia. *The American Journal of Psychiatry, 157*, 560–565.

Auerbach, C., & Silverstein, L. B. (2003). *Qualitative data: An introduction to coding and analysis*. New York, NY: New York University Press.

Ayuso-Mateos, J. L. (2012). Prototype diagnosis of psychiatric syndromes and the ICD-11. *World Psychiatry, 11*, 30–31.

Banerjee, A. (2012). Cross-cultural variance of schizophrenia in symptoms, diagnosis and treatment. *The Georgetown Undergraduate Journal of Health Sciences, 6*. Retrieved from https://blogs.commons.georgetown.edu/journal-of-health-sciences/files/Banerjee-2012-GUJHS-6-2-Cross-Cultural-Variance-of-Schizophrenia-in-Symptoms-Diagnosis-and-Treatment.pdf

Barch, D. M. (2017). Biotypes: Promise and pitfalls. *Biological Psychiatry, 82*(1), 2–3.

Bar-el, Y., Durst, R., Katz, G., Zislin, J., Strauss, Z., & Knobler, H. Y. (2000). Jerusalem syndrome. *Journal of mental science, 176*, 86–90.

Barkil-Oteo, A. (2012, August 6). Psychiatry's identity crisis, and how to start fixing it. *Discover Magazine*. Retrieved from http://blogs.discovermagazine.com/crux/2012/08/06/psychiatrys-identity-crisis-and-how-to-start-fixing-it/

Baron, M., Gruen, R., Levitt, M., & Kane, J. (1984). Platelet monoamine oxidase and clinical phenomenology of schizophrenia. *Psychiatry Research, 11*, 205–209.

Barrett, R. J. (2004). Kurt Schneider in Borneo: Do first rank symptoms apply to the Iban? In J. H. Jenkins & R. J. Barrett (Eds.), *Schizophrenia, culture, and subjectivity: The edge of experience* (pp. 87–109). West Nyack, NY: Cambridge University Press.

Bateson, G., Jackson, D. D., Haley, J., & Weakland, J. (1956) Toward a theory of schizophrenia. *Behavioural Science, 1*, 251–264.

Baudrillard, J. (1983). The ecstasy of communication. In H. Foster (Ed.), *The anti-aesthetic: Essays on postmodern culture* (pp. 145–154). New York, NY: The New Press.

Baumeister, A., & Francis, J. (2002). Historical development of the dopamine hypothesis of schizophrenia. *Journal of the History of the Neurosciences, 11*, 265–277.

Beck, A. T. (1976). *Cognitive therapy and emotional disorders*. Oxford, UK: International Universities Press.

Beng-Choon, H., Alicata, D., Ward, J., Moser, D. J., O'Leary, D. S., Arndt, S. (2003). Untreated initial psychosis: relation to cognitive deficits and brain morphology in first-episode schizophrenia. *The American Journal of Psychiatry, 160*(1), 142–148. https://doi.org/10.1176/appi.ajp.160.1.142

Benson, P. J., Beedie, S. A., Shephard, E., Giegling, I., Rujescu, D., & St. Clair, D. (2012). Simple viewing tests can detect eye movement abnormalities that distinguish schizophrenia cases from controls with exceptional accuracy. *Biological Psychiatry, 72*(9), 716–724.

Berkson, J. (1946). Limitations of the application of four-fold table analysis to hospital data. *Biometrics, 2*, 247–253.

Berrios G. E. (1989). What is phenomenology? A review. *Journal of the Royal Society of Medicine, 82*(7), 425–428.

Berrios, G. E. (1992). Phenomenology, psychopathology and Jaspers: A conceptual history. *History of Psychiatry, iii*, 303–327.

Berrios, G. E., Luque, R., & Villagrán, J. M. (2003). Schizophrenia: A conceptual history. *International Journal of Psychology and Psychological Therapy, 3*(2), 111–140.

Bhabha, H. (1992). The world and the home. *Social Text, 31/32*, 141–153.

Bhati, M. T. (2013). Defining psychosis: The evolution of DSM-5 schizophrenia spectrum disorders. *Current Psychiatry Reports, 15*, 409.

Bhavsar V., & Bhugra D. (2008). Religious delusions: Finding meanings in psychosis. *Psychopathology, 41*, 165–172.

Bhavsar, V., Fusar-Poli, P., & McGuire, P. (2018). Neighbourhood deprivation is positively associated with detection of the ultra-high risk (UHR) state for psychosis in South East London. *Schizophrenia Research, 192*, 371–376.

Bhikha, A. G., Farooq, S., Chaudry, N., & Husain, N. (2012). A systematic review of explanatory models of illness for psychosis in developing countries. *International Review of Psychiatry, 24*, 450–462.

Bhugra, D. (2007). Lumping or splitting in diagnosis – what's the point?. *International Journal of Social Psychiatry, 53*, 387–388.

Binswanger, L. (1956). Extravagance, perverseness, manneristic behaviour and schizophrenia. In J. Cutting & M. Shepherd (Eds.), *The clinical roots of the schizophrenia concepts* (pp. 83–88). Cambridge, UK: Cambridge University Press.

Binswanger, L. (1957). *Schizophrenie*. Tuebeingen, Germany: Neske.

Binswanger, L. (1963). Being-*in the-World: Selected papers of Ludwig Binswanger* (J. Needleman, Trans.). New York, NY: Basic Books.

Birenbaum-Carmeli, D. (2001). Between individualism and collectivism: The case of a middle class neighbourhood in Israel. *International Journal of Sociology and Social Policy*, *21*, 1–25.

Blaney, P. H., & Millon, T. (2009). *Oxford textbook of psychopathology*. New York, NY: Oxford University Press.

Blaney, P. H., Kreuger, R. F., & Millon, T. (Eds.) (2014). *Oxford textbook of psychopathology* (3rd edition). New York, NY: Oxford University Press.

Blankenburg, W. (1971). *Der Verlust der Naturlichen Selbstverstandlichkeit: Ein Beitrag zur Psychopathologie Symptomarmer Schizophrenien*. Stuttgart: Ferdinand Enke Verlag.

Blankenburg, W. (2001). First steps toward a psychopathology of "common sense." *Philosophy, Psychiatry, Psychology*, *8*, 303–315. (A. Mishara, Trans.) Original work published 1969.

Blashfield, R. K., Keeley, J. W., Flanagan, E. H., & Miles, S. R. (2014). The cycle of classification: DSM-I through DSM-5. *Annual Review of Clinical Psychology*, *10*, 25–51.

Bleuler, E. (1908). Die prognose der dementia praecox (Schizophreniegruppe). *Medizin*, *65*, 436–464.

Bleuler, E. (1911). *Dementia praecox, oder die Gruppe der Schizophrenien*. Leipzig, Germany: Franz Deuticke.

Bleuler, E., & Brill, A. A. (1988). *Textbook of psychiatry*. New York, NY: Classics of Psychiatry & Behavioral Sciences Library. Original work published 1924.

Bogousslavsky, J., & Moulin, T. (2011). Birth of modern psychiatry and the death of alienism: The legacy of Jean-Martin Charcot. *Frontiers of Neurology and Neuroscience*, *29*, 1–8.

Borg, M., Sells, D., Topor, A., Mezzina, R., Marin, I., & Davidson, L. (2005). What makes a house a home: The role of material resources in recovery from severe mental illness. *American Journal of Psychiatric Rehabilitation*, *8*, 243–256.

Borges, J. L. (1942). *The analytic language of John Wilkins*. Retrieved from https://ccrma.stanford.edu/courses/155/assignment/ex1/Borges.pdf

Boss, M. (1963). *Psychoanalysis and daseinsanalysis*. New York, NY: Basic Books.

Boss, M. (1975). The Daseinanalyse approach to schizophrenic 'being ill.' *Acta Psiquiátrica y Psicológica de América Latina*, *21*, 6–23.

Bourque, F., van der Ven, E., & Malla, A. (2011). A meta-analysis of the risk for psychotic disorders among first- and second-generation immigrants. *Psychological Medicine*, *41*, 897–910.

Bovet, P., & Parnas, J. (1993). Schizophrenic delusions: A phenomenological approach. *Schizophrenia Bulletin*, *19*, 579–597.

Boyd, J. H., Burke, J. D., Gruenberg, E., Holzer, C. E., Rae, D. S., George, L. K., ... & Nestadt, G. (1984). Exclusion criteria of *DSM-III*: A study of co-occurrence of hierarchy-free syndromes. *Archives of General Psychiatry*, *41*, 983–989.

Boyle, M. (2002). *Schizophrenia: A scientific delusion?* New York, NY: Taylor & Francis.

BPS. (2015). Guidelines on language in relation to functional psychiatric diagnosis. British Psychological Society Division of Clinical Psychology. Retrieved from https://

www1.bps.org.uk/system/files/user-files/Division%20of%20Clinical%20Psychology/public/Guidelines%20on%20Language%20web.pdf

BPS. (2017). *Understanding psychosis and schizophrenia*. British Psychological Society Division of Clinical Psychology. Retrieved from https://www1.bps.org.uk/system/files/user-files/Division%20of%20Clinical%20Psychology/public/CAT-1657.pdf

BPS. (2018). Introducing the Power Threat Meaning framework. British Psychological Society Division of Clinical Psychology. Retrieved from https://www.bps.org.uk/news-and-policy/introducing-power-threat-meaning-framework

Bracken, P., Thomas, P., Timimi, S., Asen, E., Behr, G., Beuster, C., ... & Yeomans, D. (2012). Psychiatry beyond the current paradigm. *The British Journal of Psychiatry*, *201*, 430–434.

Brekke, J. S., & Barrio, C. (1997). Cross-ethnic symptom differences in schizophrenia: The influence of culture and minority status. *Schizophrenia Bulletin*, *23*, 305–316.

Brentano, F. (1874). *Psychology from an empirical standpoint* (A. C. Rancurello, D. B. Terrell, & L. L. McAlister, Trans.). New York, NY: Humanities Press.

Britz, B. (n.d.). *Hearing voices with Berta Britz*. Retrieved from https://oc87recoverydiaries.org/hearing-voices-with-berta-britz/

Broome, R. E. (2011). Descriptive phenomenological psychological method: An example of a methodology section from doctoral dissertation. *The Selected Works of Rodger E. Broome*. Retrieved from http://works.bepress.com/rodger_broome/9

Broome, M. R., Harland, R., Owen, G. W., Stringaris, A. (Eds.) (2013). *The Maudsley Reader in phenomenological psychiatry*. West Nyack, NY: Cambridge University Press.

Brown, T.A., Chorpita, B.F., & Barlow, D.H. (1998). Structural relationships among dimensions of the DSM-IV anxiety and mood disorders and dimensions of negative affect, positive affect, and autonomic arousal. *Journal of Abnormal Psychology*, *107*, 179–192.

Buchanan, N. T., & Wiklund, L. O. (2021). Intersectionality research in psychological science: Resisting the tendency to disconnect, dilute, and depoliticize. *Research on Child and Adolescent Psychopathology*, *49*(1), 25–31.

Buchanan, R. W. (2007). Persistent negative symptoms in schizophrenia: An overview. *Schizophrenia Bulletin*, *33*, 1013–1022.

Buchanan, R. W., & Carpenter, W. T. (1994). Domains of psychopathology: An approach to the reduction of heterogeneity in schizophrenia. *The Journal of Nervous and Mental Disease*, *182*, 193–204.

Buckley, F. M. (1971). An approach to a phenomenology of at-homeness. *Duquesne Studies in Phenomenological Psychology*, *1*, 198–211.

Buckley, P. F., Miller, B. J., Lehrer, D. S., & Castle, D. J. (2009). Psychiatric comorbidities and schizophrenia. *Schizophrenia Bulletin*, *35*(2), 383–402.

Burston, D. (2000). *The crucible of experience: R. D. Laing and the crisis of psychotherapy*. Cambridge, MA: Harvard University Press.

Burston, D. (2018). Psychiatry, anti-psychiatry, and anti-anti-psychiatry: Rhetoric and reality. Psychotherapy and politics international. Retrieved from https://onlinelibrary.wiley.com/doi/full/10.1002/ppi.1439

Burton, R. (2001). *The anatomy of melancholy*. New York, NY: The New York Review of Books. Original work published 1621.

Buswell, G., Haime, Z., Lloyd-Evans, B., & Billings, J. (2021). A systematic review of PTSD to the experience of psychosis: Prevalence and associated factors. *BMC Psychiatry, 21*.

Butler, B. (2017). The efficacies of heritage: Syndromes, magics, and possessional acts. *Public Archaeology*, 15(2–3), 112–135.

Byrne, L., Stratford, A., & Davidson, L. (2018). The global need for lived experience leadership. *Psychiatric Rehabilitation Journal, 41*(1), 76–79. doi:10.1037/prj0000289

Calton, T., Ferriter, M., Huband, N., & Spandler, H. (2008). A systematic review of the Soteria paradigm for the treatment of people diagnosed with schizophrenia. *Schizophrenia Bulletin, 34*, 181–192.

Cardno, A. G., Thomas, K., & McGuffin, P. (2002). Clinical variables and genetic loading for schizophrenia: Analysis of published Danish adoption study data. *Schizophrenia Bulletin, 28*, 393–399.

Carlat, D. (2009, June 30). Psychiatry's *DSM-V* process: Now a bar room brawl [Web log message]. *The Carlat Psychiatry Blog*. Retrieved from http://carlatpsychiatry.blogspot.com/2009/06/psychiatrys-dsm-v-process-now-bar-room.html

Carlat, D. J. (2010). *Unhinged: The trouble with psychiatry - A doctor's revelations about a profession in crisis*. New York, NY: Free Press.

Carlstedt, R. A. (Ed.) (2010). *Handbook of integrative clinical psychology, psychiatry, and behavioral medicine: Perspectives, practices, and research*. New York, NY: Springer Publishing.

Carpenter, W. (2011a, September). *Schizophrenia: The beginning, the change, the future*. Buenos Aires, Argentina: Keynote Lecture at the World Congress of Psychiatry.

Carpenter, W. (2011b, September). Diagnostic symptoms versus core psychopathology. Lecture as part of symposium on *Rethinking psychosis: Concepts and Core Psychopathological Features* at the World Congress of Psychiatry, Buenos Aires, Argentina.

Carpenter, W. T. (2013). RDoC and DSM-5: What's the fuss? *Schizophrenia Bulletin, 39*, 945–946. Retrieved May 9, 2015 from http://www.medscape.com/viewarticle/812605

Carpenter, W. T., & Kirkpatrick, B. (2005). The heterogeneity of the long-term course of schizophrenia. In L. Davidson, C. Harding, & L. Spaniol (Eds.), *Recovery from severe mental illnesses: Research evidence and implications for practice*: *Vol. 1* (pp. 147–159). Boston, MA: Center for Rehabilitation.

Carpenter, W. T., Strauss, J. S., & Bartko, J. J. (1981). Beyond diagnosis: The phenomenology of schizophrenia. *The American Journal of Psychiatry, 138*, 948–953.

Cavallaro, R., Mistretta, P., Cocchi, F., Manzato, M., & Smeraldi, E. (2001). Differential efficacy of risperidone versus haloperidol in psychopathological subtypes of subchronic schizophrenia. *Human Psychopharmacology: Clinical and Experimental, 16*, 439–448.

Chaitin, J., Awwad, E., & Andriani, C. (2009). Belonging to the conflict: Collective identities among Israeli and Palestinian émigrés to the United States. *Social Identities: Journal for the Study of Race, Nation and Culture, 15*, 207–225.

Charcot, J. M. (1889). *Lectures on the diseases of the nervous system* (Vol. III, T. Savill, Trans.). London, UK: The New Syndenham Society.

Chidarikire, S., Cross, M., Skinner, I., & Cleary, M. (2020). An ethnographic study of schizophrenia in Zimbabwe: The role of culture, faith, and religion. *Journal of Spirituality in Mental Health, 22*(2), 173–194.

Choudry, A., & Farooq, S. (2018). Psychosis and related disorders in international classification of Disease-11 and their relationship to diagnostic and statistical Manual-5 and international classification of Disease-10. *Indian Journal of Social Psychiatry, 34*(5), 11–16.

Chubb, J. E., Bradshaw, N. J., Soares, D. C., Porteous, D. J., & Millar, J. K. (2007). The DISC locus in psychiatric illness. Molecular Psychiatry, 13(1), 36–64. https://doi.org/10.1038/sj.mp.4002106

Chung, M. C., Fulford, K. W. M., & Graham, G. (2007). *Reconceiving Schizophrenia* [International Perspectives in Philosophy and Psychiatry]. Oxford: Oxford University Press.

Cerullo, M. (2010). The end of the DSM? *Bulletin of the Association for the Advancement of Philosophy and Psychiatry, 17*, 2–3.

Clark, R. (1948). The relationship of schizophrenia to occupational income and occupational prestige. *American Sociological Review, 13*, 325–330.

Clementz, B. A., Sweeney, J. A., Hamm, J. P., Ivleva, E. I., Ethridge, L. E., Pearlson, G. D., ... Tamminga, C. A. (2016). Identification of distinct psychosis biotypes using brain-based biomarkers. *American Journal of Psychiatry* ahead of print. Retrieved from http://ajp.psychiatryonline.org/doi/full/10.1176/appi.ajp.2015.14091200

Collin, G., & van den Heuvel, M. P. (2016). Anatomical and functional brain network architecture in schizophrenia. In T. Abel & T. Nickl-Jockschat (Eds.), *The neurobiology of schizophrenia* (pp. 313–336). San Diego, CA: Elsevier Academic Press.

Compton, W. M., & Guze, S. B. (1995). The neo-Kraepelinian revolution in psychiatric diagnosis. *European Archives of Psychiatry and Clinical Neuroscience, 245*, 196–201.

Corin, E., Thara, R., & Padmavati, R. (2005). Shadows of culture in psychosis in south India: A methodological exploration and illustration. *International Review of Psychiatry, 17*(2), 75–81.

Cornblatt, B. A., Green, M. F., Walker, E. F., & Mittal, V. A. (2009). Schizophrenia: Etiology and neurocognition. In P. H. Blaney & T. Millon (Eds.), *Oxford textbook of psychopathology* (2nd ed., pp. 298–332). New York, NY: Oxford University Press.

Cornwall, M. (2018a). Introduction for special issue: "Humanistic perspectives on understanding and responding to extreme states." *Journal of Humanistic Psychology*. Retrieved from https://journals.sagepub.com/doi/full/10.1177/0022167818775579

Cornwall, M. (2018b). Merciful love can help relieve the emotional suffering of extreme states. *Journal of Humanistic Psychology*. https://journals.sagepub.com/doi/abs/10.1177/0022167818773467?journalCode=jhpa

Costello, J. (2009). *Resignation letter*. Retrieved June 18, 2011 from http://www.scribd.com/doc/17162466/Jane-Costello-Resignation-Letter-from-DSMV-Task-Force-to-Danny-Pine-March-27-2009

Crichton, P., Carel, H., & Kidd, I. J. (2017). Epistemic injustice in psychiatry. *Bjpsych Bulletin*, *41*(2), 65–70.

Cummings, C. A. (2013). DSM-5 on culture: A significant advance. *The Foundation for Psychocultural Research (FPR) Blog*. Retrieved May 6, 2015 from https://thefprorg.wordpress.com/2013/06/27/dsm-5-on-culture-a-significant-advance/

Cushman, P. (1990). Why the self is empty: Toward a historically situated psychology. *American Psychologist*, *45*, 599–611.

Culter, E. (2017). A Mad Pride perspective on borderline personality disorder. *Mad in America: Science, Psychiatry, and Social Justice*. Retrieved from https://www.madinamerica.com/2017/11/mad-pride-borderline-personality/

Cutler, E. S. (2018). In defense of victimhood. *Radical abolitionist: A cognitive literary blogspace*. Retrieved from https://www.radicalabolitionist.org/radical-abolitionist/2018/6/5/in-defense-of-victimhood

Davidson, L. (2002). Intentionality, identity, and delusions of control in schizophrenia: A Husserlian perspective. *Journal of Phenomenological Psychology*, *33*, 39–58.

Davidson, L. (2003). *Living outside mental illness: Qualitative studies of recovery in schizophrenia*. New York, NY: New York University Press.

Davidson, L. (2008). From 'Incurable' schizophrenic to person in recovery: A not so uncommon story. *Pragmatic Case Studies in Psychotherapy*, *4*, 25–34.

Davidson, L., & McGlashan, T. (1997). The varied outcomes of schizophrenia. *The Canadian Journal of Psychiatry*, *42*, 34–43.

Davidson, L., O'Connell, M., Sells, D., & Staeheli, M. (2003). Is there an outside to mental illness? In L. Davidson (Eds.), *Living outside mental illness: Qualitative studies of recovery in schizophrenia* (pp. 31–60). New York, NY: New York University Press.

Davidson, L., Rakfeldt, J., & Strauss, J. (2010). *The roots of the recovery movement in psychiatry: Lessons learned*. Hoboken, NJ: Wiley-Blackwell.

Davidson, L., Schmutte, T., Dinzeo, T., & Andres-Hyman, R. (2008). Remission and recovery in schizophrenia: Practitioner and patient perspectives. *Schizophrenia Bulletin*, *34*, 508.

Davidson, L., & Shahar, G. (2007). From deficit to desire: A philosophical reconsideration of action models of psychopathology. *Philosophy, Psychiatry, & Psychology*, *14*, 215–232.

Davidson, L., & Stayner, D. (1997). Loss, loneliness, and the desire for love: Perspectives on the social lives of people with schizophrenia. *Psychiatric Rehabilitation Journal*, *20*, 3–12.

Davidson, L., Stayner, D., & Haglund, K. (1998). Phenomenological perspectives on the social functioning of people with schizophrenia. In Mueser, K. & Tarrier, N. (Eds.), *Handbook of social functioning in schizophrenia*. Boston, MA: Allyn and Bacon.

Davidson, L., Stayner, D. A., Lambert, S., Smith, P., & Sledge, W. H. (1997). Phenomenological and participatory research on schizophrenia: Recovering the person in theory and practice. *Journal of Social Issues*, *53*, 767–784.

Davidson, L., & Strauss, J. S. (1992). Sense of self in recovery from severe mental illness. *British Journal Of Medical Psychology*, *65*(2), 131–145. doi:10.1111/j.2044-8341.1992.tb01693.x

De, S., Bhatia, T., Thomas, P., Chakraborty, S., Prasad, S., Nagpal, R., Nimgaonkar, V. L., & Deshpande, S.N. (2013). Bizarre delusions: A qualitative study on Indian schizophrenia patients. *Indian Journal of Psychological Medicine, 35*, 268–272.

Decker, H. S. (2007). How Kraepelinian was Kraepelin? How Kraepelinian are the neo-Kraepelinians? – from Emil Kraepelin to DSM-III. *History of Psychiatry, 18*, 337–360.

Deegan, P. E. (1994). A letter to my friend who is giving up. *The Journal of the California Alliance for the Mentally Ill, 5*, 18–20.

Deegan, P. E. (1996a). *Recovery and the conspiracy of hope*. Presentation at "There's a Person In Here": The Sixth Annual Mental Health Services Conference of Australia and New Zealand. Brisbane, Australia.

Deegan, P. (1996b). Recovery as a journey of the heart. *Psychiatric Rehabilitation Journal, 19*(3), 91–97.

de Jong, J. T. (2012). DSM-5 and culture. *Tijdschr Psychiatry, 54*, 807–818.

Deleuze, G., & Guattari, F. (1983). *Anti-oedipus: Capitalism and schizophrenia* (R. Hurley, M. Seem & H. R. Lane, Trans.). Minneapolis, MN: University of Minnesota Press. Original work published 1972.

Deleuze, G., & Guattari, F. (1987). *A thousand plateaus: Capitalism and schizophrenia* (B. Massumi, Trans.). Minneapolis, MN: University of Minnesota Press. Original work published 1980.

Delphin-Rittmon, M. E., Flanagan, E., Andres-Hyman, R., Ortiz, J., Amer, M. M., & Davison, L. (2015). Racial-ethnic differences in access, diagnosis, and outcomes in public-sector inpatient mental health treatment. *Psychological Services, 12*, 158–166.

Denischik, M. (2015). Temporality in psychosis: Loss of lived time in an alien world. *The Humanistic Psychologist, 43*, 148–159.

Denys, D. (2007). How new is the new philosophy of psychiatry? *Philosophy, Ethics, and Humanities in Medicine, 20*(2), 22. Retrieved from http://www.peh-med.com/content/2/1/22

Desai, M. U. (2014a). Psychology, the psychological, and critical praxis: A phenomenologist reads Frantz Fanon. *Theory & Psychology, 24*, 58–75.

Desai, M. U. (2014b). Travel as qualitative method: Travel in psychology's history and in Medard Boss' sojourn to India. *Journal of Humanistic Psychology, 54*, 494–507. doi:10.1177/0022167813517942

Descartes, R. (1996). *Meditations on first philosophy* (J. Cottingham, Trans. & Ed.). West Nyack, NY: Cambridge University Press. Original work published 1641.

Descartes, R. (2008). *Meditations on first philosophy* (M. Moriarty, Trans.). Oxford University Press. Original work published 1647.

DeVellis, R. F. (1991). *Scale development: Theory and applications*. Newbury Park, CA: Sage.

DeVylder, J. E., Narita, Z., Horiguchi, S., Kodaka, M., Schiffman, J., Yang, L. H., & Koyanagi, A. (2020). Stigma associated with the labeling of schizophrenia, depression, and hikikomori in Japan. *Stigma and Health, 5*(4), 472–476.

Dhar, A. (2020). *Madness and subjectivity: A cross-cultural examination of psychosis in the West and India*. Routledge.

Documents on the "T-4" and "14f13" Programs. (2009). In G. Eghigian (Ed.), *From madness to mental health: Psychiatric disorder and its treatment in Western*

Civilization (pp. 299–303). Piscataway, NJ: Rutgers University Press. Original work published 1939–1945.

Dohrenwend, B. P. (1990). Socioeconomic status (SES) and psychiatric disorders. Are the issues still compelling? *Social Psychiatry and Psychiatric Epidemiology, 25*, 41–47.

Dohrenwend, B. P., Levav, I., Shrout, P., Schwartz, S., Naveh, G., Link, B., ... & Stueve, A. (1992). Socioeconomic status and psychiatric disorders: The causation-selection issue. *Science, 255*, 946–952.

Dowbiggin, I. R. (1997). *Keeping America sane: Psychiatry and eugenics in the United States and Canada, 1880-1940*. Ithica, NY: Cornell University Press.

Drummond, J. (2008). *Historical dictionary of Husserl's philosophy*. The Scarecrow Press.

DuBrul, S. A. (2014). The Icarus project: A counter narrative for psychic diversity. *Journal of the Medical Humanities, 35*, 257–271.

Durgan, E. (2013). *Resistance and complexity: Solutions to urban crisis of homelessness and psychopathology through psychiatry, architecture and philosophy* (Unpublished doctoral dissertation). Vancouver: The University of British Columbia.

Durkheim, É. (1984). *The division of labor in society* (G. Simpson, Trans.). New York, NY: The Free Press. Original work published 1893.

Eghigian, G. (Ed.). (2010). Records in the case of Pyotr Grigoenko (1969-1970). In *From madness to mental health: Psychiatric disorder and its treatment in Western civilization* (pp. 317–328). Rutgers University Press.

Elkins, D. N. (2016). *The human elements of psychotherapy: A nonmedical model of emotional healing*. Washington, DC: American Psychological Association.

Ellis, A. (1989). Rational-emotive therapy. In R. J. Corsini & D. Wedding (Eds.), *Current Psychotherapies* (4th ed., pp. 197–238). Itasca, IL: Peacock Publishers.

Erhart, S. M., Marder, S. R., & Carpenter, W. T. (2006). Treatment of schizophrenia negative symptoms: Future prospects. *Schizophrenia Bulletin, 32*, 234–237.

Esima, G. E. (2017). *Keynote address:* Bridging the connection between mental health issues and spirituality. ISPS Annual Conference, Portland, OR. Retrieved from https://www.youtube.com/watch?v=ryC8uBtzofM

Faber, K. (1922). Nosography in modern internal medicine. In F. R. Packard (Ed.), *Annals of Medical History: Volume IV* (pp. 1–63).New York, NY: Paul B. Hoeber.

Fabrega, H. (1989). The self and schizophrenia: A cultural perspective. *Schizophrenia Bulletin, 15*, 277–290.

Fairburn, C. G. (1991). The heterogeneity of bulimia nervosa and its implications for treatment. *Journal of Psychosomatic Research, 35*, 3–9.

Farber, S. (2012). *The spiritual gift of madness: The failure of psychiatry and the rise of the mad pride movement*. Rochester, VT: Bear & Company.

Faris, R. E., & Dunham, H. W. (1939). *Mental disorders in urban areas: An ecological study of schizophrenia and other psychoses*. Oxford, UK: University of Chicago Press.

Farmer, P. (2005). *Pathologies of power: Health, human rights, and the new war on the poor*. Berkeley, University of California Press.

Fastovsky, N., Teitelbaum, A., Zislin, J., Katz, G., & Durst, R. (2000). The Jerusalem Syndrome. *Psychiatric Services 51*, 1052.

Fearon, P., Kirkbride, J. B., Morgan, C., Dazzan, P., Morgan, K., Lloyd, T., ... & Murray, R. M. (2006). Incidence of schizophrenia and other psychoses in ethnic minority groups: Results from the MRC AESOP study. *Psychological Medicine*, *36*, 1541–1550.

Feighner, J. P., Robins, E., Guze, S. B., Woodruff, R. A., Winokur, G., & Munoz, R. (1972). Diagnostic criteria for use in psychiatric research. *Archives of General Psychiatry*, *26*, 57–63.

Feinstein, A. R. (1970). The pre-therapeutic classification of co-morbidity in chronic disease. *Chronic Disease*, *23*, 455–468.

Fenton, W. S. (2000). Heterogeneity, subtypes, and longitudinal course in schizophrenia. *Psychiatric Annals*, *30*, 638–644.

Financial. (2012, November 30). Schizophrenia costs society 11.8 billion pounds a year, says LSE PSSRU report. *Finchannel.com*. Retrieved November 24, 2012 from http://finchannel.com/Main_News/B_Schools/119602_Schizophrenia_costs_society_11.8_billion_pounds_a_year,_says_LSE_PSSRU_report/

First, M. B. (2010a). Clinical utility: A prerequisite for the adoption of a dimensional approach in DSM. *Journal of Abnormal Psychology*, *114*, 560–564.

First, M. B. (2010b). Clinical utility in the revision of the Diagnostic and Statistical Manual of Mental Disorders (DSM). *Professional Psychology: Research and Practice*, *41*, 465–473.

First, M. B. (2010c). Paradigm shifts and the development of the diagnostic and statistical manual of mental disorders: Past experiences and future aspirations. *Canadian Journal of Psychiatry*, *55*, 692–700.

Fischer-Homberger, E. (1970). Eighteenth-century nosology and its survivors. *Medical History*, *14*, 397–403. Retrieved from http://www.ncbi.nlm.nih.gov/pmc/articles/PMC1034087/?page=1

Fisher, C. B., Busch-Rossnagel, N. A., Jopp, D. S., & Brown, J. L. (2012). Applied developmental science, social justice, and socio-political wellbeing. *Applied Developmental Science*, *16*, 1–10.

Flanagan, E. H. & Blashfield, R. K. (2002). Psychiatric classification through the lens of ethnobiology. In L. E. Beutler (Ed.), *Rethinking the DSM: A Psychological Perspective* (pp. 121–145). Washington, DC: American Psychological Association.

Flanagan, E. H., Davidson, L., & Strauss, J. S. (2010). The need for patient-subjective data in the DSM and the ICD. *Psychiatry*, *73*, 297–307.

Flanagan, E. H., Solomon, L. A., Johnson, A., Ridgway, P., Strauss, J. S., & Davidson, L. (2012). Considering DSM-5: The personal experience of schizophrenia in relation to the DSM-IV-TR criteria. *Psychiatry: Interpersonal and Biological Processes*, *75*, 375–386.

Folsom, D., & Jeste, D. V. (2002). Schizophrenia in homeless persons: A systematic review of the literature. *Acta Psychiatrica Scandinavica*, *105*, 404–413.

Ford, J. M., Morris, S. E., Hoffman, R. E., Sommer, I., Waters, F., McCarthy-Jones, S., … Cuthbert, B. N. (2014). Studying hallucinations within the NIMH RDoC framework. *Schizophrenia Bulletin*, *40*(Suppl 4), S295–S304. doi:10.1093/schbul/sbu011

Forgione, F. (2019). Diagnostic dissent: Experiences of perceived misdiagnosis and stigma in persons diagnosed with schizophrenia. *Journal of Humanistic Psychology*, *59*, 69–98.

Forgione, F., & Kamens, S. R. (2014, March). *Diagnostic discomfort: Experiences of perceived misdiagnosis and stigma in individuals carrying the "schizophrenia" label.* Paper Presentation at the Society for Humanistic Psychology Annual Conference, Palo Alto, California.

Foucault, M. (1988). *Madness and civilization*. New York, NY: Random House. Original work published 1965.

Foucault, M. (1970). *The order of things: An archeology of the human sciences*. New York, NY: Random House.

Frances, A. (2009a). A warning sign on the road to DSM-V: Beware of its unintended consequences. *Psychiatric Times*. Retrieved from http://www.psychiatrictimes.com/display/article/10168/1425378

Frances, A. (2009b). Whither DSM-V? *British Journal of Psychiatry*, *195*, 391–392.

Frances, A. (2011). Why psychiatrists should mind their language. *Culture Lab.* Retrieved 15 December, 2011 from http://www.newscientist.com/blogs/culturelab/2011/12/why-psychiatrists-should-mind-their-language.html

Frances, A. J., & Egger, H. L. (1999). Whither psychiatric diagnosis. *The Australian and New Zealand Journal of Psychiatry*, *33*(2), 161–165.

Frances, A., Mack, A. H., First, M. B., Widiger, T. A., Ross, R., Forman, L., & Davis, W. W. (1994). DSM-IV meets philosophy. *The Journal of Medicine and Philosophy*, *19*, 207–218.

Frances, A., & Spitzer, R. L. (2009). *Letter to APA Board of Trustees.* Retrieved from http://www.scribd.com/doc/17172432/Letter-to-APA-Board-of-Trustees-July-7-2009-From-Allen-Frances-and-Robert-Spitzer

Freeman, D., Emsley, R., Dunn, G., Fowler, D., Bebbington, P., Kuipers, E., ... & Garety, P. (2014). The stress of the street for patients with persecutory delusions: a test of the symptomatic and psychological effects of going outside into a busy urban area. *Schizophrenia Bulletin*, *173* [Epub ahead of print].

Frese, F. (2009, May/June). Coming out of the shadows. *Health Affairs*. Retrieved from https://www.healthaffairs.org/doi/full/10.1377/hlthaff.28.3.880

Freud, S. (1924). Neurosis and psychosis. In J. Strachey (Ed.), *The standard edition of the complete psychological works of Sigmund Freud, volume* XIX (1923-*1925): The ego and the id and other works* (pp. 147–154). London, UK: The Hogarth Press and the Institute of Psychoanalysis.

Freud, S. (1960). *The ego and the id*. New York, NY: W. W. Norton & Co. Original work published 1923.

Freud, S. (1963). The "Rat Man." In S. Freud (Ed.), *Three Case Histories* (pp. 1–81). New York, NY: Simon & Schuster. Original work published 1909

Freud, S. (1966). *Introductory lectures on psycho-analysis*. New York, NY: W. W. Norton & Co. Original work published 1917.

Freud, S. (2003). *The uncanny* (D. McLintock, Trans.). New York, NY: Penguin. Original work published 1919.

Freud, S., & Breuer, J. (2000). *Studies on hysteria*. New York, NY: Basic Books. Original work published 1895.

Fricker M. (2007). *Epistemic injustice: Power and the ethics of knowing*. Oxford University Press.

Fried, R. I. (1988) The Stendhal syndrome: Hyperkulturemia. *Ohio Medicine*, *84*, 519–520.

Friedman-Peleg, K., & Bilu, Y. (2011). From PTSD to "national trauma": The case of the Israel Trauma Center for Victims of Terror and War. *Transcultural Psychiatry*, *48*, 416–436.

Fuchs, T. (2005). Delusional mood and delusional perception: A phenomenological analysis. *Psychopathology*, *38*, 133–139.

Fuchs, T. (2007). The temporal structure of intentionality and its disturbance in schizophrenia. *Psychopathology*, *40*, 229–235.

Fulford, K. W. M., Thornton, T., & Graham, G. (Ed.). (2006). *Oxford textbook of philosophy and psychiatry*. Oxford, UK: Oxford University Press.

Fuser-Poli, P., & Politi, P. (2008). Paul Eugen Bleuler and the birth of schizophrenia (1908). *American Journal of Psychiatry*, *165*, 1407.

Gaebel, W. (2011, September). *Trends in the classification of psychotic disorders*. Symposium at the World Congress of Psychiatry, Buenos Aires, Argentina.

Galatzer-Levy, I. R., & Galatzer-Levy, R. M. (2007). The revolution in psychiatric diagnosis: Problems at the foundations. *Perspectives in Biological Medicine*, *50*, 161–180.

Gecici, O., Kuloglu, M., Guler, O., Ozbulut, O., Kurt, E., Onen, S., ... & Albayrak, Y. (2010). Phenomenology of delusions and hallucinations in patients with schizophrenia. *Bulletin of Clinical Psychopharmacology*, *20*, 204–212.

George, B. (2012). What's in a name? *Stigma Research and Action*, *2*, 119–122.

George, B., & Klijn, A. (2013a). A modern name for schizophrenia (PSS) would diminish self stigma. *Psychological Medicine*, *43*, 1555–1557.

George, B., & Klijn, A. (2013b). A sweeter smelling rose: A reply to our commentators. *Psychological Medicine*, *43*, 2015–2016.

Geronimus, A., Hicken, M., Keene, D., & Bound, J. (2006). "Weathering" and age patterns of allostatic load scores among blacks and whites in the United States. *American Journal of Public Health*, *96*(5), 826–833.

Gershon, A. A., & Weiser, M. (2009). The epidemiology of schizophrenic disorders in Israel. In I. Levav (Ed.), *Psychiatric and behavioral disorders in Israel: From epidemiology to mental health action* (pp. 233–254). Jerusalem, Israel: Gefen.

Ghaemi, S. N., & Vöhringer, P. A. (2011). The heterogeneity of depression: An old debate renewed. *Acta Psychiatrica Scandinavica*, *124*(6), p. 497.

Ginat, J. B. G. (2017). *Experiences of hospitalization in persons diagnosed with psychotic disorders: Phenomenology and relationship to symptom profiles*. Presentation at the International Society for Psychological and Social Approaches to Psychosis (ISPS), Liverpool, UK.

Giorgi, A. (1975). An application of phenomenological method in psychology. In A. Giorgi, C. Fischer & E. Murray (Eds.), *Duquesne studies in phenomenological psychology* (Vol. 2, pp. 317–342). Pittsburgh, PA: Duquesne University Press.

Giorgi, A. (2009). *The descriptive phenomenological method in psychology: A modified Husserlian approach*. Pittsburgh, PA: Duquesne University Press.

Goffman, E. (1961). *Asylums: Essays on the social situation of mental patients and other inmates*. New York, NY: Random House.

Good, B. J., & Subandi, M. A. (2004). Experiences of psychosis in Javanese culture: Reflections on a case of acute, recurrent psychosis in contemporary Yogyakara, Indonesia. In J. H. Jenkins & R. J. Barrett, *Schizophrenia, culture, and subjectivity: The edge of experience* (pp. 167–195). New York, NY: Cambridge University Press.

Gonçalves, Ó. F., Machado, P. P. P., Korman, Y., & Angus, L. (2002). Assessing psychopathology: A narrative approach. In L. E. Beutler & M. L. Malik (Eds.), *Rethinking the DSM: A psychological perspective* (pp. 149–176). Washington, DC: American Psychological Association.

Gordon, C. (1990). History, madness and other errors: a response. *History of the Human Sciences*, *3*(3), 381–396.

Gottesman, I. I. (1991). *Schizophrenia genesis: The origins of madness*. New York, NY: Freeman Press.

Gottesman, I. I., & Bertelsen, A. (1989). Confirming unexpressed genotypes for schizophrenia: Risks in the offspring of Fischer's Danish identical and fraternal discordant twins. *Archives of General Psychiatry*, *46*, 867–872.

Gottesman, I. I., & Gould, T. D. (2003). The endophenotype concept in psychiatry: Etymology and strategic intentions. *American Journal of Psychiatry*, *160*, 636–645.

Grob, G. N. (1991). Origins of DSM-I: A study in appearance and reality. *American Journal of Psychiatry*, *148*(4), 421–431.

Gross, M. L. (2012). Autonomy and paternalism in communitarian society: Patient rights in Israel. *Hastings Center Report*, *29*, 13–20.

Guarnaccia, P.J., & Rogler, L.H. (1999). Research on culture-bound syndromes: New directions. *American Journal of Psychiatry*, *156*, 1322–1327.

Gur, R. E., Keshavan, M. S., & Lawrie, S. M. (2010). Deconstructing psychosis with human brain imaging. In C. A. Tamminga, P. J. Sirovatka, D. A. Regier, & J. van Os (Eds.), *Deconstructing psychosis: Refining the research agenda for DSM-V* (pp. 109–130). Arlington, VA: American Psychiatric Association.

Guy, W. (Ed.). (1976). Clinical global impressions (CGI) scale. In *ECDEU assessment manual for psychopharmacology*, revised (pp. 218–222). Rockville, MD: National Institute of Mental Health.

Guze, S. B. (1994). Transcript: Interview I. *Washington University School of Medicine Oral History Project*. Retrieved from http://beckerexhibits.wustl.edu/oral/transcripts/guze1994.html

Haj-Yahia, M., & Abdo-Kaloti, R. (2008). Mental health consequences of Palestinian adolescents' exposure to family violence. *Journal of Loss and Trauma*, *13*, 1–41. doi: 10.1080/15325020701429130

Halim, N. (2008). Mad tourists: The "vectors" and meanings of city-syndromes. *Inter-Disciplinary.Net*. Retrieved from http://www.inter-disciplinary.net/wp-content/uploads/2008/12/halim-paper.pdf

Hammersley, P., & McLaughlin, T. (2012). Campaign for the abolition of the schizophrenia label. *Asylum Online*. Retrieved November 8, 2012 from http://www.asylumonline.netresources/campaign-for-the-abolition-of-schizophrenia-label/

Haslam, N. (2002). Kinds of kinds: A conceptual taxonomy of psychiatric categories. *Philosophy, Psychiatry, & Psychology*, *9*, 203–217.

Haslam, N. (2014). Natural kinds in psychiatry: Conceptually implausible, empirically questionable, and stigmatizing. In H. Kincaid & J.A. Sullivan (Eds.), *Classifying Psychopathology* (pp.11–28). Cambridge, MA: MIT Press.

Hayward, M. L., & Taylor, E. T. (1956). A schizophrenic patient describes the action of intensive psychotherapy. *The Psychiatric Quarterly*, *30*, 211–248.

Hearing the Voice. (2021). *About the project*. Retrieved from https://hearingthevoice.org/about-the-project/

Hearing Voices Network. (2013). *Position statement on DSM-5 & psychiatric diagnosis*. Retrieved May 31, 2015 from http://www.hearing-voices.org/wp-content/uploads/2013/05/HVN-Position-Statement-on-DSM5-and-Diagnoses.pdf

Hearing Voices Network. (2019). *About HVN*. Retrieved from http://www.hearing-voices.org/about-us/

Heidegger, M. (1962). *Being and time* (J. Macquarrie & E. Robinson, Trans.). New York, NY: Harper & Row. Original work published 1927.

Heidegger, M. (1993). Building dwelling thinking. In D. F. Krell (Ed.), *Basic Writings* (pp. 343–364). London, UK: Routledge. Original work published 1951.

Henderson, S., & Malhi, G. S. (2014). Swan song for schizophrenia? *Australian and New Zealand Journal of Psychiatry*, *48*, 302–305.

Heston, L. L. (1966). Psychiatric disorders in foster home reared children of schizophrenic mothers. *The British Journal of Psychiatry*, *112*, 819–825.

Hilker, R., Helenius, D., Fagerlund, B., Skytthe, A., Christensen, K., Werge, T. M., … & Glenthøj, B. (2018). Heritability of schizophrenia and schizophrenia spectrum based on the nationwide Danish twin register. *Biological Psychiatry*, *83*(6), 492–498.

Hill, K., & Linden, D. E. (2013). Hallucinatory experiences in non-clinical populations. In R. Jardri, A. Cachia, P. Thomas, & D. Pins (Eds.), *The neuroscience of hallucinations*. New York, NY: Springer. doi:10.1007/978-1-4614-4121-2_2

Ho, B-C., Andreasen, N. C., Ziebell, S., Pierson, R., & Magnotta, V. (2011). Long-term antipsychotic treatment and brain volumes. *Archives of General Psychiatry*, *68*, 128–137.

Hoerl, C. (2012). Jaspers on explaining and understanding in psychiatry. In T. Fuchs & G. Stanghellini (Eds.), *One century of Karl Jaspers' general psychopathology* (pp. 107–120). Oxford: Oxford University Press.

Hoffman, L., Cleare-Hoffman, H., & Jackson, T. (2015). Humanistic psychology and multiculturalism: History, current status, and advancements. In K. Schneider, J. Pierson, & J. Bugental (Eds.), *The handbook of humanistic psychology: Theory, research, and practice* (2nd ed., pp. 41–57). Thousand Oaks, CA: SAGE Publications, Inc.

Hollander, A.-C., Dal, H., Lewis, G., Magnusson, C., Kirkbride, J. B., & Dalman, C. (2016). Refugee migration and risk of schizophrenia and other non-affective psychoses: Cohort study of 13 million people in Sweden. *BMJ: British Medical Journal*, *352*, 1–8. https://www.bmj.com/content/bmj/352/bmj.i1030.full.pdf

Honnorat, N., Dong, A., Meisenzahl-Lechner, E., Koutsouleris, N., & Davatzikos, C. (2019). Neuroanatomical heterogeneity of schizophrenia revealed by semi-supervised machine learning methods. *Schizophrenia Research*, *214*, 43–50.

Hopper, K. (2003). *Reckoning with homelessness*. Ithica, NY: Cornell University Press.

Hopper, K. (2004) Interrogating the meaning of 'culture' in WHO international studies of schizophrenia. In J. H. Jenkins & R. J. Barrett (Eds.), *Schizophrenia, culture, and subjectivity: The edge of experience* (pp. 62–86). West Nyack, NY: Cambridge University Press.

Horwitz, A. V., & Wakefield, J. C. (2012). *All we have to fear: Psychiatry's transformation of natural anxieties into mental disorders*. New York, NY: Oxford University Press.

Houts, A. C. (2002). Discovery, invention, and the expansion of the modern *Diagnostic and Statistical Manuals of Mental Disorders*. In L. E. Beutler & M. L. Malik (Eds.), *Rethinking the DSM: A psychological perspective* (pp. 17–65). Washington, DC: American Psychological Association.

Howes, O. D., Roiser, J., Chaddock, C., Egerton, A., Bose, S., & McGuire, P. (2011). *Dopaminergic dysfunction: Its potential as a biomarker for schizophrenia risk and links to salience dysregulation.* Retrieved from http://discovery.ucl.ac.uk/1301727/

Hu, B., & Wertz, F. J. (2019). Into and out of exile: An integrative phenomenological understanding of attenuated psychosis syndrome. *Psychosis: Psychological, social and integrative approaches*. Retrieved from https://www.tandfonline.com/doi/abs/10.1080/17522439.2019.1693613?tab=permissions&scroll=top

Huber, G., & Gross, G., (1989). The concept of basic symptoms in schizophrenic and schizoaffective psychoses. *Recenti Progressi in Medicina, 80*, 646–652.

Hudson, C. G. (2005). Socioeconomic status and mental illness: Tests of the social causation and selection hypotheses. *American Journal of Orthopsychiatry, 75*, 3–18.

Hunter, N. (2016). Breaking news: The cause of schizophrenia finally discovered? *International Society for Ethical Psychology & Psychiatry*. Retrieved from http://psychintegrity.org/breaking-news-the-cause-of-schizophrenia-finally-discovered/

Husserl, E. (1962). *Ideas: General introduction to pure phenomenology* (W. R. B. Gibson, Trans.). New York: Collier Books. Original work published 1913.

Husserl, E. (1970). *The crisis of European sciences and transcendental phenomenology* (D. Carr, Trans.). Evanston, IL: Northwestern University Press. Original work published 1939.

Husserl, H. (1973a). *Experience and judgment* (L. Landgrebe, J. S. Churchill, K. Ameriks, & L. Eley, Trans.). Evanston: Northwestern University Press. Original work published 1948.

Husserl, E. (1973b). *Zur Phänomenologie der Intersubjektivität: Texte aus dem Nachlass Zweiter Teil: 1921-1928*. The Hague: Martinus Nijhoff. Original work published 1921–1928.

Husserl, E. (1973c). *Zur Phänomenologie der Intersubjektivität: Texte aus dem Nachlass Dritter Teil: 1929-1935*. The Hague: Martinus Nijhoff. Original work published 1929–1935.

Husserl, E. (1980). *On the phenomenology of the consciousness of internal time* (J. B. Brough, Trans.). Dordrecht, The Netherlands: Kluwer Academic Publishers. Original work published 1893–1917.

Husserl, E. (2001). *Analyses concerning passive and active synthesis: Lectures on transcendental logic* (A. J. Steinbock, Trans.). Norwell, MA: Kluwer Academic Publishers. Original work presented as a lecture series in the 1920s.

Icarus Project. (2019). Mission, vision, & principles. *The Icarus Project website*. Retrieved from https://theicarusproject.net/mission-vision-principles/

Inquiry. (2012). *The Inquiry into the 'schizophrenia'* label (ISL). Retrieved November 8, 2012 from http://schizophreniainquiry.org/

Işık, I., & Ergün, G. (2020). Hope and belonging in patients with schizophrenia: A phenomenological study. *Perspectives in Psychiatric Care, 56*(2), 235–242.

Insel, T. (2012). Director's blog: Research domain criteria -- RDoC [Web log post]. *NIMH Director's Blog*. Retrieved May 8, 2015 from http://www.nimh.nih.gov/about/director/2012/research-domain-criteria-rdoc.shtml

Insel, T. (2013, April 29). Transforming diagnosis. *NIMH Director's Blog*. Retrieved November 10, 2014 from http://www.nimh.nih.gov/about/director/2013/transforming-diagnosis.shtml

Insel, T. H., & Cuthbert, B. N. (2009). Endophenotypes: Bridging genomic complexity and disorder heterogeneity. *Biological Psychiatry*, *66*, 988–989.

Jaaro-Peled, H., Ahyan, Y., Pletnikov, M. V., & Sawa, A. (2010). Review of pathological hallmarks of schizophrenia: Comparison of genetic models with patients and nongenetic models. *Schizophrenia Bulletin*, *36*, 301–313.

Jablensky, A. (1987). Multicultural studies and the nature of schizophrenia: A review. *Journal of the Royal Society of Medicine*, *80*, 162–167.

Jablensky, A. (2010). Psychiatry in crisis? Back to fundamentals. *World Psychiatry*, *9*, 29.

Jablensky, A. (1999). The concept of schizophrenia: Pro et contra. *Epidemiologia e Psichiatria Sociale*, *8*(4), 242–247.

Jablensky, A., & Sartorius, N. (2008). What did the WHO studies really find? *Schizophrenia Bulletin*, *34*, 253–255.

Jablensky, A., Sartorius, N., Ernberg, G., Anker, M., Korten, A., Cooper, J. E., ... & Bertelsen, A. (1992). Schizophrenia: Manifestations, incidence and course in different cultures. A World Health Organization ten-country study. *Psychological Medicine Monograph Supplement*, *20*, 1–97.

Jackson, M. (2007). The clinician's illusion and benign psychosis. In M. C. Chung, K. W. M. Fulford, & G. Graham (Eds.), *Reconceiving schizophrenia* (pp. 235–254). New York, NY: Oxford University Press.

Jadhav, S. (2000). The cultural construction of western depression. In V. Skultans & J. Cox (Eds.), *Anthropological approaches to psychological medicine: Crossing bridges* (pp. 41–65). London: Jessica Kingsley Publishers.

Jameson, F. (1991). *Postmodernism, or the cultural logic of late capitalism*. Durham, NC: Duke University Press.

Janet, P. (1978). *The mental state of hystericals*. Washington, DC: University Publications of America. Original work published 1901.

Jaspers, K. (1963). *General psychopathology*. Manchester, UK: Manchester University Press. Original work published 1913.

Jaspers, K. (1968). The phenomenological approach in psychopathology. *The British Journal of Psychiatry*, *114*, 1313–1323. Original work published 1912.

Jauhar, P., & Weller, M. P. (1982). Psychiatric morbidity and time zone changes: A study of patients from Heathrow Airport. *The British Journal of Psychiatry*, *140*, 231–235.

Jenkins, J. H., & Barrett, R. J. (2004). *Schizophrenia, culture, and subjectivity: The edge of experience*. West Nyack, NY: Cambridge University Press.

Johnson, S. L., Wibbels, E., & Wilkinson, E. (2015). Economic inequality is related to cross-national prevalence of psychotic symptoms. *Social Psychiatry and Psychiatric Epidemiology*, *50*, 1799–1807.

Johnstone, L. (2017). Psychological formulation as an alternative to psychiatric diagnosis. *Journal of Humanistic Psychology*, *58*, 30–46.

Joiner, T. E., & Schmidt, N. B. (2002). Taxometrics can "do diagnostics right" (and isn't quite as hard as you think). In L. E. Beutler & M. L. Malik (Eds.), *Rethinking the DSM: A psychological perspective* (pp. 107–120). Washington, DC: American Psychological Association.

Jones, N., Godzikovskaya, J., Zhao, Z., Vasquez, A., Gilbert, A., & Davidson, L. (2017). Intersecting disadvantage: Unpacking poor outcomes within early intervention in psychosis services. *Early Intervention in Psychiatry*. Epub ahead of print. It was finally published in 2019. *13*(3), 488–494.

Jones, N., Kamens, S., Oluwoye, O., Mascayano, F., Perry, C., Manseau, M., & Compton, M. T. (2021). Structural disadvantage and culture, race, and ethnicity in early psychosis services: International provider survey. *Psychiatric Services, 72*(3), 254–263.

Jones, N., & Kelly, T. (2015). Inconvenient complications: On the heterogeneties of madness and their relationship to disability. In H. Spandler, B. Sapey, & J. Anderson (Eds.), *Madness and the Politics of Disablement*. UK: Polity Press.

Jones, N., Kelly, T., & Shattell, M. (2016). God in the brain: Experiencing psychosis in the postsecular United States. *Transcultural Psychiatry*, *53*, 488–505.

Jones, N., & Luhrmann, T. M. (2016). Beyond the sensory: Findings from an in-depth analysis of the phenomenology of "auditory hallucinations" in schizophrenia. *Psychosis: Psychological, Social, and Integrative Approaches*, *8*, 191–202.

Jones, N., Marino, C. K., & Hansen, M. C. (2016). The hearing voices movement in the United States: Findings from a national survey of group facilitators. *Psychosis: Psychological, Social and Integrative Approaches*, *8*(2), 106–117.

Jones, N., Rosen, C., Kamens, S., & Shattell, M. (2018). "It was definitely a sexual kind of sensation": Sex, sexual identity, and gender in the phenomenology of psychosis. *Psychosis: Psychological, Social and Integrative Approaches*, *10*, 122–131.

Jones, N., & Shattell, M. (2013). Engaging with voices: Rethinking the clinical treatment of psychosis. *Issues in Mental Health Nursing*, *34*, 562–563.

Jones, N. & Shattell, M. (2014). Beyond easy answers: Facing the entanglements of violence and psychosis. *Issues in Mental Health Nursing*, *35*, 809–811.

Jones, N., & Shattell, M. (2016). Not what the textbooks describe: Challenging clinical conventions about psychosis. *Issues in Mental Health Nursing*, *37*(10), 769–772.

Joyce, E. M., & Roiser, J. P. (2007). Cognitive heterogeneity in schizophrenia. *Current Opinion in Psychiatry*, *20*, 268–272.

Jung, C. (2009). *The red book* (S. Shamdasani, M. Kyburz, & J. Peck, Trans.) New York, NY: W. W. Norton & Company.

Kalathil, J., & Jones, N. (2016). Unsettling disciplines: Madness, identity, research, knowledge. *Philosophy, Psychiatry, & Psychology*, *23*(3/4), pp. 183–188.

Kalian M, & Witztum E. (1999). The Jerusalem syndrome—fantasy and reality a survey of accounts from the 19th and 20th centuries. *The Israel Journal of Psychiatry and Related Sciences*, *36*(4), 260–271.

Kalian, M., & Witztum, E. (2000). Comments on Jerusalem syndrome. *The British Journal of Psychiatry*, *176*, 492.

Kalian, M., Catinari, S., Heresco-Levi, U., & Witztum, E. (2008). Spiritual starvation in a holy space – a form of Jerusalem Syndrome. *Mental Health, Religion & Culture 11*(2), 161–172.

Kalweit, H. (1989). When insanity is a blessing: The message of shamanism. In S. Grof & C. Grof (Eds.), *Spiritual emergency: When personal transformation becomes a crisis* (pp. 77–97). Los Angeles, CA: Jeremy P. Tarcher.

Kamens, S. R. (2011, August). *Phenomenological approaches to psychiatric discourse: The DSM-5 controversies*. Paper Presentation at the American Psychological Association convention, Washington, DC. Division 32: Society for Humanistic Psychology.

Kamens, S. R. (2018). Extreme states and extreme conditions: On homelessness and the ontico-ontological difference. *Journal of Humanistic Psychology: Special Issue on Extreme States*. Online before print at http://journals.sagepub.com/doi/abs/10.1177/0022167818763734?journalCode=jhpa

Kamens, S. R., Cosgrove, L., Peters, S. M., Jones, N., Flanagan, E. H., Longden, E., ... & Lichtenberg, P. (2018). Standards and guidelines for the development of diagnostic nomenclatures and alternatives in mental health research and practice. *Journal of Humanistic Psychology*. Online before print at http://journals.sagepub.com/doi/abs/10.1177/0022167818763862

Kamphuis, J. H., & Noordhof, A. (2009). On categorical diagnoses in DSM-V: Cutting dimensions at useful points? *Psychological Assessment*, *21*(3), 294–30.

Kant, I. (1999). *Critique of pure reason* (J. M. D. Meiklejohn, Trans.). Mineola, NY: Dover Publications. Original work published 1781.

Karadzhov, D., Yuan, Y., & Bond, L. (2020). Coping amidst an assemblage of disadvantage: A qualitative metasynthesis of first-person accounts of managing severe mental illness while homeless. *Journal of Psychiatric and Mental Health Nursing*, *27*(1), 4–24. doi:10.1111/jpm.12524

Karter, J. (2018). The global 'mental health' movement—cause for concern. *Mad in America: Science, Psychiatry and Social Justice*. Retrieved from https://www.madinamerica.com/2018/10/global-mental-health-movement/

Karter, J. M. (2021). Inclusion toward transformation: Psychosocial disability advocacy and global mental health (Publication No. [Pending]). Doctoral dissertation, University of Massachusetts Boston. ProQuest Dissertations & Theses Global.

Kay, S. R. (1991). *Positive and negative syndromes in schizophrenia: Assessment and research*. New York, NY: Brunner/Mazel, Inc.

Kay, S. R., Fiszbein, A., & Opler, L. A. (1987). The positive and negative syndrome scale (PANSS) for schizophrenia. *Schizophrenia Bulletin*, *13*, 261–276.

Kay, S. R., Opler, L. A., & Fiszbein, A. (1986). Significance of positive and negative syndromes in chronic schizophrenics. *British Journal of Psychiatry*, *149*, 439–448.

Kay, S. R., Opler, L. A., & Fiszbein, A. (2006). *The positive and negative syndrome scale* (PANSS). North Tonawanda, NY: Multi-Health Systems.

Kay, S. R., Opler, L. A., & Lindenmayer, J. P. (1988). Reliability and validity of the Positive and Negative Syndrome Scale for schizophrenics. *Psychiatry Research*, *23*, 99–110.

Kay, S. R., Opler, L. A., & Lindenmayer, J. P. (1989). The positive and negative syndrome scale (PANSS): Rationale and standardization. *British Journal of Psychiatry*, *155*, 66–67.

Keeley, J. W., Morton, H. E., & Blashfield, R. K. (2014). Classification. In P. H. Blaney, R. F. Krueger, & T. Millon (Eds.), *Oxford textbook of psychopathology* (3rd edition, pp. 42–70). New York, NY: Oxford University Press.

Keller, K. D. (2008). Phenomenological understanding of psychosis. *Journal of the Society for Existential Analysis*, *19*, 17–32.

Kelman, H. C. (1999). The interdependence of Israeli and Palestinian national identities: The role of the other in existential conflicts. *Journal of Social Issues*, *55*(3), 581–600.

Kendell, R., & Jablensky, A. (2003). Distinguishing between the validity and utility of psychiatric diagnoses. *American Journal of Psychiatry*, *160*, 4–12.

Kendler, K. (2011, September). *Psychiatric genetics: An empirical and conceptual overview*. Jean Delay Prize Award Lecture at the World Congress of Psychiatry, Buenos Aires, Argentina.

Kendler, K. S., Gallagher, T. J., Abelson, J. M., & Kessler, R. C. (1996). Lifetime prevalence, demographic risk factors, and diagnostic validity of nonaffective psychosis as assessed in a US community sample. The National Comorbidity Survey. *Archives of General Psychiatry*, *53*, 1022–1031.

Kendler, K., Kupfer, D., Narrow, W., Phillips, K., & Fawcett, J. (2009). *Guidelines for making changes to DSM-V*. Retrieved November 3, 2012 from http://www.dsm5.org/ProgressReports/Documents/Guidelines-for-Making-Changes-to-DSM_1.pdf

Kendler, K. S., Muñoz, R. A., & Murphy, G. M. (2009). The development of the Feighner Criteria: A historical perspective. *American Journal of Psychiatry*, *167*, 134–162.

Kendler, K. S., & Parnas, J. (Eds.). (2008). *Philosophical issues in psychiatry*. Baltimore, MD: Johns Hopkins University Press.

Kendler, K. S., & Schaffner, K. F. (2011). The dopamine hypothesis of schizophrenia: An historical and philosophical analysis. *Philosophy, Psychiatry, & Psychology*, *18*, 41–63.

Kendler, K. S., & Zachar, P. (2008). The incredible insecurity of psychiatric nosology. In K. S. Kendler & J. Parnas (Eds.), *Philosophical issues in psychiatry* (pp. 368–385). Baltimore, MD: Johns Hopkins University Press.

Keshavan, M. S., Nasrallah, H. A., & Tandon, R. (2011). Schizophrenia, "just the facts" 6. Moving ahead with the schizophrenia concept: From the elephant to the mouse. *Schizophrenia Research*, *127*, 3–13.

Keshavan, M. S., Tandon, R., Nasrallah, H. A. (2013). Renaming schizophrenia: Keeping up with the facts. *Schizophrenia Research*, *148*, 1–2.

Kessler, R. C., Berglund, P., Demler, O., Robert, J., Merikangas, K. R., & Walters, E. E. (2005). Lifetime prevalence and age-of-onset distributions of DSM-IV disorders in the national comorbidity survey replication. *Archives of General Psychiatry*, *62*(6), 593–602.

Kessler, R. C., McGonagle, K. A., Zhao, S., & Nelson, C. B. (1994). Lifetime and 12-month prevalence of DSM-III-R psychiatric disorders in the United States: Results from the National Comorbidity Study. *Archives of General Psychiatry*, *51*(1), 8–19.

Kety, S. S. (1988). Schizophrenic illness in the families of schizophrenic adoptees: Findings from the Danish national sample. *Schizophrenia Bulletin*, *14*, 217–222.

Khattab, N. (2003). Segregation, ethnic labour market and the occupational expectations of Palestinian students in Israel. *The British Journal of Sociology*, *54*, 259–285.

Kim, M., Haney, J. R., Zhang, P., Hernandez, L. M., Wang, L., Perez-Cano, L., ... & Gandal, M. J. (2021). Brain gene co-expression networks link complement signaling with convergent synaptic pathology in schizophrenia. *Nature Neuroscience*, *24*(6), 799–809.

Kim, Y., & Berrios, G. E. (2001). Impact of the term schizophrenia on the culture of ideograph: The Japanese experience. *Schizophrenia Bulletin, 27*, 181–185.
Kimura, B. (1982). The phenomenology of the between: The problem of basic disturbance in schizophrenia. In A. J. J. de Koning & F. A. Jenner (Eds.), *Phenomenology & psychiatry* (pp. 173–184). London, UK: Academic Press.
Kincaid, H., & Sullivan, J. A. (Eds.). (2014). *Classifying psychopathology*. Cambridge, MA: MIT Press.
Kinderman, P., & Bentall, R. P. (2007). The functions of delusional beliefs. In M. C. Chung, K. W. M. Fulford, & G. Graham (Eds.), *Reconceiving schizophrenia* (pp. 275–294). New York, NY: Oxford University Press.
King, C. (2007). They diagnosed me a schizophrenic when I was just a Gemini. 'The other side of madness.' In M. C. Chung, K. W. M. Fulford, & G. Graham (Eds.), *Reconceiving schizophrenia* (pp. 11–28). New York, NY: Oxford University Press.
Kingdon, D. G., & Turkington, D. (2005). *Cognitive therapy of schizophrenia*. New York, NY: The Guilford Press.
Kirkbride, J. B., Jones, P. B., Ullrick, S., & Coid, J. W. (2014). Social deprivation, inequality, and the neighborhood-level incidence of psychotic syndromes in East London. *Schizophrenia Bulletin, 40*, 169–180.
Kirkbride, J. B., Stochi, J., Zimbrón, J., Crane, C. M., Metastasio, A., Aguilar, E., ... & Perez, J. (2014). Social and spatial heterogeneity in psychosis proneness in a multilevel case–prodrome–control study. *Acta Psychiatrica Scandinavica, 132*(4), 1–10.
Kirkpatrick, B. (2011, September). *The heterogeneity of schizophrenia: Implications for research on biomarkers*. Buenos Aires, Argentina: Keynote Lecture at the World Congress of Psychiatry.
Kirkpatrick, B., Buchanan, R. W., Ross, D. E., & Carpenter, W. T. (2001). A separate disease within the syndrome of schizophrenia. *Archives of General Psychiatry, 58*, 165–171.
Kirmayer, L. J. (2013). 50 years of transcultural psychiatry. *Transcultural Psychiatry, 50*, 3–5.
Kleinman, A. (1987). Anthropology and psychiatry. The role of culture in cross-cultural research on illness. *The British Journal of Psychiatry, 151*, 447–454.
Knapp, S. (2010). What's in a name? A history of taxonomy. *Natural History Museum of the United Kingdom*. Retrieved from http://www.nhm.ac.uk/nature-online/science-of-natural-history/taxonomy-systematics/history-taxonomy/index.html
Koehler, B. (2021). APA/WHO drop the stigmatizing term "schizophrenia". Online petition at *Change.org*. Retrieved from https://www.change.org/p/american-psychiatric-association-apa-who-drop-the-stigmatizing-term-schizophrenia
Kopala-Sibley, D. C., Zuroff, D. C., Russell, J. J., Moskowitz, D. S., & Paris, J. (2012). Understanding heterogeneity in borderline personality disorder: Differences in affective reactivity explained by the traits of dependency and self-criticism. *Journal of Abnormal Psychology, 12*, 680–691.
Kotov, R., Krueger, R. F., Watson, D., Achenbach, T. M., Althoff, R. R., Bagby, R. M., ... & Zimmerman, M. (2017). The hierarchical taxonomy of psychopathology (HiTOP): A dimensional alternative to traditional nosologies. *Journal of Abnormal Psychology, 126*, 454–477.
Kouba, P. (2006). *The phenomenon of mental disorder: Perspectives of Heidegger's thought in psychopathology*. London, UK: Springer.

Kraepelin, E. (n.d.). *Dementia praecox and paraphrenia.* Chicago, IL: Chicago Medical Book Company.

Kraeplin, E. (2011). *One hundred years of psychiatry*. Charleston, SC: Nabu Press. Original work published 1923.

Kremen, W. S., Seidman, L. J., Faraone, S. V., Toomey, R. T., & Ming, T. (2004). Heterogeneity of schizophrenia: A study of individual neuropsychological profiles. *Schizophrenia Research, 71*, 307–321.

Kremer, I., Dobrusin, M., Blanaru, M., Reshef, A., Gathas, S., Mujaheed, M., ... & Belmaker, R. H. (2008). Clinical characteristics of schizophrenia: Israeli Bedouin compared with Palestinian Arabs in Israel and the Palestinian Authority. *Neuropsychiatria i Neuropsychologia, 3*, 3–6.

Kriss, S. (2013). Book of lamentations. *The New Inquiry, 22*. Retrieved from http://thenewinquiry.com/essays/book-of-lamentations/

Krueger, R. F., & Bezdjian, S. (2009). Enhancing research and treatment of mental disorders with dimensional concepts: Toward DSM-V and ICD-11. *World Psychiatry, 8*, 3–6.

Krueger, R. F., & Eaton, N. R. (2010). Personality traits and the classification of mental disorders: Toward a more complete integration in DSM–5 and an empirical model of psychopathology. *Personality Disorders: Theory, Research, and Practice, 1*, 97–118.

Krueger, R. F., & Markon, K. E. (2006a). Reinterpreting comorbidity: A model-based approach to understanding and classifying psychopathology. *Annual Review of Clinical Psychology, 2*, 111–133.

Krueger, R. F., & Markon, K. E. (2006b). Understanding psychopathology: Melding behavior genetics, personality, and quantitative psychology to develop an empirically based model. *Current Directions in Psychological Science, 15*, 113–117.

Kuhn, H. (2013). The phenomenological concept of horizon. In M. Farber (Ed.), *Philosophical essays in memory of Edmund Husserl* (pp. 106–123). Harvard University Press.

Kuhn, T. S. (1996). *The structure of scientific revolutions* (3rd ed.). Chicago, IL: University of Chicago Press. Original work published 1962.

Kukshal, P., Thelma, B. K., Nimgaonkar, V. L., & Deshpande, S. N. (2012). Genetics of schizophrenia from a clinical perspective. *International Review of Psychiatry, 24*(5), 393–404.

Kupfer, D. F., First, M. B., & Regier, D. A. (Eds.) (2002). *A research agenda for DSM-V.* Washington, DC: American Psychiatric Association.

Kurtz, M. M. (2015). A brief history of the treatment of schizophrenia. In *Schizophrenia and its treatment: Where is the progress?* (pp. 59–84). New York, NY: Oxford University Press.

Lacan, J. (1993). *The psychoses 1955-1956 (The seminar of Jacques Lacan, book 3).* New York, NY: W. W. Norton & Co.

LaFace, H. (2014, March). *The hope of being found when one is lost: Autonomy, dignity and dehumanization in an enactive process model of psychotherapy with a schizophrenic patient.* Paper Presentation at the Society for Humanistic Psychology (American Psychological Association Division 32) Annual Conference in Palo Alto, California.

Laing, R. D. (1960). *The divided self.* New York, NY: Penguin books.

Laing, R. D., & Esterson, A. (1964). *Sanity, madness, and the family: Families of schizophrenics*. New York, NY: Penguin Books.

Lake, C. R., & Hurwitz, N. (2007). Schizoaffective disorder merges schizophrenia and bipolar disorders as one disease-there is no schizoaffective disorder. *Current Opinion in Psychiatry, 20*, 365–379.

Lambrecht, I. (2014). *Sangoma trance states*. Auckland, New Zealand: AM Publishing.

Lane, C. (2011, October 31). Saving psychiatry from itself: The DSM-5 controversy heats up again. *Psychology Today*. Retrieved September 23, 2012 from http://www.psychologytoday.com/blog/side-effects/201110/saving-psychiatry-itself-the-dsm-5-controversy-heats-again

Lasalvia, A., Penta, E., Sartorius, N., & Henderson, S. (2015). Should the label "schizophrenia" be abandoned? *Schizophrenia Research, 162*, 276–284.

Law, H., & Morrison, A. P. (2014). Recovery in psychosis: A Delphi study with experts by experience. *Schizophrenia Bulletin, 40*, 1347–1355.

Lee, S.-A., Kim, S.-M., Suh, B. K., Sun, H.-Y., Park, Y.-U., Hong, J.-H., ... & Park, S. K. (2015). Disrupted-in-schizophrenia 1 (DISC1) regulates dysbindin function by enhancing its stability. *The Journal of Biological Chemistry, 290*, 7087–7096.

LeFrançois, B. A., Menzies, R., & Reaume, G. (2013). Introducing mad studies & part 1. In B. A. LeFrançois, R. Menzies, & G. Reaume (Eds.), *Mad matters: A critical reader in Canadian mad studies* (pp. 1–26). Toronto, Canada: Canadian Scholars Press Inc.

Lehman, A. F., Alexopoulos, M. D., Goldman, H., Jeste, D., & Üstün, B. (2002). Mental disorders and disability: Time to reevaluate the relationship? In D. J. Kupfer, M. B. First, & D. Regier (Eds.), *A research agenda for DSM-V* (pp. 201–218). Arlington, VA: American Psychiatric Association.

Leitner, L. M., Faidley, A. J., & Celentana, M. A. (2000). Diagnosing human meaning making: An experiential constructivist approach. In R. A. Neimeyer & J. D. Raskin (Eds.), *Constructions of disorder: Meaning-making frameworks for psychotherapy* (pp. 175–203). Washington, DC: American Psychological Association.

Leucht, S., Kane, J. M., Kissling, W., Hamann, J., Etschel, E., & Engel, R. R. (2005). What does the PANSS mean? *Schizophrenia Research, 79*, 231–238.

Levin, T. (2006). Schizophrenia should be renamed to help educate patients and the public. *International Journal of Social Psychiatry 52*, 324–331.

Levinas, E. (1961). *Totality and infinity: An essay on exteriority* (A. Lingis, Trans.). Pittsburgh, PA: Duquesne University Press.

Lev-Wiesel, R., Al-Krenawi, A., & Sehwail, M. A. (2007). Psychological symptomatology among Palestinian male and female adolescents living under political violence. *Community Mental Health Journal, 43*, 49–56.

Levy, D. L., Holzman, P. S., Matthysee, S., & Mendell, N. R. (1994). Eye tracking and schizophrenia. *Schizophrenia Bulletin, 20*, 47–62.

Lewis-Fernández, R., Aggarwal, N. K., Bäärnhielm, S., Rohlof, H., Kirmayer, L. J., Weiss, M. G., ... & Lu, F. (2014). Culture and psychiatric evaluation: Operationalizing cultural formulation for DSM-5. *Psychiatry: Interpersonal And Biological Processes, 77*(2), 130–154.

Li, Z., Chen, J., Yu, H., He, L., Xu, Y., Zhang, D., ... & Shi, Y. (2017). Genome-wide association analysis identifies 30 new susceptibility loci for schizophrenia. *Nature Genetics, 49*, 1576. doi:10.1038/ng.3973

Liang, S. G., & Greenwood, T. A. (2015). The impact of clinical heterogeneity in schizophrenia on genomic analyses. *Schizophrenia Research*, *161*(2–3), 490–495.

Lichtenberg, P. (2017). From the closed ward to Soteria: A professional and personal journey. *Psychosis: Psychological, Social and Integrative approaches*, *9*(4), 369–375.

Lichtenberg, P., Vass, A., & Heresco-Levy, U. (2003). Politics and psychopathology in an Arab-Israeli patient. *Psychiatry*, *66*, 360–363.

Lieberman, J. A., & First, M. B. (2007). Renaming schizophrenia. *BMJ*, *334*(7585), 108. Retrieved from http://www.ncbi.nlm.nih.gov/pmc/articles/PMC1779873/

Lieberman J., Stroup, S., McEvoy, J., Swartz, M., Rosenheck, R., Perkins, D., ... & Hsiao, J. (2005). Effectiveness of antipsychotic drugs in patients with chronic schizophrenia. *New England Journal of Medicine*, *353*, 1209–1223.

Lilienfeld, S. O. (2003). Comorbidity between and within childhood externalizing and internalizing disorders: Reflections and directions. *Journal of Abnormal Child Psychology*, *31*(3), 285–291.

Lilja, L., & Hellzén, O. (2008). Former patients' experience of psychiatric care: A qualitative investigation. *International Journal of Mental Health Nursing*, *17*, 279–286. doi: 10.1111/j.1447-0349.2008.00544.x

Lindenmayer, J. P., Kay, S. R., & Opler, L. A. (1984). Positive and negative subtypes in acute schizophrenia. *Comprehensive Psychiatry*, *25*, 455–464.

Link, B. G., & Phelan, J. C. (1999). The labeling theory of mental disorder (II): The consequences of labeling. In A. V. Horwitz & T. L. Scheid (Eds.), *A handbook for the study of mental health: social contexts, theories, and systems* (pp. 361–376). West Nyack, NY: Cambridge University Press.

Linnaeus, C. (1956). *Systema naturae*. London, UK: British Museum of Natural History. Original work published 1735.

Lock, M. (1987). DSM-III as a culture-bound construct: Commentary on culture-bound syndromes and international disease classifications. *Culture, Medicine, & Psychiatry*, *11*, 35–42.

Longden, E. (2013). *Learning from the voices in my head*. Ted Conferences: Amazon Digital Services.

Longden, E., Madill, A., & Waterman, M. G. (2012). Dissociation, trauma, and the role of lived experience: Toward a new conceptualization of voice hearing. *Psychological Bulletin*, *138*, 28–76.

Lopez, M. F., Compton, W. M., Grant, B. F., & Breiling, J. P. (2007). Dimensional approaches in diagnostic classification: A critical appraisal. *International Journal of Methods in Psychiatric Research*, *16*(S1), S6–S7.

López-Ibor, J. J. (2008). The founding of the first psychiatric hospital in the world in Valencia. *Actas Españolas de Psiquiatría*, *36*, 1–9.

Lovell, A. M. (1997). "The city is my mother": Narratives of schizophrenia and homelessness. *American Anthropologist*, *99*(2), 355–368.

Luhrmann, T. H. (2007). Social defeat and the culture of chronicity: Or, why schizophrenia does so well over there and so badly here. *Culture, Medicine, and Psychiatry*, *31*, 135–172.

Luhrmann, T. (2011). Hallucinations and sensory overrides. *Annual Review of Anthropology*, *40*, 71–85. Retrieved from http://www.luhrmann.net/wp-content/uploads/2012/02/Hallucinations-and-Sensory-Overrides.pdf

Luhrmann, T. M. (2012). *When God talks back: Understanding the American Evangelical relationship with God.* New York, NY: Alfred A Knopf.

Luhrmann, T. M., & Marrow, J. (2016). *Our most troubling madness: Case studies in schizophrenia across cultures.* Oakland, CA: University of California Press.

Luhrmann, T. M., Ramachandran, P., & Tharoor, H. (2015). Differences in voice-hearing experiences of people with psychosis in the USA, India and Ghana: Interview-based study. *The British Journal of Psychiatry, 206*, 41–44.

MacDonald, A. (2014). Schizophrenia: Presentation, affect, and cognition, pathophysiology, and etiology. In P. H. Blaney, R. F. Krueger, & T. Millon (Eds.), *Oxford textbook of psychopathology* (3rd ed., pp. 333–352). New York, NY: Oxford University Press.

MacNab, F. A. (1965). *Estrangement and relationship: Experience with schizophrenia.* Bloomington, IN: Indiana University Press.

Maj, M. (2012). The self and schizophrenia: Some open issues. *World Psychiatry, 11*, 65–66.

Maj, M., & Sartorius, N. (Eds.) (2003). *Schizophrenia* (2nd ed.). Hoboken, NJ: Wiley.

Malla, A., & Payne, J. (2005). First-episode psychosis: Psychopathology, quality of life, and functional outcome. *Schizophrenia Bulletin, 31*, 650–671.

Marcel, M. (2008). *Man against mass society* (G. S. Fraser & D. MacKinnon, Trans.). South Bend, IN: St. Augustine's Press. Original work published 1962.

Marcelis, M., Navarro-Mateu, F., Murray, R., Selten, J. P., & Van Os, J. (1999). Urbanization and psychosis: A study of 1942–1978 birth cohorts in The Netherlands. *Psychological Medicine, 28*, 871–879.

Marsella, A. J. (1993). Sociocultural foundations of psychopathology: A pre-1970 historical overview. *Transcultural Psychiatric Research and Review, 30*, 97–142.

Marsella, A. J. (2016). *In pursuit of "schizophrenia": Reflections on "imprecision" in scientific and professional thought and practice.* Alpharetta, GA: Mountain Arbor Press.

Marsella, A. J., Tharp, R., & Ciborowski, T. (Eds.) (1979). *Perspectives on cross-cultural psychology.* New York: Academic Press.

Marsella, A. J., & White, G. (Eds.) (1982). *Cultural conceptions of mental health and therapy.* Boston, MA: G. Reidel Press.

Marsella, A. J., & Yamada, M. (2000). Culture and mental health: An introduction and overview of foundations, concepts, and issues. In I. Cuellar & F. A. Paniagua (Eds.), *Handbook of multicultural mental health* (pp. 3–26). San Diego, CA: Academic Press.

Martin, E. (2009). *Bipolar expeditions: Mania and depression in American culture.* Princeton, NJ: Princeton University Press.

McGlashan, T. H., & Fenton, W. S. (1992). The positive-negative distinction in schizophrenia: Review of natural history validators. *Archives of General Psychiatry, 49*, 63–72.

McGrath, J. J., Saha, S., Al-Hamzawi, A., Alonso, J., Bromet, E. J., Bruffaerts, R., ... & Kessler, R. C. (2015). Psychotic experiences in the general population: A cross-national analysis based on 31 261 respondents from 18 countries. *JAMA Psychiatry.* Retrieved from http://archpsyc.jamanetwork.com/article.aspx?articleid=2298236; doi:10.1001/jamapsychiatry.2015.0575

Meehl, P. E. (2001). Comorbidity and taxometrics. *Clinical Psychology: Science and Practice, 8*, 507–519.

Mehler, B. (1987). Eliminating the inferior: American and Nazi sterilization programs. *Science for the People*, *19*, 14–18.

Meichenbaum, D. (1977). *Cognitive-behavior modification: An integrative approach*. New York, NY: Platinum Press.

Meir-Glitzenstein, E. (2002). Our dowry – Identity and memory among Iraqi immigrants in Israel. *Middle Eastern Studies*, *38*, 165–186.

Melle, I., & Barrett, E. A. (2012). Insight and suicidal behavior in first-episode schizophrenia. *Expert Review of Neurotherapeutics*, *12*(3), 353–359.

Mensch, J. R. (1998). *Intersubjectivity and transcendental idealism*. Albany, NY: State University of New York Press.

Mergenthaler, E., & Stinson, C. (1992). Psychotherapy transcription standards. *Psychotherapy research*, *2*, 125–142.

Merikangas, K. R., Wicki, W., & Angst, J. (1994). Heterogeneity of depression: Classification of depressive subtypes by longitudinal course. *The British Journal of Psychiatry*, *164*, 342–348.

Merleau-Ponty, M. (2012). *Phenomenology of perception*. New York, NY: Routledge. Original work published 1945.

Merquior, J. G. (1985). *Foucault*. Berkeley, CA: University of California Press.

Metzl, J. M. (2009). *The protest psychosis: How schizophrenia became a black disease*. Boston, MA: Beacon Press.

Metzl, J. M., & Hansen, H. (2014). Structural competency: Theorizing a new medical engagement with stigma and inequality. *Social Science & Medicine*, *103*, 126–133.

Metzl, J. M., & Roberts, D. E. (2014). Structural competency meets structural racism: Race, politics, and the structure of medical knowledge. *American Journal of Ethics*, *16*(9), 674–690.

Mills, C. (2014). *Decolonizing global mental health: The psychiatrization of the majority world*. New York, NY: Routledge.

Minahan, J., Forgione, F., Driggs, I., Kamens, S. R., & Morrissey, M. B. (2014, August). *Collaborative phenomenological data analysis: Benefits and obstacles*. Poster Presentation at the American Psychological Association convention, Washington, DC. Division 5: Division of Quantitative and Qualitative Methods.

Minkowski, E. (1953). *La schizophrénie: Psychopathologie des schizoïdes et des schizophrènes*. Paris, France: Desclée de Brouwer à Paris. Original work published 1927.

Mirsky, A. F., Kugelmass, S., Ingraham, J., Frenkel, E., & Nathan, M. (1995). Overview and summary: Twenty-five-year followup of high-risk children. *Schizophrenia Bulletin*, *21*, 227–239.

Mishara, A. L., Lysaker, P. H., & Schwartz, M. (2014). Self-disturbances in schizophrenia: History, phenomenology, and relevant findings from research on metacognition. *Schizophrenia Bulletin*, *40*, 5–12.

Mishara, A. L., & Schwartz, M. A. (2013). Jaspers' critique of essentialist theories of schizophrenia and the phenomenological response. *Psychopathology*, *46*, 309–319.

Moran, D. (2010). Husserl and Heidegger on the transcendental "homelessness" of philosophy. In P. Vandevelde & S. Luft (Eds.), *Epistemology, archaeology, ethics: Current investigations of Husserl's corpus* (pp. 169–187). London, UK: Continuum Press.

Morawski, J. (1998). The return of phantom subjects? In B. M. Bayer & J. Shotter (Eds.), *Reconstructing the psychological subject: Bodies, practices and technologies* (pp. 214–228). Thousand Oaks, CA: Sage Publications, Inc.

Morawski, J. (2000). Just one more "other" in psychology. *Theory & Psychology, 10*(1), 63–70.

Moreira, V., & Junior, N. C. (2003) The phenomenology of schizophrenic experience: A cross-cultural critical study Brazil-Chile. *Terapia Psicológica, 21,* 75–86.

Moreira-Almeida, A. (2009). Differentiating spiritual from psychotic experiences. *The British Journal of Psychiatry, 195,* 368–371.

Morel, B. A. (1857). *Traité des dégénérescence physiques, intellectuelles, et morales de l'espèce humaine.* Paris, France: J.B. Balliere.

Morgan, C., Charalambides, M., Hutchinson, G., & Murray, R. M. (2010). Migration, ethnicity, and psychosis: Toward a sociodevelopmental model. *Schizophrenia Bulletin, 36,* 655–664.

Morgan, K. (2013). *A mind without a home: A memoir of schizophrenia.* Center City, MN: Hazelden.

Moriyama, I. M., Loy, R. M., & Robb-Smith, A. H. T. (2011). History of the statistical classification of diseases and causes of death. Center for Disease Control and Prevention. Retrieved from http://www.cdc.gov/nchs/data/misc/classification_diseases2011.pdf

Morris, S. E., & Cuthbert, B. N. (2012) Research domain criteria: Cognitive systems, neural circuits, and dimensions of behavior. *Dialogues in Clinical Neuroscience, 14,* 29–37.

Morris, J. A., Kandpal, G., Ma, L., Austin, C. P. (2003). DISC1 (disrupted-in-schizophrenia 1) is a centrosome-associated protein that interacts with MAP1A, MIPT3, ATF4/5 and NUDEL: Regulation and loss of interaction with mutation. *Human Molecular Genetics, 12,* 1591–1608.

Morrissey, M. B. & Barber, M. (2014). Phenomenology. In B. Jennings (Ed.), *Encyclopedia on bioethics* (4th ed., pp. 2391–2400). Macmillan Reference USA.

Mosher, L. R., Hendrix, V., & Fort, D. C. (2004). *Soteria: Through madness to deliverance.* Bloomington, IN: Xlibris Corporation.

Muazzam, M.G., & Muazzam, P. (1989). Important contributions of early Muslim period to medical science. II. Clinical sciences. *Journal of the Islamic Medical Association of North America, 21,* 64–70. Retrieved from http://jima.imana.org/article/viewFile/5514/21_2-6

Murali, V., & Oyebode, F. (2004). Poverty, social inequality and mental health. *Advances in Psychiatric Treatment, 10,* 216–224.

Myers, N. L. (2010). Culture, stress and recovery from schizophrenia: Lessons from the field for global mental health. *Culture, Medicine, and Psychiatry: An International Journal of Cross-Cultural Health Research, 34*(3), 500–528.

Nager, A., Johansson, L.-M., & Sundquist, K. (2006). Neighborhood socioeconomic environment and risk of postpartum psychosis. *Archives of Women's Mental Health, 9*(2), 81–86.

Nashawaty, C. (2012, February 17). The Jerusalem syndrome: Why some religious tourists believe they are the Messiah. *Wired Magazine.* Retrieved from http://www.wired.com/magazine/2012/02/ff_jerusalemsyndrome/

National Institute of Mental Health (NIMH). (2015). *Data sharing expectations for clinical research funded by NIMH.* Retrieved December 30, 2018 from https://grants.nih.gov/grants/guide/notice-files/not-mh-15-012.html

National Institute of Mental Health (NIMH). (2021). *Research domain criteria (RDoC)*. Retrieved from https://www.nimh.nih.gov/research-priorities/rdoc/index.shtml

National Institute of Mental Health (NIMH). (2023). *Research Domain Criteria (RDoC)*. Retrieved from https://www.nimh.nih.gov/research/research-funded-by-nimh/rdoc

Neighbors, H. W., Trierweiler, S. J., Ford, B. C., & Murdoff, J. R. (2003). Racial differences in DSM diagnosis using a semi-structured instrument: The importance of clinical judgment in the diagnosis of African Americans. *Journal of Health and Social Behavior*, *43*, 237–256.

Nelson, B., Parnas, J., & Sass, L. A. (2014). Disturbance of minimal self (ipseity) in schizophrenia: Clarification and current status. *Schizophrenia Bulletin*. Retrieved May 9, 2015 from http://schizophreniabulletin.oxfordjournals.org/content/early/2014/03/08/schbul.sbu034.full.pdf

Nicholson, T. R. J., Pariante, C., & McLoughlin, D. (2009). Stendhal syndrome: A case of cultural overload. *BMJ Case Reports*. Retrieved from http://www.ncbi.nlm.nih.gov/pmc/articles/PMC3027955/

Noll, R. (2007). *The encyclopedia of schizophrenia and other psychotic disorders* (3rd ed.). New York, NY: Facts on File Books.

Noll, R. (2011). *American madness: The rise and fall of dementia praecox*. Cambridge, MA: Harvard University Press.

Noorani, T. (2013). Service user involvement, authority and the 'expert-by-experience' in mental health. *Journal of Political Power*, *6*, 49–68.

Norquist, G., & Narrow, W. (2000). Schizophrenia: Epidemiology. In B. J. Sadock and V. A. Sadock (Eds.), *Kaplan & Sadock's comprehensive textbook of psychiatry* (pp. 1110–1116). New York: Lippincott Williams and Wilkins.

Nugent, N. R., Koenen, K. C., & Bradley, B. (2012). Heterogeneity of posttraumatic stress symptoms in a highly traumatized low income, urban, African-American sample. *Journal of Psychiatric Research*, *46*(12), 1576–1583.

Olbert, C. M., Gala, G. J., & Tupler, L. A. (2014). Quantifying heterogeneity attributable to polythetic diagnostic criteria: Theoretical framework and empirical application. *Journal of Abnormal Psychology*, 123, 452–462.

Olbert, C. M., Gerkin, J. S., Moseley, D. D., & Gala, G. J. (2012). *Magnitude and implications of the combinatorial heterogeneity of Major Depressive Disorder*. Manuscript submitted for publication.

Opler, L. A., Caton, C. L., Shrout, P., Dominquez, B., & Kass, F. I. (1994). Symptom profiles and homelessness in schizophrenia. *The Journal of Nervous and Mental Disease*, *182*(3), 174–178.

Opler, L. A., Opler, M. G., & Malaspina, D. (2006). Reducing the guesswork in schizophrenia treatment. *Current Psychiatry*, *9*(5). Retrieved from http://www.currentpsychiatry.com/index.php?id=22661&tx_ttnews%5Btt_news%5D=171750

Østergaard, S.D., Jensen, S. O. W., & Bech, P. (2011). The heterogeneity of the depressive syndrome: When numbers get serious. *Acta Psychiatrica Scandinavica*, *124*, 495–496.

Owen, M. J., Craddock, N., & Jablensky, A. (2007). The genetic deconstruction of psychosis. *Schizophrenia Bulletin*, *33*, 905–911. Retrieved from http://www.ncbi.nlm.nih.gov/pmc/articles/PMC2632314/

Owen, M. J., Craddock, N., O'Donovan, M. C. (2005). Schizophrenia: Genes at last? *Trends in Genetics, 21*, 518–525.

PANSS Institute. (2012). *Training*. Retrieved from http://www.panss.org/home/index.php?option=com_content&task=blogsection&id=6&Itemid=28

Parnas, J. (2011). A disappearing heritage: The clinical core of schizophrenia. *Schizophrenia Bulletin, 37*, 1121–1130.

Parnas, J., Bovet, P., & Zahavi, D. (2002). Schizophrenic autism: Clinical phenomenology and pathogenic implications. *World Psychiatry, 1*, 131–136.

Parnas, J., & Handest, P. (2003). Phenomenology of anomalous self-experience in early schizophrenia. *Comprehensive Psychiatry, 44*, 121–134.

Parnas, J., Møller, P., Kircher, T., Thalbitzer, J., Jansson, L., Handest, P., & Zahavi, D. (2005). Ease: Examination of anomalous self-experience. *Psychopathology, 38*, 236–258.

Parnas, J., Sass, L., & Zahavi, D. (2011). Phenomenology and psychopathology. *Philosophy, Psychiatry, & Psychology, 18*(1), 37–39.

Parnas, J., & Zahavi, D. (2002). The role of phenomenology in psychiatric diagnosis and classification. In M. Maj, W. Gaebel, J. J. Lopez-Ibor, & N. Sartorius (Eds.), *Psychiatric diagnosis and classification* (pp. 137–162). Chichester, UK: John Wiley & Sons.

Patel, V., Cohen, A., Thara, R., & Gureje, O. (2006). Is the outcome of schizophrenia really better in developing countries? *Revista Brasileira de Psiquiatria, 28*, 149–152.

Patterson, M. L., Moniruzzaman, A., & Somers, J. M. (2013). Community participation and belonging among formerly homeless adults with mental illness after 12 months of housing first in Vancouver, British Columbia: A randomized controlled trial. *Community Mental Health Journal, 50*, 604–611.

Patton, M. Q. (1987). *How to use qualitative methods in evaluation*. Newbury Park, CA: Sage Publications.

Pavlo, A. J., Flanagan, E. H., Leitner, L. M., & Davidson, L. (2019). Can there be a recovery-oriented diagnostic practice? *Journal of Humanistic Psychology: Special Issue on Diagnostic Alternatives, 59*, 319–338.

Perälä, J., Suvisaari, J., Saarni, S. I., Kuoppasalmi, Kimmo, Isometsä, E., Pirkola, S., Partonen, T., Tuulio-Henriksson, A., Hintikka, J., Kieseppä, T., Härkänen, T., Koskinen, S., & Lönnqvist, J. (2007). Lifetime prevalence of psychotic and bipolar i disorders in a general population. *Archives of General Psychiatry, 64*(1), 19–28. https://doi.org/10.1001/archpsyc.64.1.19.

Perona-Garcelán, S., Bellido-Zanin, G., Rodríguez-Testal, J. F., López-Jiménez, A. M., García-Montes, J. M., & Ruiz-Veguilla, M. (2016). The relationship of depersonalization and absorption to hallucinations in psychotic and non-clinical participants. *Psychiatry Research, 244*, 357–362.

Phillips, J. (Ed.) (2009). *Philosophical perspectives on technology and psychiatry* (International Perspectives in Philosophy and Psychiatry). Oxford, UK: Oxford University Press.

Phillips, J. (2013). The conceptual status of DSM-5 diagnoses. In J. Paris & J. Phillips (Eds.), *Making the DSM-5: Concepts and coontroversies* (pp. 143–158). New York, NY: Springer.

Phillips, J., Frances, A., Cerullo, M. A., Chardavoyne, J., Decker, H. S., First, M. B., ... & Zachar, P. (2012a). The six most essential questions in psychiatric diagnosis: A pluralogue part 1: Conceptual and definitional issues in psychiatric diagnosis. *Philosophy, Ethics, and Humanities in Medicine*, *7*. Retrieved from http://www.peh-med.com/content/7/1/3

Phillips, J., Frances, A., Cerullo, M. A., Chardavoyne, J., Decker, H. S., First, M. B., & Zachar, P. (2012b). The six most essential questions in psychiatric diagnosis: A pluralogue part 1: Issues of conservatism and pragmatism in psychiatric diagnosis. *Philosophy, Ethics, and Humanities in Medicine*, *7*. Retrieved from http://www.peh-med.com/content/7/1/8

Phillips, J., Frances, A., Cerullo, M. A., Chardavoyne, J., Decker, H. S., First, M. B., ... & Zachar, P. (2012c). The six most essential questions in psychiatric diagnosis: A pluralogue part 3: Issues of utility and alternative approaches in psychiatric diagnosis. *Philosophy, Ethics, and Humanities in Medicine*, *7*. Retrieved from http://peh-med.biomedcentral.com/articles/10.1186/1747-5341-7-9

Phillips, J., Frances, A., Cerullo, M. A., Chardavoyne, J., Decker, H. S., First, M. B., ... & Zachar, P. (2012d). The six most essential questions in psychiatric diagnosis: A pluralogue part 4: Issues of conservatism and pragmatism in psychiatric diagnosis. *Philosophy, Ethics, and Humanities in Medicine*, *7*. Retrieved from http://peh-med.biomedcentral.com/articles/10.1186/1747-5341-7-14

Pienkos, E. S. (2014a). *The unmooring of the world: A qualitative investigation of anomalous world experiences in schizophrenia*. Dissertation submitted to the Graduate School of Applied and Professional Psychology of Rutgers, The State University of New Jersey.

Pienkos, E. S. (2014b). Using phenomenology to understand hallucinatory experiences. *Pragmatic Case Studies in Psychotherapy*, *10*, 260–270.

Pienkos, E. (2015). Intersubjectivity and its role in schizophrenic experience. *The Humanistic Psychologist*, *43*, 194–209.

Pienkos, E. (2020). Schizophrenia in the world: Arguments for a contextual phenomenology of psychopathology. *Journal of Phenomenological Psychology*, *51*(2), 184–206.

Pienkos, E., & Sass, L. A. (2012). Empathy and otherness: Humanistic and phenomenological approaches to the psychotherapy of severe mental illness. *Pragmatic Case Studies in Psychotherapy*, *8*(1), 25–35.

Pienkos, E., & Sass, L. A. (2016). Expressions of alienation: Language and interpersonal experience in schizophrenia. *Journal of Psychopathology*, *22*(1), 62–70.

Pienkos, E., Sass, L., & Silverstein, S. (2017). The phenomenology of anomalous world experience in schizophrenia: A qualitative study. *Journal of Phenomenological Psychology*, *47*, 188–213.

Pies, R. W. (2011). Psychiatry's new brain-mind and the legend of the "chemical imbalance." *Psychiatric Times*. Retrieved Mary 8, 2015 from http://www.psychiatrictimes.com/blogs/couch-crisis/psychiatry-new-brain-mind-and-legend-chemical-imbalance

Pies, R. W. (2012a). Beyond DSM-5, psychiatry needs a "third way." *Psychiatric Times*. Retrieved from http://www.psychiatrictimes.com/blog/pies/content/article/10168/2029546

Pies, R. W. (2012b). How American psychiatry can save itself: Part 1. *Psychiatric Times*. Retrieved from http://www.psychiatrictimes.com/display/article/10168/2029641

Pinfold, V., Thronicroft, G., Huxley, P., & Farmer, P. (2005). Active ingredients in anti-stigma programmes in mental health. *International Review of Psychiatry, 17*, 123–131.

Pishva, E., Kenis, G., van den Hove, D., Lesch, K., Boks, M. M., van Os, J., & Rutten, B. F. (2014). The epigenome and postnatal environmental influences in psychotic disorders. *Social Psychiatry And Psychiatric Epidemiology, 49*(3), 337–348.

Plato. (1952). *Phaedrus* (R. Hackforth, Ed.). West Nyack, NY: Cambridge University Press. Original work composed 370 B.C.

Ponce, A. N., Clayton, A., Noia, J., Rowe, M., & O'Connell, M. J. (2012). Making meaning of citizenship: Mental illness, forensic involvement, and homelessness. *Journal of Forensic Psychology Practice, 12*, 349–365.

Popper, K. (2009). *Conjectures and refutations*. New York, NY: Routledge. Original work published 1963.

Post, R. M. (1992). Transduction of psychosocial stress into the neurobiology of recurrent affective disorder. *American Journal of Psychiatry, 149*, 999–1010.

Preston-Shoot, M. (2007). Whose lives and whose learning? Whose narratives and whose writing? Taking the next research and literature steps with experts by experience. *Evidence & Policy, 3*, 343–359.

Prince, R. & Tcheng-Laroche, F. (1987). Culture bound syndromes and International Disease classifications. *Culture, Medicine and Psychiatry, 11*, 3–20.

Project Citizenship. (2019). *About*. Retrieved January 15, 2019 from http://projectcitizenship.com/about/

Pulver, A. E., Mulle, J., Nestadt, G., Swartz, K. L., Blouin, J. L., Dombroski B., ... & McGrath J. A. (2000). Genetic heterogeneity in schizophrenia: Stratification of genome scan data using cosegregating related phenotypes. *Molecular Psychiatry, 5*, 650–653.

Raballo, A., & Parnas, J. (2012). Examination of anomalous self-experience: Initial study of the structure of self-disorders in schizophrenia spectrum. *Journal of Nervous and Mental Disease, 200*, 577–583.

Rahimi, S. (2015). *Meaning, madness, and political subjectivity*. New York, NY: Routledge.

Rains, L. S., Fallica, G., O'Daly, O., Gilleen, J., Giampetro, V., Morley, L., & Shergill, S. (2012). Exploring psychotic symptoms: A comparison of motor related neuronal activation during and after acute psychosis. *BMC Psychiatry, 12*, 102.

Raffard, S., & Bayard, S. (2012). Understanding the executive functioning heterogeneity in schizophrenia. *Brain and Cognition, 79*, 60–69.

Rank, O. (1928). *The idea of the holy: An inquiry into the non-rational factor in the idea of the divine and its relation to the rational* (J. W. Harvey, Trans.). London, UK: Oxford University Press. Original work published 1923.

Raskin, J. D., & Lewandowski, A. M. (2000). The construction of disorder as human enterprise. In R. A. Neimeyer & J. D. Raskin (Eds.), *Constructions of disorder: Meaning-making frameworks for psychotherapy* (pp. 15–40). Washington, DC: American Psychological Association.

Read, J., Mosher, L. R., & Bentall, R. P. (2004). 'Schizophrenia' is not an illness. In J. Read, L. Mosher, & R. Bentall (Eds.), *Models of madness* (pp. 3–8). New York, NY: Brunner-Routledge.

Reed, G. M. (2010). Toward ICD-11: Improving the clinical utility of WHO's international classification of mental disorders. *Professional Psychology: Research and Practice*, *41*, 457–464.

Regier, D. A., Narrow, W. E., Kuhl, E. A., & Kupfer, D. J. (2009). The conceptual development of the *DSM-V*. *American Journal of Psychiatry*, *166*(6), 645–650. Retrieved from http://ajp.psychiatryonline.org/article.aspx?articleid=100852

"Renee" (1951). *Autobiography of a schizophrenic girl: The true story of "Renee"*. New York, NY: Penguin Books.

Ricœur, P. (1975). Phenomenology and hermeneutics. *Noûs*, *9*, 85–102.

Ridley, C. R. (1984). Clinical treatment of the nondisclosing Black client: A therapeutic paradox. *American Psychologist*, *39*, 1234–1244.

Robbins, B. D., Karter, J. M., & Gallagher, K. (2015). Big pharma(kos): The stigmatized scapegoat of medicalisation and the ethics of psychiatric diagnosis. *Psychotherapy Section Review*, *56*, 84–96.

Roberson-Nahy, R., & Kendler, K. S. (2011). Panic disorder and its subtypes: A comprehensive analysis of panic symptom heterogeneity using epidemiological and treatment seeking samples. *Psychological Medicine*, *41*, 2411–2421.

Robins, E, & Guze, S. B. (1970). Establishment of diagnostic validity in psychiatric illness: Its application to schizophrenia. *American Journal of Psychiatry*, *126*, 983–987.

Romanyshyn, R. (1989). *Technology as symptom and dream*. New York, NY: Routledge.

Romanyshyn, R. (2007). *Wounded researcher: Research with soul in Mind*. Spring Journal Inc.

Ronell, A. (1991). *The telephone book: Technology, schizophrenia, electric speech*, Lincoln, NE: University of Nebraska Press. Original work published 1989.

Rosch, E., & Mervis, C. B. (1975). Family resemblances: Studies in the internal structure of categories. *Cognitive Psychology*, *7*, 573–605.

Rosen, C., Jones, N., Longden, E., Chase, K. A., Shattell, M., Melbourne, J. K., … & Sharma, R. P. (2017). Exploring the intersections of trauma, structural adversity, and psychosis among a primarily African-American sample: A mixed-methods analysis. *Frontiers in Psychiatry*, *8*. Retrieved from https://www.ncbi.nlm.nih.gov/pubmed/28469582

Rollin, H. R. (2003). Psychiatry in Britain one hundred years ago. *The British Journal of Psychiatry*, *183*, 292–298.

Rosenthal, D., Wender, P.H., Kety, S.S., Schulsinger, F., Welner, J., & Ostergaard, L. (1968). Schizophrenics' offspring reared in adoptive homes. In D. Rosenthal & S. S. Kety (Eds.), *The transmission of schizophrenia* (pp. 377–391). London, UK: Pergamon Press.

Rowe, M. (2015). *Citizenship and mental health*. New York, NY: Oxford University Press.

Rubin, E. H., & Zorumski, C. F. (2012). Perspective: Upcoming paradigm shifts for psychiatry in clinical care, research, and education. *Academic Medicine*, *87*, 261–265.

Rulf, S. (2003). Phenomenological contributions on schizophrenia: A critical review and commentary on the literature between 1980-2000. *Journal of Phenomenological Psychology*, *34*, 1–46.

Rumke, H. C., & Neeleman, J. (1990). Het Kernsymptoom der Schizophrenie en het Praecoxgevoel [The nuclear symptom of schizophrenia and the praecoxfeeling]. *History of Psychiatry*, *1*, 331–341. Original work published 1941.

Russell, J. (2018). *My story*. Retrieved from https://www.jazminerussell.com/about-1/

Russo, J., & Beresford, P. (2015). Between exclusion and colonisation: Seeking a place for mad people's knowledge in academia. *Disability & Society*, *30*(1), 153–157

Sachs, A. (2007, August). A memoir of schizophrenia. *Time Magazine Online*. Retrieved September 1, 2014 from http://content.time.com/time/arts/article/0,8599,1656592,00.html

Sadler, J. Z. (2005). *Values and psychiatric diagnosis*. New York, NY: Oxford University Press.

Sagy, S., Orr, E., & Bar-On, D. (1999). Individualism and collectivism in Israeli society: Comparing religious and secular high-school students. *Human Relations*, *52*(3), 327–348.

Sagy, S., Kaplan, A., & Adwan, S. (2002). Interpretations of the past and expectations for the future among Israeli and Palestinian Youth. *American Journal of Orthopsychiatry*, *72*, 26–28.

Saha, S., Chant, D., Welham, J., & McGrath, J. (2005). A systematic review of the prevalence of schizophrenia. *PLoS Medicine*, *2*(5), e141.

Sadock, B. J., & Sadock, V. A. (2010). *Kaplan & Sadock's concise textbook of clinical psychiatry*. Philadelphia, PA: Lippincott Williams & Wilkins.

Sadowsky, J. (2004). Delusion in Southwest Nigeria, 1945-1960. In J. H. Jenkins & R. J. Barrett (Eds.), *Schizophrenia, culture, and subjectivity: The edge of experience* (pp. 238–252). West Nyack, NY: Cambridge University Press.

Sagy, S., Orr, E., Bar-On, D., & Awwad, E. (2001). Individualism and collectivism in two conflicted societies: Comparing Israeli-Jewish and Palestinian-Arab high school students. *Youth & Society*, *33*, 3–30.

Saks, E. R. (2008). *The center cannot hold: My journey through madness*. New York, NY: Hyperion.

Santner, E. L. (1998). *My own private Germany: Daniel Paul Schreber's secret history of modernity*. Princeton, NJ: Princeton University Press.

Sartre, J. P. (1993). *Being and nothingness* (H. E. Barnes, Trans.). New York, NY: Washington Square Press. Original work published 1943.

Sass, L. (1987). Introspection, schizophrenia, and the fragmentation of self. *Representations*, *19*, 1–34.

Sass, L. (1988). The land of unreality: On the phenomenology of the schizophrenic break. *New Ideas in Psychology*, *6*, 223–242.

Sass, L. (1992a). *Madness and modernism: Insanity in the light of modern art, literature, and thought*. New York, NY: Harper Collins.

Sass, L. A. (1992b). Schizophrenia, delusions, and Heidegger's 'ontological difference.' In M. Spitzer, F. Uehlein, M. A. Schwartz, & C. Mundt (Eds.), *Phenomenology, language, & schizophrenia* (pp. 126–143). New York, NY: Springer.

Sass, L. A. (1994a). "My so-called delusions": Solipsism, madness, and the Schreber case. *Journal of Phenomenological Psychology*, *25*, 70–103.

Sass, L. (1994b). *The paradoxes of delusion: Wittgenstein, Schreber, and the schizophrenic mind*. Ithica, New York: Cornell University Press.

Sass, L. (2000). Schizophrenia, self-experience, and the so-called "negative symptoms." In D. Zahavi (Ed.), *Exploring the self: Philosophical and psychopathological perspectives on self-experience* (pp. 149–182). Philadelphia, PA: John Benjamin's Publishing Co.

Sass, L. (2001). Self and world in schizophrenia: Three classic approaches. *Philosophy, Psychiatry, & Psychology*, *8*(4), 251–270.

Sass, L. (2003a). Negative symptoms, schizophrenia, and the self. *International Journal of Psychology and Psychological Therapy*, *3*, 153–180. Retrieved from http://www.ijpsy.com/volumen3/num2/62.html

Sass, L. (2003b). Schizophrenia and the self: Hyperreflexivity and diminished self-affection. In T. Kircher & A. David (Eds.), *The self in schizophrenia: Neuropsychological perspectives* (pp. 242–271). Cambridge, UK: Cambridge University Press.

Sass, L. (2004). "Negative symptoms," commonsense, and cultural disembedding in the modern age. In J. Jenkins & R. Barrett (Eds.), *Schizophrenia, culture, and subjectivity: The edge of experience* (pp. 303–328). Cambridge, UK: Cambridge University Press.

Sass, L. (2007). Contradictions of emotion in schizophrenia. *Cognition and Emotion*, *21*, 351–390.

Sass, L. (2011). Autonomy and schizophrenia: Reflections on an ideal. In C. Piers (Ed.), *Personality and psychopathology: Critical dialogues with David Shapiro* (pp. 99–131). New York, NY: Springer.

Sass, L. (2014a). Delusion and double bookkeeping. In T. Fuchs, T. Breyer, & C. Mundt (Eds.), *Karl Jaspers' philosophy and psychopathology* (pp. 125–147). New York & Heidelberg: Springer.

Sass, L. A. (2014b). Self-disturbance and schizophrenia: Structure, specificity, pathogenesis (current issues, new directions). *Schizophrenia Research*, *152*, 5–11.

Sass, L., Borda, J. P., Madeira, L., Pienkos, E., & Nelson, B. (2018). Varieties of self disorder: A bio-pheno-social model of schizophrenia. *Schizophrenia Bulletin*, *44*(4), 720–727.

Sass, L. & Parnas, J. (2003). Schizophrenia, consciousness, and the self. *Schizophrenia Bulletin*, *29*, 427–444.

Sass, L., & Parnas, J. (2007). Explaining schizophrenia: The relevance of phenomenology. In M. C. Chung, K. W. M. Fulford, & G. Graham (Eds.), *Reconceiving schizophrenia* (pp. 64–96). New York, NY: Oxford University Press.

Sass, L., Parnas, J., & Zahavi, D. (2011). Phenomenological psychopathology and schizophrenia: Contemporary approaches and misunderstandings. *Philosophy, Psychiatry, and Psychology 18*, 37–39.

Sass, L., Pienkos, E., Nelson, B., & Medford, N. (2013). Anomalous self-experience in depersonalization and schizophrenia: A comparative investigation. *Consciousness and Cognition*, *22*, 430–441.

Sass, L., Pienkos, E., Skodlar, B., Stanghellini, G., Fuchs, T., Parnas, J., & Jones, N. (2017). *EAWE: Examination of anomalous world experience. Psychopathology*, *50*(1), 10–54.

Sass, L., & Ratcliffe, M. (2017). Atmosphere: On the phenomenology of "atmospheric" alterations in schizophrenia—Overall sense of reality, familiarity, vitality, meaning, or relevance (Ancillary article to EAWE domain 5). *Psychopathology*, *50*(1), 90–97.

Sato, M. (2006). Renaming schizophrenia: A Japanese perspective. *World Psychiatry*, *5*, 53–55.

Schatzberg, A. F., Scully, J. H., Kupfer, D. J., & Regier, D. A. (2009). Setting the record straight: A response to Frances commentary on DSM-V. *Psychiatric Times*, *26*. Retrieved from http://www.psychiatrictimes.com/dsm/content/article/10168/1425806

Schirmacher, W. (1984). The end of metaphysics - what does this mean? *Social Science Information*, *23*, 603–609.

Schneider, K. (1959). *Clinical psychopathology*. New York, NY: Grune and Stratton. Original work published 1950.

Schrader, S., Jones, N., & Shattell, M. M. (2013). Mad pride: Reflections on sociopolitical identity and mental diversity in the context of culturally competent psychiatric care. *Issues in Mental Health Nursing 34*, 62–64.

Schreber, D. P. (2000). *Memoirs of my nervous illness* (I. Macalpine & R. A. Hunter, Trans. & Ed.). New York, NY: New York Review of Books. Original work published 1903.

Schnackenberg, J. K., & Martin, C. R. (2014). The need for Experience Focused Counselling (EFC) with voice hearers in training and practice: A review of the literature. *Journal of Psychiatric Mental Health Nursing*, *21*, 391–402.

Schulman, K. A., Berlin, A. J., Harless, W., Kerner, J. F., Sistrunk, S., Gersh, B. J., … & Escarce, J. J. (1999). The effect of race and sex on physicians' recommendations for cardia catheterization. *The New England Journal of Medicine*, *340*, 618–625.

Scull, A. (2015). *Madness in civilization: A cultural history of insanity, from the bible to Freud, from the madhouse to modern medicine*. Princeton, NJ: Princeton University Press.

Scull, A., & Schulkin, J. (2009). Psychobiology, psychiatry, and psychoanalysis: The intersecting careers of Adolf Meyer, Phyllis Greenacre, and Curt Richter. *Medical History*, *53*, 5–36.

Seaton, B. E. A., Goldstein, D. N., Kelley, M. E., & van Kammen, D. P. (1999). Relations between cognitive and symptom profile heterogeneity in schizophrenia. *Journal of Nervous and Mental Disease*, *187*, 414–419.

Segall, M. H., Campbell, D. T., & Herskovitz, M. J. (1968). Chapter 14: The influence of culture on visual perception. In M. H. Segall, D. T. Campbell, & M. J. Herskovitz (Eds.), *The influence of culture on visual perception*. Indianapolis, IA: Bobbs-Merrill Company.

Sekar, A., Bialas, A. R., de Rivera, H., Davis, A., Hammond, T. R., Kamitaki, N., ... & McCarroll, S. A. (2016). Schizophrenia risk from complex variation of complement component 4. *Nature*, *530*, 177–183.

Selten, J.-P., & Cantor-Graae, E. (2005). Social defeat: Risk factor for schizophrenia. *British Journal of Psychiatry*, *187*, 101–102.

Selten, J., van der Ven, E., Rutten, B. F., & Cantor-Graae, E. (2013). The social defeat hypothesis of schizophrenia: An update. *Schizophrenia Bulletin*, *39*(6), 1180–1186. doi:10.1093/schbul/sbt134

Shapiro, S. (1977). Psychiatric syndromes and the airport. *Aviation, Space, and Environmental Medicine*, *487*, 555–557.

Shapiro, S. (1982). Airport wandering as a psychotic symptom. *Psychiatrica Clinica*, *15*(4), 173–176.

Shean, G. D. (2010). *Understanding and treating schizophrenia: Contemporary research, theory, and practice*. New York, NY: Routledge. Retrieved June 12, 2015 from https://books.google.com/books?id=8MNmAgAAQBAJ&printsec=frontcover#v=onepage&q&f=false

Sheehan, S. (1982). *Is there no place on earth for me?* New York, NY: Vintage Books.

Shorter, E. (1997). *A history of psychiatry*. New York, NY: John Wiley & Sons.

Siddle, R., Haddock, G., Terrier, N., & Faragher, E. B. (2002). Religious delusions in patients admitted to hospital with schizophrenia. *Social Psychiatry and Psychiatric Epidemiology*, *37*, 130–138.

Skinner, B. F. (1972). *Cumulative record: A selection of papers* (3rd ed.). East Norwalk, CT: Appleton-Century-Crofts.

Skodol, A. E., Schwartz, S., Dohrenwend, B. P., Levav, I., Shrout, P. E., & Reiff, M. (1996). PTSD symptoms and comorbid mental disorders in Israeli war veterans. *The British Journal of Psychiatry*, *169*, 717–725.

Söderström, O., Empson, L. A., Codeluppi, Z., Söderström, D., Baumann, P. S., & Conus, P. (2016). Unpacking 'the city': An experience-based approach to the role of urban living in psychosis. *Health & Place*, *42*, 104–110.

Söderström, O., Söderström, D., Codeluppi, Z., Abrahamyan, L. A., & Conus, P. (2017). Emplacing recovery: How persons diagnosed with psychosis handle stress in cities. *Psychosis*, *9*, 322–329.

Spandler, H., & Barker, M-J. (2016). Mad and queer studies: Interconnections and tensions. *Mad Studies Network*. Retrieved from https://madstudies2014.wordpress.com/2016/07/01/mad-and-queer-studies-interconnections-and-tensions/

Spauwen, J., Krabbendam, L., Lieb, R., Wittchen, H-U., & van Os, J. (2004). Does urbanicity shift the population expression of psychosis? *Journal of Psychiatric Research*, *38*, 613–618.

Spitzer, R. L. (2001). Values and assumptions in the development of DSM-III and DSM-III-R: An insider's perspective and a belated response to Sadler, Hulgus, and Agich's "On values in recent American psychiatric classification." *The Journal of Nervous and Mental Disease*, *189*, 351–359.

Spitzer, R. L., Endicott, J., Robins, E., Kuriansky, J., & Gurland, B. (1975). Preliminary report of the reliability of research diagnostic criteria applied to psychiatric case records. In A. Sudilovsky, S. Gershon, & B. Beer (Eds.), *Predictability in psychopharmacology: Preclinical and clinical correlations* (pp. 1–47). New York, NY: Raven Press.

Spitzer, R. L., First, M. B., Shedler, J., Westen, D., & Skodol, A. E. (2008). Clinical utility of five dimensional systems for personality diagnosis: A "consumer preference" study. *The Journal of Nervous and Mental Disease*, *196*(5), 356–374.

Spitzer, R. L., Forman, J. B., & Nee, J. (1979). DSM-III field trials: I. Initial interrater diagnostic reliability. *American Journal of Psychiatry*, *136*, 815–817.

Spivak, C. (1988). Can the subaltern speak? In C. Nelson & L. Grossberg (Eds.), *Marxism and the interpretation of culture* (pp. 271–313). Chicago: University of Illinois Press.

Stanghellini, G. (2011). Phenomenological psychopathology, profundity, and schizophrenia. *Philosophy, Psychiatry, & Psychology*, *18*, 163–166.

Starkman, M. (2013). Mad people's history, evolving culture, and language. In B. A. LeFrançois, R. Menzies, & G. Reaume (Eds.), *Mad matters: A critical reader in Canadian mad studies* (pp. 27–38). Toronto, Canada: Canadian Scholars Press Inc.

Stein, G. (2008). Did Ezekiel have catatonia? Psychiatry in the Old Testament. *British Journal of Psychiatry*, *193*, 253.

Steinbock, A. J. (1994). Homelessness and the homeless movement: A clue to the problem of intersubjectivity. *Human Studies*, *17*, 203–223.

Steinbock, A. J. (1995). *Home and beyond: Generative phenomenology after Husserl.* Evanston, IL: Northwestern University Press.

Steinbock, A. J. (1996). Homeworld/alienworld: Toward a generative phenomenology of intersubjectivity. In L. Langsdorf, S. H. Watson, & E. M. Bower (Eds.), *Phenomenology, interpretation, and community* (pp. 65–82). Albany, NY: State University of New York Press.

Strauss, J. S. (1973). Diagnostic models and the nature of psychiatric disorder. *Archives of General Psychiatry*, *29*(4), 445–449. doi:10.1001/archpsyc.1973.04200040005001

Strauss, J. S. (1989). Mediating processes in schizophrenia: Towards a new dynamic psychiatry. *British Journal of Psychiatry*, *155* (Suppl 5), 22–28.

Strauss, J. (2011). Subjectivity and severe psychiatric disorders. *Schizophrenia Bulletin*, *37*, 8–13.

Strauss, J. (2013). Reconceptualizing schizophrenia. *Schizophrenia Bulletin*, *40*, S97–S100.

Strauss, J. (2017). Uncertainty theory: A powerful approach to understanding psychiatric disorder. *Psychiatry*, *80*, 301–308.

Strauss, J. S., Bowers, M. B., & Keith, S. J. (1983). What is schizophrenia? *Schizophrenia Bulletin*, *9*, 7–10.

Strauss, J., & Carpenter, W. (1981). *Schizophrenia.* New York, NY: Springer.

Strauss, J., Carpenter, W. T., & Bartko, J. (1974). The diagnosis and understanding of schizophrenia: Part III. Speculations on the processes that underlie schizophrenic symptoms and signs. *Schizophrenia Bulletin*, *1*, 61–69.

Strauss J. S., & Dochtery, J. P. (1979). Subtypes of schizophrenia: Descriptive models. *Schizophrenia Bulletin*, *5*, 447–452.

Strauss, J. S., Hafez, H., Lieberman, P., & Harding, C. M. (1985). The course of psychiatric disorder: III. Longitudinal principles. *The American Journal of Psychiatry*, *142*(3), 289–296.

Styron, T., Davidson, L., Youins, R., Kamens, S. R., Hall, B. C., Pavlo, A., ... & Bellamy, C. (2018). Home groups: Integrating peer support and clinical care in a community mental health center. *International Journal of Group Psychotherapy.* Retrieved from https://www.tandfonline.com/doi/abs/10.1080/00207284.2018.1533408?journalCode=ujgp20

Styron, T., Kamens, S. R., Cooley Hall, B., & Youins, R. (2017, October). *'Home groups': Combining peer and clinical support at community mental health centers.* Poster Presentation at IPS: The Mental Health Services Conference of the American Psychiatric Association, New Orleans, LA.

Sue, D. W. (2001). Multidimensional facets of cultural competence. *The Counseling Psychologist*, *29*, 790–821.

Sue, D. W., Bingham, R. P., Porche-Burke, L., & Vasquez, M. (1999). The diversification of psychology. *The American Psychologist*, *54*, 1061–1069.

Summerfield, D. (2013). "Global mental health" is an oxymoron and medical imperialism. *BMJ*, *346*, f3509.

Sundararajan, L. (2015). *Task force on indigenous psychology*. Retrieved from http://www.indigenouspsych.org/index.html

Sundararajan, L., Girishwar, M., & Marsella, A. (2000). Indigenous approaches to assessment, diagnosis, and treatment of mental disorders. In I. Cuellar & F. A. Paniagua (Eds.), *Handbook of multicultural mental health* (pp. 69–87). San Diego, CA: Academic Press.

Sussman, N. (2010, August 30). Schizoaffective disorder on the DSM-V chopping block. *Psychiatry Weekly*, *5*(21). Retrieved from http://www.psychweekly.com/aspx/article/articledetail.aspx?articleid=1174

Sweeney, J. A., Haas, G. L., Li, S., & Weiden, P. J. (1994). Selective effects of antipsychotic medications on eye-tracking performance in schizophrenia. *Psychiatry Research*, *54*, 185–198.

Szasz, T. S. (1988). *Schizophrenia: The sacred symbol of psychiatry*. New York, NY: Harper & Row. Original work published 1976.

Tabb, K. (2018). Philosophy of psychiatry after diagnostic kinds. *Synthese*. Forthcoming. https://philpapers.org/rec/TABPOP

Tamminga, C. A., Sirovatka, P. J., Regier, D. A., & van Os, J. (2010). *Deconstructing psychosis: Refining the research agenda for DSM-V*. Arlington, VA: American Psychiatric Association.

Tandon, R. (2014). Schizophrenia and other psychotic disorders in diagnostic and statistical manual of mental disorders (DSM)-5: Clinical implications of revisions from DSM-IV. *Indian Journal of Psychological Medicine*, *36*, 223–225. Retrieved May 7, 2015 from http://www.ncbi.nlm.nih.gov/pmc/articles/PMC4100404/

Tandon, R., Gaebel, W., Barch, D., Bustillo, J., Gur, R. E., Heckers, S., ... & Carpenter, W. (2013). Definition and description of schizophrenia in the DSM-5. *Schizophrenia Research*, *150*, 3–10.

Tarricone, I., Tosato, S., Cianconi, P., Braca, M., Fiorillo, A., Valmaggia, L., & Morgan, C. (2015). Migration history, minorities status and risk of psychosis: An epidemiological explanation and a psychopathological insight. *Journal of Psychopathology/Giornale Di Psicopatologia*, *21*(4), 424–430.

Thornton, T. (2007, November 16). *Draft reply to Damiaan Denys*. Retrieved from http://inthespaceofreasons.blogspot.com/2007/11/draft-reply-to-damiaan-denys.html

Thornton, T. (2002). Reliability and validity in psychiatric classification: Values and neo-Humeanism. *Philosophy, Psychiatry, & Psychology*, *9*, 229–235.

Tienari, P., K.-E. Wahlberg, & L. C. Wynne (2006). Finnish adoption study of schizophrenia: Implications for family interventions. *Families, Systems & Health*, *24*(4), 442–451.

Tirupati, S., & Ramachandran, P. (2020). Schizophrenia, recovery and the individual-cultural considerations. *Australasian Psychiatry*, *28*(2), 190–192.

Trede, K. (2007). 150 years of Freud-Kraepelin dualism. *Psychiatric Quarterly*, *78*, 237–240.

Trickett, E., Watts, R. J., & Birman, D. (1994). Toward an overarching framework for diversity. In E. Trickett & R. J. Watts (Eds.), *Human diversity: Perspectives on people in context. The Jossey-Bass social and behavioral science series* (pp. 7–26). San Francisco, CA: Jossey-Bass.

Tsuang, M. T., Lyons, M. J., & Faraone, S. V. (1990). Heterogeneity of schizophrenia. Conceptual models and analytic strategies. *The British Journal of Psychiatry*, *156*, 17–26.

Tsuang, M. T., Stone, W. S., & Faraone, S. V. (2011). Genes, environment and schizophrenia. *The British Journal of Psychiatry*, *178*, s18–s24.

Ungar, T., & Knaak, S. (2013). The hidden medical logic of mental health stigma. *Australian & New Zealand Journal of Psychiatry*, *47*, 611–612.

Unick, G. J., Snowden, L., & Hastings, J. (2009). Heterogeneity in comorbidity between major depressive disorder and generalized anxiety disorder and its clinical consequences. *Journal of Nervous and Mental Disease*, *197*, 215–224.

Unsworth, S. J., Sears, C. R., & Pexman, P. M. (2005). Cultural influences on categorization processes. *Journal of Cross-Cultural Psychology*, *36*, 662–688.

Urfer, A. (2001). Phenomenology and psychopathology of schizophrenia: The views of Eugene Minkowski. *Philosophy, Psychiatry, & Psychology*, *8*, 279–289.

U.S. National Library of Medicine. (2006). Early psychiatric hospitals & asylums. *History of Medicine Online*. Retrieved from http://www.nlm.nih.gov/hmd/diseases/early.html

U.S. State Department (2012). Background note: Israel. *Bureau of Near Eastern Affairs*. Retrieved November 5, 2012 from http://www.state.gov/r/pa/ei/bgn/3581.htm

van Nierop, M., van Os, J., Gunther, N., van Zelst, C., de Graaf, R., ten Have, M., ... & van Winkel, R. (2014). Does social defeat mediate the association between childhood trauma and psychosis? Evidence from the NEMESIS-2 Study. *Acta Psychiatrica Scandinavica*, *129*, 467–476.

van Os, J. (2009). A salience dysregulation syndrome. *The British Journal of Psychiatry*, *194*, 101–103.

van Os, J. (2016). "Schizophrenia" does not exist. *BMJ*, *352*, i375. Retrieved from http://www.bmj.com/content/352/bmj.i375

van Os, J., Linscott, R. J., Myin-Germeys, I. M., Delespaul, P., & Krabbendam, L. (2009). A systematic review and meta-analysis of the psychosis continuum: Evidence for a psychosis proneness–persistence–impairment model of psychotic disorder. *Psychological Medicine*, *39*, 179–195.

van Os, J., & Tamminga, C. (2007). Deconstructing psychosis. *Schizophrenia Bulletin*, *33*, 861–862.

van Os, J., & Tamminga, C. (2010). Introduction. In C. A. Tamminga et al. (Eds.), *Deconstructing psychosis: Refining the research agenda for DSM-V* (pp. xxi–xxii). Arlington, VA: American Psychiatric Association.

Veling, W. (2013). Ethnic minority position and risk for psychotic disorders. *Current Opinion in Psychiatry*, *26*(2), 166–171.

Veling, W., Pot-Kolder, R., Counotte, J., van Os, J., & van der Gaag, M. (2016). Environmental social stress, paranoia and psychosis liability: A virtual reality study. *Schizophrenia Bulletin*, *42*(6), 1363–1371.

Velligan, D. I., & Alphs, L. D. (2008). Negative symptoms in schizophrenia: The importance of identification and treatment. *Psychiatric Times, 25*. Retrieved from http://www.psychiatrictimes.com/schizophrenia/content/article/10168/1147581

Verdoux, H., & van Os, J. (2002). Psychotic symptoms in non-clinical populations and the continuum of psychosis. *Schizophrenia Research, 54*, 59–65.

Viala, A., Ota, H., Vacheron, M. N., Martin, P., & Caroli, F. (2004). Les Japonais en voyage pathologique à Paris: Un modèle original de prise en charge transculturelle [The Japanese on a pathological voyage in Paris: An original transcultural model]. *Nervure, 17*(5), 31–34.

Wade, J. C. (1993). Institutional racism: An analysis of the mental health system. American *Journal of Orthopsychiatry, 63*, 536–544.

Wade, N. (2002, July 4). Schizophrenia may be tied to 2 genes, research finds. *New York Times Online*. Retrieved November 20, 2012 from http://www.nytimes.com/2002/07/04/health/04GENE.html

Wade, N. (2012, May 17). Many rare mutations may underpin diseases. *New York Times Online*. Retrieved November 4, 2012 from http://www.nytimes.com/2012/05/18/science/many-rare-mutations-may-underpin-diseases.html

Waddingham, R. (2012). ISPS votes to ditch the 'schizophrenia' label. *Behind the Label*. Retrieved from http://www.behindthelabel.co.uk/isps-votes-to-ditch-the-schizophrenia-label/

Wakefield, J. C. (1992). Disorder as harmful dysfunction: A conceptual critique of DSM-III-R's definition of mental disorder. *Psychological Review, 2*, 232–247.

Wang, H.-Y., Liu, Y., Yan, J.-W., Hu, X.-L., Zhu, D.-M., Xu, X.-T., & Li, X.-S. (2018). Gene polymorphisms of DISC1 is associated with schizophrenia: Evidence from a meta-analysis. *Progress in Neuro-Psychopharmacology & Biological Psychiatry, 81*, 64–73.

Watters, E. (2010). *Crazy like us: The globalization of the American psyche*. New York, NY: Free Press.

Watts, M. (2011). *The philosophy of Heidegger*. New York, NY: Routledge.

Weinberger, D. R. (1986). The pathogenesis of schizophrenia: A neurodevelopmental theory. In H. A. Nasrallah & D. R. Weinberger (Eds.), *The neurology of schizophrenia* (pp. 397–406). Amsterdam, The Netherlands: Elsevier.

Weinberger, D. R., Faith, K. B., & Frith, C. (1996). Prefrontal function in schizophrenia: Confounds and controversies. *Philosophical Transactions of the Royal Society of Biological Sciences, 351*, 1495–1503.

Weiser, M., Werbeloff, N., Vishna, T., Yoffe, R., Lubin, G., Shmushkevitch, M., & Davidson, M. (2008). Elaboration on immigration and risk for schizophrenia. *Psychological Medicine, 38*, 1113–1119.

Werner, S., Malaspina, D., & Rabinowitz, J. (2007). Socioeconomic status at birth is associated with risk of schizophrenia: Population-based multilevel study. *Schizophrenia Bulletin, 33*, 1373–1378.

Wertz, F. (1985). Method and findings in a phenomenological psychological study of a complex life event: Being criminally victimized. In A. Giorgi (Ed.), *Phenomenology and psychological research* (pp. 155–216). Pittsburgh, PA: Duquesne University Press.

Wertz, F. J. (1987). Meaning and research methodology: Psychoanalysis as a human science, *Methods: A Journal for Human Science*, *1*(2), 91–135.

Wertz, F. J. (2005). Phenomenological research methods for counseling psychology. *Journal of Counseling Psychology*, *52*(2), 167–177.

Wertz, F. J. (2010). The method of eidetic analysis for psychology. In T. F. Cloonan & C. Thiboutot (Eds.), *The redirection of psychology: Essays in honor of Amedeo P. Giorgi* (pp. 261–278l). Montréal, Québec: Le Cercle Interdisciplinaire de Recherches Phénoménologiques (CIRP), l'Université du Québec à Montréal et Rimouski.

Wertz, F. J. (2011). The qualitative revolution and psychology: Science, politics, and ethics. *The Humanistic Psychologist*, *39*, 77–104.

Wertz, F. (2015). Phenomenology: Methods, historical development, and applications in psychology. In J. Martin, J. Sugarman, & K. L. Slaney (Eds.), *The Wiley handbook of theoretical and philosophical psychology: Methods, approaches, and new directions for social sciences* (1st ed., pp. 85–101). Hoboken, NJ: John Wiley & Sons, Ltd.

Weinberger, D. R., & Berman, K. F. (1996). Prefrontal function in schizophrenia: confounds and controversies. *Philosophical Transactions of the Royal Society: Biological Sciences*, *351*, 1495–1503.

Wertz, F. J. (2018). Qualitative methods as fundamental tools: Autonomy and integration in mixed-methods research. In B. Schiff (Ed.), *Situating qualitative methods in psychological science*. Routledge/Taylor & Francis Publishing.

Wertz, F. J. (In press). Phenomenological methodology, methods, and procedures for research in psychology. In H. Cooper, M. Coutanche, L. M. McMullen, A. T. Panter, D. Rindskopf, & K. Sher (Eds.), *APA handbook of research methods in psychology* (2nd ed., Vol. 2). Research designs: Quantitative, qualitative, neuropsychological, and biological. American Psychological Association.

Wertz, F. J., & Alcee, M. (2003). A science of persons: Exploring the impact of R. D. Laing's *The Divided Self* on psychology. In R. Sternberg (Ed.), *The anatomy of impact: Great books in the history of psychology* (pp. 137–159). Washington, DC: American Psychological Association Press.

Wertz, F. J., Charmaz, K., McMullen, L., Josselson, R., Anderson, R., & McSpadden, E. (2011). *Five ways of doing qualitative analysis: Phenomenological psychology, grounded theory, discourse analysis, narrative research, and intuitive inquiry*. New York: Guilford Press.

Wertz, F. J., Desai, M. U., Maynard, E., Morrissey, M. K., Rotter, B., & Skoufalos, N. C. (2017). Research methods for person-centered healthcare science: Fordham studies of transcendence and suffering. In M. Englander (Ed.), *Phenomenology and the social foundations of psychiatry*, pp. 95–120. London: Bloomsbury.

Westen, D. (2012). Prototype diagnosis of psychiatric syndromes. *World Psychiatry*, *11*, 16–21.

Westen, D., Shedler, J., & Bradely, R. (2006). A prototype approach to personality disorder diagnosis. *American Journal of Psychiatry*, *163*, 846–856.

Whaley, A. L. (1997). Ethnicity/race, paranoia, and psychiatric diagnoses: Clinician bias versus sociocultural differences. *Journal of Psychopathology and Behavioral Assessment*, *19*, 1–20.

Whaley, A. L. (2002). The culturally-sensitive diagnostic interview research project: A study on the psychiatric misdiagnosis of African American patients. *African American Research Perspectives, 8*, 57–66.

Whaley, A. L., & Hall, B. N. (2009). Effects of cultural themes in psychotic symptoms on the diagnosis of schizophrenia in African Americans. *Mental Health, Religion, & Culture, 12*, 457–471.

Whitaker, R. (2002). *Mad in America: Bad science, bad medicine, and the enduring mistreatment of the mentally ill*. New York, NY: Perseus Publishing.

Whitaker, R. (2010). *Anatomy of an epidemic*. New York: Crown Publishers.

White, L., Harvey, P. D., Opler, L. A., Lindenmayer, J. P., & The PANSS Study Group. (1997). Empirical assessment of the factorial structure of clinical symptoms in schizophrenia. A multisite, multimodel evaluation of the factorial structure of the Positive and Negative Syndrome Scale. *Psychopathology, 30*, 263–274.

Widiger, T. A., & Clark, L. A. (2000). Towards DSM-V and the classification of psychopathology. *Psychological Bulletin, 126*, 946–963.

Widiger, T. A., & Samuel, D. B. (2005). Diagnostic categories or dimensions? A question for the Diagnostic and statistical manual of mental disorders–fifth edition. *Journal of Abnormal Psychology, 114*(4), 494–504.

Wiggins, O. P., & Schwartz, M. A. (1997). Edmund Husserl's influence on Karl Jaspers's phenomenology. *Philosophy, Psychiatry, & Psychology, 4*(1), 15–36.

Wilson, C., Smith, M. E., Thompson, E., Demro, C., Kline, E., Bussell, K., ... & Schiffman, J. (2016). Context matters: The impact of neighborhood crime and paranoid symptoms on psychosis risk assessment. *Schizophrenia Research, 171*(1–3), 56–61.

Wittgenstein, L. (2001). *Philosophical Investigations* (G. E. M. Anscombe, P. M. S. Hacker, & J. Schulte, Trans.). Malden, MA: Blackwell Publishing. Original work published 1953.

Wojcik, J., Lynda, T., Lutz, O., Mesholam-Gately, R., Sweeney, J., Pearlson, G., ... & Keshavan, M. S. (2017). SU49. Do psychosis biotypes differ across traditional schizophrenia subtypes? *Schizophrenia Bulletin, 43*(Suppl 1), S178–S179. doi:10.1093/schbul/sbx024.047

Wolfers, T., Rokicki, J., Alnæs, D., Berthet, P., Agartz, I., Kia, S. M., ... & Westlye, L. T. (2021). Replicating extensive brain structural heterogeneity in individuals with schizophrenia and bipolar disorder. *Human Brain Mapping, 42*(8), 2546–2555.

Wolitzky, R., Goudsmit, N., Goetz, R. R., Printz, D., Gil, R. Harkavy-Friedman, J., & Malaspina, D. (2006). Etiological heterogeneity and intelligence test scores in patients with schizophrenia. *Journal of Clinical Neuropsychology, 28*, 167–177.

Wolny, J., Moussa-Tooks, A., Bailey, A. J., O'Donnell, B. F., & Hetrick, W. P. (2021). Race and self-reported paranoia: Increased item endorsement on subscales of the SPQ. *Schizophrenia Research*, doi:10.1016/j.schres.2021.11.034

Woods, A. (2011). *The sublime object of psychiatry: Schizophrenia in clinical and cultural theory*. New York, NY: Oxford University Press.

World Health Organization. (n.d.). *History of the development of the ICD*. Geneva, Switzerland: World Health Organization. Retrieved from http://www.who.int/classifications/icd/en/HistoryOfICD.pdf

World Health Organization. (1979). *International classification of diseases and related health problems 9th revision*. Geneva, Switzerland: World Health Organization.

World Health Organization. (1992a). *The ICD-10 classification of mental and behavioural disorders: Clinical descriptions and diagnostic guidelines*. Geneva, Switzerland: World Health Organization. Retrieved from http://www.who.int/classifications/icd/en/bluebook.pdfs

World Health Organization. (1992b). *The ICD-10 classification of mental and behavioural disorders: Diagnostic criteria for research*. Geneva, Switzerland: World Health Organization. Retrieved from http://www.who.int/classifications/icd/en/GRNBOOK.pdf

World Health Organization. (2001). *International classification of functioning, disability and health* (ICF). Geneva, Switzerland: World Health Organization. Retrieved from http://www.who.int/classifications/icf/en/

World Health Organization. (2010). *International classification of diseases and related health problems 10th revision*. Geneva, Switzerland: World Health Organization. Retrieved from http://apps.who.int/classifications/icd10/browse/2010/en. Original work endorsed 1990.

World Health Organization. (2019). *International classification of diseases, 11th revision*. Geneva, Switzerland: World Health Organization. Retrieved from https://www.who.int/standards/classifications/classification-of-diseases

Wozniak, J., Biederman, J., Faraone, S. V., Blier, H., & Monuteaux, M. C. (2001). Heterogeneity of childhood conduct disorder: Further evidence of a subtype of conduct disorder linked to bipolar disorder. *Journal of Affective Disorders, 64*, 121–131.

Wu, E. Q., Birnbaum, H. G., Shi, L., Ball, D. E., Kessler, R. C., Moulis, M., & Aggarwal, J. (2005). The economic burden of schizophrenia in the United States in 2002. *Journal of Clinical Psychiatry*, *66*, 1122–1129.

Yang, L. H., Link, B. G., Ben-David, S., Gill, K. E., Girgis, R. R., Brucato, G., … & Corcoran, C. M. (2015). Stigma related to labels and symptoms in individuals at clinical high-risk for psychosis. *Schizophrenia Research*, *168*(1–2), 9–15.

Yen, S.-Y., Huang, X.-Y., & Chien, C.-H. (2020). The self-stigmatization of patients with schizophrenia: A phenomenological study. *Archives of Psychiatric Nursing*, *34*(2), 29–35.

Yeo, A. (2002). *When mourning breaks: Tales of hope and healing*. Singapore: Armour Publishing.

Youssef, H. A. & Youssef, F. A. (1996). Evidence for the existence of schizophrenia in medieval Islamic society. *History of Psychiatry*, *VII*, 55–62.

Zachar, P., & Kendler, K. S. (2007). Psychiatric disorders: A conceptual taxonomy. *American Journal of Psychiatry*, *164*, 557–565.

Zhu, Y., Wang, S., Gong, X., Edmiston, E. K., Zhong, S., Li, C., ... & Tang, Y. (2021). Associations between hemispheric asymmetry and schizophrenia-related risk genes in people with schizophrenia and people at a genetic high risk of schizophrenia. *The British Journal of Psychiatry*, *219*(1), 392–400.

INDEX